CITIES AND AUTOMOBILE DEPENDENCE: A SOURCEBOOK

CITIES AND AUTOMOBILE DEPENDENCE: A SOURCEBOOK

And I John saw the holy city,
New Jerusalem, coming down
from God out of heaven,
prepared as a bride adorned for
her husband.

Revelation 21:2

John saw his City descending out of heaven. It was, moreover, no strange
apparition, but a City which he knew. It was Jerusalem, a new Jerusalem....
This City, then which John saw is none other than your City, the place where
you live-as it might be, and as you are to help to make it. It is London, Berlin,
New York, Paris, Melbourne, Calcutta-these as they might be, and in some
infinitesimal degree as they have already begun to be.

*The Greatest Thing In The World
and 21 Other Addresses by Henry
Drummond (p84/5),1930*

I will return to Jerusalem, my
holy city, and live there. It will
be known as the faithful city...
Once again old men and women,
so old that they use a stick when
they walk, will be sitting in the
city squares. And the streets will
again be full of boys and girls
playing.

Zechariah 8: 3-5

**To our children,
Christy, Renée and Joshua**

Cities and Automobile Dependence:
A Sourcebook

PETER W. G. NEWMAN
Associate Professor in Environmental Science,
Murdoch University, Perth, Western Australia
and
JEFFREY R. KENWORTHY
Professional Officer in Environmental Science,
Murdoch University, Perth, Western Australia

Gower Technical

Aldershot · Brookfield USA · Hong Kong · Singapore · Sydney

Published by
Gower Publishing Company Limited,
Gower House, Croft Road, Aldershot,
Hants. GU11 3HR, England

Gower Publishing Company,
Old Post Road, Brookfield, Vermont 05036
USA

ISBN 0 - 566 - 07040 - 5

Printed and bound in Great Britain by
Courier International Ltd, Tiptree, Essex

Contents

Tables

xi

Figures

Acknowledgements

Behind the numbers which make up the main body of this book lies an enormous human effort on the part of hundreds of individuals and organisations around the world. Without the collective help of these people this book would never have been completed. It would be our sincere desire to acknowledge their often painstaking efforts in a detailed way but space would not permit. However, we believe that the city-by-city list of contributors contained in Appendix 1 provides something of a testimony to the patience, time and cooperation of the many unrewarded people who have contributed to this book over the last five years. We trust that in some small way these people may derive a sense of satisfaction in knowing that their efforts have finally been used in a constructive and hopefully beneficial way. While we are greatly indebted for all the data these people have provided, we take full responsibility for the way it has been used in this book.

A number of academics have given us encouragement and advice including Leo Klaassen, Lester Brown, Joel Darmstadter, Douglas Bohi, Vukan Vuchic, Ken Schneider, Graham Ashworth and Desmond O'Connor, for which we are very thankful.

We are also grateful for our many friends around the world who have generously provided hospitality and accomodation during our prolonged international meanderings. Without this assistance our finances would have been exhausted long before the necessary visits had been made. All these people deserve individual acknowledgement and a list appears for this purpose on the next page.

The two years work required in Australia to put all the data together was generously funded by the Australian Government's National Energy Research Development and Demonstration Program. Their financial support has been indispensible and is gratefully acknowledged, together with their many useful consultations, in particular with Associate Professor Ian Lowe and Mr Jan Kolm.

We owe a special debt of gratitude to Brad Cooper who did most of the text tabulations and solved some of the formidable problems of formatting and producing such large and difficult collections of data. The text of this book was typed by Deborah Hill who we sincerely thank for persevering with our handwriting.

Finally, but by no means least, we wish to thank our families, especially our wives and children, Ginny and Joshua Kenworthy and Jan, Christy and Reneé Newman for their patience and support particularly overseas when innumerable and sometimes tedious trips to offices could have been visits to art galleries or scenic tours.

Friends who have contributed to the making of this book

Graham and Gwyneth Ashworth
Karl Aüwarter
Göran Backstrand
Robert and Elice Baer
Freda Bell
Inger Bonneson
Kerk and Barbara Brown
Adolf and Anita Caesperlein
Libby Casey
Steve Cicerrello
Mark and Carrie Coode
Lyle and Betty Crozier
Lesley and Horst Dombrowe
Susan Ferringer
Bud and Julie Foskett
Doyle Gray
George and Mary Hartmeyer
Britta Hasselgard
Peter and Lynn Healy
John and Joy Henderson
Larry and Amber Henninger
Mel and Trudy Herrington
Chuck and Barbara Hess
Bonnie and Gary Hind
Lee and Caroline Höchstatter
Trevor and Cathy Hogan
Steve and Mary Holser
Lawrence and Carolyn Ingvarson

Bob and Shirley Jeffery
Greta Johanson
Noriko Kawai
Ruth and Bob Kiessling
Susan Kowal
Tom and Santha Kurian
Christine Ledger
Geoff and Peta Lilburne
John and Sadie Meakin
Ethel Meyer
Richard and Lois Meyer
Bill and Jeannie Miller
Edith Mojon
Duncan and Sue Murray
François and Annie Naville
Ethel and Karen Palmer
Jeff Platt
John and Aleyamma Samuel
Bonnie-Jean Schlaepfer
Franco and Lucy Sirolli
Stitt Family
Tori Takaki
Monika Tamm-Buckle
Kay and Art Thomas
Aaldert and Ineke Van der Vegt
Karla & Manfred von Malapert-Neufville
Heather Walters
Mrs Yoroi

1 Introduction: The personal basis for the book

Australian cities

The roots of this book go back some ten years to a study conducted by us of automobile dependence in the major Australian capital cities (Newman and Kenworthy, 1980 a,b,c). The variations in per capita car use, transportation energy use and public transport use identified in this study were found to relate very closely to some major land use and transport infrastructure indicators (eg. density of population and jobs, CBD parking supply, road supply etc.) As a result we were able to offer some new explanations for the specific differences in automobile dependence and gasoline use between the Australian capital cities. The more common factors used to explain urban gasoline demand such as income, city size and fuel price were included in our analysis but they failed to offer any meaningful explanations. Income variations were small and in any case went in the wrong direction for traditional transport economic theory (ie. the lower income cities tended to have higher energy use). City size was not a statistically significant explanatory factor and even so went against prevailing logic (the smaller cities had higher per capita energy use than the larger ones). Fuel price variations were not significant between the cities and appeared to play no part in understanding the 20% difference in per capita fuel use between the two extremes, Sydney and Perth.

Despite this apparent success of being able to relate significant variations in urban automobile use to physical land use characteristics and transport infrastructure factors, the realisation was always with us that the overall differences between Australian cities are very small and hence the study was of limited general application.

Although the fuel use varied by about 20%, Australian cities are all basically Automobile Cities - generally more than 90% of total passenger travel is by car. The major differences appeared to be that Melbourne and Sydney have somewhat denser inner areas built during the pre-automobile era and have good electric rapid transit systems. These cities thus tend to have significantly different transport patterns in their inner areas with greater use of walking, bicycling and public transport. But in the new post-war suburbs all Australian cities seemed to have much the same kind of transport patterns, set firmly in place by a structured low density suburbia and a car-orientated culture.

Global cities

Thus there seemed to be value in finding perspective on our cities by a comparison with US cities where it appeared that car-use was probably even higher and with European and Asian cities where it seemed car use was much less.

For a number of years we tried to collect data from the literature. An attempt was made to examine patterns of urban land use and transport in around sixty cities from over thirty countries using a range of sources (Newman and Hogan, 1987). No city-level transport energy or car ownership data could be found of significance so national data were used. However, some public transport data and land use data on a city level were available from the UN (1976) publication "Global Review of Human Settlements" and the "International Statistical Yearbook of Large Towns" (1972). The limitations in these data were rather obvious as occasionally ridiculous values would appear and all the time there was a nagging concern about whether the same methodology had been used to provide the numbers. Nevertheless there was enough there to provide a general picture of three city types - Automobile Cities, Public Transport Cities and Walking Cities (Table 1.1).

Data problems

The real drawback in using these data further lay in the unreliability of the data collection process. Even a UN bureaucracy hounding urban planners in the nations of the world to send in their data on the appropriate forms cannot guarantee that they have used the same definition of what is 'urban' or what is a 'passenger trip'. We had to find a more consistent and reliable set of data.

Other people have of course reached the conclusion that international urban comparisons can be used to develop policy. Studies like Peter Hall's"The World Cities" (Hall, 1977) or J. Michael Thomson's "Great Cities and their Traffic" (Thomson, 1977) have made major contributions to urban

Table 1.1
Relationships between urban density and transport in three city types
(Newman and Hogan, 1987).

City type	Urban density range (person per ha)	Car ownership (cars per 1000)	Gasoline consumption (annual kg per capita)	Public transport utilisation (annual passenger journeys per capita)
Automobile Cities	10 - 30 av. 20	High approx. 400	Very high approx. 870	Low approx. 90
Public Transport Cities	30 - 130 av. 90	Medium approx. 170	Medium approx. 220	High approx. 310
Walking Cities	130 - 400 av. 170	Low approx. 20	Low approx. 60	Medium approx. 180

policy. However, they tend to look at each city's data in isolation to seek a general pattern but only make qualitative comparisons between cities because their transport and land use data are not collected or presented in a systematic, uniform, or standardised way. Similar comments apply to Clark (1982) who collected a lot of urban land use data but they are not quantitatively linked to transport patterns in the cities he examines. Other urban studies like those examining the changing structure of European cities (Hall and Hay, 1980; v.d. Berg, Burns and Klaassen, 1987) or the environmental characteristics of US cities (Berry *et al.* 1974) have standardised data collection but in these cases the authors are not examining transport and land use. Hall and Hass-Klau (1985) in "Can Rail Save the City?" have compared British and German cities in some aspects of transport and land use with some very good standardised data indicating what can be done in this kind of international study. They too, however, point out that the main obstacle in their study, and one which led to a revision of their original aims, was lack of good, reliable urban data.

Thus the scene was set to pursue a study of the major world cities, collecting data on a uniform, standardised basis and bringing together transport patterns and land use to provide insight into the question of automobile dependence.

Personal problems

It became obvious fairly quickly that we would have to go to each of our cities if we were to be successful in collecting good data. It is very rare for a city to have a central source of data on land use and transport patterns - generally they are scattered through various planning and transport agencies, often at different levels of government (some have a city-wide government, others are a loosely connected series of local governments). To only *write* for such data is to invite a bureaucratic nightmare. A transnational study we came across that began at a similar time to ours, "The Future of the Automobile Study", was conducted by automobile manufacturers and was meant to look at urban land use and transport patterns. It tried to obtain data by correspondence but soon gave up and the study has since appeared emphasising only the technological aspects of the automobile (Altshuler et al., 1985).

The next question became - how do you get funding to visit thirty-two cities around the world? The answer was easy - from yourself. No-one is interested in financing a long-term 'junket'! Apart from the economic constraints there are also obvious physical constraints as it takes a rare person who is willing and able to take the best part of a year spending a week or two in each city wandering from one bureaucracy to the next seeking data. As it turns out Australians do this sort of long-term travelling quite a bit. It is a long way from Australia to anywhere so the average Aussie wanderer takes off for six months to a year whereas the average European or US tourist takes three weeks or so at a time. We therefore had a cultural advantage.

After Jeff had taken seven months off in 1983 without pay and financed his own tour (plus wife) to begin the data collection, it became clear that we were involved in more than a 'junket'. Thus the Australian Government granted funds in 1985 to continue the work, enabling us to complete much of the data collection using the contacts and studies gathered by Jeff. However, a follow up visit to nearly all cities was required by Peter (plus wife and two children) in 1986 to finalise the data - again a privately funded seven month exercise as part of his Sabbatical leave.

This history is provided to show that the data in the Sourcebook were not won easily - they proved to us at least why such a study has not been done before and is unlikely to be repeated. It is also written to show that the exercise was not an ivory-tower desk study but has involved a number of intensive visits not only to collect data but to develop a feeling for each of the cities. The data had to feel right as well as fulfil a number of standard criteria for verification.

Numbers

Anyone with this book can see that we have a fascination for numbers. Quantification provides a powerful perspective. However, it can never be for us a fascination for numbers in themselves - they are always sought and analysed for what they can tell us about the city. Thus to ride on a city's public transport, to walk its city centre, to get jammed in its traffic, to look down from its tallest buildings, to sit in the cafés and watch the people....this is what shapes our search for numbers and gives them their significance.

The project is thus a labour of love. We both have an enduring affection for the great cities of the world and would like to participate in a small way in ensuring they continue to provide the creative impetus for civilisation that they have done for millenia. In this lies a further motivation for our study - the role of transport energy.

Transport energy

Transport energy and in particular gasoline use, is a powerful reflection of how much automobile dependence there is in a city. The awareness of this at a personal level became a major motivation for this book.

In 1972/73 Peter studied in Delft, Holland and learned at first hand what a small, compact walking city is like. After that he went to Stanford and was living in the Silicon Valley suburbs of San Francisco when the OPEC oil embargo of late 1973 struck. The dislocation of the city was obvious, both economically and socially, when the car which had become the glue holding together urban life was threatened. Back in Delft little was affected as the walking, biking, public transport lifestyle continued and on car-free days people roller skated on the intercity freeways. The search for a technological solution to the energy crisis has waxed and waned since then and we have watched in vain for an easy solution to the supply of cheap transport fuels (Kenworthy and Newman, 1986 a, b).

The world continues to use oil faster than it is being found and despite short term and even medium term gluts, the spectre of an oil-short world hangs over all the world's cities. Any 'solution' promises to be an expensive one and hence reduced automobile use is virtually certain to be a major issue for nations and cities in the future. In the short term for Australian cities, as in the US, the oil-import dependence suggests a widening gap between consumption and indigenous production with the associated problems of foreign debt and political vulnerability, particularly in the 1990's.

In 1987 the US oil import bill rose to $44 billion, leading Phillip Abelson in a *Science* editorial to conclude:

> In the future our worst problem is likely to be demand for imported oil. Domestic production is down and will continue to decline. Completion of oil wells in the past 12 months have been at half the rate 2 years ago. At the same time, consumption of products has increased. This is notably true of transportation liquids, uses of which are setting all time records. (1987, p1211).

In Australia the net crude oil import bill seems tiny by comparison at A$190 million, but this is predicted to rise to over A$4 billion by 1996 when only 2 out of 10 cars will run on locally produced oil. Dependence on oil in Europe and Japan continues to be a serious problem though since the 1970's shock it has been a declining problem as oil use for non-transport functions continues to be phased out and the proportion of total energy used on transport is much less than in the US and Australia.

Conserving oil has also been strongly advocated for other environmental, economic and social reasons. Policies to reduce oil consumption in Australia and the US have concentrated on stationary uses and improving vehicle fuel efficiency, with much less attention on policies to reduce the need for motor vehicle use. For example, Phillip Abelson's response to the above oil import bill question was only directed to speed limits and mandatory vehicle efficiency standards. Studies rarely focus on cities and those that do generally suggest only minimal energy savings would be

5

associated with factors such as greater transit use and land use changes (La Belle and Moses, 1982; Sharpe, 1982; Small, 1980). A major reason for such limited conclusions has been the very meagre data base on urban energy statistics, as discussed.

Cities are being built now in patterns that last for 20 to 30 years, thus their implications for energy use should at the very least be better understood. As Beaumont and Keys state, "there has been insufficient examination of what an energy efficient urban form is actually composed of and how such a state can be reached given the present arrangements." (1982, p130). There are few who would suggest there will be as much cheap liquid fuel to use in urban transport over the next 30 years as there has been in the past 30 years.

Objectives

Apart from this energy motive there are other objectives in studying cities and collecting all these data on transport and urban form. There are so many relationships between the social, economic and environmental aspects of urban life that are determined by the city's transport patterns and how the city is shaped. Thus there are many facets of urban policy that lie behind this study all of which have a connection to the major theme - how we can reduce automobile dependence in cities. Such objectives can be listed in the following way:

•lessening the vulnerability of a city to oil supply disruptions

•transportation related inflation and increased balance of payments problems from imported oil

•growing frustration and pressures on personal freedom as urban living becomes dictated by longer and longer travel distances, traffic congestion and parking considerations

•impossibility of bicycling and walking because of sheer distances involved and the non-viability of transit for most trips

•a large proportion of transportation disadvantaged people (children, the elderly, the poor and handicapped persons who can't use cars - up to 50% in some cities)

•a high public transportation deficit and diminishing services

•high levels of environmental impact from traffic and roads including vehicular emissions (especially photochemical smog), noise, visual intrusion and social severance of neighbourhoods

•high costs of urban development as new roads, sewers, schools, community centres, transit services etc are built (and duplicated) farther from the city centre and the old inner areas decline in population and decay economically

•loss of human vitality, intimacy and neighbourliness due to lack of mixing between houses, shops and other activities (ie. excessively rigid zoning)

•central cities that are merely functional and sterile corporate centres lacking in human attractiveness, and increasingly dangerous especially after work hours

•social problems of excessive privacy and isolation and increasing crime, assisted by the lack of community (eg. the need for formal neighbourhood watch schemes to replace what was once the natural function of urban community)

Many of these issues may seem remote from the major thrust of this study on automobile dependence in cities but there are clear connections due to the fundamental way that transportation influences the shape of cities and hence how we live. The basic contention of this book is the need to reassert the importance of those who plan transport infrastructure and land use in cities as a way of addressing these problems, particularly the central question of how to make a city less dependent on the automobile.

We hope that in our data and our analysis that the fundamental importance of the planner can be seen in helping to resolve this most basic issue which affects almost every aspect of urban life.

Outline

The next chapter of the book examines the methodology used in ensuring the data were defined properly and are comparable on an international basis. It outlines the problems encountered with some parameters such as vehicle kilometres of travel (VKT), defining urban boundaries and city centres and it shows how we have attempted to overcome these.

Chapter 3 presents the main results of the study using just data from 1980. Time series data will be analysed later and added in a subsequent edition. The data are examined to show first how the patterns in gasoline use can be related to a range of transport and urban form parameters. Then the cities are examined using factor and cluster analysis to more clearly define the characteristics of high gasoline/high car use cities and low gasoline/low car use cities.

Chapter 4 examines some of the other parameters that help to explain the patterns in urban transport and in particular gasoline use and automobile dependence, across our thirty-two world cities. We look at geographic and economic parameters such as the demographic size of the city, vehicle ownership, income and gasoline price, the technological factor of vehicle efficiency, the role of climate in affecting urban lifestyles, some cultural differences in spatial traditions and political factors are assessed.

Chapter 5 analyses a series of major policy areas for reducing automobile dependence which appear to develop from the data. This is achieved under two major headings: Reurbanisation and Reorientation of Transport Priorities, along with three key focus areas to show more specifically the policies that are needed. The major policy areas to be dealt with can be summarised as follows:

•Reurbanisation - the most strategic land use policy is outlined which is to contain the city from sprawling and redevelop inside the currently underutilised urban area. Within this there are two particular focus points developed:

Focus on the central city - the central city is a key focus not only for saving energy and lessening car dependence, but to giving new life to these historic and cultural centres. The major issue examined is the question of competition between catering for automobiles in terms of parking spaces and providing more central city residences.

Focus on urban density - the issue of what minimum urban density cities need in order to reduce automobile dependence is examined, drawing together a large amount of empirical evidence from within and between international cities.

• Reorientation of transport priorities - this shows the importance of priorities for public transport, walking, and bicycling in the medium term plans for a city that is trying to reduce its dependence on the automobile. It has one major focus point:

Focus on congestion - the issue of how congestion is dealt with by traffic engineers and urban and transport planners is central to a reorientation of cities towards reduced automobile dependence. This section examines how creative use of traffic congestion needs to be developed. Congestion is seen as a potentially positive not negative force in gasoline consumption, automobile dependence, air pollution, access times and overall city life.

The final part of the book consists of the Sourcebook, containing all the data for 1960, 1970 and 1980 on the thirty-two cities in our study. This is in two sections - first parameters of raw data covering all aspects of urban transport and land use; second - parameters of standardised data deduced from the raw data, such as urban density and per capita passenger kms on various modes.

2 Methodology of Sourcebook data

Introduction

This chapter describes in detail the methods used to gather all the Sourcebook data. It commences with a general description of how the thirty-two cities were chosen and then overviews the choice of data and time periods which are the basis of the book. Following this are a general description of the approach to data collection and a more detailed explanation of the specific problems associated with deriving the individual parameters. Included in this section are detailed tables showing exactly how the CBD, inner area and whole metropolitan area are defined for each city. This is compulsory information for making sense of the mass of data contained in the Sourcebook. The chapter ends with a general statement about other detail developed by us on each city but not published in the book, plus an invitation to add to or correct any data in the book that readers feel are incorrect.

Choice of cities

In deciding to carry out an international comparison of cities the obvious first question that had to be answered was: What cities do we actually want to study? It was clear from the beginning that the five main Australian cities had to be included, since they were the basis of the study in the first place and their data were already well developed. But more than that, we wanted particularly to find out what implications the international comparisons have for future urban policy in Australia.

In order to achieve this goal and to show the full range of urban land use and transport possibilities, we did not want to limit the study to cities that were culturally similar to Australia or that were only a little denser or a little less car-orientated. Neither did we want to have cities that were just similar in population size terms, although from the point of view of practical policy development for Australian cities this might attract some criticism from those who see the patterns in very large cities, as being irrelevant to smaller cities. This criticism is answered later in the book, where we deal specifically with the question of city size and its influence on transport patterns (Chapter 4).

We did however make a conscious decision to leave out Third World cities. This was because their poverty and vastly different transport patterns based primarily around walking and other unconventional motorised and non-motorised modes (jitneys, rickshaws etc), including animal-drawn transport, put them into a very distinct class of their own. In fact Thomson (1977), in his book "Great Cities and Their Traffic", classifies them all as "Low Cost Strategy" cities, because lack of finance for major transport infrastructure such as subways has helped to create a rather chaotic transport and land use situation not seen in wealthier Western cities. In comparison to the cities in this Sourcebook they would all be very low transport energy consumers due in part to their very high densities, intensely mixed land use, short trip distances and emphasis on walking and other non-motorised transport. Evidence for this is contained in Newman and Hogan (1987) whose "Walking City" category of world cities contains mainly Third World Cities where energy use per capita is virtually rock bottom in an international perspective (see Table 1.1).

Third World cities are thus interesting in their own right and would probably reveal some useful lessons for Western cities, such as the efficiencies of mixed land use versus rigid zoning (see later). However, their transport and land use patterns are so confounded by the spectre of poverty that it is difficult to compare them in any meaningful way with more developed cities.

In keeping with our confessedly pro-urban stance and a desire to cover the full range of urban land use and transport interactions, we could not leave out a selection of the Great Cities of the world. Hence New York, Chicago, Los Angeles, San Francisco, Paris, London, Tokyo, Hong Kong and Moscow were virtually automatic inclusions. Although it could be argued that Hong Kong and Moscow are rather too different from the other cities to be included, they are clearly at one extreme of the world scale in transport/land use terms - Hong Kong because it is probably the highest density city in the world and has well developed transport infrastructure and Moscow because of its almost non-existent private car ownership and exceptional public transport system, especially rail.

Rome was initially included in the study but it was found that the chaotic urban data keeping situation made it impossible to complete. Other Southern European cities were also excluded for this reason, although with hindsight it would have been useful to have cities like Madrid, Barcelona and Athens in the study since they are good examples of hot weather, high density cities (see Chapter 4).

The other cities in the study are principal European and US cities chosen because of their prominence in an international context and for a variety of other specific reasons. For example, Amsterdam was included because of its renowned emphasis on bicycles and Zürich because of its extensive light rail system without a subway. Houston was interesting because of its explosive growth over the last twenty years with very minimal planning controls. Munich was included for its extensive central city pedestrian network and new U-Bahn and S-Bahn systems and Singapore because of its world famous traffic restraint scheme in the central area. At the time Singapore was also actively planning an electric rapid transit system which opened in 1987. It was thought that this might provide a useful before and after case study in the future.

Toronto is the only Canadian city in the study and was chosen as much for its proximity and ease of access to the US cities as for any other deeper reasons. However, after analysing its data and comparing it to the other cities we regretted that we had not included more Canadian cities at the outset. As explained in later chapters of the book, Toronto seems to sit neatly between the land use and transportation patterns of the automobile-orientated US and Australian cities and the public transport-orientated European cities. In this way it provides a very useful model for policy development, especially for the automobile cities. Our regret at not including more Canadian cities was highlighted when we discovered Professor Michael Goldberg's book comparing Canadian and US cities (Goldberg and Mercer, 1986). Goldberg's thesis is that the concept of a typical North American city is a myth and that there is really very little similarity between the Canadian and American patterns of urban development. For example, the authors show that the Canadian cities have much higher population and job densities in the inner city, they are more vital in a human sense with well-developed public spaces throughout the city, and have a far greater orientation to public transport than their US neighbours.

We have since added Montreal, Edmonton, Calgary and Vancouver to our future plans for city comparisons and some of the data have been collected.

The cities in the study are summarised in Table 2.1 by world region along with their 1980/1 populations. It can be seen that they are predominantly developed cities of the Western world with populations in excess of 700,000 people (five Australian cities, ten American, twelve European, and one Canadian). The exceptions are Singapore, Hong Kong and Tokyo which might be described as Westernised Asian cities, and Moscow which is the only city with a centrally planned economy and State restrictions on car ownership.

In terms of size, Table 2.2 shows the distribution of the total metropolitan population for the thirty-two cities. As can be seen, two thirds of the sample are under 3 million people, while only 10% are over the 10 million mark.

Table 2.1

Cities in the study by region and their 1980 population

Cities by region	1980 Population
AUSTRALIA	
Perth	898,918
Adelaide	931,918
Brisbane	1,028,527
Melbourne	2,722,817
Sydney	3,204,696
USA AND CANADA	
Phoenix	1,509,052
Denver	1,593,308
Toronto	2,137,395
Boston	2,763,357
Houston	2,905,353
Washington	2,988,100
San Francisco	3,250,630
Detroit	4,043,633
Chicago	7,103,624
Los Angeles	7,477,503
New York	17,925,200
WESTERN EUROPE AND USSR	
Frankfurt	631,287
Amsterdam	716,900
Zürich	780,502
Brussels	997,293
Munich	1,298,941
Stockholm	1,528,200
Vienna	1,531,346
Hamburg	1,645,095
Copenhagen	1,739,860
West Berlin	2,001,000
London	6,713,200
Moscow	8,015,000
Paris	10,094,000
ASIA	
Singapore	2,413,945
Hong Kong	4,986,560
Tokyo	11,597,211

Table 2.2

Distribution of total metropolitan population for the Sourcebook cities in 1980.

Population range	Number of cities	% of total
Less than 1,000,000	6	18.8%
1,000,000 to 2,000,000	8	25.0%
2,000,000 to 3,000,000	7	21.9%
3,000,000 to 4,000,000	4	12.5%
5,000,000 to 10,000,000	4	12.5%
More than 10,000,000	3	9.4%
Total	32	100.1%

Choice of data and time periods

Previous work on the Australian cities (Newman and Kenworthy, 1980 a,b,c) had laid the foundations for the kind of data we felt were necessary to characterise each city from a land use and transport perspective. Unlike the Australian cities study however, which was based on 1976 data only, we wanted to extend the analysis to show how cities have changed over a longer time period. Since a lot of the most basic data like population and employment come from Census statistics, and many countries only conduct a Census every ten years (eg. the US), it was decided to collect data for a twenty year time span characterised by the situation in 1960, 1970 and 1980 (or in the case of some cities 1961, 1971 and 1981). Twenty years appeared to be a long enough time period to see some major changes in transport and land use patterns in each of the cities, particularly since that era witnessed a very dramatic rise in the ownership and use of cars. A detailed list of the data collected is shown later in Table 2.7.

Land use patterns

Basically we wanted to be able to describe the broad land use patterns of each city including some indicators of how centralised or dispersed were these patterns. This of course necessitated collecting population, employment and physical area data for different parts of the city (CBD, inner area, outer area and the whole metropolitan region). These were then used to derive population and job density information. The fundamental nature of density in determining transport patterns such as trip length and modal split (particularly the feasibility of walking) had already been shown by many authors (Pushkarev and Zupan, 1977; Schneider, 1979; Newman and Hogan, 1981), and we had found in the Australian cities how a dense inner area can significantly alter the overall picture of transport in a city (Newman and Kenworthy, 1980 a,b,c).

At first glance getting density data on cities may seem to be a trivial exercise but it is in fact one of the more difficult tasks (see later). There is certainly lots of population density information around. Most atlases have

13

density listings but they are virtually always for the whole country or are only gross city densities. As explained in the next section, our work required only *developed* land to be included and this is where the difficulties arise.

Another broad land use characteristic which we would like to have enumerated is the degree of mixed land use, ie to what extent is there a fine-grained mixture or interspersion of different urban functions such as residences, shops, commerce and industries in different parts of the city? This however is far from easy to do, especially to come up with some simple number or "interspersion index" for a part of a city or a whole metropolitan region. Watt and Ayres (1974) attempted to do it for a large sample of US cities but found it too complex and time consuming.

Since completing the Sourcebook we have been working on this problem for selected areas of Perth in order to relate mixed land use to transport energy use and other more subjective measures of neighbourhood satisfaction (Duxbury, et al.,1988; Neville et al., 1988). The outcome of this work is that it is possible to develop good mathematical representations of how different land uses are mixed in together but is is still unfortunately not an easy exercise to extend the method to a large sample of whole cities. A number of authors have shown the transport and accessibility advantages of intensely mixed land use such as shorter trip lengths and more walking and bicycling (Cheslow, 1978). So although we haven't quantified it directly in our study, mixed land use remains a significant "background" variable which is to some extent expressed through the inner area density data. Inner areas, developed prior to dominance of the car, have much more mixed land use patterns (corner shops, apartments above shops etc) than the rigidly zoned suburban areas of the automobile era. Generally speaking, the denser an area the more mixed is the land use because the sheer numbers of people can support a rich diversity of small businesses, shops and other activities. Thus inner area density in this study remains something of a surrogate variable for mixed land use.

Transport patterns

We of course wanted to characterise in broad terms the transport patterns of each city including some measures of infrastructure provision (eg. how well are cars provided for in terms of parking and roads) and the energy use resulting from these patterns. This necessitated collecting a range of other important data such as the parking supply in the central city, the extent of the road network, the vehicles owned in the city, total kilometres of travel by the vehicles, the average speed of the traffic system, the modes used for various trips (eg. modal split for the journey to work), average trip lengths for various purposes and total consumption of gasoline and diesel fuel.

The extent of public transport and the balance between public and private transport was also of major concern. Thus we also collected key operational features of the public transport system such as the level of service provided, passengers carried and speeds of service etc. The public transport infrastructure equivalent of the road network length would perhaps have been the track lengths of rail services (tram and train) and route kilometres of buses and ferries which are readily available from public transport authorities. However, it was decided that actual service provided along the public transport routes in terms of vehicle kilometres was a more fundamental measure and so route length measures are not included in the Sourcebook. Financial details of public transport operations are of course basic to good transport planning but are not central to the main thrust of this book which attempts to get at underlying physical patterns; financial details are thus not included.

Other important data

A series of other essential parameters were collected in the course of analysing the data from the Sourcebook. These were needed to put each city in something of a socio-economic perspective and to correct for economic differences that affect the use of gasoline (eg. America's big cars). The three main extra variables were:
- Income
- Gasoline price and
- Fuel efficiency of the motor vehicle fleet.

As well, some extra data were needed to investigate a few key issues closely related to the differences in transport and land use patterns between cities. In this regard some climatic data for the cities are provided.

All of these extra variables are presented and analysed in Chapter 4 after the major transport and land use characteristics are thoroughly evaluated.

Data collection

The first attempt at gathering data for this book was made in 1982 when a series of standard letters were sent to various authorities in each of the cities. These letters requested assistance in obtaining some specific pieces of data which were highlighted on a sheet attached to the letter. Although we received reasonable responses to these requests (a few people clearly put a lot of time and effort into their reply), the replies were by no means complete (some cities failed to answer at all) and much of the data that were received remained ambiguous because of a lack of supporting explanations.

It became clear that the only way to satisfactorily gather the data and ensure that it was all precisely defined was to actually visit each city. Travel to the cities was undertaken in 1983 (excluding Moscow and West Berlin). This involved a seven month trip (Kenworthy) and visits to many transport, planning, environmental and energy agencies in each city. These included both City and State authorities. It was not unusual to be told by one authority that a particular piece of data does not exist and then to go around the corner and find that another department actually had very comprehensive data. In fact, much of the data collected was a result of not accepting the initial negative verdict even from within a single government department. At the risk of treading on bureaucratic toes, a short trip in the elevator to the next few floors often yielded what was required.

This simple anecdotal evidence says quite a lot about the state of urban data today and the coordination of important information within and between authorities. It certainly highlighted for us why such a study has not been successfully done before. It was a very rare city like London or New York that was able to provide all the data in an integrated way and this mainly through the efforts of a single, diligent and very cooperative respondent.

Even when apparently good data had been collected (or promised) it was not the end of the story. First, what initially seemed like good data on closer examination revealed errors or inconsistencies which only became obvious during the detailed comparative work in Australia. This is because raw data supplied for various parameters (eg. parking supply) can appear quite feasible in isolation from other relevant parameters. However, when examined together with other data (eg. employment) it may become apparent that the two items cannot be, for example, from the same physical area (even though they were supplied in this way).

These problems necessitated in many cases long and detailed letters seeking clarification of data supplied and often long waits for replies. Sometimes replies would not arrive at all and these had to be pursued via international telephone calls. In many cases, after replies had been received still more letters were necessary, to expand or clarify the extra data provided. This was made even more drawn out by the necessity in some cases, of writing in German and French to ensure speedier attention to the request. There have been a few particularly difficult cases where it was necessary to enlist the help of Australian and overseas diplomatic services to obtain responses. These cases, are indicative of the type of problems and delays which are experienced in research which must rely to a large extent on the good will of local and overseas authorities who see little immediate value to them in completing data for someone else's agenda.

Despite all these problems however, we have in most cases been successful in obtaining new responses from various authorities and completing the data collection on each city with what we believe is a reliable and comparable set of data.

Part of finalising the data was a follow-up trip to many of the cities in 1986 (Newman). Not only did this trip yield a lot of the outstanding data and clear up discrepancies, but also gave us some extra confidence in the general reliability and value of the study. In many cases planners not yet familiar with the study commented on the accuracy of the data for their city and hinted at the usefulness of such a compilation, although there is still room for improvement as will be seen.

At this point it is necessary to present in some detail the specific problems associated with collecting individual items of data and to give a more detailed picture of the effectiveness of the data collection procedures. An important part of this is an explanation of the way cities and parts of cities are defined.

Specific problems of data collection

One of the first exercises in data collection was to decide on the various geographical areas for which data would be compiled. This involved initially defining the metropolitan area and then the Pre World War II or inner area of that region and its central area or Central Business District (CBD). What follows is a general description of the approach taken to defining each of these areas, followed by a detailed description of how the metropolitan area, inner area and CBD were finally specified for each city (Tables 2.3, 2.4 and 2.5).

a) *Metropolitan area definitions*

The most appropriate and meaningful way of defining a metropolitan area is to take what may be termed the full functional urban region. This is usually a large, fairly contiguous built up area which may transcend any number of political or administrative boundaries such as those of Cities and States, but which functionally acts as a single, unified region. Perhaps the best example of this in the Sourcebook is the New York Tri-State Metropolitan Area. This urban region cuts across three State boundaries (New York, New Jersey and Connecticut) and embraces New York City, numerous smaller central cities and vast suburban areas which together function as one very large metropolitan area focussed primarily on Manhattan.

On the other hand the five metropolitan areas of the Australian cities are comparatively isolated and well defined, being surrounded by distinct rural hinterlands and their delineation is not complicated by crossing of political or administrative boundries. The full functional urban regions correspond almost perfectly to their respective Capital City Statistical Divisions as defined and regularly revised by the Australian Bureau of Statistics.

The approach in the Sourcebook has thus always been to try to define each metropolitan area according to its full functional urban region. This has for the most part been achieved apart from some European cities where the real functional urban region is confounded by a large number of smaller political or administrative units surrounding one large principal city (eg. Munich and Frankfurt). In these cases it was virtually impossible to obtain all the varied data required on the full urban region. Simpler items such as population and some public transport data were available, mainly because of the unique nature of public transport administration in many European cities, particularly West Germany.

Since the early 1970's all public transport services and operators in the principal European cities have joined together into large cooperatives or associations (Verkehrsverbund in West Germany). These associations which have elaborate revenue sharing arrangements provide comprehensive and well-coordinated public transport services to areas that correspond much more closely to the full functional urban region. They generally publish the population of their service area in each year, as well as a range of operational statistics, but they do not have other reliable data such as road network, vehicle registrations, actual urbanised land area etc.

For the cities where this problem occurred there was little alternative but to use the main city lying at the heart of the region (City of Munich, City of Frankfurt am Main etc) for which good comprehensive data were available. In the case of public transport data however, it was possible to obtain correct per capita figures by ensuring the data were divided by the larger population

Table 2.3
Metropolitan area definitions

Adelaide The Adelaide Statistical Division encompasses the metropolitan area and is defined by the Australian Bureau of Statistics in 1961, 1971, 1981.

Amsterdam Availability of data required the use of two metropolitan area definitions : The City of Amsterdam and Agglomeration of Amsterdam. In practise, both areas are very similar with the Agglomeration of Amsterdam having only 2.2%, 9.5% and 11.8% higher population than the City of Amsterdam in 1960, 1970 and 1980 respectively.

Boston Three major definitions of the Boston metropolitan area can be found. The Boston Urbanised Area and Boston SMSA(Standard Metropolitan Statistical Area), both of which are defined and used by the U.S Bureau of the Census. The third definition, which is used by many planning agencies is a considerably larger area known as the Boston Metropolitan Region. It comprises the Boston SMSA plus eighteen extra towns in Essex County, eighteen in Middlesex County, sixteen in Worcester County, one in Bristol County, two in Norfolk County and six in Plymouth County. In 1960, 1970 and 1980 these additional towns amounted to around an extra 1 million people on top of the SMSA population. Unfortunately, all data are not kept conistently on any one of these three areas and so a combination was used for various parameters. For example, densities are based on the Urbanised Area while vehicle registrations were only available for the Boston SMSA. Commuter Rail data on the other hand are applicable to the larger Metropolitan Region.

Brisbane Brisbane's metropolitan area is the Brisbane Statistical Division as defined by the Australian Bureau of Statistics in 1961, 1971 and 1981.

Brussels The Brussels metropolitan area is defined as the Agglomération de Bruxelles (Agglomeration of Brussels) consisting of nineteen communes (see Radioscopie de Bruxelles : Etude Statistique - Publication de l'Agglomération de Bruxelles, 1983).

Chicago Chicago's Metropolitan area is defined in two ways by the U.S. Bureau of the Census : the Urbanised Area and the SMSA. Urbanised Area has been used for densities since it gives true urban densities, while most other data are available for the SMSA on a County-by-County basis. The SMSA comprised the six Counties of Cook, Du Page, Kane, Lake, McHenry and Will in 1960, 1970 and 1980 and together are also known as the North Eastern Illinois Planning Commission Area.

Copenhagen Copenhagen's metropolitan area is generously defined as the Copenhagen Region which comprises the contiguous built up area surrounding Copenhagen proper as well as a large area of land containing isolated pieces of urban development stretching right up to and including the separate city of Helsingør in the north. Danish authorities refer to this area as the Hovedstadsregionen and good data are available for it through the Copenhagen Statistical Yearbook (see CBD definitions). The Hovedstadsregionen consists of København, Frederiksberg Kommune and Københavns amtskommune (Copenhagen suburbs), plus Frederiksborg amtskommune and Roskilde amtskommune. The contiguous built-up area is basically København, Frederiksberg and København amtskommune but most data, especially the more difficult VKT and fuel use which do not appear in the Statistical Yearbooks are provided by authorities on the basis of the Copenhagen Region. Thus for the purposes of this study the Copenhagen Region is taken as the best definition of the Copenhagen metropolitan area, although data are provided in the Sourcebook for the smaller areas in many cases .

Denver Denver's metropolitan area is defined in two ways by the U.S. Bureau of the Census : the Urbanised Area and the SMSA. Data for both these areas are used as described for Chicago. The SMSA of Denver in 1960, 1970 and 1980 consisted of the five Counties of Adams, Arapahoe, Boulder, Denver and Jefferson . In 1980 the official Census definition of the SMSA included two smaller population Counties of Gilpin and Douglas, but these have been left out for the purpose of better comparisons with previous years.

Detroit Detroit's metropolitan area is defined in the same way as described for Chicago and data are used in a similar fashion. The SMSA is defined in each year as Wayne, Oakland and McComb Counties. In 1980 the official Census definition of the SMSA was expanded to include three additional Counties: Lapeer, Livingston and St Clair. However, for comparisons with earlier years these were not included in the Sourcebook and are only a small part of the population.

Frankfurt Frankfurt is defined as the City of Frankfurt am Main , since comprehensive data are available for this area from authorities in Frankfurt and from the Frankfurt Statistical Yearbook. However, this is not the true functional urban region of Frankfurt since the City of Frankfurt is surrounded by around an additional 1,000,000 people who have Frankfurt as their major urban centre and destination for many trip purposes . Unfortunately most of the detailed data required in this study could not be obtained for this larger area. The main reason for this is that the area is comprised of many small administrative units (Landkreise and Kreisfrele Stadt) for which it would have been impossible to compile all the varied data. It was nonetheless necessary to use the larger "serviced" area" population estimates to calculate per capita public transport data. This is because the public transport operators go well beyond the boundaries of the City of Frankfurt and it is not possible to disaggregate their statistics into within and outside the City of Frankfurt.

Hamburg The Hamburg metropolitan area is defined as the City of Hamburg (Freie und Hansestadt Hamburg) for which comprehensive data are available from the Hamburg Statistical Yearbook (see CBD defintions). This area is comprised of seven major districts; Altona, Bergedorf, Eimsbüttel, Hamburg-Mitte, Hamburg-Nord, Harburg and Wandsbek. However, the Hamburg Community Transport Area (HVV or Hamburger Verkehrsverbund) is a larger area than this and so to calculate accurate per capita public transport figures, the population of the HVV area had to be used in 1970 and 1980 (in 1960 the population of the City of Hamburg was used because the HVV had not been formed at that stage). The Hamburg Community Transport Area population in 1970 is given as 2,480,000 and in 1980 as 2,440,000. No disaggregation of public transport data into that relevant to the City of Hamburg and that relevant to outside areas was available.

Hong Kong The metropolitan area of Hong Kong is defined by the Hong Kong Planning Division as comprising Hong Kong Island, Kowloon, New Kowloon, New Territories and the Marine populations (those living on boats, junks etc). Good data are available for this area through the 1961, 1971 and 1981 Hong Kong Census and other Government material.

Houston Houston's metropolitan area is defined in the same way as described for Chicago and data were used in a similar fashion. The SMSA was defined in 1960 as Harris County only, in 1970 as Harris, Brazoria, Fort Bend, Liberty and Montgomery Counties and in 1980 Waller County was added. For comparison purposes the SMSA in the Sourcebook adopts the 1980 definition for all three years (ie. six counties).

London The London metropolitan area used is the GLC area (Greater London Council) for which good Census and other data are available. The GLC area is not the full functional London Urban Region and in this sense is not an ideal definition However, compiling the comprehensive data in this study on a larger area would have been very difficult because of the diversity of sources involved, and in some cases would have probably been impossible. The data on the GLC area is as complete as any city in the world.

Los Angeles Los Angeles has two convenient metropolitan area definitions - the Urbanised Area and the Los Angeles/ Long Beach SMSA, the latter of which corresponds to Los Angeles County. Unlike the other U.S. cities where the urbanised area and SMSA populations correspond reasonably well, there is quite a large difference (2 million people) between the Urbanised Area and the SMSA of Los Angeles. Another difficulty is that like some other cities in Europe , the Los Angeles metropolitan area as defined is not the full functional urban area which comprises a series of other smaller SMSA's and Counties (e.g Orange, Riverside, San Bernadino and Ventura Counties etc). Again, the difficulties in compiling the detailed and varied data across so many separate areas would have been prohibitively time consuming and in some instances may have been impossible. The data presented are for the Los Angeles / Long Beach SMSA except for densities which are derived using Urbanised Area data as outlined in the text.

Melbourne   The Melbourne Statistical Division outlines the metropolitan area and is defined by the Australian Bureau of Statistics in 1961,1971 and 1981.

Moscow   Two defintions of the Moscow metropolitan area are available. They are: the City of Moscow whose administrative boundary is the ring Motorway and in which 1980 had a population of just over 8 million people, and the Agglomeration of Moscow, a much larger area of about 12.8m million in 1980. What little data are available on Moscow are for the City of Moscow.

Munich   Munich's metropolitan area is defined as the City of Munich (Landeshauptstadt München) comprised of thirty-seven Stadtbezirke (N°'s 1 and 5 to 41). Excellent data for this area are available from Munich's Statistical Yearbooks (see CBD defintions). Munich, like most of the European cities is however embedded within a much larger functional urban region. Planungsregion 14 is the name given to Munich's broader urban region (2,305,000 people in 1982) and some data are provided for this area in the Statistical Yearbooks. Unfortunately the comprehensive data required for this study could not be compiled on Planungsregion 14. In the case of per capita public transport data however, it was necessary to use the Planungsregion 14 population since the public transport operations extend well into this broader region.

New York   New York's metropolitan area is the true functional urban region known as the Tri-State Metropolitan Planning Region which embraces twelve counties in New York State, nine Counties in New Jersey and six planning areas in Connecticut. Extensive data are available for this area through publications of the Tri - State Regional Planning Commission and the New York Metropolitan Transportation Council.

Paris   The metropolitan area of Paris is known as the Ile de France and is comprised of three major areas; Ville de Paris, Petite Couronne and Grande Couronne. Excellent data are compiled for this area especially through the Préfecture de la Région d' Ile de France- Direction Régionale de l'Equipement, Division des infrastructures et des transports and Division de l'Urbanisme opérationnel et du Logement.

Perth   The Perth Statistical Division encompasses the metropolitan area and is defined by the Australian Bureau of Statistics in 1961,1971, 1981.

Phoenix   Phoenix's metropolitan area is defined in the same way as described for Chicago and data are used in a similar fashion. The SMSA in each year is defined simply as Maricopa County.

San Francisco   San Francisco's metropolitan area is defined in the same way as described for Chicago and data are used in a similar fashion. The SMSA of San Francisco is defined as Alameda, Contra Costa, Marin, San Francisco and San Mateo Counties in each year. In 1960 Solano County was included in the SMSA but was eliminated by the U.S. Census in subsequent years. For comparison purposes Solano County was also eliminated in 1960 in this study. An alternative definition of the metropolitan area of San Francisco is the Nine County Bay Region (Association of Bay Area Governments or ABAG), which consists of the above five Counties plus Napa, Santa Clara, Solano and Sonoma Counties. Generally good data on this area can be obtained especially through ABAG. However , it presented a much more complicated definition in terms of the comprehensive data required for this study (eg especially public transport and land use data).

Singapore   The Singapore metropolitan area is simply the whole City State or island of Singapore. Good data on Singapore are provided through the Department of Statistics (eg Yearbook of Statistics, Singapore) but most of the data in this study came through detailed enquires with numerous Government Departments and Agencies.

Stockholm   The Stockholm metropolitan area is most commonly defined as the County of Stockholm whose major built up part is the smaller Municipality of Stockholm. Raw data for this study are compiled on both areas as far as possible. However, the standardised data are for the Municipality only since the most comprehensive and reliable data were available for this area, especially through the Stockholm Statistical Yearbooks (see CBD definitions). However for public transport (per capita data), the County of Stockholm populations were used because public transport operations extend well into the County of Stockholm.

Sydney   The Sydney Statistical Division covers the metropolitan area and is defined by the Australian Bureau of Statistics in 1961,1971,1981.

Tokyo   Tokyo is commonly defined as the Tokyo Metropolis (or Tokyo-to) which in 1980 contained 11,597,000 people. However the functional urban region of Tokyo is very much larger than this and has been defined as the Tokyo Metropolitan Transportation Area which in 1980 had 25,839,000 people or over twice as many as the Tokyo Metropolis . Data availability is generally much better for the Tokyo Metropolis than it is for the Tokyo Metropolitan Transportation Area and so for this study the Tokyo Metropolis has been taken as the metropolitan area. However, public transport operations embrace the whole Tokyo Metropolitan Transportation Area and their data are published for this larger area. Thus per capita public transport data apply to the Tokyo Metropolitan Transportation Area.

Toronto   The true metropolitan area of Toronto is a large area known as the Toronto Metropolitan Region (1980 population 3,418,000). The most densely settled contiguous part of this region is the Municipality of Metropolitan Toronto incorporating 2,137,500 people in 1980, or 63% of the Region's population. Unfortunately, good data are not available for the Toronto Metropolitan Region since it embraces a number of separate administrative areas. On the other hand very comprehensive data are available for the Municipality of Metropolitan Toronto and so this has been used as the metropolitan area in this study. In the case of some public transport operations which extend beyond the Municipality (eg Go Transit), regional populations have been used in calculations.

Vienna   Vienna's metropolitan area is defined as the City of Vienna for which very good data are available through numerous sources, especially the Vienna Statistical Yearbook (see CBD definitions). The City of Vienna is not the full urban area or City Region (Umland) but data are not comprehensively available on this larger area . The "Umland" of Vienna in 1961 and 1971 had an additional 463,415 and 491,808 people respectively, although data show that in 1961 only 80,401 of these people commuted into Vienna and in 1971, 103,345.

Washington DC   Washington's metropolitan area is defined in the same way as described for Chicago and data are used in a similar fashion. The Washington SMSA is comprised of the following areas: the District of Columbia, Montgomery and Prince Georges Counties in Maryland, Arlington, Fairfax, Loudon and Prince Williams Counties in Virginia plus Alexandria, Fairfax and Falls Church cities in Virginia. In 1960 Loudon and Prince William Counties were not part of the SMSA and Fairfax City was not separated from Fairfax County. However, for comparison purposes with 1970 and 1980 these two Counties were included in the 1960 definition.

West Berlin   The metropolitan area of West Berlin is simply the City of West Berlin (which naturally has rigid, politically defined boundaries). Good data for West Berlin are provided by the Statistical Yearbook of Berlin (see inner area definitions) plus other government sources (see CBD definitions).

Zürich   The Zürich metropolitan area is defined as the Agglomeration of Zürich (as outlined by the Amt für Raumplanung des Kantons Zürich - Dr. H. Kissling, letter 30/1/1984). It consists of the City of Zürich and the following regions : Limmattal, Knonaueramt, Zimmerberg, Pfannenstil, Glattal and Furttal). Data for this area were not easy to compile and came mainly through specialised assistance supplied by the above department.

figures relevant to public transport.

Table 2.3 lists the metropolitan area definitions for each of the cities in the Sourcebook and explains clearly where trade-offs had to be made between specifying the full functional urban region and getting comprehensive data.

b) Inner area definitions

Ideally the inner area should always be defined as the urban region that was developed prior to the Second World War. This mostly represents the pre-automobile part of the present city and it generally has a different character (eg. much more mixed land use) and higher density, having been developed around the public transport system (especially trams, which have in many cases gone). However, in practice it is extremely difficult to define inner areas in this way. An obvious problem with defining inner areas as the pre World War II region is that this region is often not contiguous around the central city. Rather, it consists of scattered patches of urban development which have since been subsumed as the city filled in around them (eg. Los Angeles). It is virtually impossible to collect data on these isolated bits of the urban area. In a few cities historical documents or experienced planners were able to clearly outline urban development as of 1939/40 and present administrative units enabled this definition still to be used. However, in most cities inner areas have to be defined in a number of ways, as outlined below.

i) European cities In Europe, inner areas have mostly been defined according to groupings of administrative units clustered around and including the historical core. As a general rule, inner area administrative units are much smaller than more modern parts of the city that have developed at a lower density. In many cities it is possible to identify the post-World War II zones on a map just by their size in relation to older areas. The inner zones are generally not more than about 8km from the central city; prior to the car, travel speeds were constrained by available transport technology and 8km tended to be a comfortable travel distance, although commuter railways did permit some development further out (up to around 16km in a few cases).

ii) Australian cities In the Australian cities, inner areas have been defined according to groupings of Local Government Areas (LGAs) in close proximity to and including the CBD. These definitions are similar or identical to previous authors' definitions such as Kendig (1979) and Harrison (1977). Data are collected on a Local Government Area basis through the Australian Bureau of Statistics.

iii) Asian cities For the Asian cities, guidance was obtained from authorities within Tokyo and Hong Kong as to the areas developed before World War II, and definitions were chosen as close as possible to these based on current administrative structures. An inner area for Singapore was extremely difficult to define, and no guidance was forthcoming from authorities. Hence data for population and land area were obtained based on Census Divisions and those Divisions with high densities clustered around the

20

present day central area (traffic restriction zone) were taken as the inner area. These zones also tended to be no more than about 8km from the central area. However, the boundaries changed between each year and the inner area had to be separately defined each time. Thus Singapore's inner area is the least consistent in the study. More detail is provided on this in Table 2.4 which gives very specific definitions of the inner areas of each city.

iv) US cities In the US urban areas, administrative arrangements are quite different from the other world cities. Small scale zones comprising the urban area are not nearly so readily available. When available, they tend to be peculiar to each city and not consistent over time (eg traffic study zones or one-off land use studies). This makes it almost impossible to collect consistent data. Unlike in Australia, where small Local Government Areas comprise the metropolitan regions, the only consistent and readily available components of US urban areas which could suffice as inner areas are the old "Cities" which lie at the heart of the Metropolitan areas (eg. City of Los Angeles, City of Detroit). These have the advantage that all the data required are generally kept for them, and the boundary changes between 1960 and 1980 are negligible or non-existent. Thus for the US cities this is the definition generally adopted. The exceptions are Boston where the inner area is defined as Suffolk County, Washington where the District of Columbia has been taken as the inner area and Phoenix and Houston where better definitions of the Pre World War II area were provided by local authorities (Table 2.4).

v) Toronto and Moscow Planners in Toronto were able to specify the Pre World War II area according to current minor planning units. Moscow has so far been reluctant to give any information about its Pre World War II area and therefore no inner area data are available.

c) Central city or CBD definitions

As far as possible the CBD was defined according to the consensus view of government authorities in each city and mostly on the basis of one or more small administrative or traffic planning zones for which good data were available. However, in some cases, mainly in US and Australian cities, small modifications had to be made to accommodate the available parking data. Parking data surveys are performed irregularly in cities and the survey boundaries may change as the CBD changes. Thus, the CBD definition in a city was sometimes influenced by the availability of good parking survey data but in most cases this did not significantly affect the overall usefulness of the area finally adopted. In a few cases however, the limited extent of parking data did constrain the definition of the CBD. This was not a major problem except that it occasionally distorted the picture of the central area's residential character. In Toronto, for example, the population density of the CBD (minor planning district 1e) is given as 25.2 people per ha whereas the entire central area (planning district 1) is 43.6 people per ha. The smaller area has been used for the parking data discussion and the larger area for the population data discussion.

Table 2.4
Inner area definitions

Adelaide
Adelaide's inner area is defined as the Local Government Areas (LGA's) of Adelaide, Unley , Kensington/Norwood, St Peters, Walkerville, Prospect, Hindmarsh and Thebarton. This definition corresponds to that used by Hal Kendig in his book "New Life for Old Suburbs, George Allen and Unwin, Sydney, 1975 (p5). Data are generally available by LGA in Adelaide.

Amsterdam
Amsterdam's inner area is from the same source as the CBD definition . Again , no actual physical definition of the area is provided by the Amsterdam authorities, but comprehensive data were supplied.

Boston
Suffolk County lying at the heart of the Metropolitan Region of Boston is used as the inner area of Boston. It embraces the City of Boston plus three other smaller cities- Chelsea, Revere and Winthrop. Detailed data are available for Suffolk County from the U.S. Census and other sources.

Brisbane
Brisbane's inner area is defined as the LGA's lying within a 6km radius of the Brisbane GPO (General Post Office) in the centre of Brisbane. Maps of LGA's in each year (1961,1971,1981) were obtained and circles with 6 km radius were drawn. Each LGA lying primarily within these circles was identified and relevant data obtained from statistical sources. The LGA's for each year are as follows:
1961 and 1971: Ascot, Ashgrove, Balmoral, Camp Hill, Chatsworth, City, East Brisbane, Ekibin, Fernberg, Greenslopes, Indooroopilly, Ithaca, Morningside, Newmarket, Normanby, North City, St Lucia, South City, Toowong, Windsor, Yeronga.
1981: Albion, Alderley, Annerley, Ascot, Ashgrove, Balmoral, Bardon, Bowen Hills, Bulimba, Camp Hill, City, Coorparoo, Dutton Park, East Brisbane, Fairfield, Geebung, Grange, Greenslopes, Hamilton, Hawthorne, Herston, Highgate Hill, Indooroopilly, Kangaroo Point, Kelvin Grove, Lutwyche, Milton, Morningside, New Farm, Newmarket, Newstead, Norman Park, Paddington, Red Hill, St Lucia, South Brisbane, Spring Hill, Taringa, Toowong, West End, Wilston, Windsor, Woolloongabba, Yeronga.
It should be noted however, that Brisbane is very different from other Australian cities in its administrative structure. The majority of the Metropolitan Area or Statistical Division comes under the single authority of the Brisbane City Council. The above LGA's are thus part of the Brisbane City Council and are not the larger LGA's typical of other Australian cities.

Brussels
Brussels' inner area was one of the hardest in the study to define. This is because the Brussels region is comprised of nineteen cummunes with Bruxelles at the centre being by far the largest of these. However, it is an odd shape and the communes surrounding it could not be called completely "inner" in character. For the sake of data availability a compromise definition had to be chosen which resulted in the following eight communes being defined as Brussels' inner area: Saint- Josse-ten-Noode, Saint Gilles, Koekelberg, Etterbeek, Schaerbeek, Molenbeek-Saint-Jean, Ixelles, Bruxelles. Generally good data are available on the basis of these communes in publications such as Radioscopie de Bruxelles:Etude Statistique - Publication de L'Agglomération de Bruxelles, 1983.

Chicago
City of Chicago (in Cook County)- excellent data at local and national levels (Census)

Copenhagen
Copenhagen's inner area consists of the most densely populated part of the Copenhagen Region and is defined as the København and Frederiksberg Kommunes plus Gentofte which is part of the Københavns amtskommune (ie Copenhagen suburbs) . Detailed data are available for these areas from the Copenhagen Statistical Yearbook as cited under CBD definitions.

Denver
City and County of Denver - excellent data at local and national level (Census).

Detroit
City of Detroit (in Wayne County) - excellent data at local and national level (Census).

Frankfurt
Frankfurt's inner area definition required some detailed map work especially to obtain a consistent definition over the 1960- 1980 period. However, a satisfactory area was established based on Frankfurt's city zones (Stadtbezirke). The following zones were used to specify the inner area: CBD (ie Altstadt, Innenstadt, and Bahnhofsviertal), Westend-Süd, Westend-Nord, Nordend-West, Nordend- Ost, Ostend, Bornheim, Gutleutviertal, Gallusviertal, Bockenheim, Sachsenhausen - Nord, Sachsenhausen - Süd. Some calculations were necessary to exclude the airport zone (Flughafen) from the area of the last two zones . Good data were available from Frankfurt's Statistical Yearbooks for each of these zones (see citation in CBD definitions).

Hamburg
Hamburg's inner area was defined by the Statistisches Landesamt Der Freien Und Hansestadt Hamburg (letter dated 18/10/1982 from Herr Buch plus map of inner city obtained from Herr Buch in Hamburg). Hamburg is divided up into 7 Bezirke and 180 Ortsteile and the following Ortsteile comprise the inner area : 101-115,117, 120-126, 301-316, 401-405, 408-429, 501-507 and 510. Excellent data are provided on each Ortsteil in Hamburg's Statistical Yearbooks (see specific citation in CBD definitions).

Hong Kong
Hong Kong's inner area definition was provided by Dr Peter K.S. Pun then Acting Government Town Planner/ Conceptual, Town Planning Division of Hong Kong. It is a genuine Pre- World War II area definition which was marked on a detailed map of Hong Kong based on small zones. It consist of thirty-seven Tertiary Planning Units (TPU's) as follows: TPU 1.1.2-1.1.6, 1.2.1-1.2.4, 1.3.1-1.3.3, 1.4.4, 1.4.6, 1.5.1, 1.5.7, 1.6.1, 2.1.1, 2.1.2, 2.1.4, 2.2.1 - 2.2.5, 2.4.1 - 2.4.3, 2.5.5, 2.6.1, 2.6.4 - 2.6.7, 2.7.1, 2.8.4, 2.8.5 .
Only data for 1971 and 1981 were available. 1961 zones were completely different and could not be matched to this definition. A lot of detailed data are available on the basis of theses TPU's.

Houston
The best definition that could be found for Houston's inner area was one recommended by the Houston- Galveston Regional Transportation Study. This consisted of the area within the Interstate Loop I-610 . Data were a little harder to compile for this area but most were eventually obtained from a number of disparate sources, although 1960 and 1970 jobs could not be found.

London
A definition of "inner London" is provided in British Population Census details although no description of the physical area is published . Most of the data on London's inner area came through Mr David Bayliss of the GLC (see CBD definitions for specific citation) based on actual Census reports (eg County Reports - (Part1)Table 3).

Los Angeles
The City of Los Angeles (in Los Angeles County) is the closest administrative boundary to the pre World War II area and has excellent data from local and national sources (Census).

Melbourne
Melbourne's inner area definition is from page 5 of Kendig (1979) (see citation under Adelaide's inner area definition) and consists of eight inner metropolitan Local Government Areas as follows: Collingwood, Fitzroy, Melbourne, Port Melbourne, Prahran, Richmond, St Kilda, South Melbourne. Good data are available for Melbourne by Local Government Area in 1961, 1971, 1981.

Moscow
It has not been possible to define an inner area for Moscow due to difficulties in obtaining responses to enquiries and no published material appears to be available. No inner area data of any sort have been provided in the Sourcebook.

Munich
The inner area of Munich has been defined on the basis of zone size and distance from the CBD. The zones comprising the inner area are as follows : Stadtbezirke 1,5-14, 16, 20,21, and 26 (in earlier years zone 1 was divided into 1,2,3 and 4). This definition was validated later by the City of Munich in some parking survey data supplied by them. The only difference was that Stadtbezirke 21 was not included as an inner zone by the City of Munich.

New York
The New York Tri- State Region inner area has been defined as the whole City of New York encompassing the five Counties or Boroughs of Bronx, Kings, Queens, Richmond and New York. Excellent data are available for this area from many sources.

Paris   The Paris inner area has been defined as the Ville de Paris (City of Paris) plus the Petite Couronne (see metropolitan area definitions). It could be argued that this definition is too generous since it embraces over 60% of the total metropolitan area population. However, the only other possible definition from the point of view of reliable data collection would be the City of Paris by itself but this is definitely too constrained . There do not appear to be any intermediate size areas for which reliable data are readily available. The majority of this area appears to have been developed by the Second World War.

Perth   The inner areas of Australian cities are normally defined by LGA's. However, in Perth problems related to obtaining consistent LGA data for 1961, 1971 and 1981 meant that this method was not the best method in Perth. Rather, the inner area was defined on a more detailed basis according to Census Zones, for the sake of better data availability . The zones were as follows: 1961   101-109,130-134, 201, 204, 206, 207, 210, 213, 216, 230-233 and 300. 1971 and 1981   101-106, 108, 109, 120, 121, 130-134, 201, 204, 206, 207, 210, 216 and 230-233. Detailed data for each zone in each year were available in the respective Perth Region Data Book (see CBD definitions). In practice the above Census Zones correspond approximately to the LGA's of Cottesloe, Claremont, East Fremantle, Fremantle, Mosman Park, Nedlands, Peppermint Grove, Perth (City of), South Perth and Subiaco.

Phoenix   Unlike in other US cities it was not possible to use the whole City of Phoenix as the inner area for the Phoenix SMSA as most of the city was developed in the 1950's and 1960's. However, the City of Phoenix define their own inner city which corresponds closely to the actual core of the Phoenix region as of 1940. It is thus a more genuine Pre-World War 2 area. This area is defined as Census Tracts 1129-1133, 1139-1143, 1148-1151, and parts of 1128, 1144 and 1147. With some data manipulation (mainly to cope with the part Census Tracts) it was possible to get all the necessary data to correspond to the above definition. Details of the area can be found in Inner City Area Plan September, 1979 from the City of Phoenix (p.7 and p.14).

San Francisco   The City and County of San Francisco appears to be closest to the inner area of the San Fransisco SMSA and has excellent data from local and national sources (Census).

Singapore   Singapore's inner area was by far the most difficult to define. No authorities in Singapore seemed able to offer any suggestions about how to do it. Under the circumstances population and area data by Census Division were obtained through Singapore's Department of Statistics for 1960,1970 and 1980. Through a combination of proximity of the Census Division to the central area and the relative population density of each Census Division, an inner area was defined for each year. Basically, the chosen Census Divisions extended a maximum of around 6.5 km to the west, 5.0 km to the east and about 3.5 km to the north from the coastline in the Kampong Glam Census Division. However, Singapore's Census Divisions have changed dramatically over the 20 year period and land has been created through reclamation schemes close to the central area. Thus the best possible effort was made to define a similar inner area in each year but there are some inevitable discrepancies. The inner area in each year has been defined as follows :

   1960   Cairnhill, Farrer Park, Geylang, Havelock, Kampong Kapor, Rochore, Stamford, Tanjong Pagar, Telok Ayer and Tiong Bahru.

   1970   Alexandra, Anson, Bras Basah, Bukit Ho Swee, Bukit Merah, Cairnhill, Crawford, Delta, Farrer Park, Geylang East, Geylang Serai, Geylang West, Havelock, Hong Lim, Jalan Besar, Joo Chiat, Kallang, Kampong Glam, Kampong Kapor, Kampong Ubi, Katong, Kreta Ayer, Macpherson, Moulmein, Mountbatten, Queenstown, River Valley, Rochore, Sepoy Lines, Stamford, Tanjong Pagar, Telok Ayer, Tiong Bahru, Whampoa.

   1980   Alexandra, Brickworks, Bukit Ho Swee, Bukit Merah, Buona Vista, Cairnhill, Delta, Farrer Park, Geylang East, Geylang Serai, Geylang West, Havelock, Henderson, Jalan Besar, Kallang, Kampong Glam, Katong, Kim Seng, Kolam Ayer, Kreta Ayer, Leng Kee, Macpherson, Moulmein, Mountbatten, Queenstown, Radin Mas, River Valley, Rochore, Tanjong Pagar, Tiong Bahru, Whampoa.

Stockholm   Stockholm's inner area was defined by the Stockholm Office of Research and Statistics (Stockholms Kommun Utrednings - och statistikkontoret) in a letter from Christer Pränting (undated). It consist of the whole of Stockholm's "inre staden" (seventeen parishes) plus three parishes in the "yttre staden" (outer city) ie Brännkyrka, Enskede and Bromma. Details of these areas can be found in Stockholm's Statistical Yearbooks as cited under CBD definitions . Good data are kept for all of these area in the Statistical Yearbooks, although some extra work was required to specify the actual "urbanised " area of the inner city. This was obtained via a computerised land use data base in Stockholm.

Sydney   Kendig (1979) (see CBD definitions) defines Sydney's inner area as the LGA's of City of Sydney, South Sydney , Botany, Marrickville, Leichhardt, and North Sydney. However, three further LGA's (Randwick, Waverley and Woollahra) lie at a similar distance from the CBD and have population densities as high as the six LGA's specified by Kendig. Hence, the inner area defined here includes these three additional LGA's. Good data are available by LGA for Sydney in each year.

Tokyo   Tokyo's inner area has been defined simply as the 23 ward area of the "Tokyo Metropolis" on advice from Professor Kakumoto (see CBD definitions). Tokyo was very urbanised before World War 2 and the 23 ward area was physically and administratively the Tokyo city area . In 1940 the 23 ward area contained 92% of Tokyo's total metropolitan population (ie 6,778,804 out of a total of 7,354,971 people). Excellent data are kept for the 23 wards.

Toronto   Toronto's inner area was defined on a map by planners in the Metropolitan Planning Department of Toronto. It is a genuine Pre-World War 2 area and consists of the following Minor Planning Districts : 1a, 1b, 1c, 1d, 1e, 1f, 1g, 1h, 2a, 2b, 2c, 2d, 2e, 2f, 2g, 2h, 2i, 3c, 3e, 3g, 3h, 3i, 4b, 4c, 4d, 4g, 4h, 6a, 6b, 6c, 6e, 6f, 6g, 6h, 7b, 7c, and 14a. Excellent data are kept for these districts in each year.

Vienna   The inner area of Vienna is defined by Vienna planning authorities in Stadtentwicklungsplan für Wien: Stadterneuerung und Bodenordnung Diskussionsgrundlage by Wilhelm Kainrath, Magistrat der Stadt Wien, Geschäftsgruppe Stadtplanung, Wien, 1979 (p 4, 14, 86 and 89). It consists of Bezirke (zones) 1-9 and 20 and is broadly refered to as "Wien-Mitte". Good data are available for all of Vienna's zones through the Vienna Statistical Yearbooks (see CBD definitions).

Washington DC   The inner area of Washington is simply defined as the whole District of Columbia for which very comprehensive data are available.

West Berlin   An inner area for West Berlin was difficult to define because of problems highlighted in relation to the CBD, (Table 2.5), i.e. the division of the city into East and West. However, West Berlin is divided into twelve districts, five of which could be considered as clustered around the CBD as defined by the West Berlin authorities. Thus the inner area was defined as the following districts with their respective district numbers from the Statistical Yearbook of West Berlin. (2) Tiergarten, (3) Wedding, (6) Kreuzberg, (7) Charlottenburg, (11) Schöneberg . Good data were available for each district through the West Berlin Statistical Yearbook (Statistisches Jahrbuch Berlin) and other sources.

Zürich   The inner area of the Agglomeration of Zürich has been taken to be the whole of the City of Zürich . This was done on advice from Dr R. Ott, Assistant Director, Statistisches Amt Der Stadt Zürich. Data availability for this area is excellent, coming mainly from Zürich's Statistical Yearbook (see CBD definitions).

Population, area and employment data are on the whole more universally available (and are usually enumerated on a regular basis) and so calculations can be done to ensure these items fit the adopted CBD definition.

Table 2.5 lists detailed CBD definitions for each city in the Sourcebook and highlights where the definition was slightly too constrained resulting in an understatement of the residential character of the area.

d) Individual data items

It has been found in compiling data for each city that in general we have been able to obtain good, comprehensive data on the population, land use, employment and public transport characteristics for most of the cities in each of the years. Some additional enquiries have usually been necessary in these respects but the data were mostly obtainable. Certain aspects of the traffic system were also generally well specified such as vehicle registrations and the length of the road network. It was found that a good degree of confidence could be placed in most of these data as there are often a number of reliable sources (eg. census material, annual reports and transportation studies). As well, explanations can usually be found about how the data have been derived and exactly what they represent. However, the specification of vehicle kilometres travelled (VKT) and fuel usage in the private transport system proved to be much more difficult.

i) VKT and fuel use data

Most cities have some data on these parameters particularly from the mid 1970's and early 1980's when it became important to consider such parameters because of the oil situation. The bigger cities such as New York and Los Angeles have VKT and some fuel data back to the early sixties because of the magnitude of their traffic and automotive emissions problems. On the whole though, most overseas cities find it quite a problem to specify the VKT and fuel usage within their urban areas and, in particular, to state what it actually represents and how it is derived (eg. does it include all traffic such as trucks and other commercial vehicles or is it just for cars? Was it derived using computer modelling techniques or is it the result of travel surveys?).

A particular case concerning San Francisco came to light which highlights the uncertainties surrounding VKT data that are not accompanied by explanatory information. We are in possession of two quite different sets of VKT data for the San Francisco nine County area (Alameda, Contra Costa, Marin, Napa, Santa Clara, San Mateo, San Francisco, Solano and Sonoma) - one set from the Californian Department of Transportation for 1973 and 1980 (Caltrans) and the other from the Metropolitan Transportation Commission (MTC) for 1960, 1970 and 1980. Some time was spent trying to reconcile the two sets of data and finally a letter was sent to the MTC explaining the problems.

The reply indicated that the early Caltrans data were based on an apportionment of the State VKT data in each County and included all categories of travel (ie automobiles, trucks, vans etc). The State data were estimated from fuel sales and assumptions about average miles per gallon. After 1979 the State VKT were estimated according to a computer model based on various parameters such as income and fuel price and again allocated to the various Counties. On the other hand, the MTC data that had been supplied were in fact not for the years specified and only included personal travel (no commercial travel by trucks etc). Their data were based on household surveys from which trip matrices were generated and loaded into the road network. VKT were then estimated using travel demand simulations developed from the household surveys. In their reply the MTC provided us with a new set of VKT data for 1965 and 1979 and suggested that we use it rather than any of the other data. It can thus be seen how important it is to ensure comparability of the VKT data between cities.

On top of the above issues, many cities are embedded within a much broader urban framework (unlike for example Perth, Western Australia which is so isolated) and a significant proportion of the VKT and fuel used within their administrative boundaries can be due to travel by people who live outside these boundaries (depending on how VKT and fuel are estimated). This makes it complicated to get reliable per capita data for the population who live within the specified urban area.

Because of these problems we made extensive literature searches and wrote to various organisations in an effort to locate some consistent and reliable data base on VKT and fuel. For example, the International Road Federation in Washington DC publishes a regular digest called "World Road Statistics" which keeps national data on vehicle and passenger kilometres in private transport as well as motor spirit and diesel fuel consumption in road transport. Their reply stated that they could not provide these data for urban areas nor could they tell us of any agency who would have them.

In the end US urban VKT data were found from sources within each city and mostly confirmed later from a 1985 US Department of Transportation publication entitled "Transportation Planning Data for Urbanized Areas Based on the 1980 Census". However, there were a few cases where data in the report differed from the data obtained directly from the city. In each case the data from the city were checked and found to be much more reliable and realistic. In all cases gasoline consumption figures were checked to see how they compared with VKT data using national fleet fuel efficencies (mpg or l/100km). Gasoline consumption data were mostly obtained from specific sources within each city such as Transportation Departments or coordinating Planning Departments such as the Tri-State Regional Planning Commission and Metropolitan Transportation Council in New York.

VKT and fuel use for the Australian cities were obtained on a consistent basis from the triennial Survey of Motor Vehicle Usage (SMVU) by the Australian Bureau of Statistics. We have done independent checks on VKT data from the SMVU and found it to be in general agreement with the other sources of Australian city VKT data such as from the various Main Roads Departments around Australia (see Kenworthy, 1986a and Newman and Kenworthy, 1980 a,b,c).

For the other cities in Europe and Asia a variety of local government agencies, private consulting firms, and independent reports provided the VKT and fuel use data (or the basis for estimating them). In general these could not be cross-checked against another source because no other sources could be found, but the VKT seemed to make good sense when compared

Table 2.5
CBD definitions

Adelaide The 222 ha area defined as Adelaide's CBD from detailed block-by-block maps is bounded by North, West and East Terraces and Gouger/ Angas St in the south. The whole Central City of Adelaide is a larger area of 403 ha bounded by North, South, East and West Terraces.

Amsterdam The 640 ha CBD was provided by the Dienst Ruimtelijke Ordening Amsterdam (Amsterdam Physical Planning Department) in a letter from G.F. de Haan dated 24/5/82 . Corresponding population, employment and parking data were provided, however no actual physical definition of the area was given .

Boston The best definition of the Boston CBD was the 570 ha (2.2 square mile) area bounded by the Charles River, Boston Harbour and Massachusetts Avenue and known as Boston Proper. Boston does have a smaller area which is often called the CBD. This smaller area is bounded by Massachusetts Avenue, the Massachusetts Turnpike and Charles River but does not reflect the very large central city population of Boston, hence "Boston Proper" was chosen as the best definition for the CBD. Data on population and employment for both definitions are included in the Sourcebook, but parking data are for "Boston Proper".

Brisbane The 165 ha Brisbane CBD was standardised for employment survey purposes in 1960, 1974 and 1980 (Derek Kemp, Brisbane City Council). It consists of a small peninsula bounded on the south, east and west by the Brisbane River and in the north approximately by Roma St,Turbot St, Ann St and Boundary St. It excludes the Queensland Institute of Technology and Botanic Gardens on the tip of the peninsula. Population and parking data were matched to this definition on a block-by-block basis.

Brussels The 258.8 ha Brussels CBD was defined as six small zones (1,6,7,8,20,21). Details were provided by the Ågglomération de Bruxelles through Mr Vincent Carton in a letter dated 24/10/1986.

Chicago The 414 ha Chicago CBD is defined as Census Tracts 511 to 516 inclusive in 1960 and 3201 to 3206 inclusive in 1970. The physical area referred to is approximately the area bounded by the Chicago River in the north and west, Lake Michigan in the east and Roosevelt Rd on the south.

Copenhagen Copenhagen's 455 ha CBD is given in "Pedestrian Streets and Other Motor Vehicle Restraints in Central Copenhagen" by Kai Lemberg, Director of General Planning, Copenhagen, August 1973. This corresponds almost exactly to districts (a) and (c) (Indre by and Voldkvartererne), for which detailed data appears in the Statistik Årbog- Statistik for Hovedstadsregionen (Copenhagen Statistical Yearbook).

Denver The 382 ha Denver CBD is defined as Census Tracts 17.01,17.02, 20.00, 25.00 and 26.01. In 1960 these tracts were specified as 0017-A, 0017-B, 0020, 0025 and 0026-A, following advice from Phillip A. Plienis , City Planner with the City and County of Denver.

Detroit The Detroit CBD for 1960 and 1970 was slightly different from that for 1980. In 1960 and 1970 it has been defined as Census Tracts 1, 33, 506, 507, 508, and 530 (300 ha) and in 1980 as Census Tracts 5172, 5173, 5207 and 5208 (362 ha). The 1960/70 definition comes from the City of Detroit, Planning Department , Data Coordination Division (August 1974), which shows the CBD as subcommunity 000 with an area of 1.16 square miles(300 ha). The 1980 definition is from the State of Michigan, Department of Management and Budget (letter from Laurence S.Rosen, 9/12/1982), and is identical to the 1977 US Census of Retail Trade (Major Retail Centres Vol RC 77-C-23 Michigan) definition of the Detroit CBD.

Frankfurt Frankfurt's CBD of 239 ha in 1970 and 1980 and 227 ha in 1960 is defined as the three central zones of the City of Frankfurt - Altstadt, Innenstadt and Bahnhofsviertel. The total area of these zones in 1970 and 1980 was 254.6 ha. However this incuded "public waters" the area of which was removed for the purposes of this study . In 1960 the total area was 255.1 ha but without public waters it was 226.5 ha. The Statistical Yearbooks for the City of Frankfurt in the various years (Statistisches Jahrbuch Frankfurt am Main) show detailed data for each of these zones.

Hamburg Hamburg's CBD of 460 ha (456 ha 1960) is essentially the area which was contained within the old city walls and corresponds to Hamburg- Altsteil (ortsteil 101-103) and Neustadt (ortsteil 104-107).Detailed data were available for these small zones in Hamburg's Statistical Yearbook (Statistisches Taschenbuch - Statistisches Landesamt Hamburg).

Hong Kong The CBD of Hong Kong is generally poorly defined since Hong Kong is so dense throughout and has intensely mixed business and residential functions on both Hong Kong Island and in Kowloon. To this extent Hong Kong does not have a CBD in the usual sense. However correspondence with the Transport Department (Chiu Tak-kwong 16/12/1982) indicated that any CBD definition should generally include Tertiary Planning Units(TPU) 1.2.1 and 1.2.3 on Hong Kong Island. These are very small and almost exclusively business in character , but are surrounded by intense residential activity . To capture this residential character, the definition was extended to include TPU's 1.2.2 and 1.2.4 which,with the other two TPU comprise Secondary Planning Unit (SPU) 1.2 and is called Central District. This is still a very small area , amounting to only 102 ha in 1961 and 1971 and 108 ha in 1981, perhaps reinforcing the fact that Hong Kong does not have a traditional CBD.

Houston Houston's 392 ha CBD is defined consistently as Census Tract 121.

London London's CBD of 2697 ha is termed the "conurbation centre "and data were provided by the then Greater London Council, Transportation and Development Department through David Bayliss, Chief Transport Planner (letter dated 8/10/1982). No actual physical definition of the CBD was given .

Los Angeles Los Angeles is a multi-centred city with a relatively weak CBD in the overall context of the metropolitan region. However, the "downtown" area is generally defined as Census Tracts 2072 to 2079 and 2092 inclusive. For the purpose of this study , tract 2092 has been eliminated since parking data do not extend into this tract.The physical area is bounded approximately by Pico Boulevard in the south, Figueroa/ Harbor Freeway in the west, Sunset Boulevard in the north and Los Angeles/Maple Ave in the east.

Melbourne There are two acceptable definitions of the CBD for Melbourne. The first ,the "true" CBD is termed the Golden Mile and is the area bounded by Latrobe St in the north, Flinders St in the south, Spring St in the east and Spencer St in the west. This area is 172 ha and has been used for the population data. The other definition in use is the Central Activities District (CAD) which is a larger area (238 ha) bounded by the same streets on the south and east, Spencer Street on the west up to Latrobe but then further west to Adderley as far as Dudley. It then proceeds north east until Peel St around Queen Victoria Market to Victoria and then east to Spring St. The parking and employment data are for this area while population data are for the CBD.

Moscow The Moscow CBD of 1900 ha is the area within the Sadovoye Ring (inner ring road) which forms an almost perfect circle of radius 2.5 km.This information was supplied through the U.S.S.R embassy in Canberra and confirmed from maps.

Munich	Munich's CBD of 694 ha was specified in Munich by the "Planungsreferat" as zones (Stadtbezirke) 1,8,9,10,11,12 corresponding respectively to Altstadt, Maxvorstadt-Marsfeld, Ludwigvorstadt, Isavorstadt-Schlachthofviertel, Isavorstadt-Glockenbackviertel, Isavorstadt-Deutsches Museum . Data for each of these zones are systematically provided in Munich's Statistical Yearbooks (Statistisches Jahrbuch München and Statistisches Taschenbuch-München und seine Stadtbezirke).
New York	New York's CBD of 2331 ha is known as "The Hub" and is the total area of Manhattan south of 60th St. Consistent data are provided for this intensely developed area through the Tri-State Regional Planning Commission and New York Metropolitan Transportation Council.
Paris	The Paris CBD of 2333 ha is defined consistently as Arrondisements 1e to 10e within the Ville de Paris. Comprehensive data are kept on each arrondisement.
Perth	The Perth CBD of 759 ha is defined as Census Zones 101 and 130 to 134 inclusive.Detailed data are provided for these Census zones in the Perth Region Data Book by the Metropolitan Region Planning Authority , published for each census year. The physical area is bounded approximately by the Swan River in the south and east, Newcastle St in the north and Thomas St in the west.
Phoenix	Phoenix, like Hong Kong, does not have a CBD in the true sense . However, the reason is completely opposite to the case of Hong Kong in that Phoenix has virtually no concentrations of urban activity- it is an archetypal "dispersed" city. One definition of Phoenix's CBD takes it north-south up the Central Ave corridor which is a linear office development strip. This definition embraces seven Census Tracts (1087,1088, 1105, 1118, 1130,1131, 1141). However, this gives a CBD area of 1200 ha and is unrealistic for a city of Phoenix's size; the definition is not widely used. A better definition is that adopted by the parking surveys and includes only Census Tracts 1130, 1131 and 1141, embracing an area of 389 ha. This definition does not include the north-south office development corridor. Population, employment and parking data were available for this smaller area and it was probably the best definition that could be adopted given Phoenix's unusual urban structure.
San Francisco	San Fransisco's CBD is defined by the Department of City Planning as the C-3 district and corresponds approximately to Census Tracts 114, 115, 117, 118, 121-125, 176.01, 176.02 and 178 (see The Downtown Plan - Proposal for Citizen Review, Department of City Planning, City and County of San Fransisco, August 1983).It has a very complex physical boundary and cannot be easily described. In 1960 the Census Tracts do not readily correspond to the ones above but after some work it was possible to define a similar area. The 1960 Census Tracts numbers were A14, A15, A16, A17, A18, A21, A22, A23, K2 and K6.
Singapore	Singapore's CBD corresponds to the area traffic restraint scheme (restricted zone) and is a 772.2 ha section bounded by Lavender St, Serangoon Rd, Singapore River, Outram Rd,Cantonment Rd and includes the Orchard Rd corridor . Data were not easily obtained for this area but finally came through a number of diplomatic channels who contacted relevant departments in Singapore
Stockholm	Stockholm's 424 ha CBD was defined by the Stockholms Lans Landsting, Regionplane-Och Näringslivsnämnden, Regionplanekontoret (letter from Björn Lindfelt, 22/12/1982) and incorporates the parishes of Kungsholm, Adolf Fredrik, Gustav Vasa, Jakob, Klara and Hedvig Eleonora. Detailed data are available on all these parishes in the Stockholm Statistical Yearbook (Statistisk årsbok for Stockholm).
Sydney	Sydney's 416 ha CBD is as outlined by the Sydney City Council and is best defined in "Action Study 35: Review of Parking Policy and Control Codes - Final Draft Report" by the City Planning Department, Council of the City of Sydney, 1980. The area is too complex to describe physically but consists of the following ABS Census Collector's Districts in each year. 1961: 35CB, 35CC, 35CD, 35CE, 35CG, 35CH, 35CJ, 35CK, 35DB, 35DC, 35DD, 35DE, 35DF, 35DG. 1971: 36-02-11 to 36-02-16, 36-03-01 to 36-03-10, 36-03-12. 1981: 311401 to 311410, 311412 to 311414, 311305, 311310 to 311315. The State Transport Study Group of N.S.W was a larger definition of the CBD embracing residential parts of Surry Hills and Wooloomooloo. However, lack of parking data for this area meant that it could not be used. Nonetheless the smaller definition adopted embraced between 90% and 95% of the total jobs in the larger CBD area. The definition does explain the relatively low residential aspect to Sydney's CBD.
Tokyo	Tokyo's CBD of 4105 ha was defined through discussions with Professor Ryohei Kakumoto of the Japan Transport Economics Research Centre in Tokyo as being the three central wards lying at the heart of the 23 ward area (the major part of the Tokyo Metropolis).These wards are Chiyoda-ku, Chuo-ku, and Minato-ku. The areas of each ward have remained consistent apart from a small difference in 1960 when the total area was only 4018 ha. There is significant mixing of residential and business functions within this area with only Chiyoda being completely business in character . Detailed data are available on a consistent basis for each of these wards.
Toronto	Toronto's true CBD of 188.4 ha is defined by the Metropolitan Planning Department of Toronto as minor planning district 1e. This area however is only very minor in terms of residential functions but is surrounded by a larger "Central Area" of 2775 ha (Area 1) which has a significant mixing of residential and business activities. Because parking data were only available for MPD 1e, this smaller area has been used to characterise central city parking supply. However, for population density in the CBD data for both the small and larger CBD definition have been provided in the Sourcebook, as have the corresponding job data. The larger definition provides a truer perspective on the residential nature of Toronto's central area.
Vienna	Vienna's CBD of 301 ha is simply defined by authorities in Vienna as Bezirk 1 (District 1) and is essentially Vienna's old city core area. Systematic data are available on this district in a range of publications including The Vienna Statistical Yearbook (Statistisches Jahrbuch Der Stadt Wien).
Washington DC	The 460 ha CBD of Washington DC is generally defined by authorities as "Ring O" which embraces an area bounded on the south by Constitution Ave, on the north by Massachusetts Ave on the west by 23rd St. and on the east by 2nd St. Detailed data are kept by a number of Washington authorities for the Ring O area. A problem with this CBD definition is that it does not include close-by areas of a mixed residential/business character, hence Washington's CBD population picture is unfortunately not well represented.
West Berlin	West Berlin, like Hong Kong and Phoenix, is the other city in the study which does not have a true CBD. This is because Berlin's original central area was included in East Berlin when Berlin was divided. Consequently, West Berlin developed as a "sub-centre city" and thus has only a very small area that could be considered something of a CBD. It is defined by Der Senator für Stadtentwicklung and Umweltschutz (letter from Herr Stein 2/2/1983) as a 1.2 square kilometre (120 ha) area known as "Zoo-City". The area however has only 40,000 employees and has atypically high parking supply for a European central city. This large supply of parking supports the suggestion that "Zoo-City" is more of a sub-centre than a typical European CBD.
Zürich	Zürich's 152 ha CBD is defined by authorities in Zürich as Kreis 1 (District 1) . This area has systematic data supplied in Zürich's Statistical Yearbook (Statistisches Jahrbuch Zürich).

between cities. Certainly there were occasions when the VKT data were plainly wrong but these stood out very clearly and it was possible to resolve the issue by going back to the original source and getting more details.

Despite the difficulties outlined we are confident that the data on transport fuel use and VKT are now consistent and reliable.

ii) Land use density data: defining what is urban land Urban land use data were also open to a large degree of interpretation. A consistent definition of what constitutes 'urban' was necessary in order to make valid comparisons. Considerable effort was therefore put into ensuring that the physical land areas (ie urbanised land) took adequate consideration of what was really 'urban' ie all land was excluded that was categorised as agriculture, water bodies, forest, large open space areas (not small local open space), and undeveloped urban zoned land. Thus urbanised land was defined as all land presently developed for residential, commercial, industrial and special urban purposes (schools etc), including all streets and roads.

As an example of the kind of difficulties encountered, a case study of Paris will be presented. Despite being one of the world's great cities there was clearly no accepted urban density for Paris due to problems in defining the full extent of the city and in defining the 'urban' land use areas. It should be stressed however, that Paris was the only city that presented such a complex task. In this sense it can be taken as a "worst case" example.

The full Paris urbanised region is called the Ile de France and most data requirements are available on the basis of this large region (including gasoline use). Thus it was important to properly define the urban density of the Ile de France in 1960, 1970 and 1980. Unlike most of the other Paris data however, a close examination of all historical and current land use data revealed that they were not kept on a consistent geographical basis and in some cases included open space and in other cases did not.

The Ile de France is divided into the City of Paris (Ville de Paris), the Petite Couronne and the Grande Couronne. It was clear that some of the land use data actually excluded parts of the Grande Couronne amounting to about 1,349,000 people; data for some years included it. As well, some of the data included the land use category "open space" while other data excluded it. After many detailed calculations and reference to ancillary sources to expand and supplement missing data, four possibilities emerged for specifying Paris in density terms.
(1) More heavily urbanised section excluding open space} approx. 87%
(2) More heavily urbanised section including open space} of population
(3) Whole of Ile de France excluding open space } 100% of
(4) Whole of Ile de France including open space } population
The densities outlined in Table 2.6 resulted from these four options.

Option 4 was finally chosen as the one which best represented the density of the entire Paris region population. This was because:
   a) it was for the whole Ile de France and was thus compatible with other
      statistics and
   b) it included a local open space component which made it compatible
      with the urban density definition in other cities.
Although Paris was the worst case for defining urban area (about six days

28

were required to decipher the details), Los Angeles also had some problems. Los Angeles is defined as the Los Angeles/Long Beach SMSA (LA County); this is not the full functional urban region which embraces a number of other smaller SMSA's. The inferior definition had to be used as there are difficulties in compiling such an array of data as in this study across so many separate administrative areas (see Table 2.3). Were the true urban region to be used, as is the case in the Tri-State urban area of New York, where data are fully available, then it could be expected that the size of Los Angeles would be some 10-20% larger. However, for the purposes of the Sourcebook and the analyses carried out so far on the data, it was found that this was not a significant drawback. Some broad calculations showed that inclusion of the urbanised parts of other Counties making up the larger Los Angeles area did not significantly alter overall densities or even items like roads per capita.

Table 2.6
Possible urban densities to describe the Paris Region

	Urban density (persons/ha)		
Option	1962	1968	1982
1	97.1	94.8	83.9
2	77.6	76.1	69.1
3	72.1	67.4	63.5
4	52.7	50.2	48.3

iii) Other data items Table 2.7 contains a summary of other transport and land use data collected for the Sourcebook along with a broad description of the source. Although generally easier than defining areas of the city and getting the specific data items discussed so far, all of the data items in Table 2.7 presented some specific problems in different cities. Some of these problems are briefly mentioned in the table. The brevity of the table however belies a far more complex task especially for public transport, average vehicle occupancy and parking data which are discussed in more detail below.

•*Public transport data* Getting all the operational statistics for all the different public transport operators in each city was a nightmare in many cases. The one positive thing we found about public transport in cities like Phoenix, Houston and Detroit was the merciful simplicity of their data - one mode (bus) and mostly one operator in the 1980's. They virtually have no public transport!

The US auto-cities provided needed breathing space between compiling data on cities like New York, Chicago, Hong Kong, Hamburg and Zürich. New York has five different public transport modes and sixteen operators and Chicago has four modes, innumerable private bus operators (more than

Table 2.7
Table 2.7
Data collected for the international comparison of cities plus general data sources for each item covering 1960, 1970 and 1980.

Statistical Parameters	General Data Sources
1. Land Use Data	
(i) Population and area data	
(a) Population (total)	National census data and statistical yearbooks
(b) Actual <u>urbanised</u> area (ha) - (excluding all large non-urban uses such as undeveloped or agricultural land)	National census material on US urbanised areas, statistical yearbooks for European cities, individual land use studies and transportation studies and detailed mapping and planning data.
(c) Area of the CBD (ha)	Defined by each city or from amalgamations of small census zones or administrative units comprising the CBD (also see Parking).
(d) Population contained in the CBD	Population and area data for the CBD were usually obtained simultaneously.
(e) Inner urban area (ha)	Statistical yearbooks for European cities plus individual land use and transportation studies. US cities were frequently obtained from "Planning Agency and City Characteristics for 50 of the Nations Largest Cities" by the American Planning Association April 1982.
(f) Population contained in the inner urban area	Census data based on cities and smaller administrative zones within the city plus planning agency data.
(ii) Parking availability in the CBD (number of spaces)	
(a) Off-street	Parking surveys done irregularly by each city. Often required detailed block-by-block map work to get the correct CBD definition. Also land use/transportation studies by consulting firms.
(b) On-street	
(iii) Employment location	
(a) Number of jobs located in the CBD	Statistical yearbooks of cities in Europe CBD parking surveys which frequently enumerated employment, planning agency employment surveys and census material.
(b) Number of jobs located in the inner urban area (incl. CBD)	Census material for small zones, planning agency data and other irregular statistical surveys.
(c) Total number of jobs in the whole metropolitan area	National census data for metro areas, statistical yearbooks on cities and land use transportation studies.
2. Transportation data	
(i) Road network	
(a) Total length of road in the metropolitan area (this figure includes <u>all</u> road types from inter-state highways and freeways down to local or municipal residential streets.).	Statistical yearbooks on cities (Europe) transportation planning departments, regularly kept national statistical data on individual cities plus detailed but irregular land use transportation studies. Local roads sometimes required reference to individual municipalities and State departments.
(ii) Total vehicles on register	
(a) Passenger cars	Statistical yearbooks on cities, MotorVehicle Registry departments and national statistical material kept on cities. This was generally one of the easiest parameters to obtain except for Paris where it came through the Chamber of Automotive Manufacturers and in Washington where several different States were involved.
(b) Commercial vehicles	
(c) Trucks	
(d) Motor cycles	
(e) Others (or whatever other categories are available)	
(iii) Private transport indicators	
(a) Total annual vehicle kilometres (or vehicle miles) of travel.	Discussed in detail in text but generally from individual planning or transportation agencies in each city and often from computer models.
(b) Average vehicle occupancy (persons per vehicle). (This figure covers the 24 hour period.)	One of the most problematic of all variables. Obtained generally from transport or road authority surveys of cordon lines, transport study surveys or from detailed accident records in each city.
(c) Average speed of travel in passenger vehicles for whole metro area	Mainly from the city road authority or from major land use transportation planning studies.
(d) Total annual gasoline consumption for the metro area (incl. LPG)	Gasoline and diesel use usually obtained simultaneously from a variety of sources: National transport surveys on cities, transportation authorities, gasoline and diesel sales figures. Also estimated from VKT and vehicle fuel efficiency data, and in some cases from published statistical handbooks on cities.
(e) Total annual diesel fuel consumption for the metro area. Please note that any breakdown in (a) and (b) by vehicle type would be most valuable.	
(iv) Public transport indicators (see separate table below)	All public transport data were obtained through a combination of statistical yearbooks on each city plus very detailed enquiries within the public transport authorities in each city (eg annual reports and unpublished data within authorities).
(v) Modal split data	
(a) % of people taking public transportation for journey-to-work	Mainly national population census material on mode of travel to work - each city separately specified. Other data from detailed personal travel surveys in each city. Sometimes involved detailed calculations from raw travel survey data.
(b) % of people taking private transportation for journey-to-work	
(c) % of people walking and cycling for journey-to-work	
(d) Any other modal split data available: eg the above split for CBD oriented work trips compared to other types of work trips OR figures on modal split for other types of trips.	
(vi) Average trip lengths	
(a) Journey to work	National transportation surveys broken down for individual cities but mainly land use/transportation studies irregularly commissioned in each city.
(b) Other trip types (whatever available) Note that these data include all modes (cars, public transportation, and walking/cycling)	

2 (iv) Public Transport Indicators	Annual vehicle kilometres (1) '60 '70 '80	Annual pass-engers carried '60 '70 '80	Average distance each passenger carried (2) '60 '70 '80	Average speed of travel '60 '70 '80	Annual energy consumption '60 '70 '80
Buses					
Government) trolley					
) & diesel					
Private) where					
) relevant					
Trains					
Subway					
Surface					
Commuter rail					
Trams					
Ferries					

(1) The annual vehicle kilometres for trains is actual wagon or car kilometres not train kilometres. Similarly where articulated trams are used, actual wagon kilometres are used.
(2) Average distance travelled by each passenger is used to estimate passenger kilometres.

thirty), and seven separate commuter rail services. Hong Kong and Hamburg each have between ten and fifteen separate operators and modes and Zürich has a complex combination of municipal, national and private rail services including three separate funicular railways and an extensive government system of light rail, motor buses and trolley buses as well as private ferries.

• *Average vehicle occupancy* Average vehicle occupancy (persons per vehicle) for the 24 hour period was also a highly problematic variable. This is because of the seemingly endless variety of methods used to obtain the data in each city. Some occupancies are based on cordon counting procedures for vehicles entering the central area. Some of these are taken only in peak periods and others over a 12 hour period. In many cases the generally available data do not include evenings or weekends when average auto occupancy tends to be higher. Some data are from questionnaire travel surveys and some are from accident records in the city.

In general, average auto occupancies in peak periods (ie mainly the journey to work) tend to be between about 1.2 and 1.3 throughout the world. This apparently changes little regardless of the type of city or cultural factors. However, after a lot of searching and comparing, especially in cities where a range of values were available for various time periods and different parts of the city (CBD versus suburban), it was clear that average auto occupancy on a 24 hour basis over the full week was considerably higher than 1.3.

For example, in the Australian cities, data from transportation studies and other local governmental sources which purported to show overall average auto occupancy gave values of between 1.42 and 1.52. However, the detailed and comprehensive Survey of Motor Vehicle Usage (SMVU) conducted triennially by the Australian Bureau of Statistics showed higher auto occupancy of around 1.7 persons per vehicle. Their data cover the entire year (weekdays and weekends and all time periods) in each of the Australian cities. Because the SMVU data are calculated on a consistent basis across all five cities and appeared to provide more reliable 24 hour figures, their data were used in preference to the local sources which appeared to be underenumerating vehicle occupancies for our purposes.

For the other cities in the study the best possible available data were used, and in some cases 24 hour figures were estimated based on a range of evidence. In a few cities we are still not satisfied with the final figures which had to be adopted. For example, Brussel's figure of 1.3 we believe to be too low although the best authority we could find within the Agglomération de Bruxelles insists that it is correct. In the absence of further evidence this value has been used.

On the whole we are satisfied that the average vehicle occupancies finally adopted in most cities are reasonable, however this is one parameter where readers in some cities may find it useful to respond with better data (see end of this chapter).

• *Parking* Parking data were nearly always difficult to get. This is because parking data are never supplied in Statistical Yearbooks in the European cities and are only rarely published in readily accessible reports in the other cities. They are almost always done on an irregular basis by consultants in response to specific needs of planning authorities in cities. Where several reports are available over a long time period the boundaries of the parking inventories frequently change because the extent of the officially recognised CBD often expands. As well, parking inventories do not always correspond exactly to the CBD as defined for the purposes of population and employment data.

In quite a few cases it was a difficult task to get the parking, population, employment and physical area data to coalesce. In some cases (eg Los Angeles) it involved very time consuming calculations from a map in the parking inventory showing the numbers of different types of parking spaces on a block-by-block basis (off-street versus on-street, lot parking versus parking buildings, tenant parking versus public parking and metered versus unmetered parking).

In a number of cities the data were supplied simply by letter from a government agency without any documentary evidence or split according to off-street and on-street (eg Stockholm). This was apparently much simpler than doing rigorous calculations but often led to further queries and letters to the agency when the combination of parking spaces and employment for the same purported area did not make much sense. The parking data were generally reassessed by the respondent and as expected new data were provided. It became clear after some hard experience that it was far better to be supplied with copies of actual parking inventories than to rely on someone else to do the necessary calculations or make assumptions about what was required. We thus now have a considerable collection of parking studies.

The above comment became a generally applicable rule for virtually all data items, ie that there were fewer problems and delays requiring additional responses where actual reports or photocopies of detailed data were supplied, even if it meant laborious compilations on our part. Understandably, it would seem that it is mostly beyond reasonable expectation for government departments to do the necessary detailed work for someone else's requirements.

Final comments

It should be stressed that it would be impossible in this book to describe in detail how every individual piece of data was determined for each city. In some instances the description and accompanying calculations for just one item occupy several pages. However, these details are available from the authors since logbooks were kept for each city describing in detail, where necessary, the source of data and any assumptions, modifications or additional calculations that had to be made. Readers are welcome to write with any queries.

In addition, it is also important to note that the Sourcebook is a first attempt at gathering data on these thirty-two cities. As such it is designed to be updated. If readers have a particular interest in a city and can suggest why data are inadequate, or simply wrong, and can see how they could be improved, they are encouraged to fill out a copy of the standard form printed at the end of the book and send it back to us (Appendix 2, Table A2.1). Please also include any detailed explanations or copies of reports! Other cities are also welcome to fill out the data sheet for a recent year and so be included in any further editions of the book.

3 Main findings

This chapter is set out in two main sections. First, the key data for 1980 are extracted from the Sourcebook and compared under three major categories :
-transport patterns emphasising automobile dependence through gasoline consumption and modal split,
-parameters revealing the degree of infrastructure provision for the automobile, and
-urban form parameters.

Second, some analyses of these data are attempted, first through correlation analysis, and second through factor analysis and cluster analysis. These analyses are done in order to provide a framework for subsequent chapters on the policy implications. Only 1980 data have been analysed so far. A time-series chapter will be added in a subsequent edition of this book.

Patterns of transport and land use

The first part of this chapter examines the patterns of gasoline usage per capita and the main transport and land use patterns in the thirty-two cities for 1980. For many of the parameters Moscow is not available and hence the total is generally made up of twelve European, ten American, one Canadian, five Australian and three Asian cities. The major questions being assessed by this part of the study which are examined here are:
 •How much variation is there in the transport patterns of the world's

major cities?
  •How closely do these transport patterns relate to land use in these cities?
  •How do the transport patterns relate to the provision of transport infrastructure?

These questions have been the subject of many academic debates as well as soul-searching within transport and planning authorities. This study is hopefully able to throw some further light on the issues as it provides, probably for the first time, a reliable set of urban data for a relatively large number of cities enabling an international cross section to be examined.

Transport patterns

Table 3.1 presents twelve of the main transport variables emphasising gasoline use and the split between private and public transport. Gasoline use gives an overall feel for the transport system in each city by acting as a kind of barometer which rises with increasing automobile emphasis, as well as being of central concern in itself. Passenger kms of private car use and public transport use and their relative proportions enable a real comparison of the overall importance of these modes. The proportions of workers using private and public transport and those using non-motorised modes (walking and bicycling) for the journey to work add to this broad picture. The public transport service provision and usage variables provide a simple characterisation of the public transport system. The remaining variables summarise the magnitude of private vehicle ownership in each city (passenger cars and total vehicles).

The data are presented in their regional groupings to gain some perspective on the variations found in this international comparison.

(i) Gasoline use In 1980 the average US city was nearly double the per capita gasoline of Australian cities, a little less than double Toronto's usage, four times more than in the average European city, and ten times the average of the three "westernised" Asian cities. Moscow, which has almost no private car use manages on a mere 380 MJ per capita which is about 150 times less than US cities. There is little point in further comparisons with Moscow because not only is the rest of the data limited but its political system is so different from the rest of the cities it means that the comparison is of little value. However, it does stand as a case study that a large relatively modern city can exist on virtually no gasoline. The ten US cities also show quite a variation from Houston to New York - a difference of some 40%.

One immediate response to these international variations is to wonder how much can be due to the different technological efficiency of the cars which consume the gasoline. Apart from re-emphasising the large variations in consumption within the ten US cities (and also a 20% variation in the five Australian cities) where vehicle efficiency variations play virtually no role, a few simple calculations can be carried out.

Table 3.2 compares the regional groupings on the basis of adjusted gasoline consumption so that all the cities are made to have US vehicle efficiencies. The comparison is using national vehicle efficiencies and the second using vehicle efficiencies adjusted for average speed in each city (detailed data are

Table 3.1
Transport patterns in the world's major cities (1980).

City	Gasoline use (MJ per capita)	Total vehicles (per 1000 people)	Car ownership (per 1000 people)	Private car (passenger kms per capita)	Public transport (passenger kms per capita)	Private car/public transport balance (% of total passenger kms on public transport)	Public transport vehicle kms of service per person	Public transport passenger trips per person	Proportion of public transport passenger kms on trains (%)	Proportion of workers using public transport (%)	Proportion of workers using private transport (%)	Proportion of workers using foot or bicycle (%)
US Cities												
Houston	74,510	797	603	15,968	128	0.8	9	15	0.0	3.3	93.9	2.8
Phoenix	69,908	689	499	13,170	66	0.5	7	9	0.0	2.2	94.6	3.2
Detroit	65,978	691	594	14,017	112	0.8	17	26	2.7	4.1	93.1	2.8
Denver	63,466	853	666	11,630	218	1.8	25	27	0.0	6.5	88.1	5.3
Los Angeles	58,474	667	542	13,865	384	2.7	27	59	0.0	7.7	88.0	4.2
San Francisco	55,365	681	543	13,200	926	6.6	50	115	33.9	17.0	77.5	5.5
Boston	54,185	557	465	12,570	518	4.0	26	80	52.3	16.1	74.1	9.8
Washington	51,241	645	561	11,670	616	5.0	40	91	37.2	14.1	80.7	5.2
Chicago	48,246	518	445	11,122	971	8.0	42	115	66.7	18.3	75.5	6.2
New York	44,033	459	412	7,856	1,285	14.1	58	122	78.0	28.3	63.6	8.1
Average	**58,541**	**656**	**533**	**12,507**	**522**	**4.4**	**30**	**66**	**27.1**	**11.8**	**82.9**	**5.3**
Australian Cities												
Perth	32,610	614	475	11,477	592	4.9	53	71	14.4	12.0	84.0	4.0
Brisbane	30,653	595	458	11,721	745	6.0	48	79	55.8	16.6	78.1	5.3
Melbourne	29,104	528	446	10,128	779	7.1	53	95	63.1	20.6	73.7	5.7
Adelaide	28,791	568	475	10,625	655	5.8	51	83	33.5	16.5	77.7	5.8
Sydney	27,986	489	412	9,450	1,511	13.8	77	142	69.9	29.5	65.1	5.4
Average	**29,829**	**559**	**453**	**10,680**	**856**	**7.5**	**56**	**94**	**47.3**	**19.0**	**75.7**	**5.2**
Canadian City												
Toronto	34,813	554	463	9,850	1,976	16.7	81	178	40.2	31.2	63.0	5.8
European Cities												
Hamburg	16,671	382	344	7,470	1,516	17.0	80	248	64.4	41.0	43.9	15.3
Frankfurt	16,093	427	387	6,810	1,713	20.1	55	306	51.3	19.0	54.0	27.0
Zürich	15,709	432	375	7,254	2,157	22.9	62	363	55.6	34.0	45.0	21.0
Stockholm	15,574	390	347	6,570	2,124	24.4	119	302	60.4	46.0	34.0	20.0
Brussels	14,744	408	361	5,706	1,396	19.7	54	266	43.2	26.7	57.7	15.6
Paris	14,091	383	338	4,199	1,827	30.3	47	259	83.8	39.8	36.4	23.8
London	12,426	356	288	4,452	1,717	27.8	120	284	63.7	39.0	38.0	23.0
Munich	12,372	398	360	5,235	1,592	23.3	75	307	61.1	42.0	38.0	20.0
West Berlin	11,331	306	269	4,572	2,159	32.1	83	395	58.3	37.0	48.0	15.0
Copenhagen	11,106	296	246	6,231	1,657	21.0	110	201	48.0	31.0	36.8	32.2
Vienna	10,074	374	311	4,262	1,828	30.0	69	313	26.6	44.9	40.4	14.7
Amsterdam	9,171	342	308	4,441	1,801	28.9	74	345	45.5	14.0	58.0	28.0
Average	**13,280**	**375**	**328**	**5,595**	**1,791**	**24.8**	**79**	**299**	**55.1**	**34.5**	**44.2**	**21.3**
Asian Cities												
Tokyo	8,488	267	156	2,993	5,191	63.4	94	472	94.9	59.0	16.1	24.9
Singapore	6,003	155	65	1,789	1,942	52.1	98	353	0.0	59.6	24.6	15.8
Hong Kong	1,987	66	42	615	2,043	76.9	116	466	17.1	62.2	3.3	34.5
Average	**5,493**	**163**	**88**	**1,799**	**3,059**	**64.1**	**103**	**430**	**37.3**	**60.3**	**14.7**	**25.1**
USSR City												
Moscow	380	40	20	230	>4,262a	>95	>131	>678	>75	74.0	2.0	24.0

Note a) Moscow commuter rail data are missing

given in Table 4.1).

Three major points can be made from this table:

1. Adjusting each city to US vehicle efficiency levels means the variations in gasoline consumption between regional groupings of cities are reduced but not greatly. US cities are now less than double Australian cities; for European cities the difference drops to a little over three times and for the Asian cities the difference drops from ten times to five or eight times (depending on which efficiency is used). Obviously there are other factors besides vehicle efficiency causing the differences in gasoline use amongst these thirty-two cities. The relative importance of vehicle efficiency is further pursued in Chapter 4 along with other economic factors.

2. The difference in adjusted gasoline use becomes much reduced when using vehicle efficiencies adjusted for the average speed in each city rather than national vehicle efficiencies. The variation in efficiency from US vehicles to Asian vehicles of 50% is reduced to 22%. Average speed is the key traffic determinant of fuel efficiency in individual vehicles (Evans, Herman and Lam, 1976). This means that the vehicle efficiency factor in itself can never be isolated from the city in which it is being used, but is totally bound up in the type of traffic in which the vehicle is used. Later it will be shown that the simplistic notion of improving gasoline use by increasing average speeds is also not possible to separate from the fabric of the city, as increasing average speeds will increase automobile use and dependence.

3. The difference between the Canadian city Toronto and the Australian cities becomes much more highlighted once the vehicle efficiency factor is removed. Canadian vehicle fuel efficiency is very low so that Toronto becomes lower in gasoline usage than the average Australian city once this factor is removed. Toronto therefore becomes considerably lower than the other North American cities. Reasons for this are confirmed in the other transport parameters below.

(ii) Modal split The highly automobile orientated U.S. cities at the top of the list in Table 3.1 have virtually no public transport as a percentage of their total passenger kms of travel e.g. Houston 0.8%, Phoenix 0.5%, Detroit 0.8%. Even in a city like Denver where there is a strong policy to encourage bus usage to reduce smog levels, only 1.8% of total passenger travel is by public transport. It is only in the U.S. cities with rail systems that any significant proportion of transport is by non-automobile modes e.g. San Francisco 7%, Chicago 8%, New York 14%. The proportion of total transit passenger kms by trains in these cities is 34%, 67% and 78%. At the same time the proportion of people bicycling and walking for journey to work trips rises in these more rail-oriented cities (up to 10% in Boston, 6 to 8% in others).

Australian cities overall are a little less automobile orientated, though Perth is virtually an average U.S. city with only 5% of total passenger travel on transit, 84% of people use cars for the journey to work and only 4.0%, foot or bicycle. Sydney, with 14% of total passenger travel on public transport, is the most non-car orientated Australian city with, once again, a high proportion of public transport on rail (70%). Toronto is significantly different to its North American neighbours with 17% total transit use (in particular the comparison with its nearest neighbour Detroit at 0.8% is quite

Table 3.2
Adjusted average 1980 gasoline use per capita in cities by region to account for vehicles efficiency (relative to US vehicle efficiencies, using national values and adjusted for average speed in cities).

City	Unadjusted gasoline use per capita (MJ)	Average vehicle efficiency (National values) (L/100km)	Adjusted for average speed in cities (L/100km)	Gasoline use per capita with U.S. vehicle efficiency (MJ)	
				National values	Adjusted for average speed
US cities	58,541	15.35	19.33	58,541	58,541
Australian cities	29,829	12.50	15.33	33,446	37,612
Toronto	34,813	16.30	21.72	32,784	30,982
European cities	13,280	10.66	16.38	19,123	15,727
Asian cities	5,493	7.63	15.05	11,051	7,248

Notes: (1) Detailed data on vehicle efficiences are contained in Table 4.1 in Chapter 4.
(2) Adjustments for average speed are made by using $y = 1.0174x + 37.4291$ where $y =$ fuel consumption in ml/km and x is the inverse of average speed in s/km (Kenworthy and Newman, 1982) and national fuel efficiencies are assumed to be at an average speed of 60 km/h.

stunning).

European cities on average have 25% public transport use for the total passenger transport task (passenger kms) and for the work journey 21% of trips are by bicycling and walking. For public transport as a proportion of total travel the figures range from 17% in Hamburg to 32% in West Berlin and 30% in Vienna; for bicycling and walking to work, Copenhagen at 32% and 28% in Amsterdam are the best. In the European cities 55% of public transport passenger kms are on trains.

On average, people in U.S. cities travel nearly 7000 km further by car and over 1200 km less by public transport than in European cities. Among other things this suggests urban travel distances are shorter in Europe and in fact work journey average distances are 30 to 40% shorter in European cities (8km) compared to U.S. (13km) and Australian cities (12km).

All these comparisons are even more striking when the Asian cities are examined where 64% of the transport task is by public transport and 25% of people go to work on foot or bicycle (35% in Hong Kong). In the modern metropolis of Tokyo only 16% of people use a car to go to work and in the public transport system 95% of passenger kms are by rail.

(iii) Public transport system characteristics The two main variables used here

are the level of service provided in terms of vehicle kms per person and the annual passenger trips undertaken per person. It can be seen that the U.S. cities have by far the lowest level of public transport service (30 vehicle kms per person). This is almost half the level provided in Australian cities (56 vehicle kms), a third of the European cities (79 vehicle kms) and nearly a quarter of the Asian cities (103 vehicle kms). Use of public transport follows a similar pattern. On average, people in the U.S. cities take a public transport trip once every six days, while in the Australian cities it is once every four days, in the European cities it is almost once a day and in the Asian cities more than once a day.

(iv) Vehicle ownership Vehicle ownership is expressed as the total number of vehicles registered per 1000 people plus the actual passenger cars per 1000 people . The data follow a distinct pattern of being highest in the U.S. cities, a little lower in the Australian cities and Toronto (approx. 15%) and 38% to 42% lower in the European cities. The U.S. cities have some four to six times more vehicles per 1000 people than the Asian cities. In Houston and Denver there is the the extraordinary situation of between 8 and 9 motor vehicles for every 10 people i.e. almost as many vehicles as there are people. The role of vehicle ownership in determining transport patterns and gasoline use is considered with other factors in Chapter 4.

The next two sections deal with physical planning; parameters that relate to physical planning are divided into:
  • First, those which relate to the provision of transport and infrastructure - in this case we have chosen to compare the provision of roads per capita, the availability of car parking spaces, the level of congestion on the roads, and the relative speed of the various public transport modes.
  • Second, the physical planning of the city in terms of its urban form, in this case emphasising population and job densities in the city as a whole and then by central city, inner city and outer area, including the proportion of total population and jobs in the central and inner area .

Transport infrastructure patterns

(i) Road supply and parking Table 3.3 shows how cities provide for their transport modes in terms of road supply and central city parking. The automobile cities of the U.S. and Australia provide around three to four times as much road per capita as in European cities and nearly seven to nine times as much as in Asian cities.

Central city parking does not have quite such a large variation with the U.S. cities having some 80% more spaces per 1000 workers than European cities and six times that provided in the three Asian cities. Perth is the outstanding city in the sample as far as automobile provision is concerned with by far the highest road supply per capita and a central city parking provision second only to Phoenix which does not in fact have a true central city area (see Table 2.5).

(ii) Congestion and public transport speeds The very clear pattern

distinguishing automobile dominated US and Australian cities from those with significant public transport use (particularly rail) can be related in purely transport terms to how easy it is to travel by car and how the transit option competes in time.

The data in Table 3.3 show the automobile based cities to have average traffic speeds of 43 km/h (U.S.) and 44 km/h (Australian) compared to European cities of 30 km/h and Asian cities 24km/h. The significance of these vehicle speeds for conservation of energy will be examined in the next section on correlations and further in Chapter 5. The provision of public transport options follows the general patterns outlined so far. The bus-only cities of the U.S. provide little competition for cars with 21 to 23 km/h transit speeds. Only the rail option appears to offer any real competition with cars as the average speed of urban trains is 42 km/h in the U.S., 45 km/h in Sydney, 43 km/h in Europe and 40 km/h in Tokyo (compared to 21 km/h for cars). Tram speeds are much lower but they usually act as distributors in central areas linking in to the major train stations (Vuchic, 1981), and typically operate with very high passenger loadings, especially compared to buses. It is also interesting that the average speed of buses in U.S., Australian and European cities as well as Toronto and Moscow is 20 to 21 km/h, a remarkably constant figure considering the enormous diversity in urban conditions in these cities. In the very much denser and congested Asian cities it drops to 15 km/h. It would thus appear that, in general, bus-based public transport systems seem to have an in-built limit on operating speed of no more than 25 km/h, and thus cannot be considered genuine competitors in speed to the car in any city.

It could be concluded that any city seriously wishing to change the private car/public transport equilibrium in favour of public transport to a less automobile dependent city, must move in the direction of rail-based transport infrastructure.

Urban form patterns

(i) Total density. The main parameter describing the form of a city is its density which has significant effects on travel distances and modal split (e.g. Pushkarev and Zupan, 1977). The overall shape of the U.S. and Australian automobile city is of low density in population and jobs with European cities generally being three to four times more dense (Table 3.4). Newer cities like Houston, Phoenix, Perth and Brisbane have densities around half that of the older cities like Chicago, New York and Sydney. Toronto tends to the lower end of the European city range in its overall urban form. The Asian cities are again even more extreme with densities some ten times those of the U.S. and Australian cities. Hong Kong is by far the highest density city in the sample and probably in the world. The significance of these density patterns for automobile dependence will be examined in detail later in this chapter and again in Chapter 5.

(ii) Central city density One of the significant differences between the U.S./Australian automobile dependent cities and the more transport-balanced European and Asian cities is that the former have central cities which have become areas of very high job concentration with generally

40

Table 3.3
Provision for the automobile in the world's major cities (1980).

City	Road supply (m/person)	Parking spaces (per 1000 CBD workers)	Average speed of traffic (km/h)	Total vehicles per km of road	Car kilometres per km of road	Average speed of public transport (km/h)				
						Bus	Train	Tram	Ferry	Total system
US Cities										
Houston	10.6	370	51	76	939,428	22	-	-	-	22
Phoenix	10.4	1,033	42	66	818,455	23	-	-	-	23
Detroit	5.8	473	44	119	1,714,024	21	42	-	-	22
Denver	9.4	498	45	107	1,002,509	21	-	-	-	21
Los Angeles	4.5	524	45	158	1,989,979	21	-	-	-	21
San Francisco	4.9	145	46	140	1,923,096	22	45	15	25	29
Boston	5.2	322	39	112	1,586,674	18	45	20	-	30
Washington	5.1	264	39	127	1,562,228	18	40	-	-	26
Chicago	5.0	91	41	103	1,505,631	18	47	-	-	37
New York	4.7	75	35	99	1,267,248	15	35	-	20	31
Average	**6.6**	**380**	**43**	**111**	**1,430,927**	**20**	**42**	**18**	**23**	**26**
Australian Cities										
Perth	13.3	562	43	46	497,392	22	35	-	14	24
Brisbane	6.9	268	48	94	930,096	23	37	-	-	31
Melbourne	7.9	270	48	67	740,564	21	33	18	-	28
Adelaide	9.1	380	43	64	658,970	21	45	28	-	29
Sydney	6.2	156	39	82	870,836	20	45	-	23	37
Average	**8.7**	**327**	**44**	**71**	**739,572**	**21**	**39**	**23**	**19**	**30**
Canadian City										
Toronto	2.7	198	?	204	2,262,597	20	34	16	-	25
European Cities										
Hamburg	2.2	149	30	171	1,974,143	22	36	-	12	31
Frankfurt	2.0	242	30	214	2,136,111	22	44	17	?	37
Zürich	2.6	140	36	165	1,647,922	20	46	15	?	33
Stockholm	2.3	153	30	171	2,128,378	25	36	26	-	32
Brussels	1.7	186	?	246	2,376,794	20	38	17	-	27
Paris	0.9	201	28	410	2,997,666	13	45	-	-	40
London	1.9	130	31	186	1,321,401	18	38	-	-	31
Munich	1.7	285	35	238	1,961,237	20	55	17	-	44
West Berlin	1.5	438	28	208	1,850,153	20	32	-	11	27
Copenhagen	4.3	212	45	69	810,087	24	54	-	-	38
Vienna	1.7	190	30	216	1,539,623	19	38	17	-	23
Amsterdam	2.1	208	39	161	1,378,489	18	57	15	-	36
Average	**2.1**	**211**	**30**	**205**	**1,843,500**	**20**	**43**	**18**	**12**	**33**
Asian Cities										
Tokyo	1.9	66	21	140	1,122,092	12	40	13	-	38
Singapore	1.0	97	30	158	727,886	19	-	-	-	19
Hong Kong	0.2	37	21	290	1,518,142	15	31	10	14	17
Average	**1.0**	**67**	**24**	**196**	**1,122,707**	**15**	**36**	**12**	**14**	**25**
USSR City										
Moscow	0.4	?	45	93	281,895	21	41	18	-	>37

41

Table 3.4
Urban form in the world's major cities (1980).

City	Whole city density		Central city density		Inner area density		Outer area density		Proportion of population in CBD(%)	Proportion of jobs in CBD(%)	Proportion of population in inner area (%)	Proportion of jobs in inner area(%)
	Population	Jobs	Population	Jobs	Population	Jobs	Population	Jobs				
US Cities												
Houston	9	6	6	443	21	26	8	4	0.1	11.6	16.6	41.1
Phoenix	9	4	17	67	19	24	8	4	0.5	3.9	3.7	10.6
Detroit	14	6	11	306	48	20	11	5	0.1	6.6	31.6	29.6
Denver	12	8	11	263	19	17	10	5	0.4	11.6	30.9	49.7
Los Angeles	20	8	19	472	30	14	18	9	0.1	4.8	31.3	43.3
San Francisco	16	11	29	713	59	48	13	5	0.1	17.0	21.3	34.4
Boston	12	8	90	383	45	33	10	4	1.1	15.9	24.3	34.6
Washington	13	6	126	584	44	38	11	6	2.7	16.1	21.4	32.5
Chicago	18	8	8	938	54	26	11	5	0.1	12.3	42.3	44.9
New York	20	9	217	828	107	53	13	6	2.8	22.9	39.5	41.9
Average	**14**	**7**	**54**	**500**	**45**	**30**	**11**	**5**	**0.8**	**12.3**	**26.3**	**36.3**
Australian Cities												
Perth	11	5	8	121	16	15	10	3	0.7	24.1	22.9	51.0
Brisbane	10	4	15	346	19	16	9	3	0.3	13.9	21.7	45.7
Melbourne	16	6	25	647	29	40	16	4	0.2	15.2	9.0	33.2
Adelaide	13	5	8	251	19	25	12	4	0.2	14.4	11.6	37.3
Sydney	18	8	11	434	39	39	16	5	0.1	13.2	16.7	39.3
Average	**14**	**6**	**13**	**360**	**24**	**27**	**13**	**4**	**0.3**	**16.2**	**16.4**	**41.3**
Canadian City												
Toronto	40	20	25	757	57	38	34	14	0.2	13.4	35.7	47.9
European Cities												
Hamburg	42	24	26	407	88	106	35	12	0.7	20.0	26.8	56.0
Frankfurt	54	43	65	389	63	74	49	25	2.5	18.4	43.3	64.2
Zürich	54	33	44	422	79	66	42	17	0.9	13.6	47.4	65.2
Stockholm	51	34	97	280	58	62	46	16	6.4	26.3	49.3	74.7
Brussels	67	42	74	592	101	85	50	16	1.9	24.6	51.8	75.9
Paris	48	22	235	400	106	60	26	8	5.4	20.2	60.9	75.1
London	56	30	66	397	78	62	48	19	2.7	29.7	37.2	55.1
Munich	57	34	111	231	159	192	48	21	5.9	20.5	21.4	42.9
West Berlin	64	27	133	333	84	46	57	20	0.8	4.8	31.8	41.8
Copenhagen	30	16	85	325	59	38	24	11	2.2	16.0	37.3	44.8
Vienna	72	38	65	403	133	113	59	23	1.3	14.9	31.9	50.8
Amsterdam	51	23	108	153	83	46	32	10	9.7	29.9	59.2	71.7
Average	**54**	**31**	**92**	**361**	**91**	**79**	**43**	**17**	**3.4**	**19.9**	**41.5**	**59.9**
Asian Cities												
Tokyo	105	66	82	477	153	114	58	20	1.3	26.6	32.3	84.8
Singapore	83	37	204	339	202	?	63	?	6.6	24.3	35.2	?
Hong Kong	293	110	160	1,259	1,037	478	224	66	0.4	7.3	30.0	45.3
Average	**160**	**71**	**149**	**692**	**464**	**296**	**115**	**43**	**2.8**	**19.4**	**32.5**	**65.1**
USSR City												
Moscow	139	?	155	?	?	?	?	?	3.7	?	?	?

few residents, and the latter have a much better balance between central city jobs and residences. The central city high rise office block is a characteristic mainly of the automobile city and it gives to U.S. cities much higher average central city job concentrations than in Europe. The Australian central city is more like that in Europe in terms of job density, but it is much less in population density. The average job density profile of the U.S. city is extremely sharp going from 500 per ha in the central city to 30 per ha in the inner city and 5 per ha in the outer area, compared to European cities which have 360 per ha, 79 per ha and 17per ha. Australian cities are more like the U.S. in their profile. On the other hand, the residential density of U.S. and Australian central cities is generally less than 20 per ha (except for New York, Boston and San Francisco), whilst in Europe they average around 90 per ha and in Asia about 150 per ha.

One of the questions to examine in the next section on correlations between transport and urban form is whether this extreme pattern of job densities in U.S. and Australian cities has any significant effect on balancing automobile use patterns since public transport is favoured by strong central cities (Thomson, 1977), or whether the residential density pattern is more dominant.

(iii) Inner city and outer area density As well as being different in overall density there are clear differences in urban form between U.S./Australian cities and European/Asian cities in terms of their inner cities and their outer areas.

The U.S./Australian inner city is generally two to three times less dense than in European cities and ten times less than that in Asian cities. However, the old inner cities of San Francisco, Washington, Boston, Chicago, Sydney and particularly New York are similar to many European cities (as is Toronto), while the inner cities of newer U.S. and Australian cities are generally little more than their overall density. This confirms the generally accepted picture of older cities as having steeper population density gradients (e.g. Clark, 1982).

The outer area densities of U.S. and Australian cities are amazingly uniform in all cases with very low land use intensity. European cities are marked by much more intensively utilised outer areas - some four times more on average than in U.S. and Australian cities. Toronto is again more like a European city in its outer area: from observation it appears to develop its density through a number of intensively utilised sub-centres linked by rapid transit to the city centre. Tokyo's outer areas are similar to European outer areas, though Hong Kong is once again at the extreme in land use intensity with an overall outer area density (population and jobs) greater than the central cities of some U.S. and Australian cities.

(iv) Distribution of population and jobs The other variables in Table 3.4 relate to the proportion of population and jobs found in different parts of the city. The key point here is whether the cities are centralised or dispersed in their land use patterns. The U.S. and Australian cities clearly have very small amounts of their total population residing in the central area and are not at all centralised in this factor. The U.S. cities overall are higher than the

43

Australian cities but only because of Boston and New York which have a comparatively high proportion of central city residents. Without these two cities the U.S and Australian cities average out at 0.3% of the total population living in the CBD. The European cities on the other hand have rather a high proportion of total residents in their CBDs ranging up to 10% in Amsterdam. Overall they are more than ten times higher in this factor than the U.S. and Australian cities, while the Asian cities fall between the two extremes. The lower Asian figures are largely due to problems in defining the central area of Hong Kong.

In terms of the proportion of jobs in the central area, the data range from around 4 to 10% in the heavily suburbanised, decentralised cities like Phoenix, Denver, Houston and Los Angeles, up to to around 30% in highly centralised cities like London, Tokyo and Amsterdam. Overall, the U.S. cities are the least centralised in their jobs, followed by the Australian cities, with the European and Asian cities being about equal and the highest overall in this factor (ie approximately 20% of all jobs being located in the CBDs). Thus although the auto-based US and Australian cities have concentrated their CBD jobs into high rise towers they are not a high proportion of total employment which tends rather to be dispersed in low density patterns throughout the city.

The proportion of population in the inner area is lowest in the Australian cities, followed by the U.S and Asian cities, Toronto and European cities (16%, 26%, 33%, 36% and 42% respectively). A reason for the difference in the U.S. and Australian cities may be the somewhat more generous definitions of "inner area" in the U.S. cities compared to the Australian cities. As described in Chapter 2, the inner areas of Australian cities are much more tightly defined based on small LGA's, whereas the inner areas of US cities are based on the whole City of Detroit, Los Angeles etc.

Finally , the proportion of jobs in the inner areas is clearly lowest in the U.S. cities despite their generally larger areas (ie. 36 % compared to 41% in the Australian cities). This to some extent reflects the more economically depressed nature of the U.S. inner cities which have seen a much more vigorous suburbanisation of jobs to large industrial parks and greenfields estates. By contrast, Toronto has nearly 50% of its employment located in its inner area, followed by the European cities with 60% and the Asian cities with 65%. Although in all these cities there tends to be an outward migration of jobs, none are as far advanced in this process as the U.S. cities. In general it can be said that the US cities are the least centralised cities (apart from New York), followed by the Australian cities, Toronto, European and Asian cities.

The variations in total density and in inner/outer area patterns suggest that these may be highly significant in determining the overall transport patterns. Thus the next section analyses some of the patterns between transport and urban form as revealed by our data.

Transport and urban form correlations

Table 3.5 provides the linear correlations between the transport and urban

Table 3.5
Transport and urban form correlations.

	Urban density	Job density	CBD population density	CBD job density	Inner area population density	Inner area job density	Outer area population density	Outer area job density	Proportion of population in CBD(%)	Proportion of jobs in CBD(%)	Proportion of population in inner area (%)	Proportion of jobs in inner area(%)
Gasoline use (MJ per capita)	-0.6099 s=0.000	-0.6627 s=0.000	-0.4827 s=0.003	-0.0301 s=0.436	-0.3914 s=0.015	-0.4849 +0.003	-0.5752 s=0.000	-0.5913 s=0.000	-0.4810 s=0.003	-0.5067 s=0.002	-0.4561 s=0.005	-0.6412 s=0.000
Total vehicles (per 1000 people)	-0.7619 s=0.000	-0.7649 s=0.000	-0.6523 s=0.000	-0.2325 s=0.104	-0.5930 s=0.000	-0.6524 s=0.000	-0.7177 s=0.000	-0.7322 s=0.000	-0.4726 s=0.003	-0.3864 s=0.016	-0.4349 s=0.007	-0.5031 s=0.002
Car ownership (per 1000 people)	-0.7801 s=0.000	-0.7792 s=0.000	-0.6350 s=0.000	-0.2000 s=0.140	-0.6129 s=0.000	-0.6758 s=0.000	-0.7305 s=0.000	-0.7501 s=0.000	-0.4395 s=0.006	-0.3637 s=0.022	-0.3503 s=0.027	-0.4879 s=0.003
Private car (passenger kms per capita)	-0.7438 s=0.000	-0.7793 s=0.000	-0.6698 s=0.000	-0.1360 s=0.233	-0.5409 s=0.001	-0.6204 s=0.000	-0.6931 s=0.000	-0.7164 s=0.000	-0.5379 s=0.001	-0.4694 s=0.004	-0.5186 s=0.001	-0.6214 s=0.000
Public transport (passenger kms per capita)	+0.5234 s=0.001	+0.6773 s=0.000	+0.3959 s=0.014	+0.1452 s=0.218	+0.2927 s=0.055	+0.3675 s=0.023	+0.4602 s=0.005	+0.4897 s=0.003	+0.2981 s=0.052	+0.4500 s=0.006	+0.4185 s=0.010	+0.6935 s=0.000
Private car/public transport balance (% of total passenger kms on public transport)	+0.8537 s=0.000	+0.9077 s=0.000	+0.5948 s=0.000	+0.3155 s=0.042	+0.7405 s=0.000	+0.7810 s=0.000	+0.8402 s=0.000	+0.8458 s=0.000	+0.3549 s=0.023	+0.2902 s=0.057	+0.3639 s=0.022	+0.5352 s=0.001
Public transport vehicle kms of service per person	+0.5785 s=0.000	+0.6205 s=0.000	+0.3879 s=0.015	+0.1762 s=0.172	+0.4365 s=0.007	+0.4850 s=0.003	+0.5893 s=0.000	+0.5975 s=0.000	+0.3772 s=0.018	+0.4813 s=0.003	+0.3333 s=0.033	+0.4660 s=0.005
Public transport passenger trips per person	+0.7390 s=0.000	+0.8414 s=0.000	+0.5314 s=0.001	+0.1574 s=0.199	+0.5289 s=0.001	+0.6151 s=0.000	+0.7185 s=0.000	+0.7564 s=0.000	+0.4515 s=0.005	+0.3893 s=0.015	+0.5179 s=0.001	+0.6653 s=0.000
Proportion of public transport passenger kms on trains (%)	+0.0863 s=0.319	+0.1287 s=0.245	+0.3275 s=0.034	+0.1683 s=0.183	-0.0921 s=0.311	+0.0257 s=0.446	-0.0277 s=0.441	+0.0295 s=0.439	+0.2317 s=0.101	+0.4543 s=0.005	+0.3186 s=0.04	+0.4788 s=0.004
Proportion of workers using public transport (%)	+0.7143 s=0.000	+0.7835 s=0.000	+0.5725 s=0.000	+0.2989 s=0.051	+0.5582 s=0.001	+0.6661 s=0.000	+0.6941 s=0.000	+0.7044 s=0.000	+0.3244 s=0.037	+0.4000 s=0.013	+0.3554 s=0.025	+0.5667 s=0.001
Proportion of workers using private transport (%)	-0.7615 s=0.000	-0.8395 s=0.000	-0.6114 s=0.000	-0.2378 s=0.099	-0.5963 s=0.000	-0.6883 s=0.000	-0.7387 s=0.000	-0.7606 s=0.000	-0.4359 +0.007	-0.4334 s=0.007	-0.4685 s=0.004	-0.6239 s=0.000
Proportion of workers using foot or bicycle (%)	+0.6636 s=0.000	+0.7387 s=0.000	+0.5349 s=0.001	+0.0725 s=0.349	+0.5218 s=0.001	+0.5767 s=0.000	+0.6417 s=0.000	+0.6900 s=0.000	+0.5306 s=0.001	+0.3898 s=0.015	+0.5577 s=0.001	+0.5843 s=0.000

45

Table 3.6
Intercorrelations between the transport variables.

	Gasoline use	Total vehicle ownership	Car ownership	Private car (pass. kms per capita)	Public trans. (pass. kms per capita)	Private car/ public trans. balance	Public trans. vehicle kms per person	Public trans. pass. trips per person	Prop. of public trans. pass. kms on trains	Prop. of workers using public trans.	Prop. of workers using private trans.	Prop. of workers using foot or bicycle	Road supply	Central city parking	Average speed of traffic	Total vehicles per km of road	Car km per km of road	Average speed buses	Average speed trains	Average speed trams	Average speed ferries
Total vehicle ownership	+0.8950 s=0.000																				
Car ownership	+0.8555 s=0.000	+0.9813 s=0.000																			
Private car (pass. kms per capita)	+0.9185 s=0.000	+0.9437 s=0.000	+0.9258 s=0.000																		
Public trans. (pass. kms per capita)	-0.7328 s=0.000	-0.7328 s=0.000	-0.7450 s=0.000	-0.7633 s=0.000																	
Private car/public trans. balance	-0.7340 s=0.000	-0.8889 s=0.000	-0.9205 s=0.000	-0.8746 s=0.000	+0.8046 s=0.000																
Public trans. vehicle kms per person	-0.8305 s=0.000	-0.8256 s=0.000	-0.8082 s=0.000	-0.7981 s=0.000	+0.7028 s=0.000	+0.7347 s=0.000															
Public trans. pass. trips per person	-0.8750 s=0.000	-0.8908 s=0.000	-0.8712 s=0.000	-0.9234 s=0.000	+0.8551 s=0.000	+0.8995 s=0.000	+0.7635 s=0.000														
Prop. of public trans. pass. kms on trains	-0.5169 s=0.001	-0.4633 s=0.004	-0.3828 s=0.015	-0.4452 s=0.005	+0.5858 s=0.000	+0.3312 s=0.032	+0.4101 s=0.011	+0.4043 s=0.012													
Prop. of workers using public trans.	-0.8216 s=0.000	-0.8775 s=0.000	-0.8775 s=0.000	-0.8835 s=0.000	+0.7906 s=0.000	+0.8721 s=0.000	+0.8098 s=0.000	+0.8547 s=0.000	+0.4153 s=0.010												
Prop. of workers using private trans.	+0.8831 s=0.000	+0.9339 s=0.000	+0.9218 s=0.000	+0.9430 s=0.000	-0.8148 s=0.000	-0.9120 s=0.000	-0.8459 s=0.000	-0.9244 s=0.000	-0.4336 s=0.007	-0.9536 s=0.000											
Prop. of workers using foot or bicycle	-0.7822 s=0.000	-0.8117 s=0.000	-0.7809 s=0.000	-0.8241 s=0.000	+0.6635 s=0.000	+0.7654 s=0.000	+0.7083 s=0.000	+0.8279 s=0.000	+0.3634 s=0.022	+0.6434 s=0.000	-0.8441 s=0.000										
Road supply	+0.7081 s=0.000	+0.7737 s=0.000	+0.7026 s=0.000	+0.7854 s=0.000	-0.6621 s=0.000	-0.6744 s=0.000	-0.8205 s=0.000	-0.6257 s=0.000	-0.4563 s=0.004	-0.7559 s=0.000	+0.8033 s=0.000	-0.6960 s=0.000									
Central city parking	+0.5775 s=0.000	+0.5935 s=0.0000	+0.5271 s=0.001	+0.5574 s=0.000	-0.5795 s=0.000	-0.5394 s=0.000	-0.5694 s=0.000	-0.6238 s=0.000	-0.5699 s=0.000	-0.6546 s=0.000	+0.6472 s=0.000	-0.4800 s=0.003	+0.6489 s=0.000								
Average speed of traffic	+0.6340 s=0.000	+0.6502 s=0.000	+0.6232 s=0.000	+0.7212 s=0.000	-0.7737 s=0.000	-0.5560 s=0.001	-0.8601 s=0.000	-0.6472 s=0.000	-0.3465 s=0.030	-0.8438 s=0.000	+0.8510 s=0.000	-0.6797 s=0.000	+0.6983 s=0.000	+0.4555 s=-.006							
Total vehicles per km of road	-0.4661 s=0.004	-0.4093 s=0.010	-0.3437 s=0.027	-0.5317 s=0.001	-0.4038 s=0.012	+0.3547 s=0.023	-0.6219 s=0.000	+0.3143 s=0.042	+0.2006 s=0.135	-0.5736 s=0.000	+0.5736 s=0.000	-0.6173 s=0.000	-0.7127 s=0.000	-0.3537 s=0.000	-0.6975 s=0.000						
Car km per km of road	-0.0733 s=0.345	-0.0059 s=0.487	+0.1145 s=0.266	-0.0675 s=0.357	+0.1951 s=0.146	-0.1138 s=0.268	+0.3098 s=0.045	+0.0508 s=0.393	+0.1739 s=0.170	+0.2436 s=0.093	-0.2667 s=0.073	+0.2438 s=0.093	-0.5166 s=0.001	-0.2498 s=0.088	-0.4479 s=0.006	+0.7941 s=0.000					
Average speed buses	+0.2362 s=0.096	+0.3437 s=0.027	+0.3402 s=0.028	+0.4156 s=0.009	-0.5043 s=0.002	-0.4005 s=0.011	-0.4244 s=0.009	-0.1553 s=0.202	-0.3508 s=0.024	-0.4298 s=0.008	+0.4304 s=0.008	-0.3287 s=0.035	+0.4005 s=0.012	+0.4331 s=0.007	+0.5686 s=0.001	-0.4814 s=0.003	-0.2210 s=0.112				
Average speed trains	-0.0636 s=0.376	-0.0174 s=0.466	+0.0557 s=0.391	+0.0163 s=0.468	-0.0108 s=0.479	-0.0997 s=0.310	+0.0153 s=0.470	-0.0767 s=0.355	+0.0849 s=0.337	+0.0317 s=0.439	-0.2367 s=0.122	+0.2913 s=0.074	-0.0773 s=0.351	-0.0417 s=0.120	+0.2740 s=0.092	-0.0245 s=0.452	+0.0031 s=0.494	+0.0632 s=0.377			
Average speed trams	+0.2533 s=0.181	+0.3386 s=0.076	+0.4255 s=0.056	+0.4145 s=0.062	-0.4124 s=0.071	-0.4417 s=0.049	-0.5527 s=0.020	-0.1964 s=0.250	-0.3562 s=0.015	-0.4550 s=0.051	+0.4915 s=0.129	-0.4638 s=0.047	+0.5586 s=0.015	+0.6753 s=0.004	+0.3702 s=0.032	-0.4890 s=0.032	-0.1230 s=0.331	+0.6368 s=0.005	+0.0436 s=0.439		
Average speed ferries	+0.7962 s=0.014	+0.6123 s=0.069	+0.6095 s=0.070	+0.6297 s=0.062	-0.4504 s=0.153	-0.4483 s=0.154	-0.6257 s=0.064	-0.5159 s=0.115	-0.5196 s=0.129	-0.4915 s=0.129	+0.5196 s=0.113	-0.5458 s=0.100	+0.2380 s=0.303	-0.3846 s=0.195	+0.6853 s=0.042	-0.4678 s=0.143	-0.1532 s=0.371	+0.0236 s=0.480	+0.8810 s=0.004	: : : :	
Average speed overall	-0.3708 s=0.020	-0.2461 s=0.091	-0.1594 s=0.196	-0.2503 s=0.087	+0.4083 s=0.011	+0.0521 s=0.390	+0.2633 s=0.076	+0.2428 s=0.094	+0.1623 s=0.191	+0.1908 s=0.340	-0.2698 s=0.071	+0.3974 s=0.013	-0.2795 s=0.064	-0.3509 s=0.026	-0.1560 s=0.209	-0.1453 s=0.218	+0.2206 s=0.116	-0.1467 s=0.215	+0.6980 s=0.000	+0.1302 s=0.328	+0.5392 s=0.103

46

form variables and Table 3.6 provides the linear correlations between the transport variables so that the question of gasoline use and private car dependence can be linked to the degree of provision for the automobile. More sophisticated statistical analysis of the data is presented later but these correlations provide sufficient basis for clarifying and confirming the patterns already discussed.

Private transport and urban form

The correlations suggest that strong negative relationships exist between gasoline use or private vehicle use and all the density variables, except central city job densities. This highlights the question of the U.S. and Australian cities with their central city high rise office blocks. There is no correlation between central city job density and any of the private transport variables suggesting that this factor has little overall effect on transport patterns despite the apparent importance of peak hour CBD oriented public transport activity in these cities. It would appear to be more important to have higher residential densities mixed in with the employment activity if there is to be much less dependence on the automobile. Residential density in the central city does correlate strongly with all the transport patterns, including the amount of walking/bicycling. The case of Boston highlights this as it is the highest U.S. city for bicycling/walking to work (10%) and it has for its 72,000 central city residents ,the highest population to jobs ratio (.33) for U.S. CBD's, thus it is more like a European city in this regard. It is not hard to see that city centres with plenty of employment activity that also have high residential densities (e.g. Paris 235/ha) would have a significantly higher proportion of people walking and having little need for a car. This issue is dealt with in more detail in Chapter 5 where a focus on the central city is provided.

The relationship between density and gasoline use may be more complex than a purely linear linkage. Figure 3.1 and Figure 3.2 suggest that it may in fact be closer to an exponential relationship particularly under around 30 people per hectare. This is conceptually quite possible as a city with density in the less than 30/ha range does not just have longer distances for all types of journey; it is ensuring that non-automobile modes are not feasible due to the sheer lack of people living near a transit line and the time required for walking and biking. Thus the effects of lowering density are multiplicative. This cut off around 30/ha we have also found to be significant for transport within different parts of urban areas (Newman and Hogan, 1987). It means that in terms of transport energy saved or private car use curtailed, the effects of increasing density can be considerable if they move urban areas into at least the 30/ha density range, i.e. more like the old inner area densities.

Figure 3.1 and 3.2 suggest that if cities around 10/ha were able to consolidate and move to densities around 30/ha then fuel consumption could be reduced by half or even to around one third of its low density value. Such changes are not easy but many policy analysts using urban simulation models do not generally recognise the very large potential to alter travel patterns through land use change. For example, Small (1980) suggests that land use controls which resulted in densities of 15 units per acre (equivalent

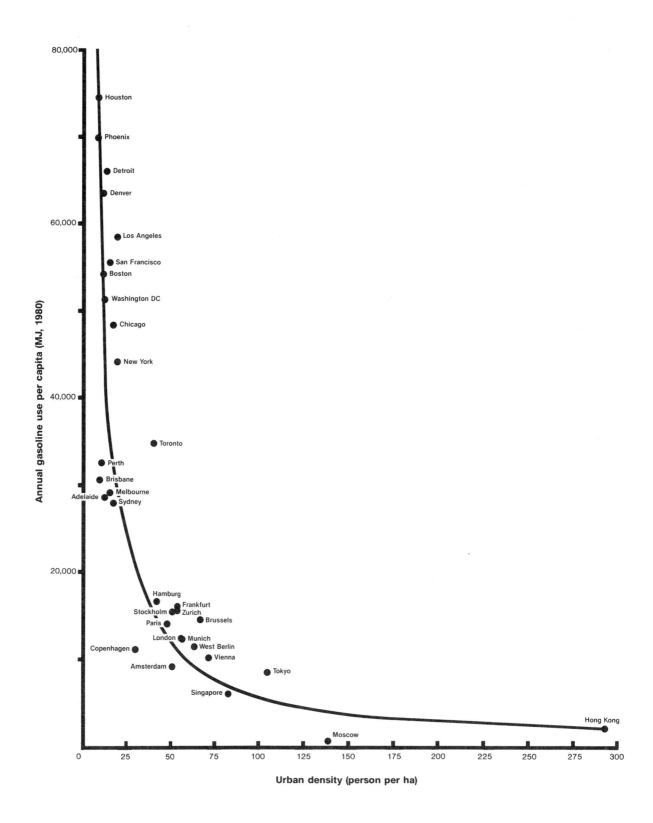

Figure 3.1   Gasoline use per capita versus urban density (1980).

48

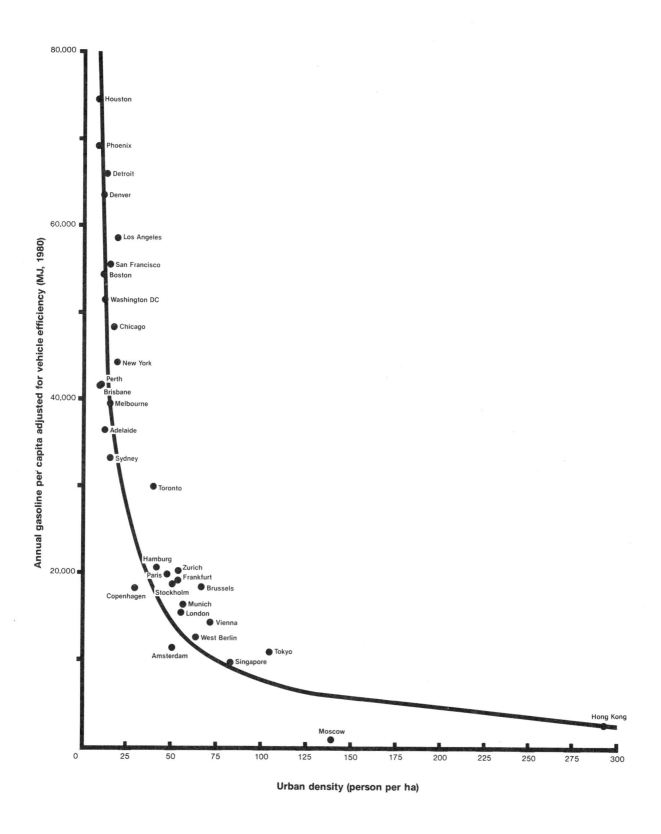

Figure 3.2   Urban density versus gasoline use per capita adjusted
for vehicle efficiency.

49

to over 50 people per ha) compared to the current US average of 5 units per acre (about 19 people per ha), would reduce automobile usage for work trips by only 1.4% after 6 years. Sharpe (1982) suggests energy savings of only 11% if urban density in Melbourne was tripled. None of these assessments take into account the sort of urban data contained in the present study. The general approach of such studies is to suggest that improving vehicle efficiencies will be far more effective than land use changes. When gasoline data are adjusted so that all cities use the most efficient cars (7 L/100km), then it is still obvious that density is more fundamental (Figure 3.2) and an exponential relationship still exists. The issue of raising urban densities to around 30/ha in order to influence transport patterns is dealt with in more detail in Chapter 5, though the evidence so far suggests this is a critical factor in urban automobile dependence.

The significance of the density factor is highlighted by transport data collected in a few U.S. cities on an inner/outer area basis. Table 3.7 shows that the New York Tri State region gasoline usage per person is 44,030 MJ, however for the inner area residents (City of New York) this reduces to 20,120 MJ and for the 1.4 million residents of Manhattan, their average gasoline consumption drops to an extraordinary 11,860 MJ, ie similar to Copenhagen, Vienna and Amsterdam. The average outer area New Yorker consumes close to 60,000 MJ and in Denver it is possible to distinguish the 240,000 ex-urban residents who live on the fringe of the city and consume some 137,000 MJ on average. The multiplicative effects on the whole pattern of transport of increasing density are confirmed by these kinds of comparison.

The other urban form variables in Table 3.5 are the centralisation variables: proportions of total population and jobs in the CBD and inner area (four variables). Again, these are all significantly negatively correlated with gasoline use and private car use, implying that the relative importance of the central and inner areas is an important factor in determining transport patterns. In other words, the less significant are the central and inner areas, the more car-orientated are cities and the higher their gasoline use. As with the density variables, these four centralisation variables are also positively associated with higher public transport performance and higher proportions of workers using foot and bicycle (nearly all are significant to ≤ 5%). This is further pursued under public transport.

Public transport and urban form

As well as the strong negative correlations with gasoline use and private vehicle use, the density variables are also significantly positively correlated with all the public transport data. In other words higher population and job densities in all parts of the city are significantly associated with more public transport passenger kms per person, a higher proportion of total passenger kms on public transport, greater public transport service provision per person, more annual trips per person and a higher proportion of workers using public transport. Similarly, higher densities are in each case associated with a greater proportion of people using foot and bicycle to get to work.

50

Table 3.7
Gasoline use and urban density by city region in the New York Tri State Metropolitan Area, 1980.

Area	Gasoline use (MJ per capita)	Urban density (persons/ha)
Outer area New York	59590	13
Whole city (New York Tri State Metro Area)	44033	20
Inner area (City of New York)	20120	107
Central city (New York County incl. Manhattan)	11860	251

Of particular note in the above correlations are the exceptionally strong correlations of all the density variables with the proportion of total passenger travel on public transport. This is a key variable since it expresses the overall balance between private and public transport and is clearly improved in favour of public transport as density increases throughout the city.

The only urban form variable that does not correlate with public transport use is central city job density (although two public transport variables do just scrape in to the significant category). This may seem surprising as it would appear that the concentration of jobs in city centres is one of the key factors behind developing a vital public transport system. However, it is probable that all the city centres have a sufficient job concentration to ensure a good public transport system for them, that the vitality of the service for the whole city depends more on other factors. For example, it may be that the actual density is less important than the total number of jobs in the city centre. Correlations with the number of jobs in the city centre and public transport do in fact show much greater significance. This suggests that centralisation of jobs may be more important for the viability of public transport than density of jobs in the central city.

This is confirmed by the fact that the proportion of jobs in the city centre (and inner area) does correlate with all the public transport variables ie. the more centralised jobs there are the more public transport is used. This centralisation factor can be understood theoretically in terms of the line-haul characteristic of public transport. Where an obvious line can be drawn leading along a corridor to a well defined city centre then public transport is clearly facilitated and on the other hand private cars become highly congested at the destination point. The opposite of centralisation is the scattering of work in many directions - no line-haul can be established for the pattern of development and car traffic is less congested.

Thus both density and centralisation appear to be clear factors which determine the viability of public transport and thus a less automobile dependent city. They appear to be additive in that a low density centralised city is likely to have more public transport than a low density decentralised

51

city but less than a high density centralised city.

This combination of density and centralisation can be used to help explain one interesting set of correlations in Table 3.5 - the proportion of public transport passenger kms on trains. As trains are the basis for line-haul public transport systems, then it is not surprising to find that this variable correlates well with the centralisation factors (proportion of jobs in CBD and inner area and also proportion of population in the inner area through which most of the line-haul routes would go). However, the proportion of public transport travel on trains does not correlate with density, apart from a weak correlation with central city population density. This is perhaps a little surprising as public transport usually increases in importance whenever trains are provided and density clearly favours public transport in general. However, three things can be said about these correlations:

(1) Linear correlations are upset by zero values and hence those cities with no train system provide a statistical artifact. When the correlations are re-done without Houston, Phoenix, Detroit, Denver, Los Angeles and Singapore, then they are clearly more significant in their linkage to the density variables.

(2) Many cities did not have well developed train systems in 1980 but instead used extensive light rail or tram systems eg. Zürich, Amsterdam, Brussels, Vienna and Boston. These systems provide a separate-way public transport and although they are not as rapid as trains (see later discussion) they are highly significant rail systems if not train systems.

(3) The 1980's has seen a resurgence in urban train systems. The following cities in our study have each constructed or commenced significant train services since the 1980 data: Hong Kong, Singapore, Vienna, Brussels, Washington, Boston and Zürich. If these cities were removed, together with those that have no train service, then there is an even stronger correlation with density eg. urban density and proportion of public transport on trains have a correlation of 0.5688 and a significance of <0.010. It would be anticipated that when the 1990 data are compared there will be a better correlation with density when all these cities show their extra train usage.

Thus density is almost certainly a factor in determining train usage along with centralisation and together they offer powerful explanations for the level of train usage in the survey.

Vehicle ownership and urban form

The remaining variables in Table 3.5 are total vehicle ownership and car ownership. It is clear that all the urban form variables apart from CBD job density are significantly and negatively correlated with these two variables ie. as population and job densities and the relative importance of central and inner areas increase, total vehicles per person and the traditional car ownership factor decrease in a statistically significant way. Put another way, the need for motor vehicles would appear to decline as cities become denser, more compact and more centralised.

52

Transport infrastructure

There are strong correlations between gasoline consumption and provision for the automobile in terms of road supply and parking (Table 3.6). Also the significant positive correlation between average speed and gasoline use highlights one of the traffic management controversies. There is clearly less gasoline use in cities with low average speeds which contradicts those traffic planners who suggest freeing up congestion to increase average speeds will save gasoline. Similarly, there is a significant negative correlation between the total vehicles per km of road and gasoline use which suggests that as the intensity of road use increases, gasoline use actually diminishes. These data suggest that although free flowing traffic may improve individual vehicle efficiencies it also causes overall fuel consumption increases, presumably due to greater private vehicle use. This will be pursed in detail in Chapter 5.

With respect to how transport infrastructure affects other transport patterns, the correlations in Table 3.6 suggest the following relationships:

• Road supply has a statistically significant relationship with virtually all the other transport variables. It is strongly and positively associated with total vehicle ownership and car ownership, passenger kms in private cars, the proportion of workers using private transport, the amount of central city parking, the average speed of traffic, the average speed of buses and the average speed of trams. Road supply is also strongly negatively linked to public transport passenger kms per capita, the proportion of total passenger travel on public transport, public transport service provision, annual public transport passenger trips per capita, the proportion of public transport travel on trains, the proportion of workers using public transport and foot and bicycle and as would be expected, the congestion measures (total vehicles per km of road and car kms per km of road).

• Central city parking provision has a virtually identical but generally weaker set of correlations with the transport variables as outlined above. The major difference is that central city parking is also significantly negatively associated with the overall average speed of public transport, ie. as central city parking increases the overall speed of public transport deteriorates. This is most likely due to the fact that it is the bus-based cities that generally have the highest central city parking and their public transport average speeds are uniformly low (between about 20km/h and 25km/h).

• Average speed of traffic which reflects the degree to which private cars are provided for in the urban system, follows the same patterns of correlations with the other transport variables as road supply and parking, ie. higher average speeds promote car use and detract from public transport.

There are a few other correlations in Table 3.6 which deserve highlighting. They can be listed as follows:

• The importance of train-based public transport appears to be supported by the correlations, in that the proportion of public transport travel on trains is uniformly associated with lower gasoline use and lower private car orientation through a series of significant negative correlations with these variables. It is also positively associated with better public transport overall through a series of significant positive correlations. Interestingly, as the proportion of public transport passenger kilometres on trains increases, the average speed of buses deteriorates. This is probably due to the fact that as buses get caught in greater congestion in cities they become slower and less reliable and segregated rail systems become the only option that can keep the public transport system competitive from a speed perspective. This is further supported by the fact that overall average speed of traffic is indeed lower in cities where the importance of a rail system is greater (significant correlation of average traffic speed with proportion of public transport passenger kms on trains). Most importantly, the correlations show that the proportion of public transport passenger kms on trains is very highly positively correlated with the overall average speed of the public transport system. This supports the idea that extensive, well-utilised rail systems are really the only way to ensure higher, more car-competitive speeds for the public transport system.

•The correlations suggest a close relationship between public transport and the non-motorised modes. The proportion of workers who walk and bicycle to work is significantly and positively associated with all the public transport variables, suggesting that as the conditions which foster public transport are supported and improved, then walking and bicycling also grows (eg. denser land use arrangements with shorter travel distances). A less automobile dependent city obviously has a range of interrelated land use and transport characteristics.

•The congestion variable, total vehicles per km of road, is negatively correlated with the vehicle ownership variables and private car use variables ie. as the actual numbers of vehicles and their use grows, congestion actually decreases, although causality can just as easily be expressed in the other direction - the lower the congestion the more the car ownership and car use. This is also supported by similar correlations of average traffic speed with private car ownership and use; average speed is better in cities with higher car ownership and use. These correlations suggest a very deliberate and marked orientation of cities towards cars, particularly in infrastructure provision, such that growth in the numbers of cars and their use is, generally speaking, more than adequately provided for by the growth in road provision and other traffic facilities. Conversely, total vehicles per km of road is positively correlated with all the major public transport variables suggesting that congestion assists the growth and orientation of a city towards public transport. Further analysis is provided on this in Chapter 5 under a Focus on Congestion.

• The final correlations worth mentioning complement the argument already presented about the significance of train systems. The average speed of buses, unlike the overall average speed of public transport, appears to have a generally negative impact on public transport and rather is associated with greater private car use (the correlations show a positive relationship between average bus speed and the private car variables such as ownership and use, and a negative relationship with the overall performance of public transport). The link here is probably the fact that the best performing bus systems in terms of speed are those in very car-orientated cities where there is a large amount of road space and comparatively low congestion. However, the speed advantage afforded to buses in these circumstances is simply not enough to offset the overwhelming orientation of the city to cars.

It should be reiterated that bus system speeds under no circumstances exceed 25km/h, whereas car speeds in cities with high average bus speeds are close to double this figure. This reinforces the previous argument that the only way to fundamentally change the orientation of a city towards greater public transport use is to improve or install rail systems which can compete on speed terms with cars.

The patterns observed in the overall sample of international cities have also been shown in the ten US cities. In all cases the same patterns can be seen as in the larger sample (Newman and Kenworthy, 1987a).

Factor and cluster analysis

This section of the book seeks to determine through a simple factor analysis and cluster analysis how the various cities can be grouped so that their transport and land use characteristics can be combined together and thus provide a framework for the final policy analysis.

Factor analysis methodology

Traditional factor analysis is generally used where a researcher is presented with a large number and broad range of variables and wishes to simplify these variables into a few key factors or dimensions. A common example is in social geography where there may be a hundred or more variables characterising a city's social and economic features; these can usually be reduced to three or four factors such as socio-economic status, family status and ethnic status (e.g. see the work of Shevky and Williams (1949) and Shevky and Bell (1955) described and analysed in Knox (1982b)). These new factors or dimensions which underly the more complex set of variables can in themselves be used as sort of pseudo-variables which greatly simplifies some statistical analyses.

A major difficulty in many factor analysis exercises is, however, actually trying to identify, or more particularly, give a name to the dimensions which the computer technique has extracted. This is usually done by looking at the variables which are heavily weighted in each factor and essentially ignoring the variables which are insignificantly weighted. The combination of variables so identified can often be seen to relate to a particular unifying concept. For example, in Kenworthy, Newman and Lyons (1983) where we did a factor analysis on a large array of land use, transportation and socio-economic data for Perth, the analysis suggested that the major factor was the degree of private transport dominance followed by four small factors such as public transport facilitation. However, it is recognised that it is not always easy to identify and name such factors and in most cases it reduces to individual researchers subjectively deciding on what the factor analysis is saying and what dimensions they intuitively believe should emerge. Of course, the dimensions obtained from any factor analysis will depend on the data that goes in and where selective control is exercised over this aspect it may be reasonably clear beforehand what the underlying unity is in the data.

In the case of the present study all the data analysed on each city had been grouped under specific headings such as traffic restraint variables and public transport variables. This, combined with previous transport energy conservation work on Australian cities (Newman and Kenworthy, 1980, a, b, c,), meant that a fairly clear conceptual foundation for understanding transport and land use in cities had already been laid. Under these circumstances it was decided not to proceed with a traditional factor analysis and thus not attempt to let a statistical routine direct the process of choosing the underlying themes in the data as they relate to transport and land use. Rather, it was decided to follow the practice of choosing the themes or factors based on previous experience and a detailed understanding of the available data from the correlation analysis, and then very simply to rank each city on each factor. The factors identified and the contributing variables were as follows:

(1) Land use intensity
(a) Urban density (resident population per ha of urbanised land).
(b) Employment density (jobs per ha of urbanised land).
(c) Inner area density (persons per ha of urbanised land).
(d) Inner area employment density (jobs per ha of urbanised land).
(e) Outer area density (persons per ha of urbanised land).
(f) Outer area employment density (jobs per ha of urbanised land).
(2) Orientation to non-automobile modes
(a) Per capita passenger kms in cars.
(b) Per capita passenger kms in public transport.
(c) Proportion of total passenger kms in public transport.
(d) Proportion of workers using public transport for the journey to work.
(e) Proportion of workers using private transport for the journey to work.
(f) Proportion of workers using walking and bicycling for the journey to work.
(g) Total vehicles per 1000 people.
(h) Cars per 1000 people.
(3) Level of traffic restraint
(a) Length of road per person.
(b) Parking spaces per 1000 central area jobs.
(c) Vehicles per km of road.
(d) Car kms per km of road.
(4) Degree of centralisation
(a) CBD density.
(b) Proportion of metropolitan population residing in the CBD.
(c) Proportion of metropolitan employment located in the CBD.
(5) Public transport performance
(a) Vehicle kms of public transport service per person.
(b) Passengers trips per person.
(c) Passenger trips per vehicle km of service.
(d) Average speed of total public transport system.
(e) Energy use per passenger km.

The method of ranking a city on a particular factor was simply to sort the thirty-two cities from lowest to highest on each individual variable and give each city a score on the variable based on the city's position in the scale (ranging from 1 to 31 or 32 depending on Moscow which has a number of missing values). The composite factor score or index was the result of adding the scores for each contributing variable.

After obtaining the composite factor score for each city the cities were ordered from lowest to highest score on each factor and their range was divided into five or six groups. For example, in the level of traffic restraint, the range was divided into cities with very unrestrained traffic, lightly restrained traffic, moderate to average traffic restraint, significantly restrained traffic and highly restrained traffic.

It should be noted that the groupings of cities in each factor are somewhat arbitrary. They are designed primarily to simplify the picture of such a large number of cities and provide a clear indication of the general trend of diminishing energy use as each factor increases. As far as possible the groupings were chosen at significant jumps in the values of the factor scores.

In order to relate the performance of each group of cities on a particular factor to automobile dependence, an average gasoline use per capita for each group was calculated. This provided a very clear picture of the trend in automobile use for each factor particularly since it smoothed out much of the scatter or variability in the data. Also, by calculating an average composite score for each group of cities on each factor, it was possible to do some simple correlations to see how closely linked each factor is with automobile use.

One minor disadvantage of this simple factor analysis method is that it did not provide the percentage of variance in the data explained by each factor. This is a major part of traditional factor analysis but since the aim here was to relate transport and land use data specifically to automobile dependence and the level of gasoline use, it was not considered essential.

Factor analysis results

As explained at the beginning of this chapter, gasoline use per capita serves as a barometer which rises with increasing automobile dependence and it has therefore been used as the focus for the factor analysis results.

The results of the simple factor analysis procedure are given in Tables 3.8 to 3.12 Each of the factors shows a marked negative relationship with gasoline use. In other words, as land use intensity, orientation to non-automobile modes, level of traffic restraint, degree of centralisation and public transport performance in cities all increase, the per capita use of gasoline diminishes in a marked way. This is confirmed by very strong correlation coefficients between per capita gasoline use and the composite factor scores for each of the five or six groupings of cities within each factor. These range between - 0.9117 (s = 0.0293) for the centralisation factor and 0.98112 (s = 0.0025) for the land use intensity factor as shown in Table 3.13. As mentioned previously, the process of grouping cities and averaging the gasoline per capita and factor scores within each group, has the effect of smoothing out some of the variance in the sample, particularly across national boundaries. Thus it might be expected that good correlations will be found. However, correlations of the gasoline data with individual factor

Table 3.8
Land use intensity index for the thirty-two world cities with corresponding gasoline use per capita (high score = high intensity).

City	Score on variable						Composite score	Rank order		Gasoline use (MJ/capita)		Composite factor score
	Urban density score	Employment density score	Outer area density score	Outer area employment density score	Inner area density score	Inner area job density score						
Adelaide	7	4	10	4	3	7	35	14	Brisbane			
Amsterdam	20	19	18	17	21	17	112	18	Perth	49,990	Extremely low density	24.8
Boston	6	7	4	6	11	10	44	18	Phoenix			
Brisbane	3	2	3	1	2	3	14	26	Houston			
Brussels	27	28	26	21	24	25	151	35	Adelaide			
Chicago	12	13	9	11	13	8	66	38	Denver			
Copenhagen	16	16	16	18	17	13	96	44	Boston			
Denver	5	10	5	9	5	4	38	49	Detroit			
Detroit	9	8	7	8	12	5	49	58	Melbourne			
Frankfurt	23	29	25	29	18	24	148	62	Washington	47,888	Low density	59.6
Hamburg	18	20	20	19	23	26	126	66	Chicago			
Hong Kong	32	31	31	30	31	30	185	68	Sydney			
Houston	2	5	1	3	6	9	26	70	Los Angeles			
London	24	22	23	24	19	22	134	78	San Francisco			
Los Angeles	15	15	15	16	8	1	70	96	Copenhagen			
Melbourne	11	6	13	6	7	15	58	98	New York	28,097	Medium density	99.5
Moscow	31	-	-	-	-	-	-	99	Toronto			
Munich	25	24	24	27	29	29	158	112	Amsterdam			
New York	14	14	12	13	26	19	98	114	Paris			
Paris	19	18	17	15	25	20	114	126	Hamburg			
Perth	4	3	6	2	1	2	18	126	Stockholm			
Phoenix	1	1	2	4	4	6	18	132	Zürich			
San Francisco	10	11	11	12	16	18	78	134	London	14,650	High density	136.4
Singapore	29	26	30	28	30	25	168	138	West Berlin			
Stockholm	21	25	22	22	15	21	126	148	Frankfurt			
Sydney	13	9	14	9	9	14	68	151	Brussels			
Tokyo	30	30	28	25	28	28	169	158	Munich			
Toronto	17	17	19	20	14	12	99	166	Vienna			
Vienna	28	27	29	28	27	27	166	168	Singapore	7,785	Very high density	169.2
Washington DC	8	12	8	13	10	11	62	169	Tokyo			
West Berlin	26	21	27	26	22	16	138	185	Hong Kong			
Zürich	22	23	21	23	20	23	132					

58

Table 3.9

Orientation to non-automobile modes index for the thirty-two world cities with corresponding gasoline use per capita (high score = high orientation to non-automobile modes).

City	Total vehicles per 1000 people	Cars per 1000 people	Per capita car passenger kms	Per capita public transport passenger kms	Proportion of passenger kms on public transport	Proportion of workers using public transport	Proportion of workers using private transport	Proportion of workers using foot and bicycle	Composite score
Adelaide	10	8	12	9	8	10	9	10	76
Amsterdam	26	25	26	22	24	7	17	26	173
Boston	11	10	6	6	5	9	12	13	72
Brisbane	9	12	7	10	9	11	8	6	72
Brussels	19	19	22	15	17	16	18	17	143
Chicago	14	14	11	13	12	13	11	11	99
Copenhagen	28	28	21	19	19	19	25	27	186
Denver	1	1	9	4	3	4	4	6	32
Detroit	3	3	2	2	2	3	3	1	19
Frankfurt	18	17	19	20	18	14	19	25	150
Hamburg	23	22	17	17	16	25	22	16	158
Hong Kong	31	31	31	27	30	31	30	28	239
Houston	2	2	1	3	2	2	2	1	15
London	25	26	25	21	23	23	24	21	188
Los Angeles	6	6	3	5	4	5	5	4	38
Melbourne	13	13	13	11	11	15	13	9	98
Moscow	32	32	32	32	31	32	31	23	245
Munich	20	20	23	18	21	26	24	19	171
New York	16	15	16	14	14	17	15	12	119
Paris	22	23	28	23	26	24	26	22	194
Perth	8	9	10	7	6	6	6	3	55
Phoenix	4	7	5	1	1	1	1	2	22
San Francisco	5	5	4	12	10	12	10	8	66
Singapore	30	30	30	25	28	30	28	18	219
Stockholm	21	21	20	28	22	28	27	19	186
Sydney	15	16	15	16	13	18	14	7	114
Tokyo	29	29	29	31	29	29	29	24	229
Toronto	12	11	14	26	15	20	16	10	124
Vienna	24	24	27	24	25	27	23	14	188
Washington DC	7	4	8	8	7	8	7	5	54
West Berlin	27	27	24	30	27	22	20	15	192
Zürich	17	18	18	29	20	21	21	20	164

Rank Order		Gasoline use (MJ/capita)	Composite factor score
15 Houston	Intensely auto-oriented	59,455	33.6
19 Detroit			
22 Phoenix			
32 Denver			
38 Los Angeles			
54 Washington			
55 Perth			
66 San Francisco	Predominantly auto-oriented	42,249	71.5
72 Boston			
72 Brisbane			
76 Adelaide			
98 Melbourne	Some orientation to non-auto modes	36,836	110.8
99 Chicago			
114 Sydney			
119 New York			
124 Toronto			
143 Brussels	Balanced auto and non-auto modes	15,118	157.2
150 Frankfurt			
158 Hamburg			
164 Zürich			
171 Munich			
173 Amsterdam	Substantially oriented to non-auto modes	11,968	186.7
186 Copenhagen			
186 Stockholm			
188 London			
188 Vienna			
192 West Berlin			
194 Paris			
219 Singapore	Intensely oriented to non-auto modes	4,215	233.0
229 Tokyo			
239 Hong Kong			
245 Moscow			

Table 3.10

Level of traffic restraint index for the thirty-two world cities with corresponding gasoline use per capita (high score = high restraint).

City	Score on variable				Composite score	Rank order			Gasoline use (MJ/capita)	Composite factor score
	Length of road per capita	Parking spaces per 1000 CBD jobs	Vehicles per km of road	Car kms per km of road						
Adelaide	5	7	2	3	17	6	Perth			
Amsterdam	21	16	20	15	72	14	Phoenix	Very unrestrained traffic	49,732	20.0
Boston	10	9	13	20	52	17	Adelaide			
Brisbane	7	12	9	9	37	26	Houston			
Brussels	27	20	30	31	108	26	Melbourne			
Chicago	12	28	11	16	67	31	Denver			
Copenhagen	16	15	5	6	42	37	Brisbane			
Denver	4	4	12	11	31	42	Copenhagen			
Detroit	9	5	14	22	50	44	Sydney	Lightly restrained traffic	40,192	47.2
Frankfurt	22	14	27	29	92	50	Detroit			
Hamburg	20	23	23	26	92	52	Boston			
Hong Kong	32	31	31	17	111	58	Washington			
Houston	2	8	6	10	26	64	Los Angeles			
London	23	26	24	14	87	66	New York			
Los Angeles	15	3	19	27	64	67	Chicago	Moderate to average traffic restraint	36,882	70.8
Melbourne	6	11	4	5	26	72	Amsterdam			
Moscow	31	-	8	1	-	78	Singapore			
Munich	25	10	29	25	89	78	San Francisco			
New York	14	29	10	13	66	82	Tokyo			
Paris	30	17	32	32	111	83	West Berlin			
Perth	1	2	1	2	6	85	Zürich	Significantly restrained traffic	15,857	86.0
Phoenix	3	1	3	7	14	87	London			
San Francisco	13	24	17	24	78	89	Munich			
Singapore	29	27	18	4	78	90	Toronto			
Stockholm	19	22	22	28	91	91	Stockholm			
Sydney	8	21	7	8	44	91	Vienna			
Tokyo	24	30	16	12	82	92	Frankfurt	Highly restrained traffic	12,748	99.4
Toronto	17	18	25	30	90	92	Hamburg			
Vienna	26	19	28	18	91	108	Brussels			
Washington DC	11	13	15	19	58	111	Paris			
West Berlin	28	6	26	23	83	111	Hong Kong			
Zürich	18	25	21	21	85					

Table 3.11

Degree of centralisation index for the thirty-two world cities with corresponding gasoline use per capita (high score = high centralisation).

City	CBD population density	Proportion of population in CBD	Proportion of jobs in CBD	Composite score	Rank order		Gasoline use (MJ/capita)	Composite factor score
		Score on variable						
Adelaide	3	7	13	23	9	Houston		
Amsterdam	24	32	30	86	11	Detroit		
Boston	26	24	16	66	15	Sydney		
Brisbane	7	10	12	29	17	Chicago		
Brussels	19	21	26	66	17	Los Angeles	53,142	17.0
Chicago	8	1	8	17	21	Washington	Almost no centralisation	
Copenhagen	21	22	17	60	23	Phoenix		
Denver	10	11	6	27	23	Adelaide		
Detroit	6	1	4	11	27	Denver		
Frankfurt	17	23	20	60	29	Brisbane		
Hamburg	13	14	21	48	29	Toronto		
Hong Kong	29	11	5	45	33	Melbourne	27,459	36.6
Houston	1	1	7	9	42	Perth	Some centralisation	
London	18	24	29	71	43	Zurich		
Los Angeles	14	1	2	17	45	Hong Kong		
Melbourne	11	7	15	33	45	West Berlin		
Moscow	28	27	-	-	48	Hamburg		
Munich	25	29	23	77	49	Vienna		
New York	31	26	24	81	59	San Francisco	21,862	55.2
Paris	32	28	22	82	60	Frankfurt	Centralised	
Perth	4	14	24	42	60	Copenhagen		
Phoenix	9	13	1	23	66	Brussels		
San Francisco	22	18	19	59	66	Boston		
Singapore	30	31	25	86	67	Tokyo	19,632	71.2
Stockholm	23	30	27	80	71	London	Strongly centralised	
Sydney	5	1	9	15	77	Munich		
Tokyo	20	19	28	67	80	Stockholm		
Toronto	12	7	10	29	81	Moscow		
Vienna	16	19	14	49	81	New York		
Washington DC	2	1	18	21	82	Paris	14,736	83.8
West Berlin	27	16	2	45	86	Amsterdam	Very strongly centralised	
Zürich				43	86	Singapore		

Table 3.12

Public transport performance index for the thirty-two world cities with corresponding gasoline use per capita (high score = high performance).

City	Score on variable						Composite score	Rank order		Gasoline use (MJ/capita)	Composite factor score
	Vehicles kms per person	Passenger trips per person	Passenger trips per vehicle km	Average speed	Energy use per passenger km	Proportion of public transport passenger kms on trains					
Adelaide	12	9	4	15	7	10	57	15	Phoenix	66,467	21.0
Amsterdam	20	26	24	24	22	15	131	17	Denver		
Boston	5	8	19	17	9	18	76	19	Houston		
Brisbane	10	7	4	18	12	20	71	22	Detroit		
Brussels	15	20	28	12	13	14	102	32	Los Angeles		
									Extremely poor public transport throughout		
Chicago	8	12	18	26	9	27	100	47	Perth	42,141	64.5
Copenhagen	28	17	8	28	15	16	112	57	Adelaide		
Denver	4	4	1	4	3	1	17	60	Washington		
Detroit	3	3	4	5	1	6	22	71	Brisbane		
Frankfurt	16	23	26	25	28	17	135	76	Boston		
Hamburg	23	18	20	19	19	26	125	76	San Francisco		
									Some good public transport features but weak overall		
Hong Kong	29	30	23	1	23	8	114	87	Melbourne	29,491	95.3
Houston	2	2	4	6	4	1	19	91	Toronto		
London	31	21	16	19	20	25	132	92	Singapore		
Los Angeles	6	5	12	3	5	1	32	100	Chicago		
Melbourne	13	11	8	14	17	24	87	100	New york		
Moscow	32	32	32	32	31	31	190	102	Brussels		
									Some excellent public transport features and good overall		
Munich	21	24	22	31	25	23	146	111	Vienna	13,454	123.4
New York	17	14	11	21	8	29	100	112	Copenhagen		
Paris	9	19	30	30	29	30	147	114	Hong Kong		
Perth	13	6	2	9	10	7	47	120	Sydney		
Phoenix	1	1	2	8	2	1	15	125	Hamburg		
San Francisco	11	13	14	16	11	11	76	131	Amsterdam		
Singapore	27	27	21	2	14	1	92	131	Stockholm		
Stockholm	30	22	17	22	18	22	131	132	London		
Sydney	22	15	8	26	21	28	120	135	Frankfurt		
									Uniformly very good public transport		
Tokyo	26	31	28	28	30	31	174	140	West Berlin	10,395	156.7
Toronto	24	16	12	10	16	13	91	143	Zurich		
Vienna	19	25	24	7	27	9	111	146	Munich		
Washington DC	7	10	14	11	6	12	60	147	Paris		
West Berlin	25	29	27	12	26	21	140	174	Tokyo		
Zürich	18	28	31	23	24	19	143	190	Moscow		
									Excellent public transport throughout		

scores for each city (i.e. 31 to 32 cases), also gave very highly significant results as also shown in Table 3.13. The levels of significance are in fact better in each case but the correlation coefficients are not as strong, due to greater scatter in the data.

The best use of Tables 3.8 to 3.12 is to take any individual city of interest and examine the categories into which it fits for each of the five factors. This gives a good overview feeling for that city in relation to other cities and provides the sort of perspective on automobile dependence in cities which is the fundamental aim of this book.

Table 3.13
Correlation coefficients and level of significance for regressions of gasoline per capita with the various factors, using groups of cities and individual cities.

Factor	Correlation coefficient with gasoline using groupings of cities (5 to 6 cases)	Level of significance	Correlation coefficient with gasoline using individual cities (31 to 32 cases)	Level of significance
Land use intensity	-0.98	0.0025	-0.79	0.0000
Orientation to non-automobile modes	-0.98	0.0014	-0.93	0.0000
Level of traffic restraint	-0.94	0.0141	-0.59	0.0007
Degree of centralisation	-0.91	0.0293	-0.63	0.0003
Public transport performance	-0.98	0.0027	-0.85	0.0000

Cluster analysis methodology

Basically, cluster analysis attempts to group items or observation units (e.g. cities) that are very similar to each other on a wide range of different variables or dimensions and to maximise the between-group differences. This is compared to traditional factor analysis which, with a few additional calculations, can be used as the basis to group items or observation units that are very similar to each other on each factor or related group of variables. Thus cluster analysis is a way of gaining an insight into the degree of similarity between various items on a multi-dimensional basis (i.e. all factors considered together), whereas factor analysis keeps the various dimensions separate. Thus cluster analysis was attempted in order to bring together the various factors and give an overall impression of which cities show a multifactor dependence on the automobile and which have a more balanced transport system.

The aims, limitations and specific problems of cluster analysis especially those related to subjectivity have been described in detail by us elsewhere (Kenworthy, Newman and Lyons, 1983).

Sophisticated computer-based cluster analysis techniques produce a range of results depending on the particular method used and these are generally accepted or rejected by the researcher based on an intuitive notion of whether they represent a helpful clustering (Everitt, 1974). However, in the present study it was decided to use a very much simpler method, which although not a formal cluster analysis technique, the end result was essentially the same. Importantly, this simple method gave a result which was intuitively very acceptable and provided what appears to be a useful grouping of cities in terms of their overall transport characteristics.

The method consisted of adding the composite factor scores for each of the five factors and arriving at a final total score for each city. Each of the five factors was designed so that a high score represented low automobile dependence, thus a high total score suggested low automobile dependence characteristics in an overall sense. The final scores for each city were then ordered from lowest to highest and the range divided into five discrete groups representing five classes of cities:

Class I - Very High Automobile Dependence, almost no role for public transport, walking or cycling, very high gasoline use.

Class II - High Automobile Dependence, minor though significant role for public transport, walking and cycling, high gasoline use.

Class III - Moderate Automobile Dependence, important role for public transport, walking and cycling, moderate gasoline use.

Class IV - Low Automobile Dependence, public transport, walking and cycling equal with cars, low gasoline use.

Class V - Very Low Automobile Dependence, public transport, walking and cycling more important than cars, very low gasoline use.

Cluster analysis results

The results of the cluster analysis are shown in Table 3.14. These are expressed in terms of decreasing automobile dependence. The most dependent Class I cities consist of a group of five American cities (Phoenix, Houston, Denver, Detroit and Los Angeles) and three Australian cities (Perth, Adelaide and Brisbane) which are very highly automobile dependent in most characteristics. The least automobile dependent are Class V cities consisting of a group of five European and Asian cities (Munich, Paris, Singapore, Hong Kong, Tokyo) which have very low automobile dependence in most characteristics.

There is an extremely strong correlation between the per capita gasoline use and the cluster analysis scores for each group of cities (5 cases), and this is only moderately weakened by doing the correlation on the basis of each individual city (31 cases). For the grouping of cities the correlation coefficient is - 0.9915 (s=0.0008) and for the individual cases it is - 0.8800 (s=0.0000).

These results appear to provide significant perspective for the development of land use and transport policies aimed at improving cities with high dependence on the automobile. To draw these policy directions out more clearly the cluster analysis results are expanded in Table 3.15 by calculating average values for each of the variables comprising the five major factors or indices. In this way it is possible to see how individual

64

Table 3.14
Overall transport energy conservation index for the thirty-two world cities with corresponding gasoline use per capita
(high score = high energy conservation).

City	Score on variable					Cluster score	Rank order	Cluster score	Gasoline use (MJ/capita)	Cluster score	
	Land use intensity index	Orientation to non-automobile modes index	Level of traffic restraint index	Degree of centralisation index	Public transport performance index						
Adelaide	35	76	17	23	57	208	92 Phoenix	208	53,049	162.9	Very poorly energy conserving in most characteristics
Amsterdam	112	173	72	86	131	574	95 Houston	574			
Boston	44	72	52	66	76	310	145 Denver	310			
Brisbane	14	72	37	29	71	223	151 Detroit	223			
Brussels	151	143	108	66	102	570	168 Perth	570			
Chicago	66	99	67	17	100	349	208 Adelaide	349			
Copenhagen	96	186	42	60	112	496	221 Los Angeles	496			
Denver	38	32	31	27	17	145	223 Brisbane	145			
Detroit	49	19	50	11	22	151	255 Washington DC	151	44,355	322.3	Generally poor energy conserving characteristics but with a few positive features
Frankfurt	148	150	92	60	135	585	302 Melbourne	585			
Hamburg	126	158	92	48	125	549	310 Boston	549			
Hong Kong	185	239	111	45	114	694	349 Chicago	694			
Houston	26	15	26	9	19	95	357 San Francisco	95			
London	134	188	87	71	132	612	361 Sydney	612			
Los Angeles	70	38	64	17	32	221	433 Toronto	221	22,846	513.2	Significant energy conserving characteritics
Melbourne	58	98	26	33	87	302	464 New York	302			
Moscow	-	245	-	-	190	-	496 Copenhagen	-			
Munich	158	171	89	77	146	641	549 Hamburg	641			
New York	98	119	66	81	100	464	567 Zürich	464			
Paris	114	194	111	82	147	648	570 Brussels	648			
Perth	18	55	6	42	47	168	574 Amsterdam	168	12,445	598.0	Strongly energy conserving in many characteristics
Phoenix	18	22	14	23	15	92	585 Frankfurt	92			
San Francisco	78	66	78	59	76	357	598 West Berlin	357			
Singapore	164	219	78	86	92	643	605 Vienna	643			
Stockholm	126	186	91	80	131	614	612 London	614			
Sydney	68	114	44	15	120	361	614 Stockholm	361			
Tokyo	169	229	82	67	174	721	641 Munich	721	8,588	669.4	Very strongly energy conserving in most characteristics
Toronto	99	124	90	29	91	433	643 Singapore	433			
Vienna	166	188	91	49	111	605	648 Paris	605			
Washington DC	62	54	58	21	60	255	694 Hong Kong	255			
West Berlin	138	192	83	45	140	598	721 Tokyo	598			
Zürich	132	164	85	43	143	567		567			

65

Table 3.15

Transportation and land use characteristics and the co-existence of transportation modes in principal world cities (1980).

Factors and variables / Category of city	Class I - Very high automobile dependence almost no role for public transport, walking or cycling, very high gasoline use	Class II - High automobile dependence, minor though significant role for public transport, walking and cycling, high gasoline use.	Class III - Moderate automobile dependence, important role for public transport, walking and cycling moderate gasoline use.	Class IV - Low automobile dependence, public transport, walking and cycling equal with cars, low gasoline use.	Class V - Very low automobile dependence, public transport, walking and cycling more important than cars, very low gasoline use.
Land use intensity					
Urban density (persons/ha)	12.2	15.4	42.1	58.0	117.3
Employment density (jobs/ha)	6.0	7.3	23.9	32.9	53.9
Outer area density (persons/ha)	10.7	12.8	32.8	48.7	83.9
Outer area employment density (jobs/ha)	4.3	5.0	12.5	18.8	28.5
Inner area density (persons/ha)	23.7	45.1	81.7	83.0	331.4
Inner area employment density (jobs/ha)	19.5	37.2	65.4	67.1	211.3
Orientation to non-automobile modes					
Total vehicles per 1000 people	684	570	422	366	254
Cars per 1000 people	539	479	367	318	192
Per capita car passenger kms	12,822	11,359	7,384	5,185	2,966
Per capita public transportation passenger kms	362	887	1,664	1,890	2,519
Proportion of passenger kms on public transportation (%)	2.9	7.4	18.6	27.2	49.2
Proportion of workers using public transportation (%)	8.6	19.3	32.0	33.3	52.5
Proportion of workers using private transportation (%)	87.2	74.4	51.7	45.4	23.7
Proportion of workers using foot and bicycle (%)	4.2	6.3	16.3	21.3	23.8
Level of traffic restraint					
Length of road per person (m)	8.8	5.7	3.0	1.9	1.1
Parking spaces per 1000 CBD jobs	514	208	160	185	137
Vehicles per km of road	91	105	159	193	247
Car kms per km of road	1,068,857	1,364,838	1,723,132	1,725,693	1,665,405
Degree of centralisation					
CBD population density (persons/ha)	14.2	45.6	78.7	89.2	158.6
Proportion of population in CBD (%)	0.3	0.7	1.5	3.9	3.9
Proportion of jobs in CBD (%)	11.4	15.0	18.4	20.7	19.8
Public transportation performance					
Vehicle kms per person	29.6	47.9	74.1	86.6	86.1
Passenger trips per person	46.1	106.3	229.6	324.3	371.4
Passenger trips per vehicle km	1.5	2.3	3.3	3.9	4.4
System average speed (km/h)	24.0	31.3	30.8	30.9	31.5
Energy use per passenger km (MJ)	2.12	1.13	0.88	0.58	0.52
Proportion public transport passenger kms on trains(%)	13.3	53.9	54.9	51.0	51.4
Transportation energy conservation status	Very poor	Generally poor but a few positive features	Significant conservation	Strongly conserving	Very strongly conserving
Gasoline use per capita (MJ)	53,049	44,355	22,846	12,445	8,588

Cities in each category and their cluster scores based on all factors.

Cities	Cluster scores	Cities	Cluster score	Cities	Cluster score	Cities	Cluster score	Cities	Cluster score
Phoenix	92	Washington	255	Toronto	433	Amsterdam	574	Munich	641
Houston	95	Melbourne	302	New York	464	Frankfurt	585	Singapore	643
Denver	145	Boston	310	Copenhagen	496	West Berlin	598	Paris	648
Detroit	151	Chicago	349	Hamburg	549	Vienna	605	Hong Kong	694
Perth	168	San Francisco	357	Zürich	567	London	612	Tokyo	721
Adelaide	208	Sydney	361	Brussels	570	Stockholm	614		
Los Angeles	221								
Brisbane	223								

parameters such as the amount of road per person or the inner area population density changes as cities move from high automobile dependent Class I cities to low automobile dependent Class V cities.

Concluding comments

The final results from the factor and cluster analysis indicate that there are five major physical planning factors or indices that can be used to distinguish cities which have high automobile dependence and gasoline use from those with low automobile dependence and gasoline use. It suggests that if a city were going to try and lower its gasoline and automobile dependence then it would need to consider :
•Increasing its land use intensity
•Increasing the orientation of its transport infrastructure to non-automobile modes
•Increasing its level of restraint to high speed traffic flow
•Increasing its degree of centralisation, and
•Increasing its public transport performance
To quantify the proportions involved in moving from the Class I highest automobile dependent cities to the Class V lowest automobile dependent cities, Table 3.16 sets out how much the five factors would need to change. Such quantities indicate how great are the differences between the cities at the two extremes. Obviously there is little likelihood of the extreme cities making such dramatic changes, indeed for many the process is more likely to be a continuing trend downward in terms of the main parameters listed. On the other hand subsequent chapters will outline policy changes that are being considered and being implemented in some cities that give hope for some changes in the directions cited.

The process of changing a major land use/transport policy direction in a city can never be just for one reason such as reducing automobile dependence or   conserving gasoline. Urban policies must include broader factors that enable all the parameters of urban life to be considered. Thus in Chapter 5 urban policies will be outlined that provide a broad urban framework incorporating many of the main issues of urban life. At the same time they will be shown to provide some potential for changing cities in the five directions highlighted by the factor and cluster analysis results from the thirty-two cities data.

Before doing this, Chapter 4 will examine the many other urban factors which help to explain the distinctive patterns outlined in this chapter separating the groups of cities into their respective levels of automobile dependence.

Table 3.16
Range of changes required in going from highest to lowest automobile dependence based on transport/land use factors and gasoline use.

Factor	Average gasoline use (MJ/capita)	Factor score	Approximate increase in each factor required between highest and lowest automobile dependent cities.
Cities with <u>lowest</u> land use intensity	49990	24.8	7 times increase
↓	↓	↓	in land use intensity
Cities with <u>highest</u> land use intensity	7785	169.2	
Cities with <u>lowest</u> orientation to non-auto modes	59455	33.6	7 times increase in orientation to
↓	↓	↓	non-auto modes
Cities with <u>highest</u> orientation to non-auto modes	4215	233.0	
Cities with <u>least</u> <u>restrained</u> traffic	49732	20.0	5 times increase
↓	↓	↓	in the level of
Cities with <u>most</u> <u>restrained</u> traffic	12748	99.4	traffic restraint
Cities with <u>lowest</u> degree of centralisation	53142	17.0	5 times increase
↓	↓	↓	in the degree of
Cities with <u>highest</u> degree of centralisation	14736	83.8	centralisation
Cities with <u>worst</u> performing public transport systems	66467	21.0	7.5 times increase in
↓	↓	↓	public transport
Cities with <u>best</u> performing public transport systems	10395	156.7	performance

4 Other factors affecting gasoline and car use patterns

This chapter will examine the more common "other factors" aside from the transport infrastructure and land use planning factors which have been suggested as major influences on car use/gasoline consumption and urban form. They are divided into economic factors and social/cultural factors though there are clearly overlaps and linkages between them all. The economic factors considered are: the demographic size of a city, vehicle ownership, income, gasoline price and vehicle fuel efficiency. The social/cultural factors considered are: climate-related lifestyle, spatial traditions and politics. It is our belief that all of these factors play a role, some very small and others are substantial factors, but that none are so dominant to make the urban planner irrelevant. Indeed it is our contention that those who plan and influence decisions on transport infrastructure and land use can be the major players in determining automobile dependence.

Economic factors

Demographic size of city

The intuitive reaction of many people is that the bigger the population of a city then the further people need to travel. Hence people in bigger cities are likely to consume more gasoline per capita. This probably does have some significance in very small cities but it does not take into consideration the distribution and density of the population and all that flows from these patterns.

The economics of city size has been investigated by many authors who conclude that increased size does lead to certain efficiencies; leaving aside the effects on commercial development, size does seem to influence the level of public transport use and through this, other transport patterns. The size of the city centre and the increased line-haul advantages are two common ways that size influences transport. Thus it is not a foregone conclusion that bigger cities are automatically going to involve more car travel and hence more gasoline use.

From our sample of large and medium sized cities there is no correlation whatsoever between population size and gasoline consumption (0.0270). This was also found to be true in our earlier study of Australian cities (Newman and Kenworthy, 1980 a, b, c) and in a study of the ten US cities (Newman and Kenworthy, 1987a). Thus the patterns of land use or how the population is distributed, appears to be more fundamental than the total population in determining how that city uses its transport, though city size may have an effect on these. As discussed in Chapter 2, this is one reason why we did not limit the choice of cities to those of similar sizes.

Vehicle Ownership

It is not hard to show from the literature that there is a relationship between vehicle ownership and vehicle use - it would be most surprising if there were none. Within our sample the correlation is significant (0.9258, s=0.000, see Table 3.6). However, this is sometimes taken by planners to mean there is really nothing you can do to control car use; the usual lament is: once people have a car they are going to use it and hence you have to provide for cars. This proposition neglects many of the subtleties in understanding the relationship between car ownership and car use.

There is evidence that car use is determined by many more fundamental urban structure parameters than car ownership. Where car ownership rates are high it is found that there are significant differences in car use between, for example, high and low density areas (see Figure 5.8). The literature suggests that there is a difference in car use patterns between those areas where cars are clearly needed as no real alternative exists and those areas where cars can be used but are not an essential item for all trips (Pushkarev and Zupan, 1977; Button, Fowkes and Pearman, 1980; Lansing and Hendricks, 1967; Hillman and Whalley, 1979).

This would probably explain why for example there is no significant correlation between vehicle ownership and income in the ten US cities studied (0.3863), even though the common argument is that wealth is the major factor in determining car ownership Again it seems that the land use patterns are more fundamental in determining the need for a car and thus in some US cities the necessity for a car (particularly second and third cars) can be overcome by particular land use arrangements. Vehicle ownership does not automatically mean automobile dependence.

Income

There is of course a clear relationship between car use and the ability to buy and use a car ie. income per capita. However, this again is only in the broad brush outline of what determines car use. Our sample of thirty-two cities shows a significant correlation between income per capita and gasoline consumption per capita (0.7994) as would be expected when comparing across large income ranges. It should be noted that only national income values were available for European cities (and Tokyo) and hence this relationship may be suspect to some degree. (data in Table 4.1). But when groups of cities are compared in the same nation and hence in the same general income bracket, the relationship between income per capita and car use is not nearly so clear. In the ten US cities median family income and gasoline use per capita had a correlation coefficient of only -0.1219 (note that this indicates a weak negative relationship!). The five Australian cities also show no significant correlation between the two parameters (-0.5328, s>0.05); note that although the correlation is not significant at the 5% level, it is again negative. This suggests that even if the correlation was statistically significant, it would imply lower energy use as income increases, which is the reverse of most accepted notions.

Thus, as with vehicle ownership, if you need to use a car you will use your income to do so, but if you don't then you may or may not. What appears to be fundamental is what determines the need for car use.

Gasoline price and vehicle fuel efficiency

Two of the key determinants of car use and hence gasoline consumption that have been isolated by econometricians using national data are gasoline price and vehicle fuel consumption (Wheaton, 1982; Archibald and Gillingham, 1981; Dahl, 1982; Pindyck, 1979). The two factors are brought together here because they are so closely related.

The thirty-two cities show significant correlations between gasoline use and price (-0.8500) and also gasoline use and national vehicle fuel efficiency (l/100km) (0.8868). This relationship is however weakened when vehicle fuel efficiency is adjusted for urban average speed. The data for these are provided in Table 4.1.

Most national policies on fuel conservation have been orientated towards these two parameters as they do clearly contribute to the consumption of gasoline. Policies to keep gasoline prices high and improve the technology of vehicles through better fuel efficiency will obviously help to conserve energy. However, if low gasoline prices in the past have contributed to very inefficient land use, then increases in fuel price may not in themselves lead to much saving if high car use is built-in to the structure of the city. People will just tend to put more of their income into fuel and less in other areas.

The same process can occur with more fuel-efficient vehicles - the extra fuel saved (and money in the pocket) could just be used to drive further. Thus little fuel is saved overall. In both cases it would appear that the actual structure of the city and its provision for cars or other modes will ultimately decide the level of car use and gasoline consumption, though these

Table 4.1
Income, gasoline price and vehicle fuel efficiency for the thirty-two cities, 1980.

City and Region	Income per Capita (US$)	Gasoline Price (US¢/per litre)	Vehicle Fuel Efficiency (L/100 km) National Data	Adjusted for urban average speed
US Cities				
Houston	8,391	21.6	15.35	17.02
Phoenix	7,047	23.6	15.35	19.42
Detroit	8,430	24.3	15.35	18.78
Denver	8,013	22.9	15.35	18.51
Los Angeles	7,560	24.2	15.35	18.51
San Francisco	8,438	24.3	15.35	18.23
Boston	7,709	22.5	15.35	20.46
Washington	9,565	23.3	15.35	20.46
Chicago	8,336	24.9	15.35	19.74
New York	7,403	24.4	15.35	22.13
Average	**8,089**	**23.6**	**15.35**	**19.33**
Australian Cities				
Perth	6,109	43.6	12.50	15.56
Brisbane	5,900	41.4	12.50	14.43
Melbourne	6,800	44.2	12.50	14.43
Adelaide	5,948	44.0	12.50	15.56
Sydney	6,784	42.2	12.50	16.66
Average	**6,308**	**43.1**	**12.50**	**15.33**
Canadian City				
Toronto	7,521	23.5	16.30	21.72
European Cities				
Hamburg	6,967	67.9	10.9	17.65
Frankfurt	6,967	67.9	10.9	17.65
Zürich	6,610	74.2	10.9	15.39
Stockholm	7,142	72.1	10.7	17.32
Brussels	6,293	85.6	10.7	17.32
Paris	6,678	83.8	8.76	14.96
London	4,990	70.0	10.7	16.90
Munich	6,967	67.9	10.9	15.72
West Berlin	6,967	67.9	10.9	18.62
Copenhagen	6,746	88.2	10.7	12.90
Vienna	6,052	73.7	10.9	17.65
Amsterdam	5,856	78.2	10.9	14.53
Average	**6,520**	**74.8**	**10.66**	**16.38**
Asian Cities				
Tokyo	5,996	76.4	7.63	16.40
Singapore	3,948	50.2	7.63	12.35
Hong Kong	3,973	57.6	7.63	16.40
Average	**4,639**	**61.4**	**7.63**	**15.05**
USSR City				
Moscow	3,943	49.9	9.1	10.97
Correlation with Gasoline Use	0.7477	-0.8500	0.8868	0.5906

Notes:

1. Income are real Gross Domestic Product data adjusted for purchasing power parities by Summers and Heston (1984). For US cities the average US figure was adjusted to account for variations in each city by a factor derived from the Median Family Income from the U.S. Census. For Australian cities the same adjustments were made based on Census data.

2. Price data were derived from "Basic Petroleum Data Book", American Petroleum Institute, 1980 (for US cities), "Oil and Australia, 1979", Australian Institute of Petroleum, 1979 (for Australian cities), "Yearbook of World Energy Statistics", United Nations 1981 (for most other cities) and Sweden, Singapore, Hong Kong and Moscow were obtained directly from the cities.

3. Vehicle efficiency data came from Chandler (1985), Energy and Environmental Analysis Inc. (1982), US Dept. of Transportation (1985) and Transport Canada (1984). Adjustments for average speed are discussed in Table 3.2.

4. All correlations are significant to <0.0005.

economic factors do have an important contribution. In addition, the broader urban policy issues concerning equity, environment and social aspects of the city are not addressed by energy conservation policies based only on gasoline price and vehicle efficiency. In terms of our analysis gasoline price and vehicle efficiencies should not be neglected as contributing to automobile dependence as reflected in our data, but they are not in themselves responsible for it.

Perspective on economic factors

In order to find some perspective on the extent to which economic factors like income, gasoline price and vehicle fuel-efficiency influence the consumption of gasoline, we have analysed how much the patterns of gasoline use in our world cities would change if all cities had:
• US incomes
• US gasoline prices, and
• US vehicle fuel efficiencies (L/100km), all adjusted for average speed.

The role of vehicle ownership is assumed to be largely subsumed under income or under the other land use factors which affect how much vehicles are needed.

To compare across the international sample requires the use of accepted price and income elasticities for gasoline consumption together with vehicle efficiencies which also vary with gasoline price and income. Table 4.2 sets out the expected gasoline consumption if US incomes, US gasoline price and US vehicle efficiency were apparent in all the thirty-one cities (Moscow is excluded due to lack of data).

If these economic and efficiency factors were the sole or primary factors then all the cities should tend to have the same gasoline use. They clearly do not. On average, the economic factors explain less than 40% of the gasoline use in the short term and around half in the long term. These are estimated using generous elasticities which are probably overestimates based on recent detailed survey work in Australia (Hensher *et al.*, 1987).

It can also be argued that these economic parameters are overestimates conceptually as they incorporate some degree of anticipated urban form change especially in the long term, but even then they do not adequately explain the variations in gasoline use in the sample. What is suggested by these results is that a purely economic approach to transport matters will be inadequate, that matters of urban form and provision for the automobile have direct and independent influence on transport patterns. We would suggest that planners who provide the transport infrastructure or who set out the physical plan of a city are directly and actively influencing transport patterns, they are not just responding to economic factors. They are of course subject to a range of social and political factors, some of which will be examined next, but first it is important to look in a little more detail at what our data suggest about economic approaches to gasoline use and automobile dependence.

Econometric models are based on correlations of variables considered to be the key determinants of gasoline use. Gasoline models have nearly all been based on national data and all find that price, income and vehicle efficiency

Table 4.2

Average value for per capita gasoline use in cities by region 1980, compared to adjusted values (for US gasoline prices, incomes and vehicle efficiency).

Cities	Actual gasoline use (MJ per capita)	Adjusted gasoline use for US gasoline prices, incomes and vehicle efficiency (MJ per capita)		% difference between US gasoline use and adjusted gasoline use by other cities	
		short term elasticities	long term elasticities	short term elasticities	long term elasticities
US cities	58,541	58,541	58,541	-	-
Australian cities	29,829	38,488	43,680	51%	25%
Toronto	34,813	29,995	26,090	49%	55%
European cities	13,280	17,082	31,080	71%	47%
Asian cities	5,493	7,676	12,340	87%	79%
Average for non US cities	**17,133**	**21,-50**	**31,160**	**63%**	**47%**

Notes :

(1) Gasoline consumption elasticities used were:

	short term	long term
gasoline price	-0.20	-1.0
incomes	+0.11	+0.6

(2) As gasoline consumption elasticities include a component due to vehicle efficiency , it is necessary to subtract this when adjusting other cities for US vehicle efficiencies otherwise it would be accounted for twice .

Vehicle efficiency elasticities used were :

	short term	long term
gasoline price	+0.11	+1.0
incomes	-0.11	-1.0

Vehicle efficiencies used were national values in Table 4.1 adjusted for average speed in each city.
In all cases vehicle efficiencies in the long term became more than equivalent to US levels and hence the vehicle efficiency factor in the long term is cancelled out .

Sources: Pindyck (1979), Dahl (1982), Archibald and Gillingham (1981) and Wheaton (1982)

74

are generally sufficient to explain their data. The problem with econometric models attempting to explain variations in *urban* gasoline consumption is that they are assuming urban spatial variations and modal split patterns can be accounted for solely by price and income variations. On a *national* basis this may broadly be the case, as rural driving will mainly be determined by these variables and in general there appears to be a correlation between wealth and urban space particularly in the US context, ie. money tends to buy space with its inherent automobile use. However, there are many important variations in this pattern, due to:

1. Constrained urban sites, such as New York.

2. Factors such as a good transit system, which concentrates land use due to its time savings and provides a real alternative to the automobile for rich and poor.

3. Social and cultural factors, such as in European cities, where frequently money buys location, not space (and a central location is often preferred).

Therefore, to leave these factors out will mean that policy developed from econometric models will have limited application to transport in cities. This would explain why in the US sample of cities there is no significant correlation between gasoline consumption and income (Newman and Kenworthy, 1987a) or between vehicle ownership and income, and the same lack of correlation was found in a previous study of Australian cities (Newman and Kenworthy, 1980 a,b,c).

In terms of policy this is extremely important. The econometric models suggest that there is little that can be done other than taxing gasoline and vehicles or legislating for better vehicle fuel efficiency. This study does not examine those policies but results so far suggest that increases in urban density and centralisation, together with the provision of a good transit option and restraint in the provision of automobile infrastructure, have important potential for saving fuel. These parameters are in the direct control of physical and transport planners.

Clearly price and income do have an effect on gasoline consumption and must be considered as part of the suite of policies to keep gasoline consumption at reasonable levels. However, it is the main thrust of this book that the urban land use and transport infrastructure variables must also be addressed.

The interactions between the transport/land use variables and the economic variables is obviously very complex. It was envisaged that regression analysis may help sort out the various factors but it is not sufficient to assume linear, non-linked relationships between each variable and gasoline. Figure 4.1 presents a picture of the interactions that would need to be evaluated to make a complete model for understanding how these variables determine gasoline consumption.

It is enough at this point to reassert the importance of the transport infrastructure and land use variables together with the more commonly accepted economic parameters.

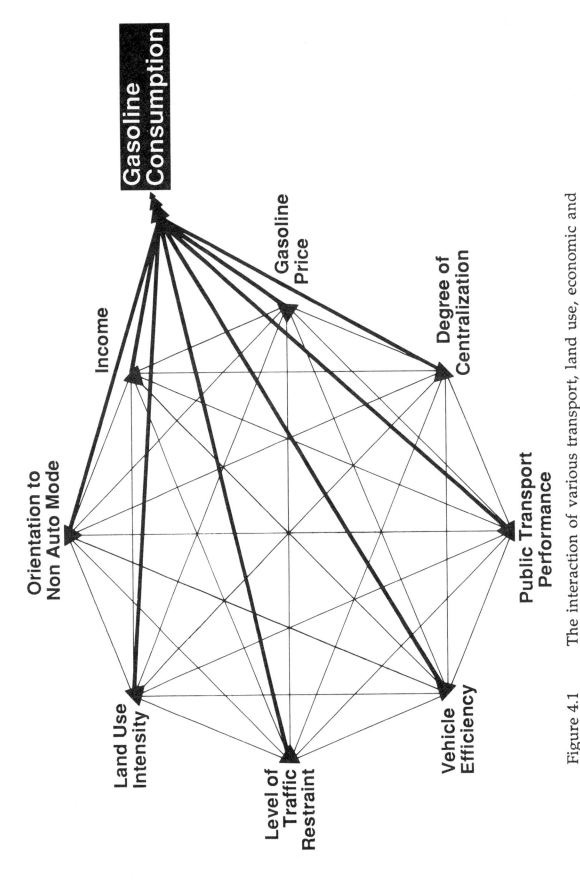

Figure 4.1   The interaction of various transport, land use, economic and technological factors in determining gasoline consumption.

Gasoline Consumption

Income

Gasoline Price

Orientation to Non Auto Mode

Degree of Centralization

Public Transport Performance

Land Use Intensity

Level of Traffic Restraint

Vehicle Efficiency

Social and cultural factors

It is difficult to separate economic factors, land use/transport and social/cultural factors as they rarely operate in isolation. Most of the questions addressed below have an economic dimension to them and a land use /transport outcome, but they are discussed here separately as they tend to operate more on the basis of human values, perceptions, traditions and processes. The first area relates to climate-related lifestyle, the second to a range of spatial traditions and the third to politics.

Climate-related lifestyle

One of the most persistent beliefs, at least in the Australian context, is that high automobile dependence is a feature of a lifestyle induced by the climate. The argument generally runs like this. A warm, low rainfall climate means that people like to spend a lot of time outdoors, this means:
  a) they travel around a lot more, and
  b) they have large private blocks of land for their house so that they can enjoy outdoor activities like gardening, barbecues, swimming in private pools and the children need extra space for sports and games. An additional argument is that the effect of snow and ice in cold climates provides extra motivation to take public transport rather than drive a car on dangerous roads (Gappert, 1987).

The first approach to this question is to suggest that there is nothing particularly attractive about a hot Australian summer, certainly nothing which would inevitably induce travel in an oppressively hot automobile. Conversely, there is nothing about cold climates that means people will inevitably stay at home, particularly considering the attractions of winter sports. Certainly hot weather can make indoor activities just as attractive as cold weather. The effect of climate on the desire for home-based outdoor activities like gardening and games seems also difficult to limit just to hotter climates. And the motivation to use public transport seems to be related to a great deal more than climate.

Nevertheless it is worth examining the data from our study to assess whether there is anything in the hypothesis. The data on average temperatures are provided in Table 4.3.

There is no significant correlation at the 5% level between gasoline consumption and average annual temperature (+0.2197) or between urban density and average annual temperature (+0.0771).

It is perhaps more instructive to widen the scope of our thirty-two cities and look at least at the general land use patterns of other cities which have hot and cold climates. When this is done it is very easy to find a range of cities that are hot and yet have a high density urban form. In Europe there are cities like Athens, Barcelona, Madrid and Rome. In the Middle East there is Istanbul, Cairo, Jerusalem, and Tehran. In South and Central America virtually every city has a hot climate, for example, Mexico City, Sao Paulo, Rio de Janeiro, Lima, Buenos Aires and all are compact and high density. In the USA there is Honolulu and the dense compact city centre of old San Francisco. In Asia again they are all dense, including the cities in our study.

Table 4.3
Annual average temperatures for the thirty-two international cities.

City	Annual average temperature (°C)	City	Annual average temperature (°C)
Moscow	4.4	Paris	11.1
Stockholm	6.6	London	11.3
Toronto	7.7	New York	12.5
Munich	8.0	San Francisco	13.9
Copenhagen	8.5	Tokyo	15.0
Zürich	8.6	Washington DC	15.6
West Berlin	8.8	Melbourne	16.1
Hamburg	9.2	Los Angeles	16.5
Detroit	9.5	Adelaide	17.1
Brussels	9.9	Perth	18.1
Frankfurt	10.0	Sydney	18.4
Amsterdam	10.1	Brisbane	20.5
Denver	10.1	Houston	20.5
Chicago	10.3	Phoenix	21.3
Vienna	10.6	Hong Kong	22.6
Boston	10.7	Singapore	27.0

On the other side of the story many of the cold northern cities of the US are low density car-orientated cities. The most obvious examples are Detroit and Denver, cities with very few of the supposed car-enhancing climate features, but cities totally dominated by the automobile and by extensive low density suburban land use.

If low density planning and high car use are encouraged in a city it is more than likely for deeper reasons than lifestyle induced by the climate.

Spatial traditions

The way that land is used in a city must have some relationship to the cultural traditions of how best to use urban space. We are unlikely to be able to do justice to the vast history of ideas that have influenced urban land use as discussed by authors like Mumford (1961), Schneider (1979) and Ellul (1970). Nevertheless, there are a few central factors that have relevance to our discussion and which underlie some of the next chapter on policy implications.

(i) *Age of city* The sheer age of a city establishes some of its important spatial traditions. Cities that were founded and grew substantially before the middle of the 19th century were basically built around walking, then public transport spread the city out and finally the car allowed even lower densities. Some data on these processes are available.

Chandler and Fox (1974) provide density estimates through their study of 3000 years of urban growth. They suggest that the ancient cities were generally in the range 100 to 200 people per ha. Some of the large ancient cities had higher densities than this range, eg Babylon was thought to have peaked at around 300 per ha in 430 BC. Rome may have reached 500 per ha in 100 AD and Woolley (quoted in Clark, 1967) estimated Ur to also have been around 500 per ha. For mediaeval cities, Chandler and Fox suggest that densities were more likely to be around 100 per ha rising to 200 per ha before crowding led to new outer walls. Genoa appears to have been the most crowded with 600 per ha in the late Middle Ages and Edinburgh was nearly as dense by 1750. Apart from these unusually crowded cities, the data from Chandler and Fox and other data from Russell (1958) support the picture of the historic walking city as generally between 100 and 200 people per ha.

Asian cities and most other cities in the Third World are presently in this urban density range. They have in fact mostly increased in density throughout this century whilst cities in the developed world have decreased in density. One of the main features that result from this high density spatial tradition is that most destinations are within walking distance (eg. see Table 4.4.). Thus there is still a strong spatial tradition within a large number of present cities like Hong Kong, Singapore and Tokyo in our sample to build and maintain a walking city with high density land use. They are not inevitably low density auto cities even though they are modern.

Most cities in Europe, USA and Australia began as walking cities and hence historical data reveal high densities. Warner's (1968) detailed study of Philadelphia showed that in 1860, when it was a walking city, its density was 364 per ha, but by 1905 the railway era had reduced its density to 129 per ha. Jefferson (1909) made a careful land use study of eight major cities in 1905 and showed the following densities: New York 227, Chicago 93, Boston 108, St Louis 89, London 154, Paris 278, Berlin 227 and Vienna 143 per ha. Sydney and Melbourne were both considered to be over 100 per ha at the turn of the century (Barrett, 1967; Powell, 1976). All these cities reflect a largely walking-based urban form that would still have been apparent at that time. Several of these type of cities have maintained a substantial commitment to their walking-based urban form particularly in their old central city areas (especially Paris, Vienna, Stockholm and other European cities). Many new areas of these cities retain a substantial walking base to their land use. Nevertheless most cities lost density as the public transport era began.

Declines in density due to the railway era began as early as 1860 in New York and Philadelphia (Blumenfeld, 1965), but were more general sometime around 1880 in the US (Guest, 1972; Edmonston, 1975). European cities also declined in density as public transport spread the city out, but the process has always been much slower than in the US. London declined to 90 per ha by 1931 (Hall *et al.*, 1973) and to 75 per ha by 1972, whilst Vienna has hardly altered from its density at the turn of the century. Eastern European cities and Russian cities have also generally maintained their density levels (Lichtenberger, 1976). The European density levels of between 30 and 130 per ha (and generally closer to 90 per ha) throughout this century are consistent with a spatial tradition of cities with a strong commitment to public transport.

Table 4.4
Density and modal split data for four suburbs in Delhi.

Suburb	Walk/Cycle	Modal Split Public Transport	Car/Motor Scooter & Other
Dakshin Puri (low income, density 310/ha)			
All Trips	73%	26%	1%
Employment	45%	53%	2%
Education	86%	10%	5%
Saket (high income, density 60/ha)			
All Trips	28%	52%	20%
Employment	4%	52%	44%
Education	25%	71%	4%
Nand Nagri (low income, density 200/ha)			
Employment	14%	81%	4%
Education	92%	7%	1%
Janak Puri (high income, density 85/ha)			
Employment	5%	82%	14%
Education	47%	49%	4%

(Source : Maunder, Fouracre and Rao, 1981; Maunder, 1983)

Most modern urban development in continental Europe has maintained the spatial tradition of a public transport city. In the UK it is a less obvious tradition in their new towns and new suburbs. US cities declined rapidly in density after 1940 (Weaver, 1977; Edmonston, 1975), with the adoption of the automobile; Australian cities were similar, though they showed lower densities generally right from their foundation (Burnley, 1980). As well, the more recently a city was established the lower is its present density (Berry and Kasarda, 1977). Canberra, the national capital of Australia, has consistently shown a density of around 10 per ha since its foundation as a car-based city 60 years ago. Old cities redeveloped for the automobile are therefore consistently found to be less than 30 per ha and are more likely to be less than 20 per ha.

Thus there are cities with strong commitments to building and maintaining the spatial traditions of a walking-city and a public transport-city, as well as the more recent automobile-city. It does appear that most US and Australian cities are part of the automobile-city tradition, though they could have been otherwise as many of their cities are quite old. Detroit was re-built from being a traditional "strong-centred", railway-based city to a totally car-based city ('fully motorised') in a period of about 30 years (Thomson, 1977).

On the other side we have seen a very rapid move away from a car-based city to a more public transport-based city in much of Canada. For example Toronto, Calgary, Edmonton, Montreal and Vancouver have made significant moves in this direction in the past 15 years (Goldberg and Mercer, 1986). Deliberate urban policies have established a new spatial tradition (see Chapter 5 for expansion of this). Also, Washington DC which continues to build an extensive Metro system, is undergoing a similar change to more use of transit and higher density land use patterns. Many other examples could be given of cities moving in this direction.

The age of a city is important in understanding its spatial traditions, but it is not sufficient nor is it fixed and inflexible.

(ii) "Plenty of space" tradition Another argument that appears to have become a cultural tradition in newer countries like USA and Australia is that such places have plenty of space and hence don't need to worry about efficient land use in their cities. As Knox (1982a) says:

> " It may be a faintly amusing concept to many of us to imagine Perth people crammed together in a transport efficient city on the edge of the wheatbelt and outback and next to the void of the Indian Ocean." (p65)

A number of points can be raised about this spatial tradition which is mainly found in Australia and the US , including the fact that there are other countries with "plenty of space" which have not developed this tradition, and there are significant human, economic, energy and environmental costs associated with such spatial attitudes.

• *Urban spatial efficiency in nations with "plenty of space"* There are many countries in the world where there is an awareness of spatial constraints; places like Japan, Hong Kong, Netherlands, England and Germany have high population densities with strong competition between industrial, urban, agricultural and natural land uses. To some extent the concentration of the city in these places reflects this need to conserve land. However, there are also a number of places where conservative urban land use is practised but there is "plenty of space". Central and South America have vast areas of rural land similar in extent to the US and Australia but their cities are all high density (Buenos Aires 80 per ha, Salvador 90 per ha, Santiago 144 per ha, Lima 171 per ha, Caracas 175 per ha and Mexico City 224 per ha (Newman and Hogan, 1987)). The USSR is also an obvious example of a nation with no shortage of space but its cities are very efficient users of space (Moscow 139 per ha and Leningrad 85 per ha).

Sweden is a clear example of a European country where there are vast expanses of rural land, mostly in forest, but the few cities of Sweden are all highly compact with very little space wasted. The basic reason for this is the long tradition in Sweden to plan urban services in an equitable and efficient manner. For example, Stockholm has no 'need' in terms of lack of space, to concentrate its land use, except that its planners believe that a good city requires that:

• a railway station for rapid urban accessibility should be within 500 to 900 metres (ie. a short walking or cycling distance) of most housing,

• a train service should not require a timetable ie. something less than a 12 minute service should be provided, and

• people should not be more than 30 minutes from the city centre.

These policies ensure a compact urban form that is based around a fast electric train with housing concentrated around stations. It is thus rare to have single detached homes in Stockholm (most of the new towns have between 3% and 14% single family housing), though most multi-family housing is no more than seven storeys (13 storeys seems to be an upper limit) (Stockholms Stadsbyggnadskontor, 1972).

Thus there are enough examples to show that if a nation has "plenty of space" it is not automatically going to have a low density urban form where land use is highly inefficient. There are likely to be many other factors involved than the availability of space, though this perception and expectation of endless space in the US and Australian context would appear to be playing some role in facilitating the low density city.

• *The costs of urban space* The idea that nations like the US and Australia have so much space that they can endlessly spread and scatter their cities is usually tempered with some awareness of the implications.

There are many commentators in the US/Australian context as well as the European context who have shown that urban space is not an independent parameter that can be toyed with depending on the whims of a city's population. In fact, there are significant costs associated with a lavish use of urban space of which planners in all countries, including the US and Australia, are becoming increasingly aware.

• *Human costs* As soon as travel distances go beyond easy walking or bicycling there is a need for mechanical transport and for the "plenty of space" enthusiasts this generally means cars. There is an immediate trade-off then in the amount of space needed to house, park and run cars - the bitumen requirements of an automobile city can be around 30% of its space (Kenworthy, 1978) and in particular the central city can be around two-thirds bitumen due to its extra need for carpark space (Antoniou, 1971). The sheer amount of extra space required in a city to accomodate the storage and movement of vehicles is highlighted when considering that cities like Denver and Houston have almost as many vehicles as they have men, women and children. This certainly must add a significant burden to the space requirements in these cities. In general, this is space not used for public purposes such as parks, central city plazas, pedestrian malls etc. As Gruen (1973) says,

"The most active, animated and significant parts of our cities, namely the cores, cannot, even by the widest stretch of the imagination and by utilizing all palliatives such as multilevel parking structures, underground garages, urban freeways, computerized signal systems, be adjusted to this disproportionate use of land without being destroyed."

It is not a coincidence that the cities with the most fuel conserving/balanced transport provision characteristics are also the cities with the most attractive city centres. Table 4.5 lists the thirty-one cities and ranks them in a highly subjective way from best to worst based on our perception of public facilities, pedestrianisation and attractive human features in their city centres (Moscow is not included since it was not visited). For our list there is a correlation of -0.8224 (s<0.0005) between the human attractiveness of the city centre and per capita gasoline use, ie the more automobile dependence in a city the less human is the central city. Others may produce a different list but it is hard to perceive hectares of bitumen and freeway overpasses as attractive urban design. Thus it is no surprise to find that the human attractiveness of the city centre is significantly and negatively correlated with the amount of automobile dominance in the city.

These human costs in the city centre are foregone fundamentally by the trade-off for lavish spatial standards in the rest of the city which generate a highly automobile dependent lifestyle. For many urban residents this trade-off is not perceived, and they choose to pursue a spatially lavish lifestyle because there are few options provided for them; the high density option is generally seen as most unattractive and unhealthy. This will be pursued in the next sections on further aspects of spatial traditions - the 'density is bad for you' tradition and the 'Anglo-Saxon pastoral' tradition.

• *Economic costs*   For each additional hectare of rural space that is converted into urban land, there are economic costs associated with the extra physical and social infrastructure that must be provided. Much of this infrastructure is a government cost. Recent calculations on Melbourne estimate that for each additional household located in central Melbourne, rather than on the urban fringe, the community saves over A$40 000 in the cost of public infrastructure such as roads, water, sewerage, electricity, education, police, fire, childcare facilities and in individual costs such as getting to work (Neilson Associates, 1987). This is because infrastructure in older parts of cities like Melbourne are underutilised as populations decline, generally due to local government restrictions on the amount of new higher density housing in established areas. The Mayor of Melbourne commenting on the Melbourne study said it showed how urban sprawl was costing the community hundreds of millions of dollars:

"Australians have blindly accepted the idea that the best housing is brick veneer on the quarter acre block in a new suburb. As a result the city is sprawling into the countryside imposing horrendous infrastructure and social costs on community institutions and individuals" (McAsey, 1987).

83

Table 4.5

Human attractiveness of the central area of each city
based on a subjective ranking by the authors.

City	Central area human attraction rating (1-31:high score=high rating)
Paris	31
Munich	30
Stockholm	29
Vienna	28
Amsterdam	27
Tokyo	26
Hong Kong	25
Singapore	24
London	23
Copenhagen	22
Zürich	21
New York	20
West Berlin	19
Toronto	18
Frankfurt	17
Hamburg	16
Brussels	15
Boston	14
San Francisco	13
Melbourne	12
Sydney	11
Chicago	10
Washington DC	9
Adelaide	8
Perth	7
Brisbane	6
Los Angeles	5
Denver	4
Detroit	3
Phoenix	2
Houston	1
Correlation with gasoline use per capita	-0.8224 (s<0.0005)

The trade-off between urban space and government costs is generally not perceived by the ordinary person seeking a new home in a new suburb. However, in these days of cost-conscious governments, the huge subsidy being provided to develop outer suburbs is not as easily rationalised away. Chapter 5 will look at some new urban policies designed to be less spatially lavish and hence less economically wasteful.

A further economic cost that flows from an automobile-dependent city is that from road accidents. In each car-based city the road toll is equivalent to a mediaeval battle cutting down a proportion of the city's youth each year (road accidents are the chief cause of death amongst young people in the US and Australia). The costs of this in terms of wasted years and health programmes is enormous.

• *Energy Costs* The trade-off between spatially lavish standards and the inevitably high use of gasoline is very evident in this study of thirty-two cities. "Space equals energy" is a growing awareness in the perception of people and urban planners, even those who follow the "plenty of space" tradition. There is an awareness of the trade-off between space and accessibility in much of the transport literature with a general acceptance that most people are happy to trade-off an hour or so of accessibility time a day in order to purchase their spatial preferences (Manning, 1978). However, there is now a growing extra cost due to the extra fuel involved.

We have outlined the transport energy costs by suburb in Perth based on household travel surveys and found the following costs involved (Newman, Kenworthy and Lyons, 1985).

Table 4.6
Estimated per capita transport energy use and cost per person based on 1976 travel data and 1988 gasoline prices.

Area of the city	Total per capita transport energy use (litres of gaso-line equivalent)	Ratio relative to Perth average	Annual cost per person (approx. 65cents /litre) $
Inner suburbs	737	0.84	479
Middle suburbs	823	0.95	535
Outer suburbs	1164	1.33	757
Perth average	873	1.00	567

Table 4.6 shows that in Perth, Western Australia, outer suburban residents use some 58% more transport energy per capita than their inner area counterparts and pay, on average, an extra $278 each per year for energy in transport. In terms of the average cost per *household*, the comparison between Fremantle, Perth's lowest transport energy consuming area and the high energy consuming outer northern suburbs emphasises the financial implications of the extra energy involved in expansive urban space. For an average household in Fremantle with 2.5 people per house (not including those under 5), the annual cost for gasoline is $895 (1988 prices of 65c/ litre),

85

while an average household in the outer northern suburbs of Hillarys with 2.8 people per house, the annual cost is $2710 or some three times higher. The equity aspects of these costs are increasingly highlighted as the wealthy in Australian cities are moving back in closer and the poor are increasingly relegated to the transport-expensive outer suburbs (King, 1982).

• *Environmental costs* The first and most obvious impact from the sprawling, spatially lavish city is the loss of rural countryside and agricultural land. The problem of land loss due to expanding cities has been examined by Brown (1978) who concluded "wherever national data are available they usually show the growth of cities to be a leading source of cropland loss" (p11). He estimates that expanding cities could consume 25 million hectares of cropland between 1978 and 2000 and although this is only 2% of the world's cropland it is generally the best soil.

Krause and Hair (1975) have shown that US cities are accelerating their expansion into farmland with the average per capita loss going from 0.08 ha in the 50's to 0.13 ha in the 60's and 70's. European cities are expanding at much slower rates (OECD,1976). Australian cities have continued to sprawl at accelerating rates. Hatwell (1976) in a study of Melbourne found that a staggering 11,400 ha of farm land was lost annually to urban sprawl ie. 4.4 ha for every extra person in the city; out of this only one fifth was lost directly to urban structures (houses, industry, and other urban facilities), the other being land used for semi-urban functions like horse agistment or it was just land being purchased for speculation on the next stage of suburban growth.

Australian cities, as noted by Wagner (1975), have had a long history of consuming some of the best agricultural land:

> "Fertile river valleys on the coastal fringe have been devoured for urbanization...Food production as a consequence has been forced inland to poorer areas....Productivity, while being maintained is only being achieved at the expense of other resources such as water, fertilizers and machinery." (p22)

The new threat to near-city agriculture in Australia and to some extent the US, has come from 'hobby farms', ie. ex-urban rural retreats for the urban commuter who wishes to lead a semi-agricultural lifestyle. Such rural subdivisions consume large areas of productive land and of course involve very high automobile dependence. In Adelaide only 17% of farms in the near urban rural sector out of a 1979 survey were in full time productive farming and apart from the loss of production there are concerns about pests, weeds, fires and marauding dogs from these partially commited land uses. Also, some of the intensive horse riding and agistment areas develop soil erosion problems with farmlets becoming what Dean (1976, p43) calls 'rural slums', destroying the very environment that the ex-urban dweller is seeking.

Thus there are significant land costs even in a nation where there is "plenty of space" and a growing awareness that these costs cannot just be assumed.

There are other environmental costs associated with the lavish use of urban space including water and air pollution that are being considered. A large and detailed study by the Real Estate Research Corporation (1974) for the US Council on Environmental Quality called the "The Costs of Sprawl" investigated the impact of three development options: high, medium and low density. The high density planned development had more public open space than the low density development and yet the study showed that the low density option used more land, water and energy as well as double the air pollution, water pollution and noise. Other simulation studies have produced similar results, including one on alternative Australian designs (Maunsell, 1975). The water factor in some US and Australian cities is a significant constraint on future urban land use. In dry areas the excessive consumption of water can be minimised by more efficient urban land use as private lawn and garden watering is by far the biggest consumer of water in such cities, eg in Perth spatially lavish suburbs use some 4 to 5 times as much water as do the medium density suburbs. Less private space and more public space can be a significant factor in determining water policies.

An additional factor in the environmental picture as it relates to urban form is solid waste. Berry *et al.*, (1974) found that there were much higher solid waste generation rates from single detached homes than from multi-unit developments. However, other studies have found that higher density neighbourhoods often have more garbage to be collected than lower density areas (Cargo, 1978; Weston, 1971). The difference appears to be due to the amount of backyard burning which occurs in low density areas, ie households often burn it themselves. While assisting waste disposal this practice gives rise to a greater local and regional source of air pollution which is not insignificant for photochemical smog generation. Ho (1983) has found similar data on waste generation in Perth. International comparisons of solid waste management and urban form seem particularly rare but it seems that the more concentrated urban form which has been outlined above is where the most effective solid waste management occurs, ie where garbage is collected and recycled rather than just being dumped. From our survey and in an assessment of the general literature, it appears that these cities mostly occur in Europe rather than in the US and Australia, and despite a lot of effort and money, few of the latter cities have gone beyond landfill, whereas European cities have been recycling for decades. The difference is probably due to lower collection costs in the higher density city and scarcity of sanitary landfill sites, thus making recycling more feasible, although there are obviously other social and political factors to do with the city which lead to a greater commitment to waste management.

The conclusions on pollution and urban design in The Costs of Sprawl and other studies are about total production of air and water pollution. However, a key question is whether actual pollution concentrations will be higher or lower. For example, individual families in a higher density environment who have less private space may also have higher concentrations of air, noise and other environmental pollution to cope with as there is less space to disperse the pollution. This has certainly been a key rationale for many local planners and local action groups wanting to retain their low density environmental amenity. Within a city this may be the case, particularly for any family moving from the high density inner area to a low density suburb on the fringe, however it is not the case when considering the total city. A detailed study of US cities by Berry *et al.*, (1974) suggests that both total and actual concentrations of pollution are less in the higher density city once density alone is the key comparison. They suggest that there are two major types of cities, those which have a high orientation towards the central city, (typically with high core city densities and a radial transportation network), and those which are basically dispersed and dependent on the automobile. They found that the first type have a more intensive use of land overall, lower percentages of land devoted to residential and commercial development, more open space and better opportunities to abate air and water pollution. They concluded:

> "All trends point in the same direction: increasing dispersion and increasing automobile usage are producing the very urban forms and land use patterns that will increase rather than decrease environmental pollution." (p424)

Thus an awareness of the trade-off between lavish spatial standards and environmental deterioration is there even in the US and Australia and it appears to be growing. There might be plenty of space, but space means money, it means energy and it means environmental damage.

What so often seems to provide the dynamic for urban spatial patterns however is not so much the above level of perception by planners of the many costs in a spacious city, but the awareness by individual householders that their quest for "plenty of space" is an essential part of a good, healthy lifestyle. Thus we move to the more subjective areas that influence our urban spatial traditions.

(iii)"Density is bad for you" tradition Most urban commentators who conclude that there are strong physical planning reasons for increasing density (eg. economic, energy and environmental costs) also suggest that this means a trade-off with the social costs of increasing density. The "Costs of Sprawl" study outlined before even makes some estimates of these negative costs. There has been a long tradition that "density is bad for you". We would like to briefly outline some of the background to this tradition which clearly has been a major motivation behind the lower density urban form characteristics outlined in this study. We would also like to look at the beginnings of a more pro-urban density tradition.

Part of the reason for this anti-density tradition is very bad scholarship on the part of urban academics in a number of disciplines. A more detailed analysis of the misconceptions they have perpetrated are analysed in a paper from which we give a brief summary here (Newman and Hogan, 1981). The studies in the "Density is bad for you" tradition have been grouped into public health, sociology and psychology.

• *Public health* The spread of disease was always thought to be through the air and hence lowering densities was seen as a way to improve health through a "wholesome supply of good air" (Jefferson, 1909, p544). The motivation for the garden suburb was often given in these terms and continues even after a century of medical evidence about sewerage and sanitary facilities being the key factors. Cities like Hong Kong and Singapore have extremely good health rates and yet some planners still talk about the need to provide plenty of space for your health (Carr, 1977).

• *Sociology* Social "ill-health" (crime, delinquency, suicide, drug taking etc.) has also been linked to higher density in people's minds, yet no consistent evidence to support the contention has been shown. Some interesting evidence on crime is available in the US Bureau of the Census publication entitled "Social Indicators" (US Bureau of the Census, 1980). They show that in 1974 New York City had a "crimes of violence" rate of 43 per 1000 for persons 12 years old and over, while in Los Angeles the same figure was 59 per 1000 (37% higher). In fact, out of the twenty-six major US cities reported, New York ranked almost the lowest, while Los Angeles ranked twelfth and yet Los Angeles is over three and a half times lower in density. The highest city for violent crime was in fact Detroit, and Denver was third; Detroit's density is two and a half times lower than New York while Denver is over five times lower.

The pattern is not peculiar to violent crime either. Theft, which is one of the major crimes in any city was very low in New York City compared to the sample of twenty-six US cities. It again ranked twenty-third with a rate of 65 per 1000 people, while Portland Oregon, a low density city considered by a lot of people to be one of the most attractive and safe US cities was ranked number one in crimes of theft (143 per 1000 or over double that of New York City). Portland was also third in crimes of violence. Los Angeles was ranked number six with 120 crimes of theft per 1000 people and San Diego and Denver were ranked second and third respectively - both very low density cities.

To examine this question in more detail we have tabulated the crime statistics of the twenty-six major US cities along with their gross population density as provided by the US Census (Table 4.7). Simple linear correlations between the density and crime figures show no significant relationship at the 5% level between violent crime and density (-0.1435), and the correlation is negative. For density and theft there is a significant correlation (-0.4673) and again it is negative. This evidence goes against the popularly held belief that increased density leads to increased crime and even suggests that there may in fact be some beneficial aspects of higher density which assist in actually keeping down some forms of crime.

At the very least, these data suggest that there is no inherent relationship between higher density and violent crime in US cities and that the common fear about increasing densities leading to an increase in violent crime may be unfounded.

The same kind of analysis has been done by others on a range of social disorder parameters without finding any significant causation. Yet the mythology about density continues to be widespread. The one main study by Schmitt (1966) which suggested a relationship between density and social disorder is widely quoted, but Schmitt's 1978 paper in which he re-examined the data and no longer found the correlation, is rarely quoted. The Australian sociologist Paul Wilson suggests: "rhetoric about the effects of high rise living must rank as one of the major hoaxes imposed by social scientists on an unsuspecting public" (1976, p45-46). High density centres like Stockholm, Paris and Vienna have had such long histories as centres of

Table 4.7
Population density and crime in twenty-six major U.S cities

City (municipality not SMSA)	Population density (persons per ha, 1980)	Victimizations of persons 12 years and over (1974)			
		Crimes of violence		Crimes of theft	
		Number per 1000 persons	Rank among major cities	Numbers per 1000 persons	Rank among major cities
Dallas	10	48	18	117	9
Houston	11	53	14	122	5
New Orleans	11	46	21	94	14
Atlanta	13	44	22	93	15
Portland	14	71	3	143	1
Denver	17	71	3	134	3
Cincinnati	19	63	9	111	10
Oakland	24	59	12	102	13
Los Angeles	25	59	12	120	6
Milwaukee	26	61	10	103	12
Minneapolis	26	70	6	120	26
San Diego	27	53	14	141	2
Cleveland	28	67	7	85	19
St Louis	28	48	18	92	16
Pittsburg	30	47	20	83	21
Buffalo	33	49	16	74	22
Detroit	34	78	1	91	17
Baltimore	38	78	1	105	11
Washington DC	39	31	25	65	23
Miami	39	22	26	44	26
Boston	46	67	7	119	8
Philadelphia	48	49	16	85	19
Chicago	51	61	10	91	17
Newark	53	38	24	45	25
San Fransisco	57	71	3	129	4
New York	91	43	23	65	23

Source : U.S. Bureau of the Census (1980) Social Indicators III : selected data on social conditions and trends in the United States p 240 and U.S. Bureau of the Census population density data from the State and Metropolitan Area Data Book 1982.

Note: For seven of the above cities the Sourcebook has provided the actual urban density , since the City of Los Angeles, City of New York etc form the inner areas of the larger metropolitan areas as defined by us. Just for the purpose of the above analysis however we have used gross population density direct from the U.S. Census. Actual urban densities for each of the above cities would be difficult and time consuming to calculate, as evidenced by the problems encountered developing these figures for only seven of them.

culture and civilisation it seems slightly ludicrous to suggest that Los Angeles, Detroit and Melbourne are more socially healthy because they are lower in density .

• *Psychology* From rats in cages, students crammed in rooms, to people walking in crowded city streets, psychologists in the Anglo-Saxon world have studied density and concluded it is bad for us. However, in recent times major critiques of these earlier studies have shown that either their results cannot be reproduced, are meaningless (rat studies), or they do not consistently show problems with density (Freedman, 1975; Baldassare, 1979). For example, crowding sometimes produces positive effects in behavioural studies, not negative as expected (Freedman, 1975) and the classic studies of New Yorkers avoiding mugged victims in the street was attributed to the density of people, but when repeated in Dutch cities did not occur (Korte, 1976). Yeung (1977) concludes that so many of the studies on density were dominated by 'half truths based on ethnocentric perspectives' (p594), suggesting that we have *wanted* to find negative aspects of density due to anti-urban bias. This will be pursued in the next section.

In more recent times there has been a significant growth in literature which emphasises not only the inadequacy of the 'density is bad for you' tradition but which sets out the positive human benefits of increasing densities.

Freedman (1975) has developed a crowding model which attempts to make some sense out of the conflicting evidence from empirical studies and which also recognises the great adaptability of humans. He suggests that "crowding is not generally negative and it does intensify human reactions to other people" (p105) ie. it is a stimulating mechanism for human interaction. This means that the human effects of density are up to us; we can let higher density produce negative effects if we design and organise it that way, and in ourselves it can be stressful if we want it to produce such effects, but we can also make higher density into something beneficial. This helps us to understand why for each example of a high density area with problems we can produce examples where the opposite is true. For example, Conway and Adams (1977) found identical apartment buildings where one had a high level of social disturbance and the other had no such problems and they attributed the difference to better management. Others have studied the role of particular individuals or collectives of residents that provided the catalyst for considerable social cohesiveness and stimulation in being part of a high density complex (Biderman *et al.*, 1963; Mercer, 1975; Baum *et al.*, 1975; Stokols *et al.*, 1978). The implication in Freedman's crowding model is that low density areas dampen the human side of cities, that such suburbs will be characterised by few outward problems but also by few of the higher aspects of human community characteristic of urban life.

There are many commentators who have made this point over a number of years: Mumford (1961) describes low density suburbia as "anti-city", Schneider (1979) suggests they are areas of withdrawal from the whole process of civilisation, whilst Britten (1977) and Pawley (1975) see the modern suburb as the spatial expression of the major ideology of our time, "privatism", which does little for the individual's growth or the development of an urban community. Many commentators have shown

91

how increased density increases the number of community interactions in a neighbourhood thus providing more potential for community development (Lee, 1971; Hillman and Whalley, 1979, 1983). Some have even gone as far as suggesting that the suburbanisation of America and the elimination of its "Greenwich Villages" has contributed to the decline of intellectual life and civic culture compared to that found in Paris and other European cities (Jacoby in Marquand, 1988).

Allen (1980) continues this positive approach to density in a paper titled "The Ideology of Dense Neighbourhood Redevelopment: Cultural Diversity and Transcendent Community Experience" where he has examined the "back-to-the-city" movement in the US. He suggests that its pro-urban, pro-density philosophy has roots in the activist movement from the 60's and 70's and is a significant change in US urban awareness through its welcoming of the cultural diversity and community that the old city can provide. It is a spark of hope in US urban literature which is often very pessimistic about American cities. Urban activists have always been the leaders of urban reforms but in the Anglo-Saxon world such activists have generally been commited to lowering densities. For example, Cherry (1969) and Davison (1983) show how the garden city movement influenced 19th and 20th century urban reformers to lower densities as a means of improving a nation's physical and moral health. It would appear to be now a time for urban activists committed to increasing densities. The presence or absence of such people will play a key role in whether US and Australian cities develop a more or less sustainable future from a number of perspectives, particularly automobile dependence.

The move towards accepting the positive benefits of density is fed by a strong architectural and urban design movement that is seeking to create better cities than the post-war US and Australian tradition of either low density privatised suburbs or high density privatised apartments. They are attempting to build what Mumford calls places that "multiply the meaningful accidents of human contact". Examples of community orientated developments are available in most cities acting as symbols and guides for those who wish to learn from them. The emphasis is almost always on concentrated, pedestrian-based land use which encourages both planned community interaction and accidental interaction. Developments by Safdie (1970, 1974), Erskine (1981), Millas (1980), Vogt et al., (1980) and Van der Ryn (1983) are just a few of these developments. But in our limited experience we seem to be only just beginning to rediscover how older European cities managed to enhance and facilitate their citizens' urbanity through urban design.

The pro-density tradition needs little support in most European and Asian urban situations where there have been long traditions of living at high density. In Hong Kong, the highest density city in the world, a survey by Pun (1979) designed to highlight the issues of most concern to the populace, found that density was ranked as 42nd in their list of problems. Obviously in the Chinese culture such dense living is not seen as a negative force. The same appears to be the case in Europe and in fact most other parts of the world, except those cities which have grown in the Anglo-Saxon tradition. A survey in Athens where neighbourhood densities are around 75 people per ha found high levels of satisfaction with their area and density did not rate a mention as one of their complaints (Athens Centre of Ekistics, 1980).

There is a growing realisation that density may not be so bad after all, a realisation with great implications for the low density automobile dependent cities of the US and Australia.

(iv) Anglo-Saxon 'pastoral' or anti-urban tradition It has not been unnoticed by some commentators that the cities which have undergone the most rapid declines in density (or have had new very low density spatial traditions) and which have the greatest commitment to the private car, have been cities with a mainly Anglo-Saxon tradition. Planners attempting to increase urban densities in Anglo-Saxon countries in recent years have been met with considerable opposition from many sections of the urban community. The reactions have been so emotional and beyond debate that they suggest a deeper human motivation is involved than just environmental or economic factors. The expression of a negative approach to density as outlined in the previous section has been traced to its roots in an anti-urban tradition in the 18th and 19th century intellectual and political leadership of the United States (White and White, 1962; Rourke, 1964; Grabow, 1977), of England (King, 1976, 1980) and of Australia (Schedvin and McCarty, 1974; Davison, 1983). Merlin (1976) points out that anti-urbanism is not a part of continental thinking (or Asian) which has a much greater acceptance of urbanity and the higher density city which this presumes. This literature suggests that we in the Anglo-Saxon world are basically scared of increasing densities because we do not come from a pro-urban tradition. Despite being a basically urban race we have never really been commited to the city. We do not have a belief in the city as a positive force for good, a place where culture can grow and all that is best in the human spirit can thrive. A minority pro-urban tradition has always existed within the big English cities (King, 1980; Briggs, 1963), but in general the English, American and Australian traditions have been to idealise places that are rural and our literary heroes are from the countryside, the prairie, the bush. Cities only serve to corrupt the purifying aspects of country life.

This literary tradition which highlights the negative aspects of the city and presents an idyllic view of rural life, is called "pastoralism". As Squires (1974) says:

"The pastoral imagination creates, as a metaphor of rebirth, a lovely country retreat in order to criticize urbanization." (p202)

It suggests that the journey from city to country provides the opportunity to find solitude, innocence and happiness. Squires suggests pastoralism, which follows a long tradition in the renaissance as 'arcadia', "represents not only a search for the good life in a remote and peaceful world but for its compliment, a retreat from ugly industrialism and artificial urban life." (p13). This tradition has been suggested as the answer to human yearnings right through the twentieth century and has its expression in some of the 60's arcadian philosophy and the deep ecology literature of today. In popular culture The Man From Snowy River and now Crocodile Dundee have perpetrated the idea that Australians are at their best in the bush and the city

93

to such rugged individualists is a foreign, artificial world.The pastoral idea reached its zenith in literature in the last half of the nineteenth century with authors like George Eliot, Thomas Hardy and D.H. Lawrence. Taylor (1973) suggests that one of the possible causes for the strength of this belief in the Anglo-Saxon world was that the British never had to live in walled cities and hence never learned to live in higher density situations. As well, the industrial revolution cities with their smoke and open sewers confirmed that they were not the way people should live. The British arcardian village has thus served as the model for urban living and the motivation for much modern Anglo-Saxon town planning. One of the main rationales for stopping urban sprawl in the UK in the 60's (documented by Hall et al., 1973) was the need to preserve the rural countryside. This motivation may have been based in the Anglo-Saxon pastoral tradition, however it led to the building of large new high rise apartment blocks in huge council estates instead of rehabilitating the old inner city housing. This in general was a terrible failure as the design and services were so bad (Ravetz, 1980). It has provided the Anglo-Saxon world with one of the worst examples of high density urban living and has been difficult to put aside in popular understanding of urban design alternatives ever since throughout the Anglo-Saxon world.

The major result of the pastoral tradition has been the development of a suburban rather than urban lifestyle in the Anglo-Saxon world. Not everyone can live in the country, in fact only a small proportion in US and Australia can, thus it appears that the pastoral anti-urban tradition has been grafted into Anglo-Saxon *cities* by people seeking as much space as possible and by withdrawing behind their private suburban walls to minimise the negative impacts of city living . A Los Angeles woman describes this spatial tradition in her city succinctly:

> "Space is very important to everyone. They are not interested in urban living. It is hard for them to conceive of someone who likes there to be people in the streets at 8 o'clock at night" (Davie, 1972, p 78).

Thus with the modern technology of automobile, telephone, TV and refrigerator providing the means, the spacious suburb and 'rural' exurb have become the urban spatial expression of the pastoral tradition. Modern advertising for new spacious suburbs and semi-rural retreats continues to use pastoral images to sell its land thus spreading the city further and further out.

The lure of automobile technology and influence of Anglo-Saxon culture is also beginning to be felt in spatial trends in European cities. In a very critical study of most American transport and land use studies, three Dutchmen - Klaassen, Bourdrez and Volmuller (1981) - express the different value system that lies behind their alternative approach:

> "We want to preserve the cores of our cities in their function as the heart of the urban communities. It is the central place where cultural and social activities concentrate, where young as well as old people go to meet each other; to experience excitement, to experience the treasures of the past. This function of the central city is what we are trying to preserve and the whole discussion on urban transport should focus on

this point. Are we able to succeed in it or are we going the same way as the American cities? Will the equilibrium between the attraction of the core and its accessibility maintain itself in a period of rapid motorisation or are all efforts to maintain accessibility only doomed to destroy its attractiveness? We are right in the middle of this struggle; the United States have passed through it and are now experiencing that there is no way back" (p164).

In support of their final statement they quote Irving Kristol (1972), who, in an article entitled "An Urban Civilisation Without Cities?", suggests that in the US "the trauma of our central cities has such deep organic causes that the proposed therapies seem trifling". The Dutch authors suggest that cities today are facing fundamental choices: one path is what they call 'disurbanisation', which is basically a US model where although a large proportion of a country's inhabitants live in spacious homes in pleasant more or less natural surroundings, the centres of old core cities are dying and their roles have been taken over by "numerous isolated specks of activity spread at random across the country". They are alarmed by this:

> "Many will feel, as do the authors, that going on along that path spells the end of western culture, a culture that has its roots in those very city centres where the variety of economic, social and cultural activities has inspired - and still does - so many to creativity. It is the authors' belief that every effort should be made to counteract the impulse that drives cities to their end, and that the ultimate goal should be to restore the old inner cities to their former glory as the centres of the economic, social and cultural life of agglomerations and their surroundings, and to revive their residential function" (p37).

The alternative path which they label 'reurbanisation' involves pedestrianisation of city centres, preserving the essential functions of these urban cores and fundamental to it all, a large commitment to the provision of housing immediately adjacent to these urban centres i.e. it is pro-urban.

This European approach to city life stands in marked contrast to much of the literature on what is seen as the ideal for cities in the Anglo-Saxon tradition (see Webber 1963, 1968, 1973), not that this link to the pastoral tradition is often seen by such authors. However, the model that is advocated, such as Webber's "non-place urban realm" for example, appears to be based on the tradition of the anti-urban Anglo-Saxon culture with its desire to find rural values via the garden suburb.

Town planners in the Anglo-Saxon world have been strongly influenced by the ideas of the Garden City movement which in the nineteenth century gave rise to a new rural vision for the smokey Industrial Revolution cities. This movement spread rapidly to all parts of the English-speaking world (King, 1976, 1978) where they found fertile soil in which to grow. In the US, Frank Lloyd Wright's low density "Broadacre City" was influenced by this movement and had its local philosophical roots in a number of anti-urban American writers (Grabow, 1977). In Australia the Garden City movement had its influence on all the main cities (Freestone, 1986) and Wilson (1976) notes that the almost universal Australian dream of a 'patch of nature' in the suburban backyard can be traced, logically at least, to the Australian desire for agrarian symbols of kinship. This is particularly poignant in a country which throughout the twentieth century has been the most urbanised in the world. Surveys of urban Australians show a very high percentage would prefer to live in the country if they had a choice (Maddox, 1978) and the exurban trend suggests a rather strong anti-urban motive.

The same pattern is evident in the US where Fuguitt and Zuickes (1973) present data that disillusioned suburban Americans tend to prefer the small agrarian community. Space has also been seen in Anglo-Saxon terms as a factor distinguishing the classes, with those in the working class in cramped, high density inner or central city areas and those in the upper class in spacious rural and semi-rural areas. Thus one of the aims of Anglo-Saxon inner city residents seeking a better life whether in the UK or as migrants, has been to seek more space in a more rural/less urban environment. This tradition is much less so in European cities where there is also an aristocratic central city tradition (Smith, 1980).

Thus a powerful spatial Anglo-Saxon tradition exists with its basis in a philosophy of anti-urbanism motivating a lot of the urban form patterns presented in our data. However, it is not the whole story by any means behind US and Australian urban spatial traditions. Some of the more positive aspects balancing this tradition are thus presented.

• *Pro-urban traditions* The pastoral myth and anti-urban tradition cannot hope to continue indefinitely as it not only leads to more and more damaging urban sprawl, but it also cannot solve the problems that are supposedly heaped up against the city. As Baldassare (1979) points out, the high density crowded city "became the non-social explanation of the society's social problems; no solution short of mass urban exodus seemed likely to alleviate the problem" (p6-7). Thus there is a substantial critique of the Anglo-Saxon pastoral tradition and its effect on cities.

The critique begins by showing that the Anglo-Saxon pastoral tradition romanticises rural life in a way that is totally unrealistic. King (1980) suggests that the suburbanite's rejection of the city is part of this romantic notion and bears little resemblance to anything in the actual life of a rural dweller. It is in fact an ideal of how things could be. This means that if an urban tradition is established which also presents an ideal of peaceful co-existence, of environmental harmony, of individual freedom and of community growth, then there is hope for the city. Such traditions have been developing for some time in literature. Squires (1974) suggests that :

> "the growth of the city as the controlling landscape of modern fiction has meant that pastoral, as I defined it, is no longer a truly viable mode of literary expression for major writers." (p217)

Popular culture such as modern music video clips, films and writing often have strong pro-urban images that were rare in the Anglo-Saxon community a few decades ago; even Crocodile Dundee is a successful though naive urbanite and his exploits in the bush reveal a certain fraudulence Australians have probably always suspected about themselves.

Social scientists have also criticised the romantic approach to rural life and negative approach to cities. Harvey (1973), Castells (1975), Wilson (1976) and Moorhouse (1980), suggest that the city, and in particular the high-density city, can be a positive force on culture and human experience, just as rural life can be a source of deprivation and that the rural-urban dichotomy has directed attention away from more fundamental sources of social disorder and loss of innocence (see especially Ellul (1970), on the latter point).That is, the city need not be a source of human alienation and environmental disaster but can in fact be the opposite .

Thus there is arising an opposing tradition which stresses the positive aspects of dense cities and tends to have an anti-suburban rather than anti-urban thrust. Allen (1980) suggests that the pro-urbanism of the above authors and others like Cox (1966) and Berger (1977) are, as already mentioned, a tradition which is linked now to the urban activism that began in the 60's and early 70's. This movement he suggests, sees much more hope and attractiveness in the mixed, dense neighbourhoods of old cities with their variety and history. The writings of Jane Jacobs (1961) have provided a strong pro-urban voice along these lines for town planners throughout the past 20 years of Anglo-Saxon urban development. The ideas are there, though perhaps not as well developed as in the anti-urban tradition. Maybe that is part of the task for this generation of town planners and urbanists alike.

Perhaps if there were more newspaper columnists like Michelle Landsberg who delight in their urban lifestyle it would highlight this pro-urban tradition:

> "Straight out the door - no front yard or walk or dreary evergreen shrubs to distance me - I am in the thick of city life. Within two blocks of my apartment building I can get my clothes cleaned, pick up hot brioches for breakfast from a French baker, sit in an airy cafe for an expresso, post a letter, buy disks for my computer, dawdle through great museums and dozens of private art galleries, stock up on bagels and lox, pick up grapefruit spoons or teenagers' socks at ritzy Bloomingdale's or dirt-cheap Alexander's, or choose among three different supermarkets....urbanologists have always deplored New York's chaotic squalor but to me it is a better place to live than to visit." (Landsberg, 1988, p A-2)

• *Multiculturalism* The other feature of societies like US, Canada, Australia and even the UK is that they are becoming increasingly multicultural. The old Anglo-Saxon anti-urban culture is being diluted by a range of much more pro-urban cultures. In Australia the old, dense inner cities have been kept alive in the post-war period first by the migrants from Southern Europe and more recently by Asian immigration (Newman, 1978; Newman, Annandale and Duxbury, 1985). In the US the blacks and Hispanics have been the major inhabitants of the inner city. In both cases there is an increasing gentrification process where a much greater mixture is occurring between races, nationalities and income groups. The possibilities for a more urban culture from this mixing seems quite high.

A number of other social factors mean that there are strong new reasons for a pro-urban tradition to have more significance in the cities of the late twentieth and early twenty-first centuries.

• *Demography* First, there is the changing demography of the city. All modern cities are facing the same patterns in changing family traditions - in all there are more older people, more single-parent families, more households without children and more adults choosing to live alone. The typical household of husband, wife and children is no longer typical in most Western cities. In Perth, for example, where most of the housing has been built for 'typical families' (couple and dependent child or children) since the war, there are in 1986 only 2 in 5 houses with children living in them.

There is thus a decreasing need for the house and yard in the suburbs with 'plenty of space for the children to play in' and an increasing need for housing close to the urban services and attractions which less-children orientated families require. Even for households with children, the majority now have mothers who work and hence an urban priority of access to childcare facilities and proximity to work becomes of higher importance for many than the need for spacious suburban surroundings.

The very least that can be said is that changing demography means a greater demand for more options in urban lifestyle - for low density suburban cities with heavy automobile dependence, this means a more urban option is required with easy access by other modes. To a greater or lesser extent the demand for this in all the US and Australian cities in our sample, has been recognised in their various planning studies, though to provide for it requires a different kind of city which will be examined further in Chapter 5.

• *Technology* Second, there is the changing technology and employment patterns in the city. The shift from manufacturing to services and more hi-tech forms of employment as well as the general availability of modern communications has been suggested as the means for even greater physical dispersal of the city: there is no further need for traditional city centres, people can live and work at home, or in garden hi-tech estates (Brotchie *et al.*, 1987).

The evidence however suggests that like the telephone, modern communications technology just increases our contacts but does not replace our need to meet with people. Thus proximity remains an important feature of the modern city, unlike Webber's claim that there could be 'community without propinquity' (Webber, 1963). The same can be said concerning hi-tech industrial estates in suburban areas which have not been found universally to be the answer (Newman, 1986). Scott and Storper (1987), when examining the whole question of high technology industry and regional development concluded:

> "Each individual nation will very probably find a different set of internal and external solutions to the problem of accommodating new industrial ensembles; the number and qualities of high technology growth centres in the countries of Western Europe are likely to differ in important ways from those of the United States depending on their own historical experiences and geographical possibilities." (p230)

Munich is an example of a city where the central and inner areas have been completely restructured in employment terms from an emphasis on the old manufacturing firms to modern services and hi-tech without the US experience of a major collapse in the employment base due to 'inevitable' suburbanisation of work (Heinritz and Klingbeil, 1986). The authors conclude:

"In Munich there simply are no areas of industrial, former or present residential blight, there is no urban decay" (p51).

Far from seeing the need for a new, more dispersed urban form arising from trends in employment, Van der Ryn and Calthorpe (1986) writing from US experience, suggest that the best urban form for contemporary functions is the traditional strong city centre with a dense housing gradient served by rapid transit links, ie a low automobile dependent city. At the least it can be said that there is nothing inevitable about the need for a particular kind of urban form to fit changing patterns in technology and employment.

The city will always exist to bring people together for their mutual benefit. Right through the era of anti-urban, low density suburbanisation in US and Australian cities there has been a pro-urban tradition for commerce. The data in our survey confirm very high job densities in all US and Australian central cities. Such a tradition does not appear to be set to change. What may change is how the residential side of the city is structured for a range of pro-urban reasons outlined here.

• *Trading-off the pastoral myth*   The tragedy of the pastoral myth as a driving force behind suburban development is never so clear as when one suburb after the other on the rural fringe becomes engulfed by urbanisation and the countryside is slowly eaten up by the city. Thus for the average suburban dwellers it is clear that whatever it is that might motivate them spatially there are certainly a lot of trade-offs they have to make. The large house and block on the edge of the city in rural surroundings may appeal but if it means a one and a half hour commute through traffic congestion, few urban services and little urban variety, then maybe a more urban lifestyle with smaller spatial demands will be preferred . Especially is this so if a more pro-urban culture is becoming accepted through the general traditions of a society.

There is evidence that this kind of trade-off is being made increasingly by the average US and Australian urban dweller. Surveys which just ask people what kind of house they prefer not surprisingly end up with statistics showing people prefer what they are used to, whether it be an Australian bungalow or a Hong Kong flat (Maddox, 1978; Michelson, 1977 and Cham-Son, 1983). However, studies which examine a range of social, physical and economic factors behind housing preference, give much more hope in resolving the main urban form issues, than studies which just list housing preferences in vague locations like city, suburb or rural area. Hempel and Tucker (1979) found that housing preferences emphasised the distance to work, shops and schools as well as social factors like neighbourhood appearance, and age of neighbours before the size of the lot. In one American town this attribute of private space was only the tenth highest attribute sought, in another it was fifteenth and in the English town it was eighteenth out of twenty-one possibilities. In an English study by Britten (1977) of the qualities in housing seen as necessary, the spatial characteristics came very low (back garden 20th, front garden 32nd and all-on-one-level [no highrise], 41st out of 42 potential attributes); after internal fittings a number of environmental factors such as clean air were considered more important than the spatial factors. These studies indicate that density increases may be considered beneficial in a future where economic, energy and environmental factors have to be traded-off against the desire for private space. Perhaps for some of the above reasons, but also no doubt for other reasons, there appears to be an increasing proportion of people favouring a medium or high density house (ABS, 1981; Department of Environment and Planning, 1983). In fact, a survey in Sydney showed a majority of the population preferred to move to the inner city area closer to the main urban facilities rather than to the outer suburbs closer to rural surroundings (ABS, 1981).

All of this suggests that generalisations should not be made about Anglo-Saxon cities being inherently low density and hence car dominated. They may have been strongly influenced by particular rural spatial traditions but they may now be easily influenced by spatial traditions of a more urban kind. The idea that the Anglo-Saxon city had little experience of an urban lifestyle due to the lack of fortified walls may need to be replaced by the Anglo-Saxon city imposing its own 'wall' due to economic, environmental and energy costs. They may also, due to their social changes and immigration, be much more willing and accepting of a new urbanity. Certainly many Canadian cities and cities like Washington and Portland are undergoing rapid changes in their urban form reflecting a new more positive urban spatial tradition. Indeed McNulty *et al.*, (1986) have documented the 'return of the livable city' in the US.

Politics

The obvious conclusion from all that has been discussed so far is that there are many competing interests with different sets of values, which have implications for the transport priorities and shape of our cities. In the end these competing interests are sorted out in the political process. Also as part of the political process are the many vested interests which are significant players in the urban decision-making system, not just because of social values, but simply because they have money or power at stake.

There is an extensive literature in this area of urban politics including the analysis by Logan and Molotch (1987) which has become the basis of the "Urban Fortunes" movement in urban studies; this movement believes cities are outcomes of human interests in wealth, power and community resources:

> "We are investigating how various kinds of people and institutions struggle to achieve their opposing goals in the creation of the metropolis...we stress not only the economic imperatives of the larger system, but the strivings of parochial elites to make money from development and ordinary people to make community a resource in their daily lives." (Logan and Molotch, 1987, pp vi-vii)

Thus politics at all its levels from the grass roots to national politics is seen as a major determinant in the process which establishes patterns of transport and land use in our cities. Such considerations can help to explain some of the large differences which occur in the patterns across regional groupings and within nations as revealed in our data. Some of the major players are thus set out in broad outline under transport politics, land politics, government politics and professional politics.

Transport politics: the road lobby versus rail and public transport lobby

The politics of transport is dominated by an acrimonious history of conflict between road and rail lobbies (Hamer, 1987). Probably the most controversial story in this conflict is the analysis by Snell (1974) on the role of the road lobby in dismantling the urban electric rail systems in US cities. Beginning in the 1930's a holding company National City Lines, made up of interests from oil, tyre and automobile industries, bought up the private electric rail systems in 45 US cities and then closed them down. "The reason for that is really a mathematical one" Snell said, "One subway car or electric rail car can take the place of from 50 to 100 automobiles" (Snell, 1975). Although in 1949 a Grand Jury ultimately convicted General Motors, Standard Oil of California and Firestone Tyres, with a criminal indictment for antitrust conspiracy, the damage had been done. Los Angeles was the worst affected with 280 million passengers a year being pushed into buses and cars, and as our analysis shows, buses rapidly lose in that league and so within a few decades there were 4 million cars in LA and the era of automobile dependent US cities had begun.

Snell also highlighted the role of the so-called "national highway users conference" which was started in 1932 bringing together companies from automobile, oil and other highway interests into a lobby for road funds and an end to mass transit funding. Thus he says the US government spent $1845 million on highways between 1952 and 1970 while rail systems received $232 million. Such priorities can be seen in our data, both in transport infrastructure and in the resulting transport and land use patterns.

Similar conflicts are seen through to the present with enormous political fighting over relative road and transit funding including problems over the rebuilding of rail systems in Los Angeles (Connell, 1986). Other countries have such road and rail lobby conflicts (Hamer, 1987) and in Australia there were similar implications from increased road funding through the post war period (Neutze, 1977; Beed, 1981).

The political power base of organisations such as those in the road lobby is very strong and their influence on decision-making is difficult to match. However, matching can and does occur. Governments everywhere have to be answerable to the wider public as well as to their lobbyists and in many European and Asian countries with strong private industry lobbies their influence on city transport has been minimised by equally powerful lobbies for public transport. Our data indicates that public transport political support and funding can be given a high priority and recent trends in transit (especially new rail systems such as on the west coast of the USA), suggests that such publicly oriented transport can be a major factor in the future direction of our cities (Vuchic, 1981). There is nothing inevitable about the power and influence of the road lobby.

Land politics: The private land development industry versus public planners

In the same way that transport politics can determine transport priorities and hence urban land use, it is possible to examine land politics and see how it determines urban land use and hence transport patterns. There has been a long urban studies tradition examining the politics of urban land use, particularly since the early 1970's as a reaction to mechanistic urban models (Harvey, 1973; Castells, 1978; Cox, 1978). For these people it is possible to explain the patterns observed in our data by considering how land is owned and developed in relation to broad economic trends.

Capitalism is based on the accumulation of wealth and then its investment into physical assets that help produce further accumulation. In the economy as a whole the city appears to be built in a series of cycles with most construction patterns related to the level of capital accumulation. Suburbanisation is explained in terms of the need to invest capital in both the land and transport systems necessary to service that land. Thus most suburbanisation follows economic booms and as the economy contracts so the city turns back into itself rather than expanding on its fringe.

Detailed explanations can be given for centuries of urban growth and technological change, eg. Walker (1978) examined two major boom cycles with their accompanying suburban growth though the analysis tends to be rather culturally biased with a particularly US version of suburbs seen as almost inevitable. Likewise Australian cities have been analysed to show how suburban land has been developed in response to capital accumulation (Sandercock, 1975, 1979; Badcock, 1984). In all cases urban planning is seen as a virtual puppet that might attempt to regulate property development in minor ways but in essence has virtually no power to direct urban growth for public purposes. Private capital in this perspective drives cities under an inevitable process that maximises private gains.

Once again it is possible to glance at our data on the huge differences between urban land use; despite all cities showing suburbanisation not all cities have so optimised conditions for private gain whilst subjugating public purposes. All cities show some evidence to the contrary. In particular, European cities, Asian cities and even Toronto have managed to impose a public direction to urban growth when it is occuring so that there is some balance between private and public gain. The planner has a role to play and given some priority in the political process they can assert values of more compact, community-oriented housing, closer links between homes and work, public transport facilities, public places for enjoyment of the urban and the natural, and the redevelopment and consolidation of existing urban areas, instead of further outer fringe suburbanisation. Whilst not underestimating the power of private capital, cities can be bigger than the wealth and power of their collective private citizenry.

Government politics: Metropolitan versus municipal priorities and inner versus outer area government.

Land use politics and transport politics are not just a question of private versus public but frequently major decisions concerning the city are questions of government versus government within the city.

For a metropolitan-wide government that needs to direct development, their responsibility is to ensure that urban infrastructure is efficiently and equitably distributed. Each local government is trying to optimise their own development goals and that is not always consistent with the goals of the wider city. Frequently in the past the resolution of this conflict has led to a more automobile-dependent city.

In Australian cities this conflict is mainly expressed in a conflict over the municipal priority to redirect population growth to inner areas where extensive urban infrastructure is often underutilised, in contrast to the local government priority of inner areas which do not want any changes to their perceived amenity and character (Bunker, 1983).

In US cities, where metropolitan-wide government is not as strong, the conflict is often a question of inner versus outer area local government priorities. Decisions on land use become competitions between local authorities seeking or not seeking development (Cervero, 1986a).

The 60's and 70's in most cities, and particularly in US and Australian Class I cities, saw most development moved to outer areas with declining populations (and jobs) in inner areas. Government priorities often were responsible for the extent of these changes. Now in the late 80's and 90's with a new set of priorities the conflicts between the levels of government are heightened.

There is however no necessary or inevitable outcome that government politics will ensure a continuation of the automobile-dependent policies of previous decades. Resolution has been obtained in some cities that places priority, as in European and Asian cities, on maintenance and redevelopment of older more central locations rather than at the urban fringe (Heinritz and Klingbeil, 1986).

Government politics need not inhibit the development of less automobile-dependent policies in cities.

Professional politics: road planning versus comprehensive land use/transport planning.

The development of cities is clearly influenced by politics acting through governmental dealings with the financial actors and power brokers in the urban system, as well as relationships between different levels of government. However, there is another dimension of politics which is perhaps not as obvious or so open to public scrutiny and that is the political agendas of individual government agencies and the technical advice they give to policymakers on transport and land use.

This political dimension, which we have termed "professional politics", is partly seen in the biases that can be built into the seemingly objective technical procedures used to model the future transport needs and land use patterns of a city. Some of these biases will be described in this section. However, it is first necessary to set out a little background to this whole area which enables the political dimensions to begin to be seen.

The most important of the technical procedures in transport planning is the land use/transport modelling process which emerged in the mid 1950's as a distinct area of study. The watershed for land use/transport modelling was the publication in 1954 of Mitchell and Rapkins' "Urban traffic - A function of land use" which ushered in a period of multi-million dollar transportation studies, some of which took up to three years to complete. The purpose of these studies was to plan for anticipated growth in population, jobs and traffic flows as far ahead as 20 years, such that there would continually be an equilibrium between the supply of transport facilities and demand for travel as it arises out of land use.

The concept of the "grand transportation study" was embraced with enormous enthusiasm with virtually every developed city at some point between 1955 and 1975 undertaking at least one major transportation study. In the US since 1962, urban areas over 50,000 people have been required to do land use/transportation studies on a regular basis to qualify for Federal road funds. Governments vigorously promoted them partly because they were a high profile exercise which appeared to be tackling transport issues and partly because of the political influence brought to bare on Governments by a handful of international transport consulting firms who very quickly adopted, and to some extent monopolised, the then esoteric technical procedures. There was an almost endless amount of money to be made from "grand transportation plans" during the 1950's and 1960's, and transport consulting firms were only too eager to adapt their technical expertise to fit the political expectations of the time. The 1950's and early 1960's were a very optimistic and prosperous period characterised by booming car ownership and the political expectation, at least in the US and Australia, was that the automobile would be the future of urban transport. Thus right from the outset land use/transport studies tended to be strongly associated with planning for roads and cars rather than a balance of transport modes, and most of the US and Australian land use/transport studies pioneered the building of elaborate highway and freeway systems.

The first major transportation plans to appear were the Chicago and Detroit Transportation Studies which were very much along the lines just described. These two studies pioneered the technical procedures we know today as the land use/transport modelling process (Black, 1981). These technical procedures have been refined and tuned over the years but have evolved into what is generally known as the "conventional" land use/transport planning study. It has in fact been said that there is "a generalised international urban transportation planning process" (Ben Bouanah and Stein, 1978).

This process can be characterised by the following major tasks, (1) formation of goals and objectives, (2) inventories of the present situation which are then used to undertake the four key mathematical steps - traffic generation, traffic distribution, modal split and traffic assignment, (3) forecasting of new land use plans and their resulting traffic, (4) analysis of alternative transport networks to cope with predicted travel and (5) evaluation of various alternatives according to costs, benefits, impacts and practicality. These tasks however are by no means value-free, objective technical procedures and there are numerous ways that they can be biased to facilitate certain directions. Some of these ways will now be outlined since they most clearly demonstrate "professional politics" in action.

As already stated, the transportation studies of the 1950's and 1960's pioneered large scale road and highway planning and in the process public transport, especially rail, was glossed over and almost eliminated from many cities, (eg. Detroit, Phoenix, Houston, etc). Stopher and Meyburg (1975) show this clearly when they comment about how public transport was dealt with technically in the modal split stage of the US studies...."The earlier in the process that transit trips could be estimated and removed from further consideration, the more efficient would be the resulting highway travel forecasting procedure." The analysis would then proceed with most forecasting based on private transport growth and land use patterns based around this. Once such land use is in place the only public transport that can service it is an inefficient bus service and hence the conclusion is inevitably that a massive increase in road funding is needed to provide the "grand plan" needs.

Early traffic assignment methods were another source of bias in favour of road planning. Traffic assignment is one of the final steps in land use/transport modelling where, having established the level of trip making between each zone and the modal split, traffic must be assigned to specific routes in the road system. An algorithm for doing this was developed and became known as the "all-or-nothing" traffic assignment method (Moore, 1959). Basically this method assigns traffic to the "minimum path" between two zones which generally means the path that requires the least time (though it may incorporate other vehicle costs etc). In its early uses such as the Chicago Area Transportation Study it had some serious deficiencies which were nevertheless accepted. It was for example, very sensitive to small time differences of as little as 2 seconds between routes. This would cause all traffic to load onto one route with none on any other almost equally preferable route. It did not build-in the obvious congestion effects that would occur under these circumstances where drivers on the heavily loaded route would spill over onto a series of other existing routes to avoid delays ie. there was no multiple routing in the early traffic assignment techniques and calibration or verification of the results was very difficult. Congestion effects did not feedback into modal choice either, where it is likely that unfavourable road conditions would have improved the role of railway systems (eg. Chicago's rapid transit and commuter rail systems in this case).

The result of the "all-or-nothing" method was that engineers were virtually able to conclude anything they liked. It was very easy for them to over-justify new freeways because the culminating effect of this traffic assignment method was to predict overloaded road routes.

Another possible way that traffic assignment could generate a high demand for new roads was simply not to include some existing key roads in the model. In any transport modelling exercise, the existing road system is considerably simplified to include only major or significant traffic arteries. However, in building the road network in the model, a line has to be drawn between which roads warrant inclusion and which ones do not; simplicity and minimising the cost of running the model are important considerations.

If too few roads are included too much of the predicted traffic will be loaded onto key major roads and the results will call for new major roads which, if constructed, would be seriously overdesigned or simply not really needed. However, such roads soon became self-fulfilling prophecies as discussed next.

Building large road systems changes the nature of the city into a more automobile-dependent one. This awareness of how transport is related to land use is another dimension of land use/transport modelling which has a definite "professional political" dimension to it. In general, modelling has assumed that land use is "handed down" by land use planners and that transport planners are merely shaping the appropriate transport system to meet the needs of the land use forecast. This is not the case. One of the major reasons why freeways around the world have failed to cope with demand is that transport infrastructure has a profound feedback effect on land use, encouraging and promoting new development wherever the best facilities are provided (or are planned). Most of the major US cities such as Chicago, New York and Detroit which built extensive freeway systems as proposed by their grand transportation studies, found that the freeways spread land use and generated more and more traffic until very soon after completion the freeways were already badly congested.

However, once locked into a primarily road-based system a momentum develops which is very hard to stop. The obvious response to the failure of freeways to cope with traffic congestion is to suggest that still further roads are urgently needed. The new roads are then justified again on technical grounds in terms of time, fuel and other perceived savings to the community from eliminating the congestion (see Chapter 5). This sets in motion a vicious circle or self-fulfilling prophecy of congestion, road building, sprawl, congestion and more road building. This is not only favourable to the vested interests of the road lobby and land developers but it also builds large and powerful government road bureaucracies whose professional actors see their future as contingent upon being able to justify large sums of money for road building. This commitment translates into direct political activity where policy makers are influenced by what can be very biased technical advice. In this way road authorities can become de facto planning agencies directly shaping land use in a city and having a large vested interest in road-based solutions to the transport problem.

A simple example of the way professional politics in government agencies can operate in favour of roads and to the detriment of public transport is seen in the Brisbane Transport Study of 1965, where the Main Roads Department was closely involved. The final results of the modal choice model indicated that some 88% of all trips plus or minus 8% were by private vehicle. In terms of road planning this may be sufficiently accurate but the Brisbane public transport agencies found the results unusable for their planning purposes because 12% public transport trips plus or minus 8% could mean the difference between halving or doubling their activities (Clark, 1987). They were thus unable to participate in any meaningful way in the grand transportation plan.

Up to 1982 the MRD in Brisbane also employed "short design years" specifically to avoid taking into account the possibility of transport infrastructure feedback, effects on land use. This may have improved the short term accuracy of their modelling, which would have been one of their aims but it certainly cloaks the effect that major new roads will have on future land use and to some extent disguises the longer term ineffectiveness of new roads in coping with traffic.

In summary, there is nothing inherent in the actual techniques of the land use/transport modelling process which will inevitably produce road-biased results. It is more the way decisions are made about how to use the techniques. Historically road planners have dominated this exercise. If a genuine attempt is made to consider alternatives to urban sprawl and more freeways it is possible to build in more sophisticated feedback mechanisms where transport and land use are dealt with in an iterative manner, one progressively affecting the other. Alternative traffic assignment and modal choice models are also available which deal better with non-automobile modes.

Ultimately it comes back to the first stage of the process - the formation of goals and objectives. In the past land use/transport modelling has chased something of a fairy-tale world where transport demand and supply were going to be kept in equilibrium by planning road systems to cope with projected traffic volumes - a sort of "transport utopia". The pressing requirement was to keep ahead of congestion. Developing alternative transport systems and different land use patterns - a comprehensive approach to land use/transport planning aimed at minimising unnecessary movement - was not really seriously considered as long as the road planning treadmill was dominant

A change to more comprehensive planning requires better specification of the goals and objectives of transport studies and this is also where urban planners can play a key role. There are new imperatives developing in the transport arena, spurred on partly in the US by the failure of the grand freeway schemes to deliver satisfactory levels of accessibility - cities are awash in traffic and over the past few years "suburban gridlock" has taken the traffic problem to the outer suburbs (Cervero, 1986a). For example, in the San Francisco Bay Area polls have shown for the' fourth consecutive year that transportation is the single-most pressing urban problem (Eno Foundation, 1988).

Paralleling this failure of the road system there has been a rapid growth in new light rail systems along the West Coast of the USA and in Canada over the last 10 years. Many of these systems have been introduced as political decisions rather than as technical decisions from the landuse/transport modelling process. This reflects the widespread disenchantment with the grand plan and its overwhelming automobile dependence which resulted. Unbridled personal mobility is being questioned since it is being increasingly seen that mass prosperity and the automobile rather than promoting greater freedom, have created traffic congestion and high levels of individual frustration (Eno Foundation, 1988). In Australia the sheer cost of infrastructure to maintain suburban sprawl is becoming prohibitive and the gridlocked freeways in peak hours has become the norm for most cities following through on their "grand plans".

Thus urban planners are now in a key position to assert their role in the development of cities. New goals and objectives can be given to the transport/land use modelling process based around balancing the roles of various modes of transport, minimising total travel in the urban system and reducing the costs of urban land development. Other important issues can also play a role in the formulation of tasks for land use/transport modelling. For example, revitalisation of central cities is a major concern in many urban areas, as are the issues of environment and the livability of neighbourhoods.

Professional politics will always play a role in this area, with rivalries between government departments pulling in different directions, but there is certainly no compulsive reason why this should favour roads and suburban sprawl to the exclusion of other transport modes and more compact patterns of development. As stated by the last major Australian transport study, the Sydney Area Transport Study (SATS, 1974) concerning landuse/transport modelling, "some of the inputs into the models are based on assumptions of a political nature or those containing value judgements" (p II-1), obviously these political and value judgements are subject to change. And further on SATS reminds users of the study that "Transport models cannot directly give answers to policy questions, nor can they derive transport system alternatives. Final decisions cannot be reduced to a set of mathematical equations." (pII-1).

Quite clearly the urban planner has an important and decisive role to play in the formulation of goals, objectives and outcomes of transport modelling whether they use computer models or not.

Conclusion

It is hoped that enough evidence has been presented in this chapter to reassert the fundamental role of the urban planner in shaping the city. The urban planner must take into consideration the perspective and the data from the economist, the engineer, the social planner, the real estate agent, even the novelist and poet, and all the other players mentioned in this chapter. However, it is the contention of this book that, in the end the policies which decide on the relative priorities for various transport infrastructure, and the policies which determine the land use characteristics of a city, must depend to a very large extent on the vision of the urban planner. The outcome of policy development lies of course with politics and it is in that arena where the various policy lobbies are weighed and decided. Lobby groups for the automobile, roads and greenfield urban development are powerful and persuasive but the problems of the automobile-dependent city as outlined have become much clearer and the prospects of a city with less of these characteristics has much appeal. This chapter has suggested there are no real social or technical questions which should prevent an urban planner developing more pro-urban, less auto-based policies. We thus turn in the next chapter to the major conclusions outlined in Chapter 3 from our thirty-two cities and to some thoughts on what ought to be the major policy elements in transport infrastructure and land use guiding our cities in the short term and into the next century.

5 Urban planning and transport policy implications

The results of factor and cluster analyses outlined in Chapter 3 show that we need to consider five physical planning factors to enable our cities to become less automobile and gasoline dependent. They need to develop:

- more intensive land use
- more orientation in transport infrastructure to non- automobile modes
- more restraint on high speed traffic flows
- more centralised land use, and
- better performing public transport.

Chapter 4 suggested that there was a primary role for physical planners in the urban process rather than seeing their role as secondary to economic or social forces. Having emphasised this to highlight the importance of the physical planner's role it is also necessary to recognise that urban planning in any city never involves just setting out the physical parameters and adjusting the city according to a physical blueprint. Thus this chapter attempts to provide some urban policy directions that have been highlighted by many of the cities in our survey for a range of physical reasons but also economic and social reasons. They are developed here because they have obvious potential for easing urban dependence on the automobile by moving cities in the five directions outlined above. But they also appeal as they appear to offer concurrent solutions to many other urban problems.

The policies are set out under two broad headings, one *reurbanisation*, which addresses the question of more intensive and centralised land use and the other, *reorientation of transport priorities,* addresses the question of transport infrastructure, traffic restraint and public transport. However it will also be shown how each of the general policy areas of *reurbanisation* and *reorientation of transport priorities* assist with each of the five physical planning factors set out above. Land use and transport policies are inseparable.

Reurbanisation

The concept of reurbanisation has been developed primarily in Europe (see van den Berg *et al.,* 1981; van den Berg, Burns and Klaassen, 1987). As shown in the data from this study, European cities are much more 'urbanised' than cities in the US and Australia which have dispersed rapidly in the twentieth century. However, their concern is that the same dispersal processes are underway in their cities (see quotes in Chapter 4). They identify these processes as spatial cycles and describe them as follows:

> "An urban population begins to grow and by its very growth it attracts people from the surrounding countryside, setting a townward migration, often on a large scale, in motion. It is mainly the abundance of workplaces in the city that attracts migrants for, by moving to town, they can greatly improve their living conditions. There comes a moment, however, when rising incomes and increased car density induce a shift of residential locations towards suburban areas, basically the very areas from which migrants used to come. Things keep shifting and changing; at a certain movement the core city becomes so crowded with workplaces that their very density impedes the proper functioning of the economic activities they represent; from then on an exodus of workplaces from the city begins, following that of residents. Part of the activities locate on newly built industrial estates, others settle in recently constructed residential areas. In the last phase of the cycle both workplaces and inhabitants are leaving the agglomeration.
>
> This cyclical process is first manifest in the old historical city (within the mediaeval defence ramparts); in the stage of suburbanisation it can be recognised in the city core, and in the disurbanisation stage, has spread across the whole agglomeration. It is at this stage that most West European agglomerations have now arrived; the stage where they suffer the loss of population and workplaces" (p 21).

They describe reurbanisation in the following way:

> "The process thus set going is one of once more turning degenerated urban patches into city quarters with living cores, fulfilling a real economic, social and cultural function, a process of reurbanisation. Its ultimate fascinating objective is the revival of the old core cities, fascinating to many individuals who have learnt in hard practice that living near to nature means mowing the lawn every week, driving downtown in long queues every morning and driving out of town in

long queues in the evening; that a suburban home means buying a second car for their wives so that they may flee the periphery, etc. The more people realise all this, the less they will want to leave the inner city if they are still there, and the stronger will become the desire to live just there, leading a modern life in an old town full of atmosphere" (p 36).

A stylised summary of the stages in urban development is thus set out in Figure 5.1 to highlight what is meant by this term reurbanisation.

Most European cities have had significant experience at reurbanisation policies in terms of better using urban land and containing urban sprawl. Almost all of the twelve cities in the study have policies to try and reverse population decline in their central and inner areas. There is evidence that in Stockholm and in Dutch cities this process has occurred and to that extent reurbanisation is well underway (eg. Poelstra, 1987; van den Berg, Klaassen and van der Meer, 1983).

The same trend to redevelop, restore, reuse and more intensively develop urban land can be seen in US cities but it is largely in its infancy. Brian Berry calls it "islands of renewal in seas of decay" (Berry, 1985). The potential for reurbanisation of US cities is therefore recognised and from this study it can be seen by comparison with other global cities to be quite considerable. Recent data suggest that the deconcentration of people and jobs from US cities has reached the slowest rate since the 1920's and the return of younger people to the city is becoming demographically evident (Macauley, 1985). As well, there is beginning to be a recognition that this reversal could now be favoured by trends in technology (towards more office and service-oriented employment) and demography (towards more households with no children), but that it will probably proceed initially through behavioural, rather than straight economic factors (Dynarski, 1986).

Working against a revival of the inner city in the US is the combination of problems from concentrated racial and poorer communities that are in the majority in most US inner cities; at the same time, these communities have expressed fear of gentrification by upper middle class whites taking over cheap inner city housing. The resolution, at least in theory, would appear to be in reurbanisation by building additional inner city housing. Gentrification can be a social problem if only replacement of low income households by high income households occurs, but this is not what reurbanisation aims to do. Reurbanisation is a process whereby population increases begin to occur in areas that have been depopulating for many years. In terms of many US and Australian central cities in our study it is a process whereby resident populations begin to fill-in the population "crater" that has characterised most automobile dependent cities since the 1950's. As such it can be a positive economic force, revitalising areas that have been depressed for a long period. Creative ways of building more central and inner city housing and then forging new and more integrated communities appears therefore to be a crucial policy for more than just energy conservation and reducing dependence on the automobile in US cities. Experience in Sacramento and Philadelphia as detailed in Van der Ryn and Calthorpe (1986) appears to offer some guidelines for this in a US context. Fremantle

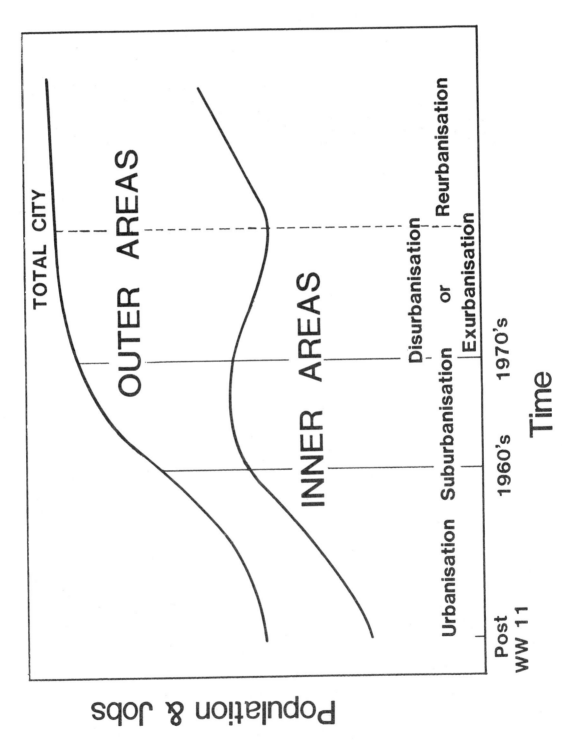

Figure 5.1   Stages of urban development.

112

has shown that rapid reurbanisation in an Australian inner area can occur without negative social impacts (Newman, 1987).

Toronto is an example of a city that has taken seriously the need for land use policies which can ease dependence on the automobile. Such policies have not been called reurbanistion but in essence have been. In 1984 they produced a major study on transport energy conservation for their city and Table 5.1 sets out the policies considered necessary to lower gasoline use. They correspond to the kind of policies outlined here as reurbanisation and build on urban policies first developed in the mid 70's in most Canadian cities to develop less automobile dependence in their cities.

Australian cities have been attempting to come to terms with their sprawl and declining inner areas over the past decade. A range of studies and policy documents have been produced for nearly all of the cities (Australian Institute of Urban Studies, 1983; Bunker, 1983; Wilmoth, 1982) under the general approach of "urban consolidation". This has been taken by Paul Landa a former Minister for Planning in New South Wales to mean "an emphasis in planning on the fuller use of the established urban areas." He went on:

> "...there is some confusion about what urban consolidation means... To some, it signified an intention to redevelop the inner areas to high-rise skyscrapers; others saw it as putting up a barbed-wire fence around the metropolitan area and erecting signs 'this far and no further'. There were those who wanted to achieve it by discouraging people to consume more housing than they need; as well as those who saw consolidation as forcing everyone to live in a flat. Some thought it was a guise for the ruthless imposition of the State bureaucracy's view over the wishes of local communities to preserve the Australian way of life; while to others it appeared as an underhand conspiracy to boost the fortunes of flat developers. I would like to assert my belief that urban consolidation is none of these things, but rather a change of approach in urban management which removes the many constraints which now impede the adaptation of built-up areas." (Reid [Ed], 1981 p1)

Although there has been some success in Australian cities with consolidation policies there have been two major problems: one is local government which controls most land use decisions and which has been very reticent to allow density increases, and the other is the lack of adequate integration of these land use policies with transport policies, particularly new high speed roads which automatically drain development away to the ends of these arteries. This will be further addressed in the next policy section on transport infrastructure.

The specifics of reurbanisation in terms of the data contained in this study are now presented for each region of the city using comparisons between the five classes of city.

Table 5.1
Compatibility of Metropolitan Toronto planning direction with transportation energy conservation principles.

Energy conservation planning principle	Metro Toronto planning direction
Urban form and structure	
• Compact and contiguous form	- no large blocks of land by-passed - encouragement for redevelopment and intensification - emphasis on transit
• High overall density	- completion of redevelopment within Scarborough and Etobicoke - high density redevelopment encouraged at specific locations - continued growth in employment
• Nodes and corridors	- major development strategy within Metro - transit routes planned to support high density sub-centres - local policies encourage higher densities at nodes and along main travel corridors
Land Use	
• Integrated land use pattern	- trend to more diversification at Metro scale - housing in central areas and waterfront - greater employment opportunities, amount and type, in suburbs - maintenance of manufacturing jobs - development of major retail facilities in suburbs

Source: The Municipality of Metropolitan Toronto, Toronto Transit Commission and Energy Ontario (1984).

Inner area land use

Figure 5.2 sets out the comparative inner area population and job densities for the five classes of cities. It shows that there is a very large difference (almost 100%) between the Class I and Class II cities. This highlights the importance of inner area redevelopment for the highly auto-orientated Class I cities. Here lies an enormous potential for reurbanisation as densities are so low (see Figure 5.3). Huge potential exists for infill developments, intense mixed use developments of vacant or underutilised land, redevelopment of existing poorly used industrial and warehousing sites etc.

In particular, development on or near rail reserves would appear to be crucial as a part of an integrated approach to lowering automobile dependence and providing a viable alternative to the car. It is clear from the data that the Class II cities with their stronger inner area have a major advantage over Class I cities. This is obviously one of the main reasons that they have less automobile dependence and lower gasoline use. The inner area provides not only a distinctively different, less auto-dependent lifestyle, but it provides the backbone for a rail system which extends into the lower density outer areas. This rail service is then able to provide a significant option to many in the outer areas, though without the dense inner areas it is

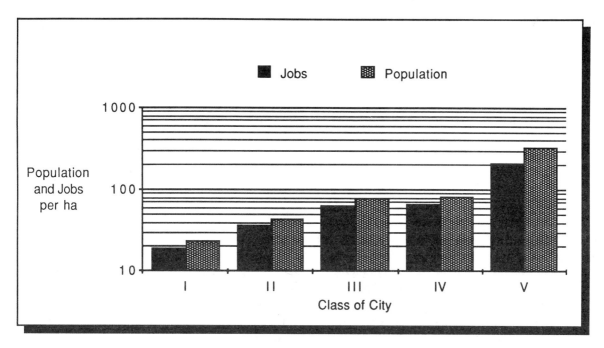

Figure 5.2   Inner area population and job densities in each
                  class of city.

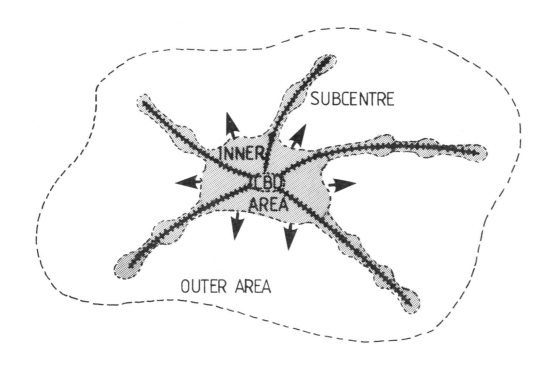

Figure 5.3   Conceptual plan for reurbanisation.

unlikely that the rail service would have much viability.

Inner areas in Class I cities are often heavily blighted by large highways or planned freeway reserves which are designed to bring outer area motorists into the central city. These are a significant obstacle to reurbanisation, though the redevelopment of planned freeway zones provides a rapid and highly cost-efficient option as it is government owned land. Examples where such a process have been successful can be found in Adelaide, Portland (Oregon) and Toronto. The Portland experience has been well documented and is summarised as it shows how effective reurbanisation in an inner urban area can be.

Portland is an ideal case study since it demonstrates how a city can fundamentally begin to change its transportation priorities away from cars towards public transport. Summarising the decision to build a light rail system instead of a freeway and to reurbanise the corridor, Edner and Arrington (1985) made the following remarks:

> "...it was not just a simple matter of evaluating transit and highway alternatives, but rather more broadly a revolution in metropolitan thinking regarding preferred transportation systems" (p1).

The Tri-Met transit authority in Portland recognised from the start that transport planning required important land use planning as well:

> "The case being made is that the introduction of major new transportation assumptions requires new land-use assumptions. The two are too inextricably linked to do otherwise. The revised land-use case presented here addresses the need for coordinated land-use and transportation planning and investments to realize the best possible result. A variety of creative implementation mechanisms, including Transportation Corridor Development Cooperation, are potentially available to encourage the level of development desired. Along with incentives for development in station areas, some disincentives to development outside the corridor would be necessary" (p 3).

The expected changes from the reurbanisation of the area have been summarised based on Edner and Arrington (1985):
• The conversion of a considerable portion of the corridor's vacant land and some lower value structures to higher intensity uses (multiple family, commercial, office);
   • A rapid conversion to higher density uses within the corridor;
   • A shift of multiple-family development into the LRT corridor;
   • A reduction in the growth rate outside the corridor;
   • The need for significantly improved urban services within the corridor;
   • A general positive impact on property values;
   • A total reduction in energy utilization from development in an energy-efficient area;
   • A reduction in automobile use and ownership;
   • A reduction in public costs associated with both development and environmental pollution.

116

The Portland experience is thus particularly instructive in that it is an automobile city undergoing some fundamental reorientations. It is very relevant to Class I cities for a number of important reasons:

(1) The light rail system was built in place of an interstate urban freeway which was to cut through the Portland area removing 1% of Portland's housing stock (over 3000 homes). The US interstate freeway funding system provides for withdrawal of planned freeways with an option to use the total funds that would have been expended on other transportation projects including public transport. Boston was the first city to take advantage of this option and improve public transport and Portland followed their experience.

(2) In land use terms Portland is particularly applicable to Class I cities being very low density (11.4 persons/ha in 1980) and the eastern corridor through which the light rail system runs from downtown is predominantly single-family housing. The Portland central area is very similar to several Class I cities having 82,140 jobs in 1980 compared to, for example, Perth's CBD which had 81,016 and Adelaide with 55,663 in the CBD (and 69,076 in the whole central city).

(3) The land use changes predicted to occur for specific areas in response to the light rail system after five to seven years are very significant. Some of the more major ones along the LRT route can be summarised as follows:
- Downtown
  - 2 to 2.6 million square feet of new office space (186,000 to 241,540 m^2)
  - 240,000 to 400,00 square feet of new retail space (22,300 to 37,200 m^2)
  - 550 to 700 new residential units.
- East Multnomah County - 20% of all new residential development envisioned to be within five minutes walk of the LRT stations.
- Gresham - this is at the end of the line and is predicted to attract 2000 to 2300 multi-family units around the stations and 400,000 - 700,000 square feet of office space in the same area (37,200 to 65,000 m^2).

(4) The fundamental change away from cars towards public transport in Portland between 1973 and the present has been characterised by a number of other important developments which have strong potential for reducing dependence on automobiles and gasoline.
- The Portland central area has undergone a revitalisation in terms of urban design based around more human-orientated developments. Part of this process has been a strong emphasis on central city housing with a number of notable mixed use developments and a considerable number of high rise apartment buildings.
- A ceiling on the number of parking spaces allowed in downtown Portland has prevented a blow out in this factor and assisted the viability of public transport.
- Portland has won priority for its light rail system at traffic lights where it runs on the normal road system. It has also created special bus transit streets which give buses a clear run through the traffic.

As a total system therefore, Portland has a number of valuable lessons which it can teach Class I cities about reurbanisation. Other cities have had similar experiences but none appear to have been so well documented. Edner and Arrington (1985) conclude with a comment that shows reurbanisation is not just a technical matter:

> "On a comprehensive level, the Banfield decision represented a major shift in the functional and philosophic role of transit in the region. This shift was a wrenching experience which set a context of opportunity in terms of exploring new transportation systems. It also ruptured the political fabric of transportation decisionmaking, realigning the roles and responsibilities of many political and technical actors" (p 2).

Inner area redevelopment in Class II to V cities is an on-going process which has generally had quite a high priority as the areas are so vital to each city. For some cities, efforts to reurbanise will have to be increased as pressures to develop elsewhere occur. One of the ways that some cities like Stockholm and Hong Kong are finding to do this is to highlight development opportunities on and around railway land. The obvious places are on rail stations but most cities have large railway marshalling yards in inner areas with enormous redevelopment potential above or on the yards. For example, Melbourne is moving its marshalling yards in the central area to permit a whole range of central city redevelopments and Denver has a vast expanse of disused railway land in the central area with plans for its redevelopment.

One of the ways that Toronto has found to increase its population and job densities in the inner area is by the development of several sub-centres. These centres mean that there are high density nodes of activity within the medium density suburbs, again making public transport and walking more viable. The sub-centres are linked by a range of public transport options and developers are given bonus incentives to locate their various projects in certain key areas on or adjacent to the subway system.

Middle area land use

Middle areas are those suburbs which have been built after World War II, generally at quite low densities but which now are beginning to disurbanise ie they are losing population and in some cases jobs, as they age and no longer have vacant greenfield land for new development.

Such areas exist in most of the Class I, II and III cities, though most European cities developed their post-war suburbs at much higher density than in the US and Australia. In many ways the European post-war suburb continued the tradition of a public transport-oriented land use with often quite high density developments. However, in US and Australian cities middle suburbs were unlike the pre World War II inner suburbs as they were generally very low density and deliberately eliminated the fine grain mix of activities characteristic of the older areas. They are therefore different to European cities in that they are disurbanising much quicker.

The planning priority for middle suburbs in US and Australian cities should therefore be to reurbanise at higher densities. The type of land use in the old inner suburbs needs to be pushed out through the middle suburbs as shown in Figure 5.3.

This will require the full range of reurbanisation policies including in-fill, redevelopment of industrial and warehousing sites, resubdivision of old declining low density precincts, intense mixed use developments, air-rights development over rapid transit routes and conversion of un-needed road reserves. Opposition to reurbanisation does occur (Bunker 1983) but it need not be seen as a fundamental problem; studies in Fremantle (an old area of Perth) have shown that its low energy, low automobile land use with higher density and mixed activities (Neville et al., 1988) is just as satisfactory as a residential neighbourhood to those who live there as the post-war outer and middle suburbs of Perth with their low density, rigidly zoned land use (Duxbury et al., 1988). The residents of Fremantle appear to make the simple trade-off that less private space and more mixed activities means they have more easy access to urban facilities and a more interesting and active community.

Outer area land use

Figure 5.4 shows the variation between the five classes of cities in outer area density.

Class I and Class II cities are not very different and both will need to be aware that these areas are where the major automobile dependence and high gasoline use have become in-built.

From the analysis here it would be important to stress the need for containing any further outer area growth. There would need to be restrictions on the subdivision of rural land for hobby farms and other very low density development. Taxation incentives for rural land owners at the urban fringe need to reflect the economic importance of not developing their land.

The direction for development needs to be inwards not outwards, and hence outer areas need to be concentrated at least initially by filling in the various parts of their area that have been leap frogged or by-passed. For many Class I cities this alone can mean large savings in infrastructure costs compared to continued outer fringe development. Another way of consolidating development in outer areas is to establish a few key sub-centres around rapid transit lines which then provide something of a focus for future developments.

Central city land use

Figure 5.5 shows that the density of central city land use in Class I cities is significantly less than Class II cities. The most pressing requirement in this regard appears to be a major increase in the number of people residing in the central area. CBD population densities in Class II cities are more than three times those in Class I cities, suggesting that policies to attract people to densities of around 40 to 50/ha would be appropriate. Such population increases seem entirely achievable whilst attracting more jobs at the same time; note that central city job density in Class II cities is over twice that of Class I cities. Despite this lower job density in Class I cities, they seem better able to attract jobs than they do resident population, suggesting a need for

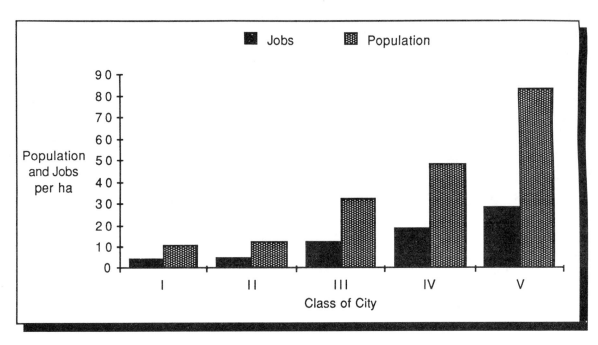

Figure 5.4   Outer area population and job densities in each
class of city.

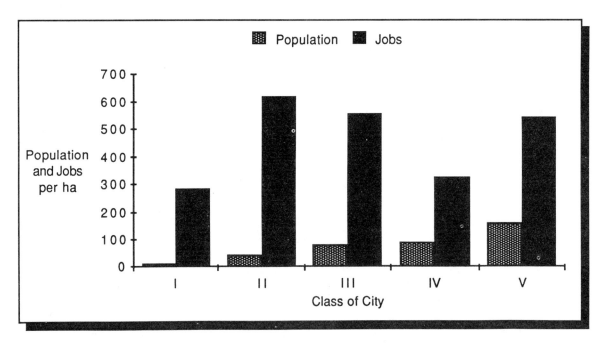

Figure 5.5   Central city population and job densities in each
class of city.

very strong conscious policies to develop central area housing.

San Francisco, a Class II city, provides something of a case study for Class I cities wanting to encourage more central city housing. San Francisco has a CBD of 383 ha with a resident population of 34,338. By comparison, the average size of the CBD in Class I cities is almost identical (374 ha) but with an average of only 5028 residents (ie. San Francisco has almost seven times more residents in the same size central area). Interestingly, San Francisco's central area population has remained relatively stable, declining by only 6% from 1960 to 1980 (ie. 36,620 to 34,338). By contrast, the overall decline in central city resident population in the Class I cities from 1960 to 1980 was 46% (excluding Brisbane for which no 1960 central area resident population is available).

Despite this large resident population in a relatively small area, it has not been at the expense of jobs. San Francisco's jobs numbered 273,000 in 1980 compared to an average of 96,000 for the eight Class I cities.

Part of the key to San Francisco's success in creating not only a very diversified and economically vital CBD in employment terms, but also a 'living' centre in population terms, has been its very strong pro-residential policies in the central area - to have as many people as possible living close to the major centre of employment, culture and retail activity. A recent policy of renewing the Mission Bay area provides a perspective on the priorities of the city.

The Mission Bay redevelopment is of particular note and relevance to cities wanting to develop their central areas; this waterfront area of 300 acres (121 ha) adjacent to and south of the downtown area is being redeveloped into a "new urban neighbourhood with an integrated living and working environment to be built out over the next 20 to 30 years along with a system of parks, recreation and natural resource areas" (Department of City Planning, City and County of San Francisco, 1987). The area will be redeveloped with:

- no buildings over eight stories
- 7,577 residential units (including 30% "affordable")
- up to 2.6 million square feet (241,540m^2) research and development space
- up to 4.1 million square feet (381,900m^2) of office space
- up to 200,000 square feet (18,600m^2) of retail space, and
- parks, lagoons, canals, waterways and public open spaces.

If the residential units were to achieve an average occupancy of 2 persons this would imply an extra 15,154 people in what is essentially the central area of San Francisco. This would give an overall urban density for the area of 125 persons per ha, which when compared to the world cities in this survey, is 36% higher than the average central city density of the twelve European cities and only 16% lower than the Asian cities. This gives some perspective on how underutilised are the central areas of many Class I cities compared to this Californian model (which is usually associated with dispersal rather than concentration of urban activities).

San Francisco has also enacted quite stringent regulations on central city project developers whereby they are required to provide a certain amount of residential floorspace with every new office development. This can be within the actual office building or on another site within a prescribed area.

Such policies are the key to their central city residential vitality.

One of the key policy areas highlighted here has been the need for more population in the central city. This section concludes by making a detailed assessment of this question using the Sourcebook data. It is done to show not only the importance of the policy and to seek to find why it works in some cities and not others, but also to show how the Sourcebook data can be used to cast light on a critical policy question.

Focus on the central city

"Unfortunately, the sum of all these dispersals does not produce a new urban constellation. Though potentially they provided the elements for a new kind of multi-centred city, operated on a regional scale, their effect has so far been to corrode and undermine the old centres, without forming a pattern coherent enough to carry on their essential cultural functions on anything like the old level. Within a generation, when they lose the momentum they now derive from the historic city, the resulting deterioration will be serious. Left to themselves, as Los Angeles already demonstrates, these forces will automatically destroy the city" (Lewis Mumford, 1961; p573).

The population-parking trade off

The central city is a symbol of the whole city - it reflects the city's basic values and priorities in its physical layout and general attractiveness. It can be a featureless group of office blocks set in a sea of bitumen and congested traffic or it can be a buzz of human activity with a diversity of compact buildings and easy access to traffic-free, attractive pedestrian precincts. Our view of the central city is summed up by the British Bishop, E.R. Wickham:

"Integral to the spirit of the good city is its public and social life, its zest and gaiety and the capacity for intermingling....It should be a place of exuberance and exaltation of the human spirit, a place for celebration and public 'happenings', for rich and easy encounter, for relaxation and enjoyment. It must not be simply functional and utilitarian" (Wickham, 1977; p262).

In Chapter 4 we set out a list of what we regarded were the best and worst central city areas from this perspective of simple human attractiveness. It was shown to correlate significantly with the level of gasoline use and private car use. The list is again presented in Table 5.2, this time it includes data on central area population, central area parking and a ratio of the two. Figure 5.6 graphs the relationship between central city 'human attractiveness' and the ratio of central city population to parking. There is a significant correlation between the two of 0.86.

The reason for examining these data was a subjective sense that those central cities which we found to be the most attractive seemed to have controlled the private car so that although there may have been areas of

Table 5.2
Central area population and parking and
their relationship to the human attractiveness
of the central area.

Cities in order of central area human attractiveness		Central Area Population	Central Area Parking (spaces)	Population/ Parking (ratio)
Paris	31	548,620	187,000	2.93
Munich	30	77,172	45,750	1.69
Stockholm	29	41,146	12,000	3.43
Vienna	28	19,537	23,000	0.85
Amsterdam	27	69,400	20,400	3.40
Tokyo	26	337,644	112,998	2.99
Hong Kong	25	17,287	5,076	3.41
Singapore	24	157,300	25,327	6.21
London	23	179,000	138,843	1.29
Copenhagen	22	38,571	31,400	1.23
Zürich	21	6,750	9,000	0.75
New York	20	506,100	144,926	3.49
West Berlin	19	16,000	17,500	0.91
Toronto	18	4,742	28,193	0.17
Frankfurt	17	15,572	22,484	0.69
Hamburg	16	12,153	27,900	0.43
Brussels	15	19,180	28,400	0.68
Boston	14	71,557	70,200	1.02
San Francisco	13	34,338	39,665	0.87
Melbourne	12	?	41,600	?
Sydney	11	4,440	28,151	0.16
Chicago	10	6,462	35,374	0.18
Washington DC	9	3,458	70,943	0.05
Adelaide	8	1,819	21,146	0.09
Perth	7	6,392	51,500	0.12
Brisbane	6	2,531	15,315	0.17
Los Angeles	5	9,516	80,074	0.12
Denver	4	7,050	49,919	0.14
Detroit	3	4,046	52,400	0.08
Phoenix	2	6,724	26,772	0.25
Houston	1	2,145	64,194	0.03

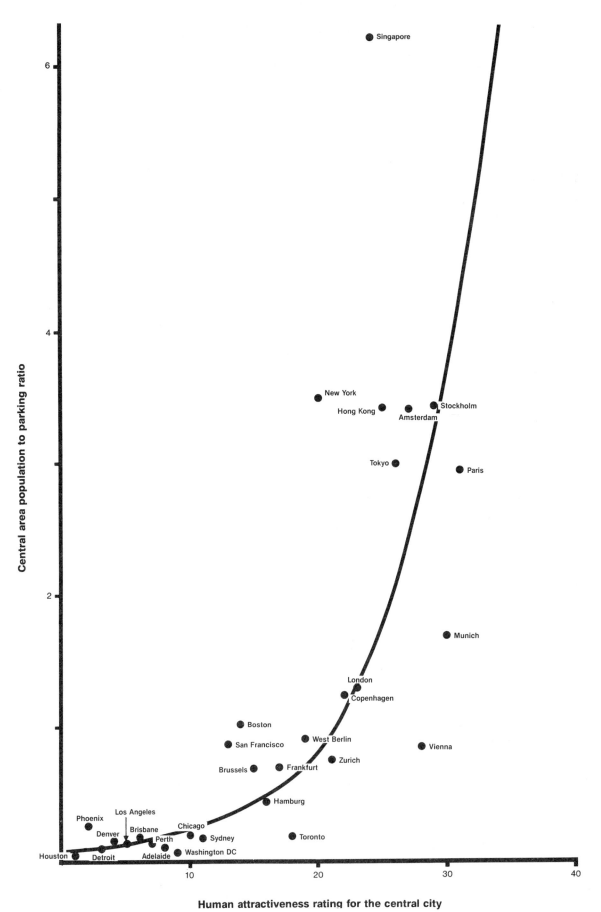

Figure 5.6   The population/parking trade-off.

124

congested traffic, it was generally possible to escape from cars and enjoy the urbanity of the place at a pedestrian scale. It seemed to us that these cities did not place parking as a high priority in the functioning of their city.

The obverse of this parking policy was also a subjective impression that much more attention was given to two things:

a. Public places, parks, pedestrian areas, arcades, ie. in general, places for people rather than places for cars, and

b. Central city residences within 5 to 10 minutes walk of all these attractive public facilities. It is not an easy task to obtain numbers on the public places though it is easy to observe many cities, where Mumford's lament is obvious: "Instead of buildings set in a park we now have buildings in a parking lot" (Mumford, 1961; p576). But we did have numbers on the central city population and as the data show there is a clear correlation to back up our subjective assessment.

What these data suggest and the subjective impressions from the thirty-two central cities, is that there is a trade-off between areas for people and areas for cars. In particular there appears to be a trade-off between population and parking.

One of the important and easily observed features of a central city is that those cities where there is a significant residential community tend to have a built-in 24 hour city. Such places invariably are more safe and attractive to the general population, at all times because they are people-places. In Oscar Newman's terms they have much more 'defensible space' with much less space that is abandoned at night to gangs. Central city populations tend to own their public places and provide the community-watching and caring which no police force can ever really replace (see Jacobs (1961) for further on this).

It is not hard to see how in a small central city why a trade-off exists between population and parking. Parking areas for a small work force of say 50,000 would take up around 150 ha of land. If such land were used instead for housing it could provide a home for around 7,500 people at reasonable medium to high densities (50/ha). This comparison is based on an average of 30m² of land per parking bay (including all ancillary land such as aisles etc.) For the population side of the calculation, the 50 persons per ha is total urban land (ie roads, dwellings, shops etc.) As suggested in Chapter 4, Antoniou (1971) has made calculations on the amount of bitumen given over to cars in central Los Angeles and found it to be around $2/3$ of the city area. It is not hard to see why many writers become so caustic about such a city:

"Los Angeles...a nightmarish sprawling anti-city peopled by a rootless and lonely crowd, in which all the rich, multifarious and interdependent functions of the traditional city have been eliminated by the means of transport" (in Ashworth, 1973; p62).

"People escape to suburbs and abandon the city. 'Los Angelization' of the earth turns it into a mass habitat of defensive privacy and incessant movement" (Schneider, 1979).

How do such differences in central city areas occur? Obviously there are no simple answers but a combination of factors including the priority given to public transport, (especially a train service), the priority given to parking and the priority given to housing. Most central city office developments involve a certain amount of parking and city planners use this as one of the means to control the development for various public purposes. The amount of parking in such developments can easily rise to quite high levels for the whole city centre unless strictly held limits are kept to. As with the 'tragedy of the commons' (Hardin, 1968), the public good of the pedestrian scale in the central city can be easily eroded by each individual development having a parking allowance that by itself seems quite small but multiplied many times over just creates a crush of cars.

Central area land values are generally not going to easily lend themselves to housing developments unless they are at enormously high rents. Although penthouses in central cities obviously have their role there is an important place for a full range of housing close to the city centre. This provides walking access to many major urban facilities and thus in equity terms as well as energy and environmental terms, such housing is important. Such housing can only be provided by the use of public land or by the use of incentives to encourage a proportion of all developments to be residential. For each individual development the provision of housing should be seen as part of their public responsibility in maintaining an attractive, good city centre. San Francisco appears to have adopted such an approach.

The extreme case of a city which adopted the exact opposite approach would appear to be Detroit. General Motors, who have remained in the sea of parking which is downtown Detroit today, have found it necessary to set up a whole arm of corporate activity designed specifically to revitalise central Detroit. This has involved renovating whole streets of rundown Victorian houses and selling them at a financial loss. They have also had to renovate the street environment with landscaping, new street furniture and some public spaces. Their activities have even extended to installing an old tourist tram using 1890's streetcars bought back from Lisbon after they were removed and sold some 40 to 50 years ago. As well, GM have been very involved in building a downtown peoplemover to link up major parts of the downtown area. Ironically, one of the initial motivations for this activity was the fact that their own employees were finding it so unattractive and dangerous just walking from their cars to the office that GM was forced to take action to regenerate the human character of their section of downtown which cars had helped to destroy. This included trying to encourage people to actually live in and around the area again.

This demonstrates that there is clearly a degree of social responsibility involved in how a central city is allowed to develop. If it is seen as a purely financial matter, then extreme cases can occur, like in Detroit, of individual decisions gradually destroying the fabric of the city, and ultimately backfiring on those who may have been key actors in the whole process.

A city centre which restricts parking, provides incentives for public transport use, and incentives for residential development will be moving towards a less automobile-orientated, more human-orientated city. For

126

many Class I cities the obvious first step in this is to locate some central parking lots and build housing over them. In the longer term, if high parking cities like Detroit, Los Angeles and Perth were to move towards greater public transport access in the central city and more emphasis on the pedestrian scale, then there remains the possibility that some parking lots could be dispensed with altogether for housing.

A further area of policy that is necessary for reurbanisation is centred on urban density and what levels of development are likely to influence cities (and areas of cities) to be less car dependent.

Focus on urban density

". . . in America space-eating has become almost a national pastime. . .The standards that Frank Lloyd Wright projected in 'The Disappearing City' - at least an acre of land per family - are taken as universally desirable even if not achievable. As a result the city itself is fast disappearing: its scattered parts 'lost in space'." (Lewis Mumford, 1961; Note to Plate 48   p424-425)

In Chapter 3 the relationship between urban density and gasoline use was examined. It was suggested that there seemed to be a density for the city overall of around 30 to 40 people per hectare where a completely different less-auto based kind of urban transport occurred. Cities below this kind of density showed an exponential increase in automobile use. The graphs supporting this were of gasoline versus density and gasoline (adjusted for vehicle efficiency) versus density. In Figure 5.7 we have presented the relationship between gasoline (adjusted for US gasoline price, US incomes and US vehicle efficiencies) versus density. The same exponential relationship is clear though now there are fewer cities scattered away from the main curve ie the economic factors reduce the variations and highlight the fundamental link between urban land use and automobile dependence.

Chapter 3 also gave the data from New York and Denver by region which suggest the same exponential relationship with a major shift in patterns of travel in the higher density inner and central areas and the outer areas under 20 to 30 people/ha having large automobile dependence.

For practical land use planning purposes it may be very useful if a particular minimum density range could be determined which provided a significant potential for a more public transport/walking/biking lifestyle. Thus the literature was examined to see if the sort of range suggested by our data was confirmed by the density-transport data in other cities.

Density and public transport in cities overall

In the study mentioned in Chapter 1 based on data provided by the UN "Global Review of Human Settlements", density and public transport data were compared for approximately sixty cities. The data were not as reliable as ours but they show the same pattern ie. a fundamental shift in the region around 30 to 40 people/ha. There may also be another shift which occurs in

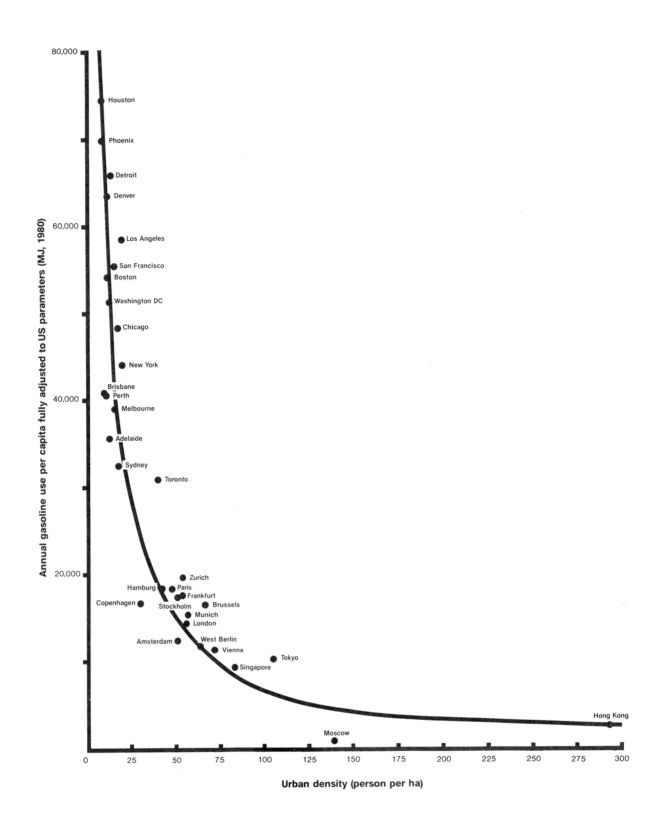

Figure 5.7 — Gasoline use per capita versus urban density adjusted to US income, vehicle efficiencies and gasoline prices.

128

the region over 100/ha whereby public transport goes down due to the large increase in walking (and biking). At densities over 100/ha it is easy to imagine that the vast majority of trips would be within an easy walk. This density corresponds with the traditional walking city density of 100/ha or more that occurred right through history (and is briefly reviewed in Chapter 4 under the "Age of City" factor).

Density and transport within cities

If this 30-40/ha cut off point for a more public transport orientated urban lifestyle were true, then it should be possible to isolate the same patterns within the regions of a variety of cities. Inner city areas in our Sourcebook data consisently show much reduced automobile dependence to the rest of the city and are invariably more than 30 to 40/ha. The same pattern can be seen in a range of studies within various cities around the world.

Figure 5.8 shows the density and transport patterns in a number of UK cities. It is a detailed breakdown of travel characteristics by density provided by Hillman and Whalley (1979 and 1983) who examined UK settlements based on the National Travel Survey 1978/79. Figure 5.8 shows the following:

(i)There is a rapid increase in total distance travelled (by all modes) as density declines: people in low density areas travel almost twice as far as in high density areas and there appears to be a discontinuity at around 30/ha whereby travel distances go from around 150 km/week to 190 km/week for less than 10/ha areas.

(ii) When car travel alone is compared, people in low density areas travel by car three times as far as those in high density areas.

(iii) Below 20/ha there is a marked increase in travel per person by car only.

(iv) Auto ownership increases as density declines, especially in areas less than 20/ha where there are rapid increases in households owning two or more cars (the same pattern with car ownership and density was found in each income bracket).

(v)The proportion of households having a frequency of bus service better than half hourly decreases markedly as density declines: the bus service becomes very poor under 30/ha.

(vi) The proportion of walking trips decreases as density declines.

Low density areas under 20 to 30 persons/ha thus generate automobile dependence due to a combination of factors including greater distances to travel and little option to walk or use public transport. Above 30/ha the percentage of households with no car is more than 40% and at the highest density range (over 75/ha), 67% have no car. Densities below the 30/ha range, particularly in the less than 20/ha range, mean that the lack of an automobile would severely erode the ability to participate fully in urban life. Public transport-dependent people in low density cities, as shown dramatically by the Hillman and Whalley data in Figure 5.9, can expect little in the way of a bus service and rail is very unlikely. For those in cities or parts of cities where densities are over 20/ha (and especially over 40/ha) then public transport can be a strong travel option and the automobile is not quite so essential to participate in urban life.

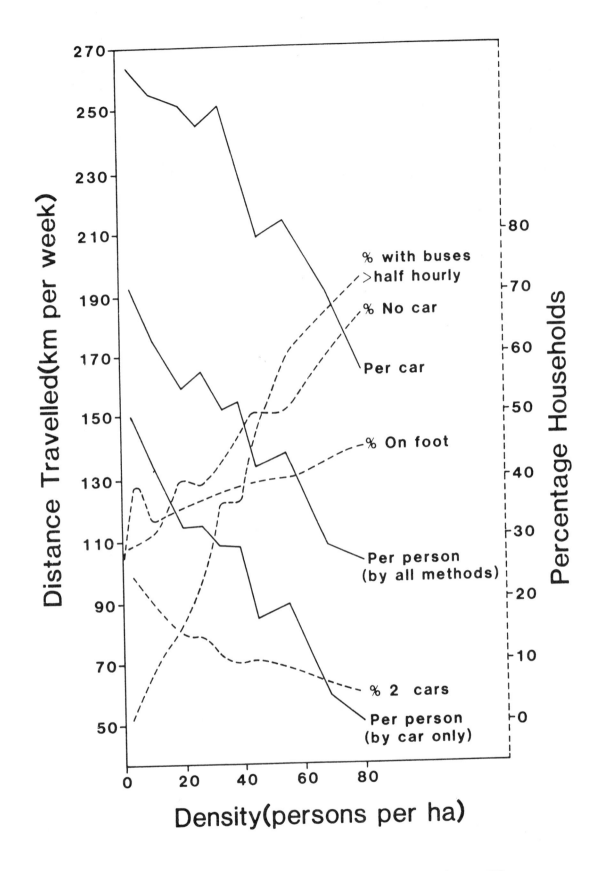

Figure 5.8   Travel characteristics by density in UK (1978-79).

Clark (1967), based on a study in Chicago, suggested that a density of 48/ha is likely to be the limit 'below which public transport will be unremunerative without a subsidy' (p366). As most public transport systems have some subsidy, the limit may therefore be reducible to around 30/ha before public transport is either a major financial burden or is reduced to insignificant service levels. Pushkarev and Zupan (1977) in a survey of US cities suggest that cities with less than 25/ha are associated with insignificant public transport and in those places or parts of cities where densities are between 25 and 90/ha there is a sharp increase in transit use; more than half of all work trips are by public transport in the latter part of this density range.

In the 1969 San Francisco Bay Area Transportation Study, urban areas over 36/ha had a modal split with 21% transit and 37% walking, compared to suburban areas with densities between 12 and 36/ha which had only 14% transit and 19% walking. And where the outer suburban fringe had densities below 12/ha then it reduced to 5% transit and 13% walking (Bay Area Transportation Study Commission, 1969). The inner cities of Sydney and Melbourne in 1971 had densities of 40/ha and 37/ha repectively in 1971 and had significantly different transport patterns to those of their low density outer suburbs (Newman and Kenworthy, 1980a,c); these inner city areas had journey to work proportions by public transport and walking of 55% and by car of 38%, while the proportions were reversed in the outer suburbs. Moreover, shopping and school journeys reflect similar patterns, with even lower automobile dependence in the inner city.

Numerous studies have shown how the density factor within a city reduces auto ownership and auto use, even after adjusting for other socio-economic variables (eg. Lansing and Hendricks, 1967; Guest and Cluett, 1976). Neels et al., (1977) found in a study of Household Travel Surveys in eight US cities, that on average you could expect that a low density development in an outer area at a density of around 7/ha would generate around 103 auto miles (166 km) of travel per household per day, compared to a high density development in an inner area which would generate around 50 miles (81 km) of auto travel per day. Fels and Munson (1974), in their study of Trenton, New Jersey found that the old central area with a density of 54/ha had a per capita transport energy of 41 GJ per year but in the outer suburbs where densities averaged around 7/ha the per capita energy was 94 GJ per year. Pushkarev, Zupan and Cumella (1982) in their study of US cities with and without rail, conclude that the direct transfer of travel between rail and car cannot explain the differences in travel between these cities. They suggest that higher density associated with the rail corridors means lower ownership and lower use of automobiles which creates an indirect travel saving of some four times the 19 billion vehicle kms of auto travel directly saved by rail in the nation each year in urban areas. This is still however only a small proportion of annual US urban travel which is highly dependent upon the automobile.

Low density areas under 30 people/ha and especially under 20/ha thus generate automobile dependence due to a combination of factors including greater distances to travel and little option to walk or use public transport. Behnman and Beglinger (1976) also showed that when density is reduced, the level of automobile occupancy decreases. Thus this combination of factors appears to substantiate the evidence in this book that there is an exponential increase in automobile use as density declines. In particular, with densities less than 20/ha, automobile-dependence seems almost complete.

Conclusion to urban density

For practical planning, if a region or corridor were to be built with a minimum urban density of 20 and preferably 30 to 40 people per ha, then it appears that there may be a corresponding pattern of urban activity which is more public transport/walking/biking based. The reasons for this could include the combination of shorter distances, a more viable concentration for transit collection and greater congestion for cars. However, it should also be added that each of these factors can be abused by bad planning so that transport patterns can be pushed more towards cars despite having increased densities. The kinds of "bad planning" could include:

(i) placing higher density housing development a long way from all other major urban activity (obviously it would be better to build close to a railway station or within walking distance of a range of urban employment and other activities);

(ii) making all such housing for high income earners only (a social mix is always better for a balanced transport system as well as for equity reasons); and

(iii) forcing the development into more of an auto-mode by large adjacent roads and by excessive parking that makes the development less human in its scale and orientation.

Despite these other potential directions, in general it should be possible to make urban regions or corridors where densities are 30 to 40/ha, much less auto-dependent. If development at this density were made for a corridor leading to a central city, then the line-haul effect outlined in Chapter 3 would add to the public transport viability of the corridor.

For a uniformly low density city, as in Class I cities, higher density urban regions or corridors would provide a choice of lifestyle for their populace which may only suit certain people initially eg. older people not wanting to use a car anymore, single people who only want accessibility, poorer people who can not afford to buy and run a car. As such areas develop they can attract an increasing number of people to such a lifestyle thus making reurbanisation an increasingly popular option. Without good quality models of urban lifestyle like this it is often difficult for a low density city to project the necessary image which makes a higher density more urban lifestyle an attractive option.

There are of course a range of possible architectures to achieve a density of 30 to 40/ha. A combination of housing types could be incorporated as in the Real Estate Research Corporation (1974) study, which with 40% six storey apartments, 30% two storey apartments, 20% town houses and 10% single family clustered homes, with 30% of the developed area devoted to open space and recreation, had a density of 37.5/ha. This is in comparison to the low density sprawl community with only 9.0% open space/recreation. It is possible to build with all 2 storey town houses and achieve densities above

30 to 40/ha, especially if families can be attracted through sufficient internal space and features such as children's playgrounds. However, with modern low levels of dwelling occupancy it is unlikely that such densities can be reached without some component of medium or high rise apartments.

This should not mean a loss of aesthetic quality, as of course such developments can be built very attractively and integrated with good urban design and landscaping into a high quality development. One only has to look at the urban landscape of Canadian cities such as Toronto and Vancouver to see how effectively they have juxtaposed good quality, high rise residential developments throughout their urban areas with typical single-family residential neighbourhoods. There appears to be no evidence in these Canadian cities that such a mixture of different residential types leads to feelings that residential areas are developing into slums. In many parts of the US and Australia this would be the reaction. Some further studies of Canada's successful integration of medium to high rise apartments in single family areas would appear to be worthwhile.

Reurbanisation - concluding comments

Reurbanisation as outlined here offers a land use package which should assist with each of the five factors (from the factor analysis) as key determinants of gasoline use and automobile dependence. They are described in Table 5.3 highlighting the direct and indirect linkages between land use and transport.

The way that reurbanisation land use policies have clear transport implications is also set out in Figure 5.9. The combination of these effects is then shown in a summary way (in this Figure) to have other implications for the city in assisting resolution of the broad urban problems which beset automobile-dependent cities. Chapter 4 developed some of the analysis behind these linkages and undoubtedly each simple link requires further development and substantiation; these are shown as examples of how reurbanisation as an urban policy has a number of rationales and that a less automobile and gasoline dependent city is probably a better city on many grounds.

Reorientation of transport priorities

Although land use provides the framework for a city's transport system, the actual patterns which emerge can of course be altered by the priority given to various modes. Many European cities are as compact as Amsterdam and Copenhagen but these two are noted for strong commitments to bicyclists and pedestrians. They also have a much higher priority for public transport, for example, Vienna's priorities were summed up by its Mayor when he stated that "unlimited individual mobility . . . is an illusion", that the "future belongs to the means of public transport" and that this will be "a driving force of city renewal" (Gratz, 1981). Australian cities show a greater commitment to transit than most US cities with comparable land use.

Table 5.3
The major elements in reurbanisation policies in terms of the five factor analysis conclusions stressing the overlap between land use and transport policies.

- **More intensive land use**.

Reurbanisation by definition intensifies land use in inner, outer and central city areas by techniques such as infill, redevelopment, dual occupancy housing, air rights over transit lines, incentives for central city housing....

- **More orientation in transport infrastructure to non-automobile modes.**

This is the major thrust of the next policy area to be discussed but reurbanisation provides the opportunity for non-automobile modes to flourish. The provision of infrastructure by itself will not be successful eg cycle paths can help promote bicycle use but in very low density cities distances are just too far for any significant bicycle use. Thus reurbanisation is the land use component which will help to make public transport, bicycling and walking feasible options . It is necessary to provide the infrastructure but it is generally not sufficient unless accompanied by the land use changes suggested by reurbanisation.

- **More restraint on high speed traffic flows.**

This again relates primarily to the next policy area but it can be seen that where you have low density scattered land use then high speed roads appear more necessary to ensure economic transport linkages; on the other hand if land use is intensified then not only is there less need for the high speed road alternative but there is less possibility for it to be built through more developed areas. Thus reurbanisation works against the need and the possibility of high speed road alternatives and enables a more balanced transport system to be achieved.

- **More centralised land use.**

Reurbanisation as outlined highlights the role of the city centre. It also suggests that strong sub-centres (as in Toronto) can be developed to intensify land use in inner and middle suburbs. To reurbanise is to highlight the centre and sub-centres rather than scattered land uses which can only be serviced by the automobile.

- **Better performing public transport.**

Reurbanisation as already mentioned provides the opportunity for public transport to perform better. If the land use is not conducive to public transport then all the transit management techniques and customer incentives in the world can do little more than start a process which induces land use change.

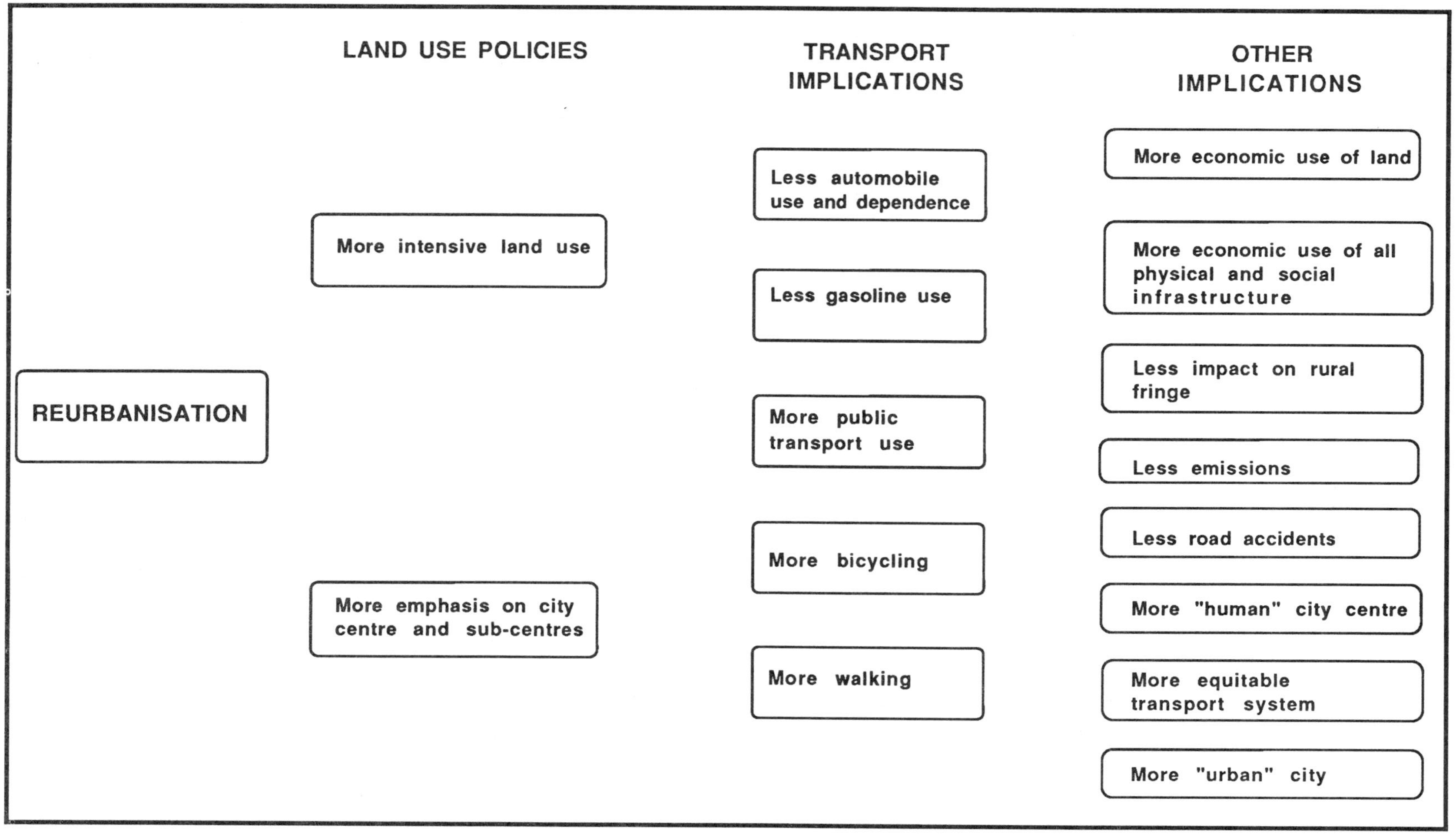

LAND USE POLICIES

REURBANISATION

More intensive land use

More emphasis on city centre and sub-centres

TRANSPORT IMPLICATIONS

Less automobile use and dependence

Less gasoline use

More public transport use

More bicycling

More walking

OTHER IMPLICATIONS

More economic use of land

More economic use of all physical and social infrastructure

Less impact on rural fringe

Less emissions

Less road accidents

More "human" city centre

More equitable transport system

More "urban" city

Figure 5.9   Reurbanisation: Its major policy components and implications for transport and other socio-economic and environmental factors.

Within the US, the urban structure of cities such as Los Angeles and Detroit could support much more transit use but they have obviously directed their priorities in the past to automobiles, eg Detroit has an inner area population density which approaches that of Toronto yet it has only one fifth of the transit service provision per person. Transport priorities have tended in the past, especially in Class I and II cities, to emphasise the provision of facilities for automobile travel. Thus a reorientation of transport priorities in cities would include elements of the following policies.

Parking limitations

The level of parking in the CBD is almost a litmus test of the whole provision of automobile-infrastructure. Thus, it needs to be accepted that controls over the level of parking is a necessary policy, particularly in Class I cities. These cities in the worst category of automobile dependence have a massive two and a half times more central area parking per 1000 jobs than cities in the next category (see Figure 5.10). There would appear to be a need to move towards parking provision in these cities to no more than 200 spaces per 1000 CBD jobs.

This would require a concurrent policy that provides good public transport access and a series of central city policies on housing, cultural attractions, urban design, pedestrianisation and commercial activity that allows a central city to compete strongly with suburban areas where easy parking is available (McNulty, *et al.*, 1986).

Upgraded and extended public transport

The differences between the five city classes in terms of public transport provision are quite dramatic, as shown in Figure 5.11. Obviously the provision of good transit gives a city far more than just another transport option - it provides the focus for land use development which facilitates a whole urban lifestyle orientation that is less automobile based and enables a city to become much more economic in its use of land.

The second category of cities shows significant improvements in their orientation away from cars towards public transport and also considerable improvements in the performance of public transport in terms of speed, energy efficiency and passenger attraction. For example, the number of passenger kms per person on public transport and the proportion of the total passenger transport task on public transport are more than two and a half times greater for Class II cities than for the Class I cities. The proportion of people using public transport to go to work is over twice as high. Most significantly however, is a dramatic increase in the importance of rail systems - the proportion of the public transport task performed by trains increases by over four times that in the very highly automobile dependent cities. The difference in energy use between these cities is obviously not due just to a more efficient rail mode, but is due to the fact that rail systems facilitate more energy-conserving land use in general. The technology and management structures for high-cost or low-cost modern separated-way

136

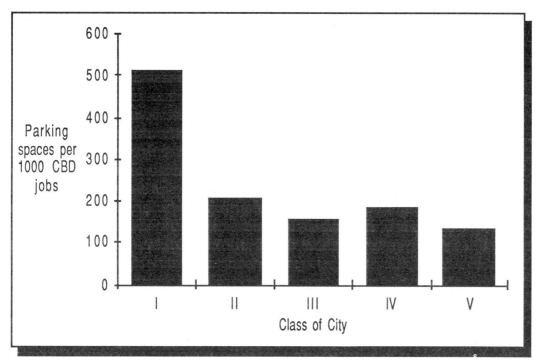

Figure 5.10   Parking supply in the CBD in each class of city.

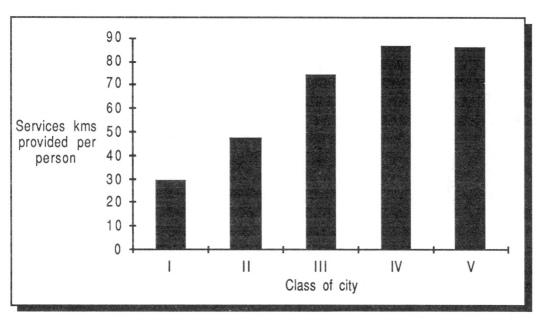

Figure 5.11   Public transport provision in each class of city.

transit systems have been adequately demonstrated in all continents, with both positive and negative assessments (Vuchic, 1981). However, such systems (in particular new light rail options), are increasing in popularity as a means of coping with high and medium capacity transport requirements, especially in Canada and on the West Coast of the United States (Vuchic,

137

1981; Cervero, 1986b). To make transit a more fundamental part of the Class I cities will require a major commitment of planning and capital but it would not be unlike the type of commitment that has been more recently shown to highway building. The full benefits of such transit systems will only be realised when land use is allowed and encouraged to concentrate around transit stations. This has occurred around Washington's Metro and in most Canadian cities as they have introduced their modern rail systems (Kenworthy, Newman and Lyons, 1987; MWCOG and NCRTPB, 1983). Transit authorities can also help to pay for their systems by entreprenaurial activity on their land, such as development above and around stations. This is an important part of most US rail system developments.

The sheer inadequacy of totally automobile-dependent transportation is seen in the fact that many Californian cities like Los Angeles, San Jose, Sacramento and San Diego after years of growing car use, have recognised the need for a rail system. In Australia, Brisbane and now Perth (from 1989) have electrified their rail systems, with Brisbane showing large increases in patronage as a result. Such changes will only play a minor part in the short term future of these cities but it would appear that they are making a step towards a less automobile dependent city and as oil stocks dwindle in the 1990's such cities are likely to want to accelerate the process of building a less fuel-hungry, less automobile-dependent city.

For Class II cities which make the necessary changes to become more like Class III cities, the general performance of public transport would tend to rise commensurate with its greater role in the transport system. The data suggest for example, around 50% greater service provision per person, a doubling in the annual trips made per person from about 1 trip every three and a half days to around 2 trips every 3 days, more passengers picked up for every km of service provided, greater energy efficiency per passenger km, and a continuing emphasis on rail.

The combination of changes outlined here appear very large. However, they are not beyond reach, particularly over, say, a 30 year period. In order to see the possibility of such changes it is useful to consider Toronto, a city in the Class III category. Toronto is easy for Americans and Australians to relate to in cultural terms, having a preponderance of suburban style living (approximately 60% of dwellings are single family housing) and having high car ownership. The main difference appears to be however that Toronto has achieved overall population and job densities within the lower part of the European range. It has done this through a series of dense sub-centres based chiefly around the subway system and a planning direction which emphasises urban consolidation (ie redevelopment and intensification with mixed land use throughout the urban area).

While the private car and suburbia are still major parts of Toronto and lifestyles are on the whole visibly more akin to Australia and America than to Europe, Toronto has achieved a remarkable balance in its land use/ transportation system. Transport choices in Toronto are probably better developed than in any city in the world. They include long haul diesel commuter trains, a subway system, modern on-street trams, new light rail systems on separated tracks, electric trolley buses and diesel buses. In this context, Toronto functions with 53% less road per person than the Class II cities, but still has a major circumferential freeway system. However, plans for radial freeways have been replaced by subway lines (eg the Spadina line).

The process of change indicated by Toronto offers considerable encouragement to cities in Class I and Class II categories. Toronto made a deliberate policy in the 70's to shift its land use and transport infrastructure away from the automobile orientation of cities further south of the border to a more public transport orientation. Its success in doing this suggests that other cities beginning now can also make such rapid changes in orientation.

Pedestrianisation and bicyclisation

The cheapest and most fuel-efficient transport modes rarely achieve much priority in an automobile-oriented society, but where land use is sufficiently concentrated, the opportunities for more walking and biking can be greatly encouraged by better facilities. This can include better separation through pathways, bike lanes and particularly central city pedestrianisation. Planning for linkages between public transport and cycleway facilities are particularly important, as they provide the flexibility to an inflexible transit route, thus increasing the door-to-door competitiveness of transit (eg Bowden, Campbell and Newman, (1984) showed that the catchment for a train service can be more than doubled by cycleway links and better cycle facilities at stations).

The other low-cost method is the European 'Woonerf' treatment of high density residential streets, which allows complete car access, but by careful landscaping and provision of angle parking, it narrows and meanders streets to give greater priority to pedestrians and bicyclists (Tanghe, Vlaeminck and Berghoef, 1984; Cresswell, 1979; White *et al.*, 1978 and van Vliet, 1983).

It is worthwhile noting that Class I and Class II cities are rather similar in their use of bicycling and walking, at least in the proportion of workers using these modes as their principal means of getting to work (Class I cities are 4% on average, while Class II are 6%). The real change however comes in the Class III cities where the proportion of workers using foot and bicycle increases by around three times to 16% and continues to rise to 21% and 24% in Class IV and V cities.

This basically reflects the clear difference between European travel patterns and those in the Australian and US cities (Class III cities are dominated by European cities plus New York and Toronto). It would appear from this that although the Class II cities are considerably better than the Class I cities in public transport, they both have a lot of changing to do along the lines outlined above before they achieve the levels of walking and bicycling found in the Class III cities. Fundamental land use changes as detailed in previous sections, would also be essential for greater walking and bicycling to occur in Class I and Class II cities. Toronto is the least orientated to walking/bicycling of the Class III to V cities and could benefit from a new commitment to these modes in a similar way to their program on public transport. Such a change would confirm its continuing role as a model in North America for reduced automobile dependence.

The 'Woonerf' technique described above is an example of traffic restraint or planned congestion, as it accepts that there is a limit on private vehicle movement and adjusts priorities to give advantage to other modes. Traffic restraint and planned congestion primarily limit the provision of high speed road alternatives as the main way of achieving accessibility in a city. The policy means an integrated approach involving land use decisions and the provision for other modes.

The level of road provision is over 50% higher in Class I cities than Class II cities (see Figure 5.12), and would imply the need for a policy of curtailing roads to around 5 to 6m per person as one of the strategies for reducing automobile dependence. This would mean curtailing major new urban road projects but more importantly would also depend upon the general land use directions just outlined. In particular, since roughly three quarters of the road kilometrage in a city is comprised of minor and local streets, this would imply a shift of emphasis from the single family house with a typical wide street frontage, towards innovative family housing which shares road access more intensively (and which also has less need of roads because of its public transport and walking/bicycling orientation). For example, in Toronto road provision is only 2.7m per person due in part to the fact that single family housing is around 60% compared to a Class I city like Perth where it is 78%. Another reason for Toronto's lower road provision is again related to land use. Much of Toronto's older style single-family residential area is comprised of houses with very narrow frontages, compared to the more common suburban practise of a wide street frontage. Blocks are deep and houses are frequently two storeys, thus the length of residential street required to service the houses is much reduced. According to the Real Estate Research Corporation (1974), single family housing requires on average around seven times as much road length as that for high rise apartments. Considerable road savings could thus be anticipated if a reurbanisation policy is instituted.

If Class II cities further restrained their traffic to levels associated with Class III cities then the international data indicate there would also be dramatic offsetting moves away from the relative importance of cars. The data suggest that if the combination of transport infrastructure and land use changes occurred, then the associated transport patterns could lead to:

(a) a doubling in the number of passenger kms on public transport and the proportion of the total passenger transport task performed by public transport,

(b) journey to work trips that are a third by public transport, half in cars and around 16% on foot and bicycle, ie virtually a tripling in the importance of non-motorised modes,

(c) a reduction in the number of passenger kms per person in cars by around 35% (ie almost 4000 passenger kms per person less each year). This reduction in overall mobility is much more than the approximate 800 extra passenger kms on public transport suggested by the data. The difference would most likely be due to overall shorter trip lengths in a much denser, integrated urban setting as well as a greater all round role for walking and bicycling, ie.

land use changes associated with strong traffic restraint measures as indicated in the next best group of cities can make large differences in the dependence of a city on the automobile.

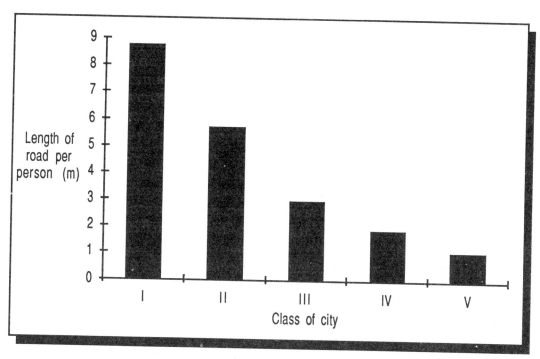

Figure 5.12   Road provision in each class of city.

Traffic restraint and planned congestion shift the orientation of planners from road construction to traffic system management. The money generated from road project savings and from selling of major road reserves could be used for better traffic management of the existing road system and general improvements in public transport necessary to assist these cities in moving towards a less automobile dependent model. The policy should also mean less environmental impact from large highways in urban areas and thus has a number of positive public aspects. On the other hand, the policy does mean transport planners accepting lower average traffic speeds and using this as the opportunity for providing better accessibility through better linking of activities rather than more mobility.

There is however some controversy that a policy of lowering average traffic speeds would in fact increase gasoline use and hence this issue will be examined in some detail for two reasons. First, it highlights the need to integrate transport planning and land use planning as assumed throughout this book, and second, the issue provides an ideal case study of how the Sourcebook data can be used to give perspective on these transport/land use matters.

Focus on congestion

"The only effective cure for urban congestion is to so relate industrial and business zones to residential areas that a large part of their personnel can either walk, or cycle to work, or use a public bus, or take a railroad train. By pushing all forms of traffic on to high speed motorways, we burden them with a load guaranteed to slow down peak traffic to a crawl; and if we try to correct this by multiplying motorways, we only add to the total urban wreckage by flinging the parts of the city ever farther away in a formless mass of thinly spread semi-urban tissue." (Lewis Mumford, 1961; p579)

Congestion is a central focus for transport planners. It is almost always seen in a negative light as something which must be removed, generally by providing a bigger road or by some traffic management technique that allows more free flowing movement. This orientation for transport planners can often mean that they lose sight of the broader objectives in managing a city, ie creating accessibility to achieve the most public good in an economic, social and environmental sense. If freeing up congestion leads to the city referred to by Mumford (above) then it has lost its way as a policy for urban management.

This focus attempts to put congestion into a broader urban context. It attempts to show that congestion can be a force for good, particularly in lessening automobile dependence. It will examine in detail the effect of congestion on energy and emissions, and on time savings. It will attempt to show that the central question is an automobile-dependent land use pattern and any policy to ease congestion without considering this will be counterproductive.

Congestion, energy and emissions

Does free flowing traffic save fuel (and lowers emissions) in a city? This question is often asked in response to our contention that traffic restraint will ease automobile dependence and gasoline use; it is generally asserted that building up congestion will in fact make cars use more fuel and we will be worse off than before. This section will attempt to answer that question. It examines a brief history of the issue and then analyses the question in terms of the thirty-two cities data and some more detailed data within a few of the cities in our study.

Background There is a longstanding observation that automobiles get high miles per gallon in smooth, free-flowing traffic and poor miles per gallon in stop-start, congested traffic. It appears that this observation was first systematically examined in Detroit by Carmichael and Haley (1950) using a vehicle set up with various statistical instruments. Their work was later extended by Stonex (1957) in a study of Los Angeles' traffic characteristics in order to document how emissions from automobiles vary according to traffic conditions.

Since that time (especially after the 1974 and 1979 oil shocks) there has been a growing research and popular literature on how improved average traffic speeds can reduce automotive fuel consumption and emissions. The research approach has generally been based on instrumented vehicles floating in the traffic stream recording fuel use and driving patterns (speeds, idle times, stops, etc.) under various traffic conditions. Driving pattern data gathered in this way have been formulated into standardised 'driving cycles'. These cycles, which can be modified to reproduce any kind of driving pattern, are used in emissions laboratories to study how emissions and fuel use vary under different conditions of traffic flow for different vehicles. In these ways predictive fuel and emissions models have been developed for vehicles based on the traffic conditions in which the vehicles are driven. The key parameter in both fuel and emissions models is average speed (Chang and Herman, 1978; Bowyer, Akcelik and Biggs, 1985); the higher the average speed the lower the fuel use and emissions in individual vehicles (for fuel this applies up to average speeds of about 60 km/h). Thus Chang and Herman for example claim: "We expect that improvements in traffic quality can reduce travel time which, in turn, can directly produce a reduction in fuel consumption" (1978, p. 75). Hence there is a strong research basis for the belief that free flowing traffic saves fuel and lowers emissions.

We have argued in detail elsewhere (Newman and Kenworthy, 1984) that this research is useful in as much as it provides a good explanation of the way fuel is used and emissions are produced by vehicles in urban traffic. This can assist, for example, in comparing scientific advances in motor vehicle engineering, new fuels, new engines and various add-on modifications to vehicles. However, when the results of this work are assumed to apply at a total urban system level (ie improving average speeds will reduce fuel and emissions overall in a city) there are very serious questions to be asked.

In order to see more clearly the basis for this questioning of traffic engineering results as they apply to urban systems, a number of models can be considered. The first shows how there are clearly different "levels of knowledge" involved in studying urban transportation energy and emissions issues (Figure 5.13). Basically we can identify a level of research involving the vehicle and one involving the city. These two levels can be further subdivided into four levels summarised as follows:

1. *Within the vehicle* Mechanical engineers seek to define how engines use fuel and produce emissions under different traffic conditions and different driving techniques.

2. *Vehicle to vehicle level.* Traffic engineers seek knowledge on how traffic patterns can be characterised and what quantities of fuel and emissions these represent (ie, the production of a "driving cycle" that attempts to freeze in time and space a city's driving patterns).

3. *City zone level* Transport planners seek to isolate some of the more dynamic aspects of traffic management by modelling and predicting traffic patterns due to changes like new highways or signalling systems, and linking them to energy and emissions.

4. *Whole city level* Urban planners seek to measure, calculate and model total energy and emissions quantities and to see how they would alter under various spatial strategies.

The basic problem arises when research at the first and second levels in the model involving the vehicle (mechanical and traffic engineering) is accepted as necessarily valid in the higher levels of the model involving corridors of a city or the whole city; in other words when a quantum jump is made from

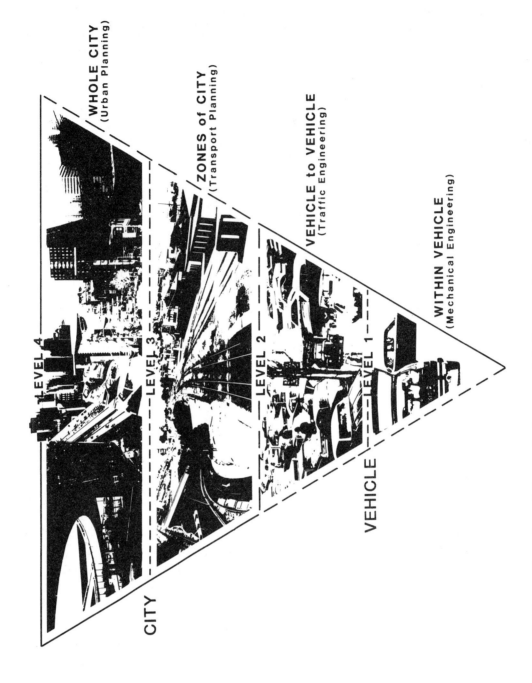

LEVEL 4 — WHOLE CITY
(Urban Planning)

LEVEL 3 — ZONES of CITY
(Transport Planning)

LEVEL 2 — VEHICLE to VEHICLE
(Traffic Engineering)

LEVEL 1 — WITHIN VEHICLE
(Mechanical Engineering)

CITY

VEHICLE

Figure 5.13   Levels of knowledge model for studying urban transport energy use.

144

confined areas of research within the vehicle or in a traffic stream to a broader level involving the operation of an entire urban system. The complex processes occurring at these higher urban levels include those that affect the various modes of transportation, the patterns of land use (density and mixture of various functions), and travel distances; these processes are clearly not just due to how well a vehicle can move through traffic which is the focus of the traffic engineer. All these processes are obviously crucial in determining gasoline use and emissions. Thus the results from within and between vehicles produced by traffic engineers do not stand alone, they must be integrated with knowledge from the city level, not merely superimposed upon it. Some further models help to clarify this situation.

Figure 5.14 (Model 1) summarises the way in which traffic engineering research using results from single instrumented vehicles has been assumed to apply to the urban system level. Essentially this research treats the road traffic system as an independent factor, capable of being modified in isolation from feedback effects within the rest of the urban system, for example changes in land use patterns. The reasoning tends to assume a simple, linear flow on of effects from improving average traffic speeds, as shown in the model.

However, urban systems are rarely that simple. It is therefore possible to suggest a series of likely feedback effects of free-flowing and congested traffic which might characterise the processes operating within zones of the city or the city as a whole (Figure 5.14, Models 2a and b). Note the way the results of the traffic engineering research have been incorporated into this more involved picture.

At present the simpler traffic engineering approach in Model 1 is the one which has gained credence among the policy making levels of national governments and other institutions and the provision of smoother, freer-flowing traffic systems for reasons of energy conservation and emissions abatement is now an established goal in many cities. Most major cost-benefit models justifying road proposals incorporate significant community benefits from fuel savings (and sometimes emissions) based on predicted savings due to improvements in average speed. Such models have had virtually universal acceptance for around 40 years. The following statements are indicative of this acceptance and show clearly how basic traffic engineering research, based on Model 1 assumptions, is used to formulate urban policy on roads and congestion.

The National Association of Australian State Road Authorities (NAASRA, 1984) in a major roads study concluded the following about Australia's urban road system:

"In 1981, eight per cent of travel was on roads with very low peak hour travel speeds of less than 20 kilometres per hour. Almost half was on roads with peak hour speeds less than 40 kilometres per hour. Projections of future travel speed show that a 25 per cent funding increase would be required to prevent a reduction in already low travel speeds. A 25 per cent increase would also save 110 million litres of fuel, representing a large proportion of all savings which could be achieved by any practical means." (p. 4)

145

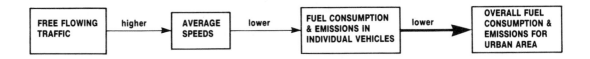

Model 1: Linear Assumptions

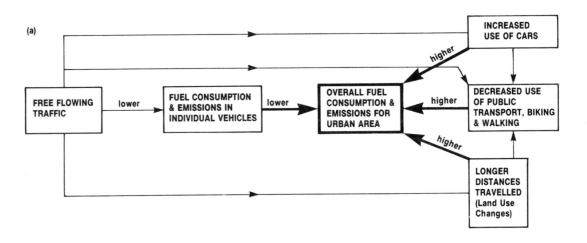

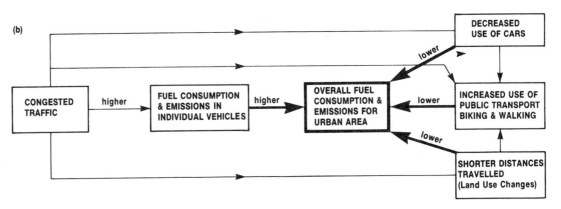

Model 2: Feedback Assumptions (a) Freeflowing Traffic, &
(b) Congested Traffic

Figure 5.14   Conceptual models for understanding transport energy use
                in cities.

146

In Melbourne a proposed major freeway project to link two existing freeways was partially justified on the basis that it would save significant quantities of fuel. The following statement by the Royal Automobile Club of Victoria summarises the argument.

"Fuel savings by private and business vehicles are estimated at 8.5 litres per 100 km on a freeway link, which means that if the two freeways were joined, an annual 1.7 million litres of petrol valued at $0.6 million, based on a price of 35 cents per litre, would be saved. For commercial vehicles, the estimated quantity of fuel saved is an annual 210,000 litres valued at $73,000. The annual fuel saving bill is some $0.67 million for all vehicles which is regarded as conservative as it is based on the performance of a single passenger vehicle and does not take into account the extra distance travelled on the arterial road system." (Royalauto, July, 1982, p. 4)

The strength of feeling about how important extra road funding is in terms of fuel savings is shown by an article in the Royal Automobile Club of Western Australia journal:

"About 96,500 litres of fuel a day are wasted in Sydney morning peak hour traffic congestion, according to the Australian Road Research Board ... An audit of 5 studies showed that better traffic management could save up to 10% of fuel used in peak hours in cities ... What the Bureau did not say is that improved urban road systems are also significant contributors to fuel saving, a point which the RAC and its sister organisations in Australia have been making with successive Federal Governments on the issue of road funding ... Perhaps one day the penny will drop!" (The Road Patrol, October-November, 1985, p. 8).

In terms of urban policy on roads, congestion, fuel conservation and emissions abatement, it is therefore, important to answer the question "Does free flowing traffic actually save energy and lower emissions in the overall city?" To provide the answer requires an approach which tests the conceptual models in Figure 5.14 by integrating real data from the traffic engineering, transport planning and urban planning levels outlined in Figure 5.13.

This section will attempt to do this by:
(1) looking at the overview data from the thirty-two cities,
(2) examining a detailed set of data from Perth which enables the trade-off between fuel-efficient vehicles and a fuel-efficient city to be examined,
(3) assessing some "internal evidence" from surveys related to public transport and sub-optimal vehicle usage, and
(4) comparing Perth and New York to see how two very different cities compare on this issue.

1. Data from international cities study   Table 5.4 contains the data on average traffic network speeds, average public transport speeds and gasoline use for the thirty-two cities. These data suggest that it is the cities with the highest average traffic speeds that have the highest per capita gasoline consumption. Thus free flowing traffic is not associated with lower fuel use in this global survey. It is in fact cities with the most constrained traffic flows that have the lowest per capita gasoline use as hypothesised by us. The positive correlation between the two parameters is statistically significant.

In order to better understand how the Sourcebook data provides perspective on the two models and confirms the hypothesis regarding free flowing traffic, it is necessary to reiterate the findings outlined in previous chapters. As outlined in Chapter 3, the range of fuel consumption in the survey is very large from the US cities with an average of around 58,500 MJ per capita to Australian cities around 29,800 per capita, European cities 13,300 MJ per capita and Asian cities 5,500 MJ per capita. The variation in gasoline use was analysed in Chapter 3 and 4 and the following general relationships found:

• Not more than half of the variation can be explained by vehicle size, income and gasoline price;

• There is a close association with urban form factors such as density of jobs and residents and central city strength;

• Gasoline use is also closely linked to the degree to which the city provides automobile infrastructure in the form of roads and car parking.

The various factors and cities in the global study were clustered and the resulting total picture is presented again in Table 5.5 outlining the key variables that do influence transport energy (and emissions). Note especially the systematic way in which transport energy use per capita diminishes from left to right across the table as the whole city and transportation system becomes less oriented to private vehicles and more oriented to public transport, walking and cycling. In particular, road provision per capita declines from a high of 9m per person for the highest energy consuming group (53000 MJ per capita annually) to a low of about 1m per person in the lowest energy consuming cities (8500 MJ per capita annually). Congestion, as measured by vehicles per km of road and car kms per kilometre of road, also increases progressively as gasoline use declines. Here again is evidence that greater provision of urban roads and free-flowing traffic systems are not energy conserving policies. Rather they appear to be part of a broader urban process which creates greater automobile dependency in cities through progressively less dense, less centralised land use patterns, greater overall provision for cars and diminishing viability of public transport, walking and bicycling.

In terms of public transport speeds, Table 5.4 also shows that those cities with the lowest overall public transport operating speeds have the highest energy. This is because they tend to be totally or predominantly bus-based and buses simply can't compete in speed terms with private automobiles. As already pointed out, the range of bus speeds for the cities is remarkably small, tending to be around 20 to 21 km/h and never exceeding 25 km/h. On the other hand, those cities with significant rail-systems tend to have much faster overall public transport operating speeds because train systems have average speeds typically above 40 km/h and up to 55 km/h in some cases. Such systems provide very good competition to the automobile for speed of access. Thus the only high average speed which appears to correlate with

Table 5.4
Gasoline use and average transportation speeds for the thirty-two cities.

City	Gasoline Use (MJ per person)	Average speed of traffic (km/h)	Average speed of public transport (km/h)			
			Bus	Train	Tram	Overall
US cities						
Houston	74510	51	22	-	-	22
Phoenix	69908	42	23	-	-	23
Detroit	65978	44	21	42	-	22
Denver	63466	45	21	-	-	21
Los Angeles	58474	45	21	-	-	21
San Francisco	55365	46	22	45	15	29
Boston	54185	39	18	45	20	30
Washington	51241	39	18	40	-	26
Chicago	48246	41	18	47	-	37
New York	44033	35	15	35	-	31
Average	58541	43	20	42	18	26
Australian cities						
Perth	32610	43	22	35	-	24
Brisbane	30653	48	23	37	-	31
Melbourne	29104	48	21	33	18	28
Adelaide	28791	43	21	45	28	29
Sydney	27986	39	20	45	-	37
Average	29829	44	21	39	23	30
Canadian city						
Toronto	34813	?	20	34	16	25
European cities						
Hamburg	16671	30	22	36	-	31
Frankfurt	16093	30	22	44	17	37
Zürich	15709	36	20	46	15	33
Stockholm	15574	30	25	36	26	32
Brussels	14744	?	20	38	17	27
Paris	14091	28	13	45	-	40
London	12426	31	18	38	-	31
München	12372	35	20	55	17	44
West Berlin	11331	28	20	32	-	27
Copenhagen	11106	45	24	54	-	38
Vienna	10074	30	19	38	17	23
Amsterdam	9171	39	18	57	15	36
Average	13280	30	20	43	18	33
Asian cities						
Tokyo	8488	21	12	40	13	38
Singapore	6003	30	19	-	-	19
Hong Kong	1987	21	15	31	10	17
Average	5493	24	15	36	12	25
USSR city						
Moscow	380	45	21	41	18	>37
Correlation coefficients with gasoline use (excluding Moscow)		.703*	.273	-.048	-.260	-.376*

Table 5.5

Transportation and land use characteristics and the co-existence of transportation modes in principal world cities (1980).

Factors and variables / Category of city	Class I - Very high automobile dependence almost no role for public transport, walking or cycling, very high gasoline use	Class II - High automobile dependence, minor though significant role for public transport, walking and cycling, high gasoline use.	Class III - Moderate automobile dependence, important role for public transport, walking and cycling moderate gasoline use.	Class IV - Low automobile dependence, public transport, walking and cycling equal with cars, low gasoline use.	Class V - Very low automobile dependence, public transport, walking and cycling more important than cars, very low gasoline use.
Land use intensity					
Urban density (persons/ha)	12.2	15.4	42.1	58.0	117.3
Employment density (jobs/ha)	6.0	7.3	23.9	32.9	53.9
Outer area density (persons/ha)	10.7	12.8	32.8	48.7	83.9
Outer area employment density (jobs/ha)	4.3	5.0	12.5	18.8	28.5
Inner area density (persons/ha)	23.7	45.1	81.7	83.0	331.4
Inner area employment density (jobs/ha)	19.5	37.2	65.4	67.1	211.3
Orientation to non-automobile modes					
Total vehicles per 1000 people	684	570	422	366	254
Cars per 1000 people	539	479	367	318	192
Per capita car passenger kms	12,822	11,359	7,384	5,185	2,966
Per capita public transportation passenger kms	362	887	1,664	1,890	2,519
Proportion of passenger kms on public transportation (%)	2.9	7.4	18.6	27.2	49.2
Proportion of workers using public transportation (%)	8.6	19.3	32.0	33.3	52.5
Proportion of workers using private transportation (%)	87.2	74.4	51.7	45.4	23.7
Proportion of workers using foot and bicycle (%)	4.2	6.3	16.3	21.3	23.8
Level of traffic restraint					
Length of road per person (m)	8.8	5.7	3.0	1.9	1.1
Parking spaces per 1000 CBD jobs	514	208	160	185	137
Vehicles per km of road	91	105	159	193	247
Car kms per km of road	1,068,857	1,364,838	1,723,132	1,725,693	1,665,405
Degree of centralisation					
CBD population density (persons/ha)	14.2	45.6	78.7	89.2	158.6
Proportion of population in CBD (%)	0.3	0.7	1.5	3.9	3.9
Proportion of jobs in CBD (%)	11.4	15.0	18.4	20.7	19.8
Public transportation performance					
Vehicle kms per person	29.6	47.9	74.1	86.6	86.1
Passenger trips per person	46.1	106.3	229.6	324.3	371.4
Passenger trips per vehicle km	1.5	2.3	3.3	3.9	4.4
System average speed (km/h)	24.0	31.3	30.8	30.9	31.5
Energy use per passenger km (MJ)	2.12	1.13	0.88	0.58	0.52
Proportion public transport passenger kms on trains(%)	13.3	53.9	54.9	51.0	51.4
Transportation energy conservation status	Very poor	Generally poor but a few positive features	Significant conservation	Strongly conserving	Very strongly conserving
Gasoline use per capita (MJ)	53,049	44,355	22,846	12,445	8,588

Cities in each category and their cluster scores based on all factors.

Cities	Cluster scores	Cities	Cluster score	Cities	Cluster score	Cities	Cluster score	Cities	Cluster score
Phoenix	92	Washington	255	Toronto	433	Amsterdam	574	Münich	641
Houston	95	Melbourne	302	New York	464	Frankfurt	585	Singapore	643
Denver	145	Boston	310	Copenhagen	496	West Berlin	598	Paris	648
Detroit	151	Chicago	349	Hamburg	549	Vienna	605	Hong Kong	694
Perth	168	San Francisco	357	Zürich	567	London	612	Tokyo	721
Adelaide	208	Sydney	361	Brussels	570	Stockholm	614		
Los Angeles	221								
Brisbane	223								

150

low fuel use is that of public transport, not private transport.

2. *Data from the Perth driving cycle study* These data enable a closer look at the hypothesis by examining in one city how there is a trade-off between vehicle fuel efficiency and more fuel- efficient land use patterns.

Between 1980 and 1983, Perth Western Australia was the subject of an intensive traffic study using a computer-instrumented vehicle (Kenworthy, Newman and Lyons, 1983). The purpose of this study was to develop a driving cycle for Perth by collecting a range of representative driving pattern data on all types of roads from the central city to the urban fringe. The instrumented vehicle was used to "chase" vehicles in morning, evening and off-peak periods to record traffic conditions, and the fuel consumed by the instrumented vehicle in all these conditions was recorded using an accurate fuel meter. These data, which amounted to over 3000km of urban driving, are one of the most detailed sets of data on urban traffic conditions and vehicular fuel consumption to date and more importantly the data are able to provide perspective on average speeds and vehicle efficiency in a cross sectional area through the city.

As part of this traffic study a comprehensive survey was also made of the broader land use and transportation characteristics of the Perth Metropolitan Area, including per capita gasoline use on a small zone basis from central to outer areas. In fact the same spatial framework (thirty-eight zones amalgamated into six larger homogeneous areas) was used for the traffic study and this broader analysis. Hence, it was possible to combine the detailed traffic engineering work involving fuel consumption of individual vehicles (vehicle level research) with an understanding of the land use patterns and transportation processes and their resulting per capita gasoline use (city level research), as outlined in Figure 5.13. Details of per capita gasoline use in Perth on a small area basis and the corresponding land use and transportation analysis (Newman, Kenworthy and Lyons, 1985) were linked with the vehicle level research and city level research in order to assess if there is in fact a trade-off between the provision of freer-flowing traffic and more fuel-efficient vehicles and the development of a more fuel-efficient city overall (Newman and Kenworthy, 1986). The following summarises this research and extends it in a simple way to include emissions and then time savings.

Tables 5.6 and 5.7 capture the major results of the traffic pattern and vehicular fuel consumption analysis as well as the per capita gasoline use in each of the six major areas of Perth. It is clear from these tables that while congestion diminishes significantly from central to outer areas (eg average speeds improve 54%) and vehicle fuel consumption improves, actual per capita fuel use by residents in these areas increases significantly. Vehicles in central areas have 19% lower fuel efficiency than the Perth average due to congestion but the central area residents use 22% less actual fuel, and conversely, congestion-free outer suburban driving is 12% more fuel efficient than average but residents use 29% more actual fuel. It is important to stress that the per capita fuel data incorporates the factor of vehicle fuel efficiency due to traffic conditions.

Table 5.6

Traffic patterns and distance from the CBD in the six areas of Perth, 1981.

Area	Distance from central city (km)	Average speed (km/h)	Stops per km	Positive kinetic energy (m/s^2)
1	2	33.8	1.57	0.53
2	5	41.3	0.89	0.46
3	9	45.5	0.56	0.39
4	11	46.7	0.67	0.39
5	13	44.9	0.76	0.38
6	19	52.2	0.32	0.33
Perth average	-	43.4	0.84	0.42

Table 5.7

Variations in vehicular fuel consumption and per capita fuel use with   3D
distance from the CBD in the six areas of Perth, 1981.

Area	Distance from central city (km)	Vehicle fuel cons. (ml/km)	% Diff. rel. to Perth average	Per capita fuel use (MJ/person/yr)	% Diff. rel. to Perth average
1	2	147.0	+18.6%	23,624	-22.0%
2	5	128.5	+3.7%	25,634	-15.4%
3	9	118.5	-4.4%	28,930	-4.5%
4	11	117.4	-5.2%	27,785	-8.3%
5	13	119.0	-4.0%	32,783	+8.5%
6	19	108.9	-12.1%	39,015	+28.8%
Perth average	-	123.9	-	30,286	-

These results are depicted graphically in Figure 5.15 which suggests that there is indeed a trade-off in energy terms between attempting to improve the fuel-efficiency of the traffic system through raising average speeds and trying to foster an urban system which is more fuel-efficient overall. Looking at these results in terms of the models in Figure 5.14 it appears that the feedback parameters such as land use factors and modes of travel exert an influence on gasoline use far in excess of the fuel efficiency of vehicles as determined by traffic conditions. In other words, in the congested but denser and more compact central and inner areas travel distances are shorter for all modes and there is greater use of public transport, walking and cycling. In outer areas densities of development are low, travel distances are long and a much higher proportion of travel is by automobile with less public transport, walking and cycling. Tables 5.8 and 5.9 support this analysis by providing the average trip length, public transport service and modal split data for the six areas.

The interpretation that locational, land use and modal split factors are the overriding influence in determining actual gasoline use in a city and that these tend to swamp the effects of vehicle fuel efficiency are further supported by Figure 5.16. This figure draws together data on per capita gasoline use for Perth based on more finely detailed areas (thirty-eight

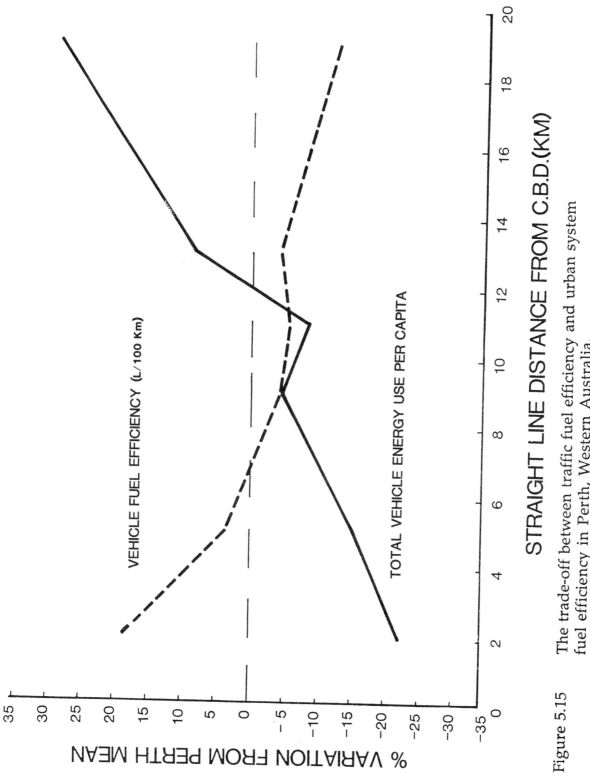

Figure 5.15   The trade-off between traffic fuel efficiency and urban system fuel efficiency in Perth, Western Australia.

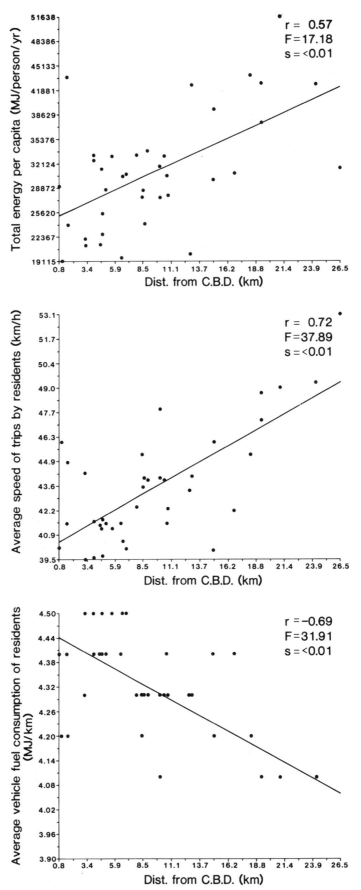

Figure 5.16   Variation of total transport energy per capita, average trip speed and average vehicle fuel consumption as a function of distance from the Perth CBD.

154

zones). However, unlike in Figure 5.15 where driving pattern and fuel consumption data are based on the instrumented vehicle survey, the average speed and fuel consumption of vehicles come from independent government transport surveys and are based on resident's trips anywhere in the city. As can be seen, the average speed of trips by people living at various distances from the CBD improves markedly from central to outer areas and the fuel efficiency of their vehicles improves in the same way. However, their total gasoline use actually increases in a complete reversal of the linear assumptions model underlying the traffic engineering research. It is important to note also that the gasoline usage patterns by suburban area do not follow income patterns.

Table 5.8
Variations in average trip length for various trip types with distance from the CBD in the six areas of Perth.

| Area | Distance from CBD | 1976 average trip lengths (km) | | | | |
		Work	Social/ Recreational	Shopping	Other	Overall
1	2	7.0	5.9	2.7	4.8	5.0
2	5	6.8	7.4	3.7	5.3	5.7
3	9	9.3	6.6	3.8	5.3	6.0
4	11	13.0	6.9	4.2	5.7	6.9
5	13	11.9	7.8	5.4	6.2	7.2
6	19	13.0	9.7	5.9	7.9	8.8
Perth average	-	10.0	7.2	4.4	5.9	6.6

Table 5.9
Variations in public transport service and modal split with distance from the CBD in the six areas of Perth.

Area	Distance from CBD	Public transport service kilometres per hectare of urbanised land (km)	%Total trips by car	%Total trips by public transport, walking and cycling
1	2	12.0	61.2	38.8
2	5	2.5	71.2	28.8
3	9	2.7	73.5	26.5
4	11	1.3	64.7	35.3
5	13	0.9	72.7	27.3
6	19	0.4	78.1	21.9
Perth average-		1.7	71.4	28.6

This analysis can be extended to include emissions (Figure 5.17). Like fuel consumption, emissions of CO (carbon monoxide) and HC (hydrocarbons or unburnt gasoline) from automobile tailpipes are dependent upon the average speed of travel with obvious improvements as average speed increases. NOx (nitrogen oxides) are only slightly dependent on vehicle speed (Kent and Mudford, 1979). By using the speed dependent equations for CO and HC of Australian vehicles (CO (g/km) = 0.8 + (510/V) and HC (g/km) = 0.6 + (34/V) from Taylor and Anderson (1982) where V is the average speed in km/h), it is possible to calculate the vehicle emission production rates and

155

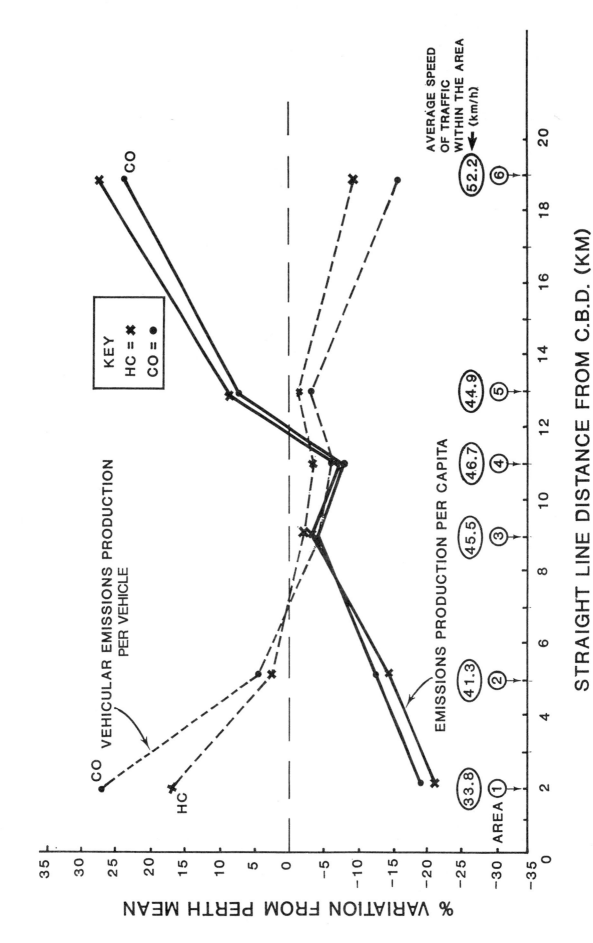

Figure 5.17   The trade-off between low polluting traffic and a low polluting urban system in Perth, Western Australia.

156

per capita emissions for each of the six areas in Perth. The per capita figures of course incorporate an emissions factor based on average speed of travel.

Figure 5.17 shows clearly that while vehicles driven in the Perth central area at 33.8 km/h average speed have 17% to 27% more HC and CO emissions respectively per kilometre of travel relative to the average for Perth, residents of the area actually generate 19% to 21% less total CO and HC respectively due to their smaller use of the automobile and greater use of other modes. Conversely in outer areas there is a positive benefit in terms of emissions from vehicles with the average speed of 52.2 km/h yielding 9% to 16% lower emissions per kilometre (HC and CO respectively) than the average for Perth. However, residents of the outer suburbs actually generate some 24% to 27% more CO and HC respectively than the average for Perth residents due to their longer auto travel distances and less use of other modes.

As with fuel, a pattern emerges of a significant trade-off between attempting to control emissions through improving traffic flows and the overall effect this has on the actual amount of emissions produced. In other words higher average traffic speed appears to spread the city, creating lower density land use, a greater need for cars, longer travel distances and reduced use of other less polluting or pollution-free modes. The benefits gained in terms of less polluting traffic streams appear to be overwhelmed by the sheer amount of extra travel and the resulting bulk of emissions. These results are also in broad keeping with Berry et al., (1974) as detailed earlier in the book. Berry et al., showed that it is the lower density, more automobile orientated US cities that have the worst total environmental pollution.

Thus the evidence from the Perth Driving Cycle study suggests that in Perth at least, free flowing traffic is associated with increased fuel use and increased emissions.

3. *Data from corridor studies in Perth* Supportive evidence on the mechanism as to how this effect of free flowing traffic works its way back into greater use of the automobile and also non-optimal use of the automobile, are provided by some corridor studies in Perth.

(i) The effects of free flowing traffic on public transport use

An attitudinal survey was conducted of bus and train passengers who use a transportation corridor in Perth (Kenworthy and Newman, 1985). The aim of this study was to assess the importance of road congestion in their decision to use public transport. In particular the survey attempted to find out how many people might transfer from public transport to cars should congestion be significantly reduced or eliminated in the corridor. The survey showed some 17% of bus passengers and 11% of train passengers would transfer if the congestion was eased. It was calculated that if only half of these passengers actually did transfer to cars, the extra gasoline use would be enough to cancel out the savings from a computer-coordinated set of traffic signals along the corridor designed to smooth out traffic flows. It should be remembered that Perth is the least congested city in our sample so that the congestion factor here is likely to be the bare minimum of what could be expected in other cities. The congestion factor should also be possible to find in patronage comparisons between corridors.

157

Bus patronage in Perth was examined in freeway corridors and corridors without freeways to see if congestion levels were impacting on patronage. Freeway related bus services in Perth were found to be declining faster in the average number of passengers carried per service than other bus services, some of which in the relatively congested inner areas were found to be actually improving their passenger carrying performance (Kenworthy and Newman, 1985). This was in a period shortly after the Freeway was opened and little congestion was obvious. After a few years congestion at peak periods began to occur and the bus services again began to pick up patronage. These surveys show in practical terms the shortcomings of confining traffic management or engineering strategy assessments to the immediate effects on the road traffic stream. They show that reducing congestion can have important feedback effects particularly on public transport which may significantly alter the picture of gasoline savings (or emissions reductions) derived from simple fuel consumption and traffic models.

(ii) The effects of free flowing traffic on vehicle efficiency

Not all free flowing traffic improves the fuel efficiency of a vehicle. As mentioned before, vehicles are generally engineered to perform in a fuel-optimal way at speeds of around 55 to 60 km/h. A study in Perth was designed to find the fuel and time implications of freeway speed limits and examined how optimal were the driving conditions in freeway and other driving conditions (Kenworthy et al., 1986).

The study found that increases in the speed limit above 80 km/h involve progressively greater fuel penalties of up to 31% at 110 km/h for an 8 km length of freeway. Our investigation into driving patterns in Perth during 1980 to 1983, found that Perth already has over a third of its daily travel at speeds above the fuel-optimal speed of 55 km/h (Kenworthy, Newman and Lyons, 1983). Using some simulated urban trips under controlled cruise conditions it was found that average speed alone is actually a misleading criterion, even in assessing the energy efficiency of a road system per se. This is because higher average speeds are often achieved by merely increasing the potential for higher cruise speeds between stops. Thus two trips can have the same average speed with very different fuel economy, ie one trip achieves its average speed by higher cruise speeds to offset idle periods and has much poorer fuel economy than a trip which has low cruise speeds but fewer stops and idle periods.

This Perth study suggests therefore that traffic policies which encourage further increases in cruise speeds such as increasing speed limits, freeway building and road widening will be counter-productive for energy conservation. On the other hand, traffic policies that minimise stops and idling periods while keeping cruise speeds close to 55 km/h will save fuel. This means that for energy conservation, roads and signal systems should be designed to encourage low travel speeds with fewer stops and shorter idle periods. Policies that seek to achieve a "blanket" increase in average speeds by increasing cruise speeds (eg raising speed limits or building more freeways), will more than likely be counter-productive in energy terms.

The Perth evidence suggests that the conditions under which a policy of constrained cruise speeds might be more practicable would most likely include:

1. Higher traffic levels along arterial roads with computer-linked traffic signals;

2. A more compact urban form where travel distances are much shorter and more suitable to a reduction in cruise speeds.

Higher density activity also means more intensively used roads which lower cruise speeds so that if at the same time stops can be lowered it would lead to better fuel efficiency. As already shown, high density areas are also fundamentally lower in their use of transport energy because of greater walking, cycling and public transport and short trip lengths. It may therefore be possible to optimise land use and traffic systems as far as energy conservation is concerned, by pursuing the same policy of increased concentration of urban activity.

The sort of traffic patterns and urban form which appear in the above analysis to be associated with lower energy use (and emissions) are therefore very different from the city with low congestion and high average speed like Perth. This therefore leads us to the final study - a comparison of Perth with New York.

4. Data from a comparison of Perth and New York As part of the data collection for the Sourcebook, average speed, per capita fuel use and urban density data were found on New York by region which enabled a simple comparison with Perth concerning how transport energy use patterns change from congested central areas to free-flowing outer areas. New York is a very different type of city to Perth as it has extreme levels of congestion in its high density central and inner areas. It thus offers the potential for a comparison at the other end of the traffic spectrum from Perth.

Table 5.10 presents data on New York in terms of gasoline use, average traffic speed and urban density for the central, inner and outer areas as well as the whole city and compares them with Perth. The overall energy efficiency of New York clearly improves as congestion gets worse, despite the obvious deterioration in the energy efficiency of the traffic system that would occur from New York's outer areas to the centre of Manhattan.

Table 5.10
Gasoline use, average traffic speed and urban density by city region in the New York Tri-State Metropolitan Area, 1980.

Area	Gasoline use (MJ per capita)	Average traffic network speed (km/h)	Urban density (persons/ha)
Outer area New York	59590	40.1	13
Whole city (New York Tri-State Metro area)	44033	34.9	20
Inner area (City of New York)	20120	25.8	107
Central city (New York County incl. Manhattan)	11860	16.1	251

159

Figure 5.18 pictures this contrast between Perth and New York. The same qualitative pattern is evident linking lower overall fuel use with slower traffic speeds, however in New York it is even more extreme. Further detailed studies on New York or on a European or Asian city would help to delineate the patterns developed here. However, the evidence suggests that other cities, most of which have greater congestion than Perth, are likely to have an even more positive relationship between congestion and the fuel-efficiency of their city.

Conclusion to the four sets of data on energy and emissions The studies of Perth as a whole system and by corridor and the global cities comparison confirm the picture that free flowing traffic does not lead to savings in fuel or lowering of emissions in a city overall. The means of achieving these savings appears to lie in more fundamental transport and land use planning related to travel distances and modes as well as in changes at the vehicle level. In other words, the central focus needs to be on automobile dependence rather than any tinkering with how well a vehicle is performing in the traffic stream. Land use patterns which give rise to automobile dependence, as discussed in this book, are usually promoted by most attempts at easing congestion and are thus counterproductive in the longer term.

Congestion and time savings

It is generally perceived that the major disbenefit of urban traffic congestion is the extra travel times involved in gaining access to the range of urban facilities. Congestion is removed or reduced by building new roads, widening existing ones, creating one way traffic systems and coordinating traffic signals; overall savings in travel time are virtually always predicted to result from such projects. Time savings are given an appropriate dollar value, and together with the dollar value of fuel savings and other savings such as reduced wear and tear on vehicles, they form the major part of the community benefits estimated to accrue from the project.

We have examined this question of net community time savings from free-flowing traffic by examining our international cities data from the perspective of the vehicle and passenger hours implied by the data in each city. Vehicle hours for cars were simply derived by dividing the total VKT in cars by the average speed of the traffic network; for public transport, vehicle hours were obtained by dividing the vehicle kilometres for each mode by the average speed of that mode. Passenger hours were derived in the same way except that passenger kms by each mode formed the numerator of the calculation of the two items. Passenger hours is probably the fairest since it can be thought of as representing the total personal time commitment in motorised modes necessary to gain access to urban needs in each city. It also takes into account the much greater importance of public transport in the European and Asian cities.

Table 5.11 contains the data resulting from these calculations expressed as annual vehicle and passenger hours per capita by car and public transport. It can be seen very clearly that there are much higher total per capita vehicle

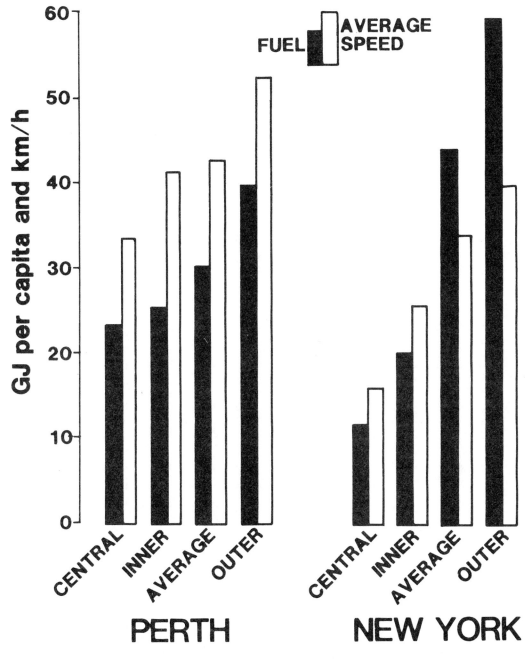

Figure 5.18   Comparison between Perth and New York showing how gasoline use per capita and average traffic speeds varies across the two urban areas.

Table 5.11
Vehicle and passenger hours per capita in cars and public transport in the international cities (1980).

City	Car vehicle hours per capita	Public transport vehicle hours per capita	Total vehicle hours per capita	Public transport as % of total	Car passenger hours per capita	Public transport passenger hours	Total passenger hours per capita	Public transport as % of total
US Cities								
Houston	194	0.4	194.4	0.2	312	5.9	317.9	1.9
Phoenix	218	0.3	218.3	0.1	294	2.8	296.8	0.9
Detroit	261	0.8	261.8	0.3	316	5.1	321.1	1.6
Denver	209	1.2	210.2	0.6	258	10.3	268.3	3.8
Los Angeles	200	1.2	201.2	0.6	307	17.8	324.8	5.5
San Francisco	205	2.2	207.2	1.1	289	39.0	328.0	11.9
Boston	225	1.2	226.2	0.5	319	20.4	339.4	6.0
Washington	206	1.9	207.9	0.9	302	27.5	329.5	8.4
Chicago	185	1.8	186.8	1.0	271	33.1	304.1	10.9
New York	169	2.6	171.6	1.5	225	46.8	271.8	17.2
Average	**207**	**1.4**	**208.4**	**0.7**	**289**	**20.9**	**309.9**	**6.8**
Australian Cities								
Perth	153	2.2	155.2	1.4	266	25.4	291.4	8.7
Brisbane	135	1.7	136.7	1.2	246	25.5	271.5	9.4
Melbourne	122	2.1	124.1	1.7	213	30.1	243.1	12.4
Adelaide	141	2.2	143.2	1.5	251	25.4	276.4	9.2
Sydney	138	2.6	140.6	1.9	243	45.8	288.8	15.9
Average	**138**	**2.2**	**140.2**	**1.6**	**244**	**30.4**	**274.4**	**11.1**
Canadian City								
Toronto	?	3.6	?	?	?	88.4	?	?
European Cities								
Hamburg	147	2.9	149.9	1.9	247	52.0	299.0	17.4
Frankfurt	142	2.2	144.2	1.5	227	63.6	290.6	21.9
Zürich	120	2.8	122.8	2.3	201	83.7	284.7	29.4
Stockholm	106	4.0	110.0	3.6	143	68.7	211.7	32.5
Brussels	?	2.6	?	?	?	59.0	?	?
Paris	100	2.4	102.4	2.3	150	63.1	213.1	29.6
London	81	4.5	85.5	5.3	142	64.5	206.5	31.2
Munich	93	2.8	95.8	2.9	150	52.3	202.3	25.9
West Berlin	98	3.3	101.3	3.3	164	84.3	265.3	31.2
Copenhagen	77	3.2	80.2	4.0	138	50.9	188.9	27.0
Vienna	89	3.7	92.7	4.0	142	92.9	234.9	39.6
Amsterdam	75	3.2	78.2	4.1	129	76.7	205.7	37.3
Average	**103**	**3.1**	**106.1**	**2.9**	**167**	**67.6**	**234.6**	**28.8**
Asian Cities								
Tokyo	100	3.5	103.5	3.4	140	146.4	286.4	51.1
Singapore	24	5.2	29.2	17.8	59	103.1	162.1	63.6
Hong Kong	17	7.7	24.4	31.6	30	129.9	159.9	81.2
Average	**47**	**5.5**	**52.5**	**10.5**	**76**	**126.5**	**202.5**	**62.5**
USSR City								
Moscow	3	+5.1	8.1	63.0	5	+133.1	138.1	96.4

162

and passenger hours (ie cars and public transport) in the American and Australian cities where average road network speeds are around 44 km/h, than there are in the European and Asian cities where traffic is much more congested and average speeds are around 24 to 30 km/h. The US cities involve a time commitment of some 310 passenger hours per capita of which only 7% is in public transport; the Australian cities are 12% less than this with 274 passenger hours (11% on public transport), while the European cities involve 24% less time than the US cities with 235 passenger hours per capita (29% on public transport) and the Asian cities are the lowest with a total of 203 hours per capita or 35% less than the US cities (63% of this is public transport). A similar though more extreme pattern is in evidence for total vehicle hours per capita (cars and public transport). Obviously there is a travel time commitment for walking and bicycling which is not taken into consideration in Table 5.11. This will increase the transport time commitment for all cities but in particular for European and Asian cities. It may smooth out the differences between the cities so that all end up with a fairly equivalent travel time budget. However, what the table does indicate is that the more auto-dependent a city is, the more massive is the infrastructure for mechanised private travel and yet no obvious time savings for the city as a whole are apparent. People just spend more time in cars.

Relating these findings back to the level of congestion in each of the cities, it is found that total passenger hours per capita has a significant positive correlation with average speed of the road network (0.4562, s<0.10) and total vehicle hours per capita is similar (0.5774, s<0.005). In other words, the results suggest that as the speed of the traffic system increases, so does the actual personal time commitment necessary to maintain participation in the urban system, which would appear to be the reverse of the common assumption about reducing congestion to save time.

The implication here would appear to be similar to that outlined for gasoline use, ie extra speed is not used to save time but to travel further in response to more far flung land uses, and this extra travel involves time expenditure in excess of that saved by travelling faster.

Conclusion to congestion and time savings The conclusion to this section is similar to what we deduced from the energy/emissions section. The apparent benefits to the individual vehicle (and driver) from more free flowing traffic is only a very short term and illusory benefit. The city as a whole will be altered by traffic changes which induce more automobile dependence, particularly land use changes. These changes soon add up to an overall effect of greater energy use, more emissions and as shown in this section, increased travel times (particularly automobile time). Thus the central issue becomes an awareness that congestion need not be a totally negative factor but that it can be used to help a city become less automobile dependent. Some ideas on how this could be begun are outlined below.

Implications

1. Urban road project justification The cost-benefit analyses of major road projects usually incorporate time savings fuel savings and occasionally emissions in their justification. The research outlined here suggests that in urban situations the simple assumptions used in these models are probably wrong. Abelson (1986) in his review of the economics of roads seriously questions the conceptual and data basis of these models, though he only considers the effects on individual vehicles.

As millions of dollars of investment are directed annually into urban roads it would appear to be essential for their justification to be valid. The research conducted here would suggest that fuel (and emissions) would probably be a cost and not a benefit in any calculation that involved all the factors in Model 2. As an interim measure, while better cost-benefit models were being developed, it would seem prudent not to include fuel (or emissions) in road project justification. Similarily with time savings which are generally the major perceived community benefits, it is not a simple matter of predicting vehicle times before and after a new road is constructed and concluding that the road will save x hours of travel time. It has been amply demonstrated over the years that cars expand to fill the available road space and our data certainly suggest that time is not saved in cities with the biggest and best road systems. What appears to be necessary is a more dynamic feedback process built into land use/transport modelling (See Professional politics section in Chapter 4), which incorporates the fact that the new road will influence land use, which will in turn detract from the initial time savings predicted by the model. Without such "real world" effects predicted, time savings will be illusory.

2. Traffic engineers and congestion To most practising traffic engineers these conclusions may seem largely academic since they do not really go far enough in explaining how traffic engineering practice can be modified to cope with them. Traffic engineers must daily confront the problem of how to assess the impacts of traffic congestion and what solutions to offer. Their responses are very much conditioned by a general approach that traffic congestion is always a negative thing and must be eliminated as far as possible; the way they deal with congestion is necessarily determined by the way they think about it.

The data in this study and especially the broad perspective gained from the international comparisons offer an alternative way of viewing congestion: that rather than being something which must always be gotten rid of, congestion can actually be creatively exploited as a tool in helping a city progress towards lower car dependency and lower energy use through a better balance between cars, public transport, walking and bicycling. This concept has sometimes been referred to as "planned congestion" (Hensher, 1977).

Developments along these lines occurred in Europe in the 1960s when it was recognised that building more roads was destroying cities and not ultimately helping the congestion situation either (Hall and Hass-Klau, 1985). This was followed by a change of priorities in transportation policy towards public transport and something of an acceptance that certain levels of congestion are a fact of life in cities. The same awareness has become much more common in Canadian cities in the past decade.

164

A similar recognition would appear to be needed in the Class I and II cities of Australia and the US, at least with regard to major new roads in urban areas. "Planned congestion" could be seen as an opportunity to help contain the outer growth of cities, develop more efficient concentrated nodes of urban activity, shorten travel distances, give priority to public transport and fundamentally lower the automobile dependence and transport energy use of our cities. Obviously, this approach would not preclude managing or alleviating congestion using established traffic management techniques, especially where environmental amenity or the livability of neighbourhoods was at stake, eg the Dutch Woonerf concept (OECD, 1973; OECD Road Research Group, 1978). Neither would it interfere with efforts to optimise traffic systems for fuel efficiency by reducing stops and idle periods without raising cruise speeds and average speeds. However, it would mean a fundamentally different approach to the assessment of major urban traffic problems taking into account the positive benefits of congestion as outlined above. Thus the role of the traffic engineer can change from one of being primarily concerned with alleviating congestion to one of creatively managing congestion. This would place the role of traffic engineers in a much broader context where all actions are closely linked to the broader transportation and land use planning goals of the city. This new approach would appear to be essential if we are to have correct assessments of the role of congestion in many aspects of city planning as well as in the issues examined here.

3. *Congestion and the public* Many will say that accepting congestion is a fundamental denial of their rights, but others have suggested that far from being an economic disincentive, 'automobile restraint' can be a tool to improve a city's 'viability as a business centre' (Small, 1986, p219), that a less car-dependent transport system is far more equitable, especially for the young (Schaeffer and Sclar, 1975) and that such cities provide the opportunity for a more convivial, community-orientated urban society (Illich, 1973). At the very least, it could be suggested that the transition to a lower automobile-using city need not be painful, if the perceived problems from congestion are consistently being offset by real gains in access through new transit systems and new more centrally-located housing.

Reorientation of transport priorities - concluding comments

Reorientation of transport priorities, as outlined here, offers a package of changes which, if integrated with the previous land use changes, should improve each of the five factors outlined in the factor analysis and presented at the start of this chapter as the guide to our policy analysis. The five factors are summarised in Table 5.12 stressing how the transport and land use policies are so closely linked. Figure 5.19 also sets out these links and then shows how the reorientation of transport priorities has a range of other urban policy implications as outlined previously for reurbanisation. The transport infrastructure policies have direct implications for land use and together the two policy areas have a range of economic, environmental and

Table 5.12
The major elements in reorientation of transport priorities in terms of the five factor analysis conclusions, stressing the overlap between transport and land use policies.

- **More intensive land use.**

A rail oriented transit system offers enormous potential for intensification of land use as it can deliver large numbers of people within walking distance of stations. Pedestrian and bicycle facilities supplement this intensification process. The shift from high speed road services will have a large impact on containing land use rather than the urban sprawl associated with freeway extensions.

- **More orientation in transport infrastructure to non-automobile modes.**

This is the major thrust of the re-orientation policy as outlined for parking, roads, transit and infrastructure for other non-auto modes.

- **More restraint on high speed traffic flows.**

The re-orientation policy accepts this directly and redirects funding from high speed roads into traffic management and infrastructure for other non-auto modes. It also uses the land which would have been set aside for such road projects to intensify urban land uses thus encouraging other non-automobile modes.

- **More centralised land use.**

The provision of rapid transit to central city and sub-centres will centralise land use. Especially if this is also done in conjunction with a policy to reduce parking and increase populations in central areas.

- **Better performing public transport.**

The re-orientation policy will undoubtedly improve the performance of public transport through its combination of improved infrastructure, less provision for automobiles and better land use to enhance the use of public transport.

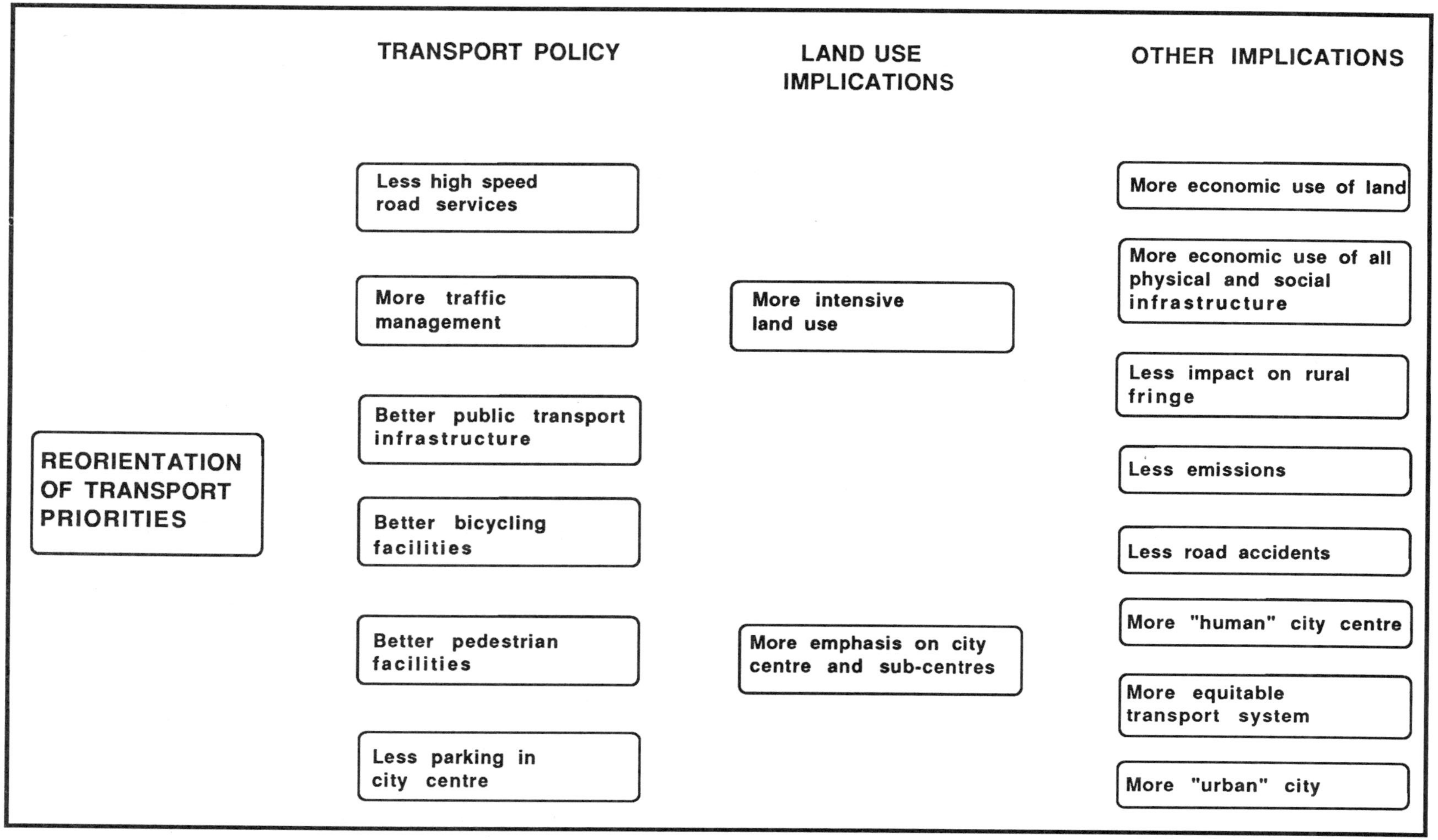

Figure 5.19   Reorientation of transport priorities: Its major policy components and implications for land use planning and other socio-economic and environmental factors.

167

social implications. Reducing dependence on the automobile and gasoline can mean a much better city from many perspectives.

Conclusion

This book suggests that physical planning and transport agencies have a major contribution to make in the reduction of automobile and gasoline dependence in cities. Policies that relate to prices, income and technology as generated by econometricians undoubtedly have their role, as do policies related to more social objectives, but without direction in land use and commitment of transport resources to non-automobile modes, these policies will not be sufficient. The data in this study suggest that there is a large potential for reducing automobile dependence and conserving gasoline in US and Australian cities by changes towards patterns of land use and transport that are evident in other cities around the world and also within some US and Australian cities. They also show other cities how they can further enhance their ability to achieve a more balanced, less vulnerable transport system. The more precise data that are now available provide perspective for physical planners and transport planners to establish achievable goals.

The policies outlined of reurbanisation and reorientation of transport priorities should have value in reducing gasoline and automobile dependence, but a number of other benefits also seem apparent in economic, social and environmental concerns through lower automobile use. Indeed, it is arguable that the reduced dependence on gasoline and the automobile in general is just one element in McNulty's 'return of the livable city' (McNulty *et al.*, 1986).

This book has not attempted to outline in detail the implementation of such policies, it merely attempts to suggest what are feasible goals. The time scale for such changes could possibly be gauged from cities like Detroit and Los Angeles which over a 30 to 40 year period were transformed from being comparatively compact, rail-orientated cities to dispersed, automobile-orientated cities. The process of reurbanisation and reorientation of transport priorities could arguably be even faster with modern technology and more rapid turnover of buildings. Some of the evidence presented here from Toronto, other Canadian cities and from US cities like Washington DC, San Fransisco and Portland suggest that rapid urban change is possible.

The forces of dispersal and greater automobile reliance are obviously very powerful and to overcome them cities must first benefit by recognising what is possible. This book has attempted to set out the patterns of transport and urban form which currently exist in less automobile dependent cities and which could thus be emulated in substance, but in a style and manner fitting to the social, cultural and environmental conditions peculiar to each city.

SOURCEBOOK OF URBAN LAND USE, TRANSPORT AND ENERGY DATA FOR PRINCIPAL CITIES OF NORTH AMERICA, EUROPE, ASIA AND AUSTRALIA, 1960, 1970 AND 1980

PART I   RAW DATA

Adelaide

POPULATION AND AREA	1960	1970	1980
Total population	587,957	842,693	931,886
Urbanised area(ha)	35,067	57,758	72,221
Population of the CBD	4,121	2,660	1,819
Area of the CBD(ha)	222	222	222
Population of the inner city	140,980	128,276	108,140
Area of the inner city(ha)	5,760	5,760	5,760

EMPLOYMENT LOCATION			
Number of jobs in the CBD	56,500	56,156	55,663
Number of jobs in the inner city	?	140,066	144,464
Number of jobs in the outer area	?	194,040	242,750
Number of jobs in the metro.area	?	334,106	387,214

PARKING SUPPLY IN THE CBD			
Off street parking spaces	7,367	?	17,126
On street parking spaces	6,595	?	4,020
Total parking spaces	13,962	17,000	21,146

ROAD NETWORK (km)			
Sealed	?	4,833	6,888
Formed and surfaced	?	?	1,134
Formed only	?	?	165
Unformed	?	?	319
Total roads in the metro.area	3,420	7,598	8,506

MOTOR VEHICLES ON REGISTER			
Cars and station wagons	146,537	293,115	456,740
Utilities and panel vans	19,237	?	40,929
Rigid trucks	?	?	19,088
Articulated trucks	?	?	2,525
Other truck types	667	?	4,199
Total trucks(***)	11,049	?	25,812
Total commercial vehicles(***)	30,286	36,222	66,741
Motor cycles	10,127	12,051	21,386
Buses	1,040	1,737	1,406
Total vehicles on register	187,990	293,115	546,273

*(items marked***are sub totals)*

PRIVATE TRANSPORT INDICATORS			
Total annual V.K.T.	$2.3218*10^9$	$4.5521*10^9$	$6.5301*10^9$
Total annual V.K.T.in cars	$1.8308*10^9$	$3.8778*10^9$	$5.6052*10^9$
Average vehicle occupancy	1.9	1.9	1.78
Car occupant kilometres	$3.4785*10^9$	$7.3678*10^9$	$9.9921*10^9$
Average road network speed(km/h)	?	?	42.8

TRANSPORTATION ENERGY USE			
Motor spirit consumption (Joules)	$1.0600*10^{16}$	$2.0624*10^{16}$	$2.7667*10^{16}$
Diesel fuel consumption (Joules)	$1.1937*10^{15}$	$2.0149*10^{15}$	$5.1917*10^{15}$
Total fuel consumption (Joules)	$1.1794*10^{16}$	$2.2639*10^{16}$	$3.2859*10^{16}$

MODAL SPLIT FOR THE JOURNEY TO WORK (% of workers)

Public transport	?	19.6	16.5
Private transport	?	75.0	77.7
Walking and cycling	?	7.0	5.8

AVERAGE TRIP LENGTHS (km)

Journey to work	?	?	?
Other trip purposes	?	?	?

PUBLIC TRANSPORT INDICATORS

VEHICLE KILOMETRES

-Buses			
Municipal motor bus	16,607,150	16,718,240	37,197,000
Municipal trolley bus	1,138,270	0	0
Private motor bus	5,625,340	10,743,530	0
Total	*23,370,760*	*27,461,770*	*37,197,000*
-Trains			
Suburban rail	17,430,000	11,882,000	9,620,000
-Trams			
Municipal tramways	874,230	669,760	802,000
-Ferries	0	0	0
Grand total	*41,674,990*	*40,013,530*	*47,619,000*

PASSENGERS CARRIED

-Buses			
Municipal motor bus	52,549,504	38,559,000	61,007,000
Municipal trolley bus	3,593,632	0	0
Private motor bus	10,490,000	14,856,000	0
Total	*66,633,136*	*53,415,000*	*61,007,000*
-Trains			
Suburban rail	14,584,000	13,393,000	13,815,000
-Trams			
Municipal tramways	2,768,864	2,700,000	2,678,000
-Ferries	0	0	0
Grand total	*83,986,000*	*69,508,000*	*77,500,000*

AVERAGE TRIP LENGTH (km)

-Buses			
Municipal motor bus	4.5	5.0	6.4
Municipal trolley bus	4.5	0.0	0.0
Private motor bus	6.0	7.0	0.0
-Trains			
Suburban rail	13.0	12.8	14.8
-Trams			
Municipal tramways	6.5	6.5	6.5
-Ferries	0.0	0.0	0.0

PASSENGER KILOMETRES
-Buses

Municipal motor bus	236,472,768	188,745,000	388,004,520
Municipal trolley bus	16,171,344	0	0
Private motor bus	62,940,000	103,992,000	0
Total	*315,584,112*	*292,737,000*	*388,004,520*

-Trains

Suburban rail	189,008,640	170,760,750	204,462,000

-Trams

	17,997,616	17,550,000	17,407,000

-Ferries

	0	0	0
Grand total	*522,590,368*	*481,047,750*	*609,873,520*

AVERAGE SPEED (km/h)
-Buses

Municipal motor buses	18.0	18.0	21.0
Municipal trolley bus	16.0	0.0	0.0
Private motor bus	23.0	23.0	0.0
Overall bus speed	*18.9*	*19.8*	*21.0*

-Trains

Suburban rail	28.0	30.0	45.0

-Trams

Municipal tramways	29.0	28.0	28.0

-Ferries

	0.0	0.0	0.0
All modes average	*22.5*	*23.7*	*29.2*

ENERGY CONSUMPTION
-Buses

Municipal motor bus			
Diesel (litres)	4,982,100	5,517,000	15,283,094
Municipal trolley bus			
Elec.(kWh)	2,390,400	0	0
Private motor bus			
Diesel (litres)	0	3,008,200	0
Petrol(litres)	2,193,900	0	0
Total(Joules)	*2.7548*10^{14}*	*3.2643*10^{14}*	*5.8519*10^{14}*

-Trains

Suburban rail			
Diesel(litres)	4,159,800	4,191,800	9,230,074
Total(Joules)	*1.5928*10^{14}*	*1.6050*10^{14}*	*3.5342*10^{14}*

-Trams

Municipal tramways			
Elec.(kWh)	2,089,400	1,634,200	1,783,920
Total(Joules)	*7.5218*10^{12}*	*5.8831*10^{12}*	*6.4221*10^{12}*

-Ferries

	0	0	0
Grand total(Joules)	*4.4228*10^{14}*	*4.9281*10^{14}*	*9.4503*10^{14}*

Amsterdam

POPULATION AND AREA	1960	1970	1980
Total population			
City of Amsterdam	869,600	831,500	716,900
Agglomeration of Amsterdam	889,400	918,700	812,500
Urbanised area(ha)(City of Amsterdam)	8,918	12,956	14,122
Population of the CBD	131,700	93,500	69,400
Area of the CBD(ha)	640	640	640
Population of the inner city	596,800	498,600	424,600
Area of the inner city(ha)	5,100	5,100	5,100
EMPLOYMENT LOCATION			
Number of jobs in the CBD	180,000	168,000	98,000
Number of jobs in the inner city	295,000	310,000	235,000
Number of jobs in the outer area	60,500	69,800	93,000
Number of jobs in the metro.area	355,500	379,800	328,000
PARKING SUPPLY IN THE CBD			
Off street parking spaces	?	?	?
On street parking spaces	?	?	?
Total parking spaces	**11,000**	**15,700**	**20,400**
ROAD NETWORK (km)			
Total roads in the metro.area	407	1,375	1,522
MOTOR VEHICLES ON REGISTER			
Cars	56,230	174,615	220,664
Vans	?	?	14,095
Trucks	?	?	3,157
Special vehicles	0	?	1,138
Buses	444	?	552
Two wheeled motor bikes	17,956	?	5,667
Vans and trucks***	10,400	?	17,252
All "other vehicles"***	28,800	19,385	24,609
Total vehicles on register	**85,030**	**194,000**	**245,273**

(items marked***are sub totals)

PRIVATE TRANSPORT INDICATORS	1960	1970	1980
Total annual V.K.T.	?	?	?
Total annual V.K.T.in cars	$6.1509*10^8$	$1.9043*10^9$	$2.0981*10^9$
Average vehicle occupancy	1.72	1.72	1.72
Car occupant kilometres	$1.0580*10^9$	$3.2753*10^9$	$3.6086*10^9$
Average road network speed(km/h)	?	?	39.0

TRANSPORTATION ENERGY USE	1960	1970	1980
Motor spirit consumption (Joules)	$1.836*10^{15}$	$5.629*10^{15}$	$5.080*10^{15}$
Diesel fuel consumption (Joules)	?	$1.097*10^{15}$	$2.350*10^{15}$
Total fuel consumption (Joules)	$1.836*10^{15}$	$6.726*10^{15}$	$7.830*10^{15}$

MODAL SPLIT FOR THE JOURNEY
TO WORK (% of workers)

Public transport	20.0	21.0	14.0
Private transport	24.0	52.0	58.0
Walking and cycling	56.0	27.0	28.0

AVERAGE TRIP LENGTHS (km)

Journey to work	?	7.3	?
Evening peak (all trips:agglomeration)			
Public transport	7.3	7.9	?
Autos	4.7	7.9	?
Bikes and mopeds	2.3	3.3	?
Overall	3.9	6.4	6.6

PUBLIC TRANSPORT INDICATORS

VEHICLE KILOMETRES
-Buses

Gemeentevervoerbedrijf(GVB)	10,600,000	16,537,000	21,492,000

-Trains

Metro(GVB)	0	0	2,991,000
Suburban rail(National:NS)	17,402,199	20,727,716	21,354,868
Total	*17,402,199*	*20,727,716*	*24,345,868*

-Trams

Gemeentevervoerbedrijf(GVB)	15,904,000	8,173,000	10,188,000

-Ferries

-Ferries	0	0	0
Grand total	*43,906,199*	*45,437,716*	*56,125,868*

PASSENGERS CARRIED
-Buses

Gemeentevervoerbedrijf(GVB)	48,473,000	68,938,000	80,840,000

-Trains

Metro(GVB)	0	0	27,900,000
Suburban rail(National:NS)	20,000,000	18,100,000	20,000,000
Total	*20,000,000*	*18,100,000*	*47,900,000*

-Trams

Gemeentevervoerbedrijf(GVB)	96,792,000	111,339,000	121,260,000

-Ferries

-Ferries	0	0	0
Grand total	*165,265,000*	*198,377,000*	*250,000,000*

AVERAGE TRIP LENGTH(km)
-Buses

Gemeentevervoerbedrijf(GVB)	4.0	4.2	4.5

-Trains

Metro(GVB)	0.0	0.0	6.0
Suburban rail(National:NS)	20.0	24.1	23.8

-Trams

Gemeentevervoerbedrijf(GVB)	2.5	2.6	2.8

-Ferries

-Ferries	0.0	0.0	0.0

PASSENGER KILOMETRES
-Buses

GVB	193,900,000	289,500,000	363,800,000

-Trains

Metro(GVB)	0	0	167,400,000
Suburban rail(National:NS)	400,000,000	435,305,000	476,200,000
Total	*400,000,000*	*435,305,000*	*643,600,000*

-Trams

GVB	242,000,000	289,500,000	339,500,000

-Ferries	0	0	0
Grand total	*835,900,000*	*1,014,305,000*	*1,346,900,000*

AVERAGE SPEED (km/h)
-Buses

Gemeentevervoerbedrijf(GVB)	15.4	17.4	18.0

-Trains

Metro(GVB)	0.0	0.0	35.0
Suburban rail(National:NS)	65.0	65.0	65.0
Overall train speed	*65.0*	*65.0*	*57.2*

-Trams

Gemeentevervoerbedrijf(GVB)	17.3	15.8	15.0

-Ferries	0.0	0.0	0.0
All modes average	*39.7*	*37.4*	*36.0*

ENERGY CONSUMPTION
-Buses
Gemeentevervoerbedrijf(GVB)

Diesel (litres)	4,439,091	7,132,113	10,273,151
LPG(cubic metres)	0	0	296,000
Total (Joules)	*$1.6997*10^{14}$*	*$2.7309*10^{14}$*	*$4.2136*10^{14}$*

-Trains
Metro(GVB)

Elec.(kWh)	0	0	20,083,193
Suburban rail(National:NS)			
Elec.(kWh)	38,790,000	46,202,079	47,600,000
Total(Joules)	*$1.3964*10^{14}$*	*$1.6633*10^{14}$*	*$2.4366*10^{14}$*

-Trams
Gemeentevervoerbedrijf(GVB)

Elec.(kWh)	27,907982	37,259,892	51,745,000
Total(Joules)	*$1.0047*10^{14}$*	*$1.3414*10^{14}$*	*$1.8628*10^{14}$*

-Ferries	0	0	0
Grand total(Joules)	*$4.1008*10^{14}$*	*$5.7356*10^{14}$*	*$8.5130*10^{14}$*

Boston

POPULATION AND AREA	1960	1970	1980
Total population			
SMSA	2,589,301	2,753,800	2,763,357
Urbanised area	2,413,236	2,652,575	2,678,473
Metropolitan region	3,401,217	3,630,098	3,701,114
Urbanised area(ha)	133,592	171,976	221,880
Population of the CBD[1]			
Boston Proper	79,615	65,116	71,557
Boston CBD	2,949	3,722	8,382
Area of the CBD(ha) (Boston Proper)	570	570	570
Population of the inner city	791,329	735,190	650,142
Area of the inner city(ha)	14,504	14,504	14,504

EMPLOYMENT LOCATION			
Number of jobs in the CBD			
Boston Proper	273,000	245,600	218,205
Boston CBD	246,000	182,600	119,189
Number of jobs in the inner city	424,300	429,400	474,707
Number of jobs in the outer area	494,100	632,100	898,853
Number of jobs in the metro.area	918,400	1,061,500	1,373,560

PARKING SUPPLY IN THE CBD			
Public off street parking spaces	16,300	29,500	35,200
Private off street parking spaces	4,300	9,600	20,300
Total off street (Boston Proper)	**20,600**	**39,100**	**55,500**
On street parking spaces (Boston Proper)	8,700	14,700	14,700
Total parking spaces (Boston Proper)	**29,300**	**53,800**	**70,200**

ROAD NETWORK (km)			
0 lanes	?	?	53
1 lane	?	?	686
2 lanes	?	?	12,310
3 lanes	?	?	35
4 lanes	?	?	406
5 lanes	?	?	14
6 lanes	?	?	224
7 lanes	?	?	11
8 lanes	?	?	61
Total roads in the metro.area	**?**	**?**	**13,800**

MOTOR VEHICLES ON REGISTER			
Passenger cars	705,967	926,600	1,285,777
Other vehicles	144,596	187,267	252,952
Total vehicles on register	**850,563**	**1,113,867**	**1,538,729**

PRIVATE TRANSPORT INDICATORS			
Total annual V.K.T.	$1.1831*10^{10}$	$1.9506*10^{10}$	$2.7180*10^{10}$
Total annual V.K.T. in cars	$1.0648*10^{10}$	$1.7555*10^{10}$	$2.4462*10^{10}$
Average vehicle occupancy	1.51	1.42	1.42
Car occupant kilometres	$1.6078*10^{10}$	$2.4928*10^{10}$	$3.4736*10^{10}$
Average road network speed(km/h)	?	?	39.4

TRANSPORTATION ENERGY USE

Motor spirit consumption (Joules)	$6.0811*10^{16}$	$1.0543*10^{17}$	$1.4973*10^{17}$
Diesel fuel consumption (Joules)	$1.3378*10^{16}$	$2.0932*10^{16}$	$2.7741*10^{16}$
Total fuel consumption (Joules)	$7.4189*10^{16}$	$1.2636*10^{17}$	$1.7747*10^{17}$

MODAL SPLIT FOR THE JOURNEY TO WORK (% of workers)

SMSA

Public transport	25.6	19.7	16.1
Private transport	62.2	68.2	74.1
Walking and cycling	12.2	12.1	9.8

City of Boston only

Public transport	45.8	39.7	34.4
Private transport	39.7	45.1	48.4
Walking and cycling	14.5	15.2	17.3

AVERAGE TRIP LENGTHS (km)

Journey to work	?	?	9.8
Other trip purposes	?	?	?

PUBLIC TRANSPORT INDICATORS

VEHICLE KILOMETRES

-Buses

Municipal motor bus (MBTA)[1]	20,836,098	31,288,838	38,669,009
Municipal trolley bus (MBTA)	10,608,123	7,339,357	1,258,991
Total	*31,444,221*	*38,628,195*	*39,928,000*

-Trains

Rapid transit (MBTA)	16,063,295	18,691,062	18,032,000
Commuter rail (MBTA)[2]	1,294,303	3,298,423	5,840,000
Total	*17,357,598*	*21,989,485*	*23,872,000*

-Trams

Municipal tramways (MBTA)	14,622,571	12,680,603	7,728,000
Ferries	0	0	0
Grand total	*63,424,390*	*73,298,283*	*71,528,000*

PASSENGERS CARRIED

-Buses

Municipal motor bus (MBTA)	65,115,252	72,670,283	61,865,880
Municipal trolley bus (MBTA)	33,544,220	17,046,116	2,774,020
Total	*98,659,472*	*89,716,399*	*64,639,900*

-Trains

Rapid transit (MBTA)	95,935,412	86,900,000	90,501,000
Commuter rail (MBTA)	7,337,143	8,017,000	9,339,015
Total	*103,272,555*	*94,917,000*	*99,840,015*

-Trams

Municipal tramways (MBTA)	54,464,508	49,800,000	52,105,000
-Ferries	0	0	0
Grand total	*256,391,559*	*234,433,399*	*216,584,915*

AVERAGE TRIP LENGTH (km)
-Buses
Overall Buses (MBTA)	6.0	6.5	7.0

-Trains
Rapid transit (MBTA)	5.8	5.8	5.8
Commuter rail (MBTA)	24.0	26.1	29.6

-Trams
Municipal tramways (MBTA)	4.0	4.0	4.0

-Ferries
	0.0	0.0	0.0

PASSENGER KILOMETRES
-Buses
Municipal motor bus (MBTA)	390,691,509	472,356,841	434,380,128
Municipal trolley bus (MBTA)	201,265,323	110,799,753	18,099,172
Total	*591,956,832*	*583,156,594*	*452,479,300*

-Trains
Rapid transit (MBTA)	556,041,648	503,672,400	524,542,830
Commuter rail (MBTA)	176,091,432	209,098,750	276,346,840
Total	*732,133,080*	*712,771,150*	*800,889,670*

-Trams
Municipal tramways (MBTA)	219,219,645	200,445,000	209,723,430

-Ferries
	0	0	0
Grand total	*1,543,309,557*	*1,496,372,744*	*1,463,092,400*

AVERAGE SPEED (km/h)
-Buses
Municipal motor bus (MBTA)	17.9	18.0	18.2
Municipal trolley bus (MBTA)	19.0	19.0	19.4
Overall bus speed	*18.0*	*18.0*	*18.2*

-Trains
Rapid transit (MBTA)	35.0	35.0	35.0
Commuter rail (MBTA)	?	?	45.0
Overall train speed	*?*	*?*	*38.5*

-Trams
Municipal tramways (MBTA)	21.3	20.7	20.2

-Ferries
	0.0	0.0	0.0
All modes average	*?*	*?*	*29.6*

ENERGY CONSUMPTION
-Buses
Municipal motor bus (MBTA)

Diesel (litres)	?	?	25,440,138
Petrol(litres)	?	?	0
Municipal trolley bus (MBTA)			
Elec.(kWh)	?	?	?
Total (Joules)	?	?	?

-Trains
Rapid transit (MBTA)

Elec.(kWh)	?	?	66,718,400
Commuter rail (MBTA)			
Diesel(litres)	?	?	?
Total(Joules)	?	?	?

-Trams
Municipal tramways (MBTA)

Elec.(kWh)	?	?	?
Total(Joules)	?	?	?

-Ferries	0	0	0
Grand total(Joules)	?	?	?

Note:
(1)MBTA is the abbreviation for *Massachusetts Bay Transportation Authority* , formerly the *Metropolitan Transit Authority*.
(2)The MBTA currently controls the operation of the eight commuter rail lines. however, previously the commuter rail services were operated by individual companies such as *Boston and Maine railroad*.

Brisbane

POPULATION AND AREA	1960	1970	1980
Total population	621,550	867,784	1,028,527
Urbanised area(ha)	29,662	77,000	100,718
Population of the CBD	?	1,816	2,531
Area of the CBD(ha)	165	165	165
Population of the inner city	280,299	269,790	223,352
Area of the inner city(ha)	11,142	11,140	12,060
EMPLOYMENT LOCATION			
Number of jobs in the CBD	55,324	56,838	57,065
Number of jobs in the inner city	161,000	?	188,272
Number of jobs in the outer area	51,270	?	223,715
Number of jobs in the metro.area	212,270	?	411,987
PARKING SUPPLY IN THE CBD			
Off street parking spaces	5,999	10,960	13,936
On street parking spaces	2,972	1,976	1,379
Total parking spaces	**8,971**	**12,936**	**15,315**
ROAD NETWORK (km)			
Total roads in the metro.area	4,824	6,478	7,084
MOTOR VEHICLES ON REGISTER			
Cars and station wagons	129,112	255,384	514,974
Utilities and panel vans	28,880	38,248	95,288
Rigid trucks	?	?	17,424
Articulated trucks	?	?	2,838
Other truck types	165	?	1,856
Total trucks(***)	10,353	17,486	22,118
Total commercial vehicles(***)	39,233	55,734	117,406
Motor cycles	5,917	10,455	33,360
Buses	777	1,495	3,328
Total vehicles on register	**175,039**	**323,068**	**669,068**

*(items marked***are sub- totals)*

PRIVATE TRANSPORT INDICATORS	1960	1970	1980
Total annual V.K.T.	$2.4102*10^9$	$4.0655*10^9$	$8.1987*10^9$
Total annual V.K.T.in cars	$1.8812*10^9$	$3.2871*10^9$	$6.5888*10^9$
Average vehicle occupancy	2.04	1.93	1.83
Car occupant kilometres	$3.8376*10^9$	$6.3441*10^9$	$1.2058*10^{10}$
Average road network speed(km/h)	36.7	?	47.6

TRANSPORTATION ENERGY USE			
Motor spirit consumption (Joules)	$1.1179*10^{16}$	$1.8369*10^{16}$	$3.4460*10^{16}$
Diesel fuel consumption (Joules)	$8.5535*10^{14}$	$1.5973*10^{15}$	$6.5150*10^{15}$
Total fuel consumption (Joules)	$1.2034*10^{16}$	$1.9966*10^{16}$	$4.0975*10^{16}$

MODAL SPLIT FOR THE JOURNEY TO WORK (% of workers)			
Public transport	?	28.5	16.6
Private transport	?	65.2	78.1
Walking and cycling	?	6.3	5.3

AVERAGE TRIP LENGTHS (km)

Journey to work	?	?	?
Other trip purposes	?	?	?

PUBLIC TRANSPORT INDICATORS

VEHICLE KILOMETRES

-Buses			
Municipal motor bus	7,869,680	22,114,960	19,664,179
Municipal trolley bus	1,830,570	0	0
Private motor bus	7,151,620	9,970,730	7,700,000
Total	*16,851,870*	*32,085,690*	*27,364,179*
-Trains			
Suburban rail	18,760,042	17,526,569	22,327,724
-Trams			
Municipal tramways	12,788,230	0	0
-Ferries	0	0	0
Grand total	*48,400,142*	*49,612,259*	*49,691,903*

PASSENGERS CARRIED

-Buses			
Municipal motor bus	23,558,000	65,220,000	41,341,017
Municipal trolley bus	9,642,000	0	0
Private motor bus	12,661,000	16,853,000	9,921,844
Total	*45,861,000*	*82,073,000*	*51,262,861*
-Trains			
Suburban rail	24,582,000	27,621,000	30,329,707
-Trams			
Municipal tramways	73,659,000	0	0
-Ferries	0	0	0
Grand Total	*144,102,000*	*109,694,000*	*81,592,568*

AVERAGE TRIP LENGTH (km)

-Buses			
Municipal motor bus	4.4	5.5	6.6
Municipal trolley bus	4.4	0.0	0.0
Private motor bus	4.4	5.5	6.6
-Trains			
Suburban rail	12.8	13.6	14.1
-Trams			
Municipal tramways	4.4	0.0	0.0
-Ferries	0.0	0.0	0.0

PASSENGER KILOMETRES
-Buses

Municipal motor bus	103,655,200	358,710,000	272,850,712
Municipal trolley bus	42,424,800	0	0
Private motor bus	55,708,400	92,691,500	65,484,170
Total	*201,788,400*	*451,401,500*	*338,334,882*

-Trains

Suburban rail	314,649,600	375,645,600	427,648,869

-Trams

	324,099,600	0	0

-Ferries

	0	0	0
Grand Total	*840,537,600*	*827,047,100*	*765,983,751*

AVERAGE SPEED (km/h)
-Buses

Municipal motor bus	21.3	20.0	23.0
Municipal trolley bus	?	0.0	0.0
Private motor bus	?	?	?
Overall bus speed	*21.3*	*20.0*	*23.0*

-Trains

Suburban rail	28.4	33.8	37.0

-Trams

Municipal tramways	17.6	0.0	0.0

-Ferries

	0.0	0.0	0.0
All modes average	*22.5*	*26.3*	*30.8*

ENERGY CONSUMPTION
-Buses

Municipal motor bus			
Diesel (litres)	2,810,600	8,845,984	8,680,436
Municipal trolley bus			
Elec.(kWh)	5,491,710	0	0
Private motor bus			
Diesel (litres)	2,554,150	3,988,292	3,392,070
Total(Joules)	*$2.2519*10^{14}$*	*$4.9142*10^{14}$*	*$4.6226*10^{14}$*

-Trains

Suburban rail			
Diesel(litres)	1,024,021	10,057,519	9,400,620
Elec.(kWh)	0	0	15,919,953
Coal(tonnes)	59,259	0	0
Total(Joules)	*$1.5343*10^{15}$*	*$3.8510*10^{14}$*	*$4.1726*10^{14}$*

-Trams

Municipal tramways			
Elec.(kWh)	25,960,000	0	0
Total(Joules)	*$9.3456*10^{13}$*	*0*	*0*

-Ferries

	0	0	0
Grand total(Joules)	*$1.8530*10^{15}$*	*$8.7652*10^{14}$*	*$8.7952*10^{14}$*

Brussels

POPULATION AND AREA	1960	1970	1980
Total population	1,022,795	1,075,136	997,293
Urbanised area(ha)	10,200	13,500	14,800
Population of the CBD	51,000	19,381	19,180
Area of the CBD(ha)	259	259	259
Population of the inner city	595,386	582,179	516,594
Area of the inner city(ha)	5,141	5,141	5,141

EMPLOYMENT LOCATION			
Number of jobs in the CBD	?	?	153,082
Number of jobs in the inner city	539,882	523,469	472,155
Number of jobs in the outer area	140,492	144,329	150,310
Number of jobs in the metro.area	680,374	667,798	622,465

PARKING SUPPLY IN THE CBD			
Off street parking spaces	?	?	?
On street parking spaces	?	?	?
Total parking spaces	?	22,293	28,400

ROAD NETWORK (km)			
Total roads in the metro.area	1,450	1,550	1,651

MOTOR VEHICLES ON REGISTER			
Cars and station wagons	160,868	282,021	360,073
"Other" types of vehicles	34,498	38,737	46,608
Total vehicles on register	**195,366**	**320,758**	**406,681**

PRIVATE TRANSPORT INDICATORS			
Total annual V.K.T.	$2.5480*10^9$	$3.8735*10^9$	$4.6239*10^9$
Total annual V.K.T.in cars	$1.8339*10^9$	$3.1375*10^9$	$3.9248*10^9$
Average vehicle occupancy	1.6	1.5	1.45
Car occupant kilometres	$2.9342*10^9$	$4.7063*10^9$	$5.6910*10^9$
Average road network speed(km/h)	?	?	?

TRANSPORTATION ENERGY USE			
Motor spirit consumption (Joules)	$5.5984*10^{15}$	$1.1211*10^{16}$	$1.4704*10^{16}$
Diesel fuel consumption (Joules)	$6.8357*10^{15}$	$7.0454*10^{15}$	$6.6921*10^{15}$
Total fuel consumption (Joules)	$1.2434*10^{16}$	$1.8256*10^{16}$	$2.1396*10^{16}$

MODAL SPLIT FOR THE JOURNEY TO WORK (% of workers) [1]			
Public transport	58.6	35.0	26.7
Private transport	23.5	41.8	57.7
Walking and cycling	17.9	23.2	15.6
Public transport	64.0	50.0	43.0
Private transport	15.0	33.0	46.0
Walking and cycling	21.0	16.0	11.0

AVERAGE TRIP LENGTHS (km)			
Journey to work	?	?	4.4
Other trip purposes	?	?	?

PUBLIC TRANSPORT INDICATORS

VEHICLE KILOMETRES

-Buses			
MIVB	8,680,041	15,902,306	20,776,460
NMVB	937,000	3,554,000	5,723,000
Trolley buses	1,164,407	0	0
Total	*10,781,448*	*19,456,306*	*26,499,460*
-Trains			
Metro(STIB)	0	0	4,255,274
Suburban rail(National:SNCB)	6,780,000	6,800,000	7,200,000
Total	*6,780,000*	*6,800,000*	*11,455,274*
-Trams			
MIVB	46,652,147	23,601,121	15,461,792
NMVB	1,318,000	554,000	0
Total	*47,970,147*	*24,155,121*	*15,461,792*
-Ferries	0	0	0
Grand total	*65,531,575*	*50,411,427*	*53,416,526*

PASSENGERS CARRIED

-Buses			
MIVB	33,241,879	44,614,484	70,735,526
NMVB	25,589,000	26,254,000	24,336,000
Trolley buses	4,952,401	0	0
Total	*63,783,280*	*70,868,484*	*95,071,526*
-Trains			
Metro(STIB)	0	0	34,219,294
Suburban rail(National:SNCB)	61,000,000	57,700,000	33,200,000
Total	*61,000,000*	*57,700,000*	*67,419,294*
-Trams			
MIVB and NMVB	214,618,895	122,692,723	102,606,907
-Ferries	0	0	0
Grand Total	*339,402,175*	*251,261,207*	*265,097,727*

AVERAGE TRIP LENGTH (km)

-Buses			
MIVB and NMVB	3.5	3.8	4.0
-Trains			
Metro(STIB)	0.0	0.0	4.0
Suburban rail(National:SNCB)	14.0	14.0	14.0
-Trams			
MIVBandNMVB	3.5	3.8	4.0
-Ferries	0.0	0.0	0.0

PASSENGER KILOMETRES

-Buses			
MIVB and NMVB	223,241,480	269,300,239	380,286,104

-Trains			
Metro(STIB)	0	0	136,877,176
Suburban rail(National:SNCB)	854,000,000	807,800,000	464,800,000
Total	*854,000,000*	*807,800,000*	*601,677,176*
-Trams			
MIVB and NMVB	751,166,133	466,232,347	410,427,628
-Ferries	0	0	0
Grand total	*1,828,407,613*	*1,543,332,586*	*1,392,390,908*

AVERAGE SPEED (km/h)

-Buses			
Overall bus speed	18.8	18.7	19.8
-Trains			
Metro(STIB)	0.0	0.0	30.8
Suburban rail(National:SNCB)	40.7	40.7	40.7
Overall train speed	*40.7*	*40.7*	*38.4*
-Trams			
Overall tram speed	17.1	16.1	17.3
-Ferries	0.0	0.0	0.0
All modes average	*28.3*	*29.4*	*27.1*

ENERGY CONSUMPTION

-Buses			
MIVB			
Diesel (litres)	3,972,925	8,099,412	11,722,174
NMVB			
Diesel (litres)	429,817	1,813,265	3,233,333
Trolley buses			
Elec.(kWh)	2,475,763	0	0
Total(Joules)	$1.7749*10^{14}$	$3.7956*10^{14}$	$5.7265*10^{14}$
Trains			
Metro(STIB)			
Elec.(kWh)	0	0	59,030,096
Suburban rail(National:SNCB)			
Elec.(kWh)	53,901,000	58,208,000	59,976,000
Total(Joules)	$1.9404*10^{14}$	$2.0955*10^{14}$	$4.2842*10^{14}$
-Trams			
MIVB and NMVB			
Elec.(kWh)	101,999,153	79,470,348	92,770,752
Total(Joules)	$3.6720*10^{14}$	$2.8609*10^{14}$	$3.3397*10^{14}$
-Ferries	0	0	0
Grand total(Joules)	$7.3873*10^{14}$	$8.7520*10^{14}$	$1.3350*10^{15}$

Note:
(1) The first set of modal split data are based on a number of different sources and appear to be reasonable when compared to other European cities. However, the second set of data from the INS based on the 1961, 1970 and 1981 censuses are probably more comparable over time.

Chicago

POPULATION AND AREA	1960	1970	1980
Total population			
SMSA	6,220,913	6,978,947	7,103,624
Urbanised area	5,959,213	6,714,578	6,779,799
Urbanised area(ha)	248,588	330,743	387,951
Population of the CBD	4,377	4,936	6,462
Area of the CBD(ha)	414	414	414
Population of the inner city	3,550,404	3,366,957	3,005,072
Area of the inner city(ha)	49,935	52,707	55,509
EMPLOYMENT LOCATION			
Number of jobs in the CBD	322,695	364,548	388,283
Number of jobs in the inner city	1,624,713	1,475,493	1,417,381
Number of jobs in the outer area	819,906	1,341,983	1,741,957
Number of jobs in the metro.area	2,444,619	2,817,476	3,159,338
PARKING SUPPLY IN THE CBD			
Off street parking spaces	25,281	33,109	32,484
On street parking spaces	1,500	2,000	2,890
Total parking spaces	**26,781**	**35,109**	**35,374**
ROAD NETWORK (km)			
State roads	5,020	?	5,268
County roads	2,882	?	2,779
Local roads	22,206	?	27,651
Total roads in the metro.area	**30,108**	**34,745**	**35,698**
MOTOR VEHICLES ON REGISTER			
Passenger cars	1,914,476	2,728,443	3,161,165
Trucks and buses	170,961	240,748	395,306
Motor cycles and scooters	10,765	59,690	117,477
Other vehicles	9,865	9,633	8,505
Trailers etc.(non-motorised)[1]	77,671	190,311	203,120
Total vehicles on register	**2,106,067**	**3,038,514**	**3,682,453**
PRIVATE TRANSPORT INDICATORS			
Total annual V.K.T	$2.6786*10^{10}$	$4.2383*10^{10}$	$5.6577*10^{10}$
Total annual V.K.T.in cars	$2.5447*10^{10}$	$4.0264*10^{10}$	$5.3748*10^{10}$
Average vehicle occupancy	1.56	1.47	1.47
Car occupant kilometres	$3.9697*10^{10}$	$5.9188*10^{10}$	$7.9010*10^{10}$
Average road network speed(km/h)			
Urbanised area of Chicago	?	?	41.0
City of Chicago(inner area)	?	?	29.5
TRANSPORTATION ENERGY USE			
Motor spirit consumption (Joules)	$1.6629*10^{17}$	$2.9128*10^{17}$	$3.4272*10^{17}$
Diesel fuel consumption (Joules)	$1.5142*10^{16}$	$2.2735*10^{16}$	$2.6582*10^{16}$
Total fuel consumption (Joules)	$1.8143*10^{17}$	$3.1401*10^{17}$	$3.6930*10^{17}$

MODAL SPLIT FOR THE JOURNEY
TO WORK (% of workers)

SMSA

Public transport	33.0	23.6	18.3
Private transport	57.3	68.5	75.5
Walking and cycling	9.7	7.9	6.2
City of Chicago only			
Public transport	44.2	36.5	32.8
Private transport	46.2	54.4	58.9
Walking and cycling	9.6	9.1	8.3

AVERAGE TRIP LENGTHS (km)

Journey to work	?	11.3	12.6
Other trip purposes			
Shopping	?	4.8	?
Social/recreational	?	9.2	?
School	?	5.0	?
Personal business	?	11.9	?
Business related to work	?	11.9	?

PUBLIC TRANSPORT INDICATORS

VEHICLE KILOMETRES

-Buses

Motor buses(CTA)	148,088,019	143,814,992	141,311,310
Trolley buses(CTA)	28,449,677	14,470,279	0
Total CTA buses	**176,537,696**	**158,285,271**	**141,311,310**
Private motor bus cos.	21,155,666	22,000,000	23,476,221
Total	*197,693,362*	*180,285,271*	*164,787,531*

-Trains

Rapid rail(CTA)	72,188,088	82,897,280	79,852,780
Commuter railroads			
Burlington Northern	3,500,000	5,127,703	7,146,790
Chicago&North Western	17,000,000	18,329,850	19,986,540
Chicago,Milwaukee,St Paul&Pac.	3,000,000	4,026,071	8,656,970
Chicago,South Shore&South Bend	6,324,887	4,100,462	3,235,068
Illinois Central Gulf	20,000,000	14,207,767	7,665,210
Norfolk&Western	100,000	113,853	303,968
Chicago,Rock Island,Pacific	4,000,000	3,866,846	3,883,320
Sub total(commuter rail)	**53,925,000**	**49,772,552**	**50,877,866**
Total	*126,113,088*	*132,669,832*	*130,730,646*

-Trams	0	0	0
-Ferries	0	0	0
Grand total	*323,806,450*	*312,955,103*	*295,518,177*

PASSENGERS CARRIED

-Buses

Motor buses(CTA)	504,808,010	?	537,691,910
Trolley buses(CTA)	125,414,225	?	0
Total CTA buses	**630,222,235**	**503,341,685**	**537,691,910**
Private motor bus cos.	39,663,289	31,596,000	38,235,494
Total	*669,885,524*	*534,937,685*	*575,927,404*

-Trains

Rapid rail(CTA)	169,425,105	158,081,410	154,737,131
Commuter railroads			
Burlington Northern	9,262,000	9,726,000	14,433,154
Chicago&North Western	20,107,000	25,046,000	30,373,204
Chicago,Milwaukee,St Paul&Pac.	5,037,000	5,954,260	11,445,553
Chicago,South Shore&South Bend	4,112,979	2,682,705	2,102,794
Illinois Central Gulf	19,675,000	18,785,272	16,861,023
Norfolk&Western	small ?	197,600	1,152,722
Chicago,Rock Island,Pacific	6,995,000	6,196,000	7,160,115
Sub total(commuter rail)	**65,188,979**	**68,587,837**	**83,528,565**
Total	*234,614,084*	*226,669,247*	*238,265,696*

-Trams	0	0	0
-Ferries	0	0	0
Grand total	*904,499,608*	*761,606,932*	*814,193,100*

AVERAGE TRIP LENGTH (km)

-Buses

Motor buses(CTA)	3.7	3.7	3.7
Trolley buses(CTA)	3.7	3.7	0.0
Private motor bus cos.	6.0	6.3	8.1

-Trains

Rapid rail(CTA)	11.8	11.8	11.8
Commuter railroads			
Burlington Northern	?	?	30.8
Chicago&North Western	?	?	34.5
Chicago,Milwaukee,St Paul&Pac.	?	?	36.7
Chicago,South Shore&South Bend	?	?	49.6
Illinois Central Gulf	?	?	31.7
Norfolk&Western	?	?	25.8
Chicago,Rock Island,Pacific	?	?	27.0
Overall commuter rail	**26.8**	**29.8**	**33.2**

-Trams	0.0	0.0	0.0
-Ferries	0.0	0.0	0.0

PASSENGER KILOMETRES

-Buses			
Motor buses(CTA)	1,867,789,637	?	1,989,460,067
Trolley buses(CTA)	464,032,633	?	0
Total CTA Buses	**2,331,822,270**	**1,862,364,235**	**1,989,460,067**
Private motor bus cos.	237,979,734	199,054,800	309,707,501
Total	*2,569,802,004*	*2,061,419,035*	*2,299,167,568*

-Trains			
Rapid rail(CTA)	1,999,216,239	1,865,360,638	1,825,898,146
Commuter railroads			
Burlington Northern	?	?	444,541,143
Chicago&North Western	?	?	1,046,699,076
Chicago,Milwaukee,St Paul&Pac.	?	?	420,051,795
Chicago,South Shore&South Bend	?	?	104,298,582
Illinois Central Gulf	?	?	534,494,429
Norfolk&Western	?	?	29,740,228
Chicago,Rock Island,Pacific	?	?	193,323,105
Sub total(commuter rail)	**1,747,064,637**	**2,043,917,543**	**2,773,148,358**
Total	*3,746,280,876*	*3,909,278,181*	*4,599,046,504*

-Trams	0	0	0

-Ferries	0	0	0
Grand total	*6,316,082,880*	*5,970,697,216*	*6,898,214,072*

AVERAGE SPEED (km/h)

-Buses			
Motor buses(CTA)	16.3	14.4	16.1
Trolley buses(CTA)	15.2	12.7	0.0
Private motor bus cos.	18.8	25.0	32.2
Overall bus speed	*16.4*	*15.0*	*18.2*

-Trains			
Rapid rail(CTA)	35.4	35.4	36.1
Commuter railroads			
Burlington Northern	?	?	57.3
Chicago&North Western	?	?	56.2
Chicago,Milwaukee,St Paul&Pac.	?	?	54.4
Chicago,South Shore&South Bend	?	?	67.8
Illinois Central Gulf	?	?	49.9
Norfolk&Western	?	?	36.7
Chicago,Rock Island,Pacific	?	?	45.9
Overall commuter rail	**54.0**	**54.0**	**54.1**
Overall train speed	*44.1*	*45.1*	*46.9*

-Trams	0.0	0.0	0.0

-Ferries	0.0	0.0	0.0
All modes average	*32.9*	*34.7*	*37.4*

ENERGY CONSUMPTION

-Buses

Motor buses(CTA)			
Diesel (litres)	20,122,911	47,247,572	108,133,131
Petrol(litres)	19,348,155	0	0
LPG(litres)	98,848,454	79,378,267	0
Trolley buses(CTA)			
Elec.(kWh)	69,140,696	35,303,420	0
Private motor bus cos.			
Diesel (litres)	9,921,473	16,233,918	39,042,956
Petrol(litres)	501,770	433,342	64,474
Total(Joules)	$4.6837*10^{15}$	$4.6589*10^{15}$	$5.6376*10^{15}$

-Trains

Rapid rail(CTA)			
Elec.(kWh)	207,109,902	240,546,810	283,788,000
Commuter railroads			
Burlington Northern			
Diesel (litres)	6,755,000	9,896,467	13,793,305
Chicago&North Western			
Diesel (litres)	29,580,000	31,893,939	34,776,580
Chicago,Milwaukee,St Paul&Pac.			
Diesel (litres)	6,210,000	8,333,967	17,919,928
Chicago,South Shore&South Bend			
Elec.(kWh)	31,909,519	20,707,333	16,337,093
Illinois Central Gulf			
Diesel (litres)	8,276,400	5,879,458	3,172,000
Elec.(kWh)	141,273,000	100,358,000	54,161,920
Norfolk&Western			
Diesel (litres)	226,000	257,308	686,968
Chicago,Rock Island,Pacific			
Diesel (litres)	7,600,000	7,347,007	7,378,308
Total(Joules)	$3.6147*10^{15}$	$3.7374*10^{15}$	$4.2516*10^{15}$

-Trams	0	0	0
-Ferries	0	0	0
Grand total(Joules)	$8.2984*10^{15}$	$8.3963*10^{15}$	$9.8892*10^{15}$

Note:
(1) Excluded from total vehicles.

Copenhagen

POPULATION AND AREA	1960	1970	1980
Total population			
Copenhagen-Frederiksberg	835,666	724,647	581,938
Copenhagen-Frederiksberg & suburbs	1,321,805	1,339,990	1,206,622
Copenhagen Region	1,607,526	1,752,631	1,739,860
Urbanised area(ha)			
Copenhagen-Frederiksberg	7,781	8,226	8,414
Copenhagen-Frederiksberg & suburbs	26,695	30,017	31,806
Copenhagen Region	40,124	52,449	57,179
Population of the CBD	65,000	52,607	38,571
Area of the CBD(ha)	455	455	455
Population of the inner city	923,974	802,391	648,720
Area of the inner city(ha)	9,872	10,078	10,944
EMPLOYMENT LOCATION			
Number of jobs in the CBD	185,780	155,200	147,920
Number of jobs in the inner city	513,000	446,200	415,000
Number of jobs in the outer area	204,000	365,500	512,000
Number of jobs in the metro.area	717,000	811,700	927,000
PARKING SUPPLY IN THE CBD			
Off street parking spaces	?	?	?
On street parking spaces	?	?	?
Total parking spaces	28,000	30,800	31,400
ROAD NETWORK (km)			
Total roads in the metro.area			
Copenhagen/Frederiksberg	784	806	816
Copenhagen/Frederiksberg & suburbs	1,900	2,549	3,402
Copenhagen Region	4,500	6,034	7,435
MOTOR VEHICLES ON REGISTER			
Private cars			
Copenhagen/Frederiksberg	81,722	126,678	108,642
Copenhagen/Frederiksberg & suburbs	?	257,238	274,195
Copenhagen Region	142,200	349,634	428,701
Vans, lorries, trucks			
Copenhagen/Frederiksberg	27,705	27,310	20,776
Copenhagen/Frederiksberg & suburbs	?	50,796	44,635
Copenhagen Region	38,000	75,857	72,332
Motor cycles			
Copenhagen/Frederiksberg	24,676	9,082	3,869
Copenhagen/Frederiksberg & suburbs	?	16,124	7,712
Copenhagen Region	40,900	20,295	11,837
Buses and other vehicles			
Copenhagen/Frederiksberg	428	749	1,080
Copenhagen/Frederiksberg & suburbs	?	1,090	1,586
Copenhagen Region	800	1 424	2,467
Total vehicles on register			
Copenhagen/Frederiksberg	134,531	163,819	134,367
Copenhagen/Frederiksberg & suburbs	?	325,248	328,128
Copenhagen Region	221,900	447,210	515,337

PRIVATE TRANSPORT INDICATORS

Total annual V.K.T.	$2.5320*10^9$	$6.2760*10^9$	$7.2480*10^9$
Total annual V.K.T.in cars	$2.0310*10^9$	$5.3790*10^9$	$6.0230*10^9$
Average vehicle occupancy	2.7	1.7	1.8
Car occupant kilometres	$5.4837*10^9$	$9.1443*10^9$	$10.8414*10^9$
Average road network speed(km/h)			
Copenhagen/Frederiksberg	?	30.0	36.0
Copenhagen region	?	45.0	45.0

TRANSPORTATION ENERGY USE

Motor spirit consumption (Joules)	$1.0789*10^{16}$	$1.8663*10^{16}$	$1.9322*10^{16}$
Diesel fuel consumption (Joules)	$2.8335*10^{15}$	$7.2751*10^{15}$	$8.0409*10^{15}$
LPG (Joules)	0.0	$0.4335*10^{15}$	$0.7395*10^{15}$
Total fuel consumption (Joules)	$1.3622*10^{16}$	$2.6372*10^{16}$	$2.8103*10^{16}$

MODAL SPLIT FOR THE JOURNEY TO WORK (% of workers)

Public transport	?	26.5	31.0
Private transport	?	39.4	36.8
Walking and cycling	?	34.1	32.2

AVERAGE TRIP LENGTHS (km)

Journey to work	?	7.3	7.5
Other trip purposes			
Car work trips	?	9.3	9.5
Public transport work trips	?	10.6	11.0
Bicycle work trips	?	3.6	3.6
Walking work trips	?	0.9	0.9
Private car (all trips)	?	7.7	?
Public transport (all trips)	?	8.5	?
Bicycle and moped (all trips)	?	2.0	?
Walking (all trips)	?	0.7	?

PUBLIC TRANSPORT INDICATORS

VEHICLE KILOMETRES

-Buses

Municipal motor bus	10,800,000	29,464,000	0
Municipal trolley bus	3,100,000	1,385,000	0
Metropolitan area buses	14,300,000	29,151,000	0
HT[1] buses			
Municipal	0	0	68,692,000
Private contractors	0	0	18,685,000
Total	*28,200,000*	*60,000,000*	*87,377,000*

-Trains
Suburban rail
S-Tog (National:DSB)

Electric	19,000,000	48,200,000	62,800,000
Diesel	0	0	2,500,000
Other National:DSB	33,200,000	33,200,000	33,200,000
Private (5 companies)	4,000,000	4,000,000	4,700,000
Total	*56,200,000*	*85,400,000*	*103,200,000*

-Trams

Municipal tramways	31,800,000	5,451,000	0

-Ferries

	0	0	0
Grand total	*116,200,000*	*150,851,000*	*190,600,000*

193

PASSENGERS CARRIED

-Buses

Municipal motor bus	37,500,000	142,889,000	0
Municipal trolley bus	10,600,000	5,143,000	0
Metropolitan area buses	48,832,000	41,968,000	0
HT buses	0	0	250,000,000
Total	*96,932,000*	*190,000,000*	*250,000,000*

-Trains
Suburban rail

S-Tog (National:DSB)	52,600,000	57,000,000	76,800,000
Other National:DSB	26,400,000	15,000,000	16,700,000
Private (5 companies)	5,160,000	5,160,000	6,070,000
Total	*84,160,000*	*77,160,000*	*99,570,700*

-Trams

Municipal tramways	129,500,000	21,836,000	0

-Ferries	0	0	0
Grand total	*310,592,000*	*288,996,000*	*349,570,000*

AVERAGE TRIP LENGTH (km)

-Buses

Overall buses	5.5	5.7	6.0

-Trains
Suburban rail

S-Tog (National:DSB)	13.6	14.6	12.0
Other National:DSB	22.5	22.5	22.5
Private (5 companies)	14.4	14.4	14.4

-Trams

Municipal tramways	4.4	4.4	0.0

-Ferries	0.0	0.0	0.0

PASSENGER KILOMETRES

-Buses

Overall buses	533,126,000	1,083,000,000	1,500,000,000

-Trains
Suburban rail

S-Tog (National:DSB)	716,800,000	830,200,000	921,600,000
Other National:DSB	594,000,000	337,500,000	375,750,000
Private (5 companies)	74,304,000	74,304,000	87,418,000
Total	*1,385,104,000*	*1,242,004,000*	*1,384,768,000*

-Trams

Municipal tramways	569,800,000	96,078,400	0

-Ferries	0	0	0
Grand total	*2,488,030,000*	*2,421,082,400*	*2,884,768,000*

AVERAGE SPEED (km/h)

-Buses
Overall bus speed	?	21.8	23.8

-Trains
Suburban rail
All DSB trains in region	60.0	60.0	55.0
Private (5 companies)	44.0	44.0	43.8
Overall train speed	*59.1*	*59.0*	*54.3*

-Trams
Overall tram speed	?	?	0.0

-Ferries
	0.0	0.0	0.0
All modes average	*?*	*?*	*38.4*

ENERGY CONSUMPTION

-Buses
Municipal motor bus			
Diesel (litres)	3,900,000	12,100,000	0
Municipal trolley bus			
Elec.(kWh)	8,153,000	3,324,000	0
Metropolitan area buses			
Diesel (litres)	4,433,000	10,494,000	0
HT buses (Diesel: litres)			
Municipal	0	0	31,000,000
Private contractors	0	0	7,300,000
Total(Joules)	*3.4842*10^{14}*	*8.7709*10^{14}*	*1.4665*10^{15}*

-Trains
Suburban rail
S-Tog (National:DSB)
Elec.(kWh)	50,500,000	91,300,000	139,200,000
Other National:DSB			
Elec.(kWh)	?	?	?
Private (5 companies)			
Elec.(kWh)	?	?	?
Total(Joules)(S-Tog only)	*1.8180*10^{14}*	*3.2868*10^{14}*	*5.0112*10^{14}*

-Trams
Municipal tramways
Elec.(kWh)	83,634,000	14,336,000	0
Total(Joules)	*3.0182*10^{14}*	*5.1610*10^{14}*	*0*

-Ferries
	0	0	0
Grand total(Joules)	*8.3130*10^{14}*	*1.2574*10^{15}*	*1.9676*10^{15}*

Note:

(1) HT is the name of the public transport coordinating authority-*Hovedstadsomradets Trafikselskab.*

195

Denver

POPULATION AND AREA	1960	1970	1980
Total population			
SMSA	929,383	1,227,529	1,593,308
Urbanised area	803,624	1,047,311	1,352,070
Urbanised area(ha)	43,149	75,887	113,613
Population of the CBD	15,525	9,070	7,050
Area of the CBD(ha)	382	382	382
Population of the inner city	493,887	514,678	492,365
Area of the inner city(ha)	17,321	22,663	25,496
EMPLOYMENT LOCATION			
Number of jobs in the CBD	53,430	67,250	100,327
Number of jobs in the inner city	234,500	297,900	428,733
Number of jobs in the outer area	150,100	218,100	434,684
Number of jobs in the metro.area	384,600	516,000	863,417
PARKING SUPPLY IN THE CBD			
Off street parking spaces	?	?	44,554
On street parking spaces	?	?	5,365
Total parking spaces	31,800	38,890	49,919
ROAD NETWORK (km)			
Freeway and expressway	189	228	232
Arterial	?	1,684	1,729
Collector	?	877	924
Local	5,970	8,696	9,867
Total roads in the metro.area	8,178	11,485	12,752
MOTOR VEHICLES ON REGISTER			
Passenger	445,288	641,678	1,061,513
Trucks	70,053	118,927	236,545
Motor cycles	6,673	23,670	60,167
Mobile homes	10,717	12,063	?
Total vehicles on register[1]	532,731	796,338	1,358,225
PRIVATE TRANSPORT INDICATORS			
Total annual V.K.T.	5.1220×10^9	8.4620×10^9	13.4220×10^9
Total annual V.K.T.in cars	4.7320×10^9	7.4860×10^9	12.7840×10^9
Average vehicle occupancy	1.50	1.40	1.23
Car occupant kilometres	7.0980×10^9	10.4804×10^9	15.7243×10^9
Average road network speed(km/h)	?	?	45.1
am peak	?	?	43.0
pm peak	?	?	39.9
off peak	?	?	50.1
TRANSPORTATION ENERGY USE			
Motor spirit consumption (Joules)	2.7024×10^{16}	4.4958×10^{16}	6.8062×10^{16}
Diesel fuel consumption (Joules)	4.4080×10^{15}	5.2720×10^{15}	1.4726×10^{16}
Total fuel consumption (Joules)	3.1432×10^{16}	5.0230×10^{16}	8.2788×10^{16}

MODAL SPLIT FOR THE JOURNEY TO WORK (% of workers)

SMSA

Public transport	10.4	4.5	6.5
Private transport	80.5	89.1	88.1
Walking and cycling	9.1	6.3	5.3

City (County) of Denver only

Public transport	16.0	8.1	10.3
Private transport	74.2	83.7	82.1
Walking and cycling	9.8	8.2	7.6

AVERAGE TRIP LENGTHS (km)

Journey to work	?	?	11.1
Other trip purposes			
All trips			
Transit	5.7	?	8.1
Automobile	7.6	?	8.5

PUBLIC TRANSPORT INDICATORS

VEHICLE KILOMETRES
-Buses

Municipal motor bus	14,490,000	11,149,776	39,720,310
-Trains	0	0	0
-Trams	0	0	0
-Ferries	0	0	0
Grand total	*14,490,000*	*11,149,776*	*39,720,310*

PASSENGERS CARRIED
-Buses

Municipal motor bus	40,000,000	16,490,000	42,800,000
-Trains	0	0	0
-Trams	0	0	0
-Ferries	0	0	0
Grand total	*40,000,000*	*16,490,000*	*42,800,000*

AVERAGE TRIP LENGTH (km)
-Buses

Municipal motor bus	5.7	6.9	8.1
-Trains	0.0	0.0	0.0
-Trams	0.0	0.0	0.0
-Ferries	0.0	0.0	0.0

PASSENGER KILOMETRES

-Buses			
Municipal motor bus	228,000,000	113,783,291	346,680,000
-Trains	0	0	0
-Trams	0	0	0
-Ferries	0	0	0
Grand total	*228,000,000*	*113,783,291*	*346,680,000*

AVERAGE SPEED (km/h)

-Buses			
Overall bus speed	?	17.7	21.1
-Trains	0.0	0.0	0.0
-Trams	0.0	0.0	0.0
-Ferries	0.0	0.0	0.0
All modes average	*?*	*17.7*	*21.1*

ENERGY CONSUMPTION

-Buses			
Municipal motor bus			
Diesel (litres)	8,516,250	5,864,823	22,558,600
Total(Joules)	*$3.2609*10^{14}$*	*$2.2456*10^{14}$*	*$8.6377*10^{14}$*
-Trains	0	0	0
-Trams	0	0	0
-Ferries	0	0	0
Grand total(Joules)	*$3.2609*10^{14}$*	*$2.2456*10^{14}$*	*$8.6377*10^{14}$*

Note:
(1) Excludes all tractors, farm trucks, trailers and special equipment.

Detroit

POPULATION AND AREA	1960	1970	1980
Total population			
SMSA	3,762,360	4,199,931	4,043,633
Urbanised area	3,537,709	3,970,584	3,809,327
Urbanised area(ha)	189,562	225,848	270,336
Population of the CBD	7,681	6,428	4,046
Area of the CBD(ha)	300	300	362
Population of the inner city	1,670,144	1,514,063	1,203,339
Area of the inner city(ha)	24,662	24,662	25,019

EMPLOYMENT LOCATION			
Number of jobs in the CBD	?	103,724	110,700
Number of jobs in the inner city	744,000	610,775	497,932
Number of jobs in the outer area	570,000	922,747	1,186,392
Number of jobs in the metro.area	1,314,000	1,533,522	1,684,324

PARKING SUPPLY IN THE CBD			
Off street parking spaces	32,900	?	47,100
On street parking spaces	3,700	?	5,300
Total parking spaces	**36,600**	**44,500**	**52,400**

ROAD NETWORK (km)			
Total roads in the metro.area	19,721	21,814	23,485

MOTOR VEHICLES ON REGISTER			
Passenger	1,375,151	1,894,564	2,401,199
Commercial	125,542	193,115	313,966
Motor cycles	10,094	58,276	79,119
Other (municipal, farm, trailer,coach)	21,453	3,373	?
Total vehicles on register[1]	**1,510,787**	**2,145,955**	**2,794,284**

PRIVATE TRANSPORT INDICATORS			
Total annual V.K.T.	?	$3.8161*10^{10}$	$4.6798*10^{10}$
Total annual V.K.T.in cars	?	$3.3692*10^{10}$	$4.0199*10^{10}$
Average vehicle occupancy	1.51	1.46	1.41
Car occupant kilometres	?	$4.9190*10^{10}$	$5.6681*10^{10}$
Average road network speed(km/h)	37.9	41.9	44.4

TRANSPORTATION ENERGY USE			
Motor spirit consumption (Joules)	?	$2.0234*10^{17}$	$2.6679*10^{17}$
Diesel fuel consumption (Joules)	?	$0.4961*10^{17}$	$0.1209*10^{17}$
Total fuel consumption (Joules)	?	$2.5195*10^{17}$	$2.7888*10^{17}$

MODAL SPLIT FOR THE JOURNEY TO WORK (% of workers)

SMSA

Public transport	13.8	8.4	4.1
Private transport	79.8	87.0	93.1
Walking and cycling	6.4	4.6	2.8

City of Detroit only

Public transport	23.6	18.5	12.0
Private transport	69.2	75.8	83.8
Walking and cycling	7.2	5.7	4.2

AVERAGE TRIP LENGTHS (km)

Journey to work (all modes)	10.2	12.1	13.8
Journey to work (autos only)	10.6	12.5	14.3
Other trip purposes			
Shopping (hb)	3.6	4.2	?
Social/recreational (hb)	7.5	7.9	?
Non-home based	6.3	6.8	?

PUBLIC TRANSPORT INDICATORS

VEHICLE KILOMETRES

-Buses

Municipal[2] motor bus

Diesel	38,188,479	59,523,753	?
Petrol	26,805,779	93,915	?
Total municipal	**64,994,258**	**59,617,668**	**46,458,656**
SEMTA (normal service)	0	0	18,745,088
SEMTA (demand responsive)	0	0	11,584,476
Total	*64,994,258*	*59,617,668*	*76,788,220*

-Trains

Commuter rail (SEMTA)[3]	negligible	259,550	413,834

-Trams

Municipal tramways (DSR)	3,269,438	0	0

-Ferries

	0	0	0
Grand total	*68,263,696*	*59,877,218*	*77,202,104*

PASSENGERS CARRIED

-Buses

Municipal motor bus	171,147,560	158,610,420	106,408,000
SEMTA (normal service)	0	0	11,883,872
SEMTA (demand responsive)	0	0	1,764,542
Total	*171,147,560*	*158,610,420*	*120,056,414*

-Trains

Commuter rail (SEMTA)	negligible	323,000	515,000

-Trams

Municipal tramways (DSR)	11,874,341	0	0

-Ferries

	0	0	0
Grand total	*183,021,901*	*158,933,420*	*120,571,414*

AVERAGE TRIP LENGTH (km)
-Buses

Municipal motor bus	2.5	2.6	2.6
SEMTA (normal service)	0.0	0.0	14.3
SEMTA (demand responsive)	0.0	0.0	8.1

-Trains

Commuter rail (SEMTA)	0.0	23.4	27.4

-Trams

Municipal tramways (DSR)	2.53	0.0	0.0

-Ferries

	0.0	0.0	0.0

PASSENGER KILOMETRES
-Buses

Municipal motor bus	433,003,327	410,800,988	280,917,120
SEMTA (normal service)	0	0	169,989,648
SEMTA (demand responsive)	0	0	14,204,563
Total	*433,003,327*	*410,800,988*	*465,111,331*

-Trains

Commuter rail (SEMTA)	0	7,541,240	14,084,280

-Trams

Municipal tramways (DSR)	30,042,083	0	0

-Ferries

	0	0	0
Grand total	*463,045,410*	*418,342,228*	*479,195,611*

AVERAGE SPEED (km/h)
-Buses

Municipal motor buses	20.2	20.5	20.5
SEMTA (normal service)	0.0	0.0	29.0
SEMTA (demand responsive)	0.0	0.0	24.7
Overall bus speed	*20.2*	*20.5*	*21.4*

-Trains

Commuter rail(SEMTA)	0.0	41.9	41.9

-Trams

Municipal tramways	15.2	0.0	0.0

-Ferries

	0.0	0.0	0.0
All modes average	*19.9*	*20.5*	*21.5*

ENERGY CONSUMPTION

-Buses

Municipal motor bus			
Diesel (litres)	22,766,071	33,869,217	29,155,374
Petrol (litres)	19,568,885	59,678	689,544
SEMTA (normal service)			
Diesel (litres)	0	0	11,051,273
SEMTA (demand responsive)			
Petrol (litres)	0	0	4,588,745
Total(Joules)	$1.5506*10^{15}$	$1.2989*10^{15}$	$1.7226*10^{15}$

-Trains

Commuter rail (SEMTA)			
Diesel(litres)	0	677,126	1,079,630
Total(Joules)	*0*	$2.5927*10^{13}$	$4.1339*10^{13}$

-Trams

Municipal tramways			
Elec.(kWh)	9,180,200	0	0
Total(Joules)	$3.3049*10^{13}$	*0*	*0*

-Ferries	0	0	0
Grand total(Joules)	$1.5836*10^{15}$	$1.3248*10^{15}$	$1.7639*10^{15}$

Note:

(1) Total excludes the "other" category.

(2) In 1960 and 1970 these were the *Department of Street Railways* (DSR) and in 1980 the *Detroit Department of Transportation*(DDOT).

(3) SEMTA took over *Grand Trunk Western Railroad* 1974...service terminated in 1983.

Frankfurt

POPULATION AND AREA	1960	1970	1980
Total population	670,048	669,751	631,287
Urbanised area(ha)	7,682	8,982	11,695
Population of the CBD	23,944	19,426	15,572
Area of the CBD(ha)	227	239	239
Population of the inner city	411,077	319,155	273,116
Area of the inner city(ha)	3,424	3,602	4,373

EMPLOYMENT LOCATION			
Number of jobs in the CBD	116,162	114,922	92,992
Number of jobs in the inner city	384,777	398,702	324,747
Number of jobs in the outer area	101,719	139,771	181,038
Number of jobs in the metro.area	486,496	538,473	505,785

PARKING SUPPLY IN THE CBD			
Off street parking spaces	3,082	12,000	12,740
On street parking spaces	9,744	9,744	9,744
Total parking spaces	**12,826**	**21,744**	**22,484**

ROAD NETWORK (km)			
Total roads in the metro.area	894	1014	1258

MOTOR VEHICLES ON REGISTER			
Motor cars	89,320	187,527	244,255
Motor cycles	15,038	1,739	6,514
Motor lorries and other vehicles	13,950	18,414	18,697
Total vehicles on register	**118,308**	**207,680**	**269,466**

PRIVATE TRANSPORT INDICATORS			
Total annual V.K.T.	?	?	?
Total annualV.K.T.in cars	$1.3398*10^9$	$2.3341*10^9$	$2.6868*10^9$
Average vehicle occupancy	1.6	1.6	1.6
Car occupant kilometres	$2.1437*10^9$	$3.7346*10^9$	$4.2989*10^9$
Average road network speed(km/h)			
City of Frankfurt	?	?	30.0
City of Frankfurt & surrounding areas	?	?	45.0

TRANSPORTATION ENERGY USE			
Motor spirit consumption (Joules)	$4.0900*10^9$	$8.3399*10^{15}$	$1.0159*10^{16}$
Diesel fuel consumption (Joules)	?	?	?
Total fuel consumption (Joules)	?	?	?

MODAL SPLIT FOR THE JOURNEY TO WORK (% of workers)			
Public transport	36.7	34.4	19.0
Private transport	14.0	24.5	54.0
Walking and cycling	49.3	41.1	27.0

AVERAGE TRIP LENGTHS			
Journey to work	?	?	?
Other trip purposes	?	?	?

PUBLIC TRANSPORT INDICATORS[1]

VEHICLE KILOMETRES
-Buses

Stadtwerke motor bus	7,746,679	10,955,960	11,463,271
DB motor bus	?	?	8,000,000
Total	*?*	*?*	*19,463,271*

-Trains

S-Bahn	0	0	22,353,158
U-Bahn	0	?	9,500,208
R-Bahn[2]	?	?	2,500,000
Total	*?*	*?*	*34,353,366*

-Trams

Stadtwerke tramways	30,133,552	26,924,797	12,778,358

-Ferries

-Ferries	0	0	0
Grand total	*?*	*?*	*66,594,995*

PASSENGERS CARRIED
-Buses

Stadtwerke motor bus	29,807,125	30,445,759	42,604,550
DB motor bus	?	?	13,759,200
Total	*?*	*?*	*56,363,750*

-Trains

S-Bahn	0	0	81,010,800
U-Bahn	0	?	62,883,600
R-Bahn	?	?	8,975,200
Total	*?*	*?*	*152,869,600*

-Trams

Stadtwerke tramways	166,555,073	141,851,333	100,276,854

-Ferries

-Ferries	0	0	0
Grand total	*?*	*?*	*309,510,204*

AVERAGE TRIP LENGTH (km)
-Buses

Stadtwerke motor bus	3.9	3.9	3.9
DB motor bus	?	?	8.6

-Trains

S-Bahn	0.0	0.0	15.0
U-Bahn	0.0	?	4.8
R-Bahn	?	?	22.9

-Trams

Stadtwerke tramways	3.9	3.9	3.9

-Ferries

-Ferries	0.0	0.0	0.0

PASSENGER KILOMETRES
-Buses

Stadtwerke motor bus	116,247,788	118,738,460	166,157,745
DB motor bus	?	?	118,329,120
Total	*?*	*?*	*284,486,865*

-Trains

S-Bahn	0	0	1,212,731,676

U-Bahn	0	?	301,841,280
R-Bahn	?	?	205,442,328
Total	*?*	*?*	*1,720,015,284*
-Trams	649,564,785	553,220,199	391,079,731
-Ferries	0	0	0
Grand total	*?*	*?*	*2,395,581,880*

AVERAGE SPEED (km/h)
-Buses

Stadtwerke motor buses	?	?	21.5
DB motor bus	?	?	?
Overall bus speed	*?*	*?*	*21.5*

-Trains

S-Bahn	0.0	0.0	45.8
U-Bahn	0.0	?	31.3
R-Bahn	?	?	50.0
Overall train speed	*?*	*?*	*43.8*

-Trams

Stadtwerke tramways	?	?	16.7

-Ferries

-Ferries	0.0	0.0	0.0
All modes average	*?*	*?*	*36.7*

ENERGY CONSUMPTION
-Buses
Stadtwerke motor bus

Diesel (litres)	3,424,000	4,843,000	5,067,000
DB motor bus			
Diesel (litres)	?	?	1,443,200
Total(Joules)	*?*	*?*	*2.4926*10^{14}*

-Trains
S-Bahn

Elec.(kWh)	0	0	137,000,000
U-Bahn			
Elec.(kWh)	0	?	32,899,220
R-Bahn			
Elec.(kWh)	?	?	15,322,000
Total(Joules)	*?*	*?*	*6.6680*10^{14}*

-Trams
Stadtwerke tramways

Elec.(kWh)	?	?	48,698,322
Total(Joules)	*?*	*?*	*1.7530*10^{14}*

-Ferries

-Ferries	0	0	0
Grand total(Joules)	*?*	*?*	*1.0914*10^{15}*

Note:

(1) Populations used for the public transport data are: Trams- City of Frankfurt populations; 1,002,837 for Stadtwerke buses and U-Bahn (1980); 2,451,321 for DB buses, S-Bahn and R-Bahn (1980).

(2) Before the S-Bahn, the major train service was the R-Bahn (14 lines). However, by 1982 all these were converted to S-Bahn (in 1980/81 there was only 1 R-Bahn line of 13.8km).

Hamburg

POPULATION AND AREA	1960	1970	1980
Total population	1,832,346	1,793,782	1,645,095
Urbanised area(ha)	26,838	31,204	39,433
Population of the CBD	26,914	16,714	12,153
Area of the CBD(ha)	456	460	460
Population of the inner city	693,284	542,524	440,014
Area of the inner city(ha)	4,966	4,975	4,975

EMPLOYMENT LOCATION			
Number of jobs in the CBD	202,153	199,134	187,400
Number of jobs in the inner city	566,740	540,080	524,720
Number of jobs in the outer area	438,790	430,641	412,280
Number of jobs in the metro.area	1,005,530	970,721	937,000

PARKING SUPPLY IN THE CBD			
Off street parking spaces	?	?	?
On street parking spaces	?	?	?
Total parking spaces	**25,000**	**27,700**	**27,900**

ROAD NETWORK (km)			
Municipal roads	2,832	3,201	3,411
Freeways	15	35	60
Federal roads	75	157	157
Private roads	291	135	46
Total roads in the metro.area	**3,213**	**3,528**	**3,674**

MOTOR VEHICLES ON REGISTER			
Motor cars and station wagons	175,321	433,079	566,641
Trucks	28,633	33,681	34,986
Motor bikes/scooters/mopeds	28,669	3,288	13,235
Buses	903	1,403	1,754
Articulated vehicles (eg tractors)	2,426	3,817	4,757
Other vehicles (eg special vehicles)	1,543	3,919	7,710
Total vehicles on register	**237,495**	**479,187**	**629,083**

PRIVATE TRANSPORT INDICATORS			
Total annual V.K.T.	$3.7207*10^9$	$7.1515*10^9$	$8.2230*10^9$
Total annual V.K.T.in cars	$2.8577*10^9$	$6.2363*10^9$	$7.2530*10^9$
Average vehicle occupancy	1.68	1.68	1.68
Car occupant kilometres	$4.8009*10^9$	$1.0477*10^{10}$	$1.2185*10^{10}$
Average road network speed(km/h)	?	?	30.0

TRANSPORTATION ENERGY USE			
Motor spirit consumption (Joules)	$8.7283*10^{15}$	$2.2283*10^{16}$	$2.7425*10^{16}$
Diesel fuel consumption (Joules)	?	?	?
Total fuel consumption (Joules)	?	?	?

MODAL SPLIT FOR JOURNEY TO WORK (% of workers)			
Public transport	53.0	45.7	40.8
Private transport	15.4	35.7	43.9
Walking and cycling	31.6	18.6	15.3

AVERAGE TRIP LENGTHS (km)

Journey to work	?	?	?
Other trip purposes	?	?	?

PUBLIC TRANSPORT INDICATORS[1]

VEHICLE KILOMETRES

-Buses			
HHA stadt-bus [2]	?	31,010,000	49,000,000
HHA schnell-bus	?	9,260,000	7,200,000
DB-bus[3] (1970) PVG (1980)[4]	?	1,800,000	1,200,000
VHH-bus [5]	?	11,910,000	15,200,000
DBP-bus [6]	?	480,000	600,000
Sub-total	**28,717,000**	**54,460,000**	**73,200,000**
Private	11,670,000	13,128,000	21,368,000
Total	*40,387,000*	*67,588,000*	*94,568,000*

-Trains			
U-Bahn (HHA)	?	53,710,000	50,800,000
S-Bahn (DB)			
Electric	?	35,010,000	40,000,000
Diesel	?	8,530,000	7,300,000
AKN[7]	?	1,470,000	2,300,000
ANB[8]	?	400,000	500,000
EBO[9]	?	280,000	300,000
Total	*44,626,000*	*99,400,000*	*100,900,000*

-Trams			
Municipal tramways (HHA)	35,408,000	12,590,000	0

-Ferries			
Alsterschiffe (HHA)	?	200,000	124,000
Hadag schiffe (HADAG)[10]	?	720,000	462,000
Total	*1,395,000*	*920,000*	*586,000*
Grand total	*121,816,000*	*179,578,000*	*196,054,000*

PASSENGERS CARRIED

-Buses			
HHA stadt-bus	?	138,600,000	219,200,000
HHA schnell-bus	?	14,000,000	12,400,000
DB-bus (1970) PVG (1980)	?	4,800,000	4,400,000
VHH-bus	?	27,500,000	32,100,000
DBP-bus	?	800,000	900,000
Sub-total	**96,039,000**	**185,700,000**	**269,000,000**
Private	8,925,000	3,405,000	3,399,000
Total	*104,964,000*	*189,105,000*	*272,399,000*

-Trains			
U-Bahn (HHA)	?	190,300,000	183,200,000
S-Bahn (DB)			
Electric	?	111,700,000	113,500,000
Diesel	?	26,100,000	23,500,000
AKN	?	3,000,000	3,500,000
ANB	?	1,200,000	1,400,000
EBO	?	700,000	800,000
Total	*283,662,000*	*333,000,000*	*325,900,000*

207

-Trams			
Municipal tramways (HHA)	212,066,000	63,315,000	0
-Ferries			
Alsterschiffe (HHA)	?	1,400,000	1,300,000
Hadag schiffe (HADAG)	?	9,800,000	6,200,000
Total	*22,387,000*	*11,200,000*	*7,500,000*
Grand total	*623,079,000*	*596,620,000*	*605,779,000*

AVERAGE TRIP LENGTH (km)

-Buses			
HHA stadt-bus	?	4.2	4.1
HHA schnell-bus	?	7.7	7.7
DB-bus (1970) PVG (1980)	?	7.0	3.4
VHH-bus	?	8.6	7.6
DBP-bus	?	9.5	9.5
Sub- average (buses)	**5.0**	**5.2**	**4.7**
Private	10.0	10.0	10.0
-Trains			
U-Bahn (HHA)	?	5.6	5.1
S-Bahn (DB)			
Electric	?	9.9	9.3
Diesel	?	11.8	12.6
AKN	?	13.2	11.2
ANB	?	5.9	6.6
EBO	?	9.0	7.8
Overall average trains	*7.5*	*7.6*	*7.2*
-Trams			
Municipal tramways (HHA)	4.3	4.3	0.0
-Ferries			
Alsterschiffe (HHA)	?	3.7	3.7
Hadag schiffe (HADAG)	?	3.0	3.0
Overall average ferries	*3.1*	*3.1*	*3.1*

PASSENGER KILOMETRES

-Buses			
HHA stadt-bus	?	580,900,000	899,700,000
HHA schnell-bus	?	107,200,000	95,300,000
DB-bus (1970) PVG (1980)	?	34,100,000	14,900,000
VHH-bus	?	234,300,000	240,800,000
DBP-bus	?	7,700,000	8,600,000
Sub-total	480,200,000	964,200,000	1,259,300,000
Private	89,250,000	34,050,000	33,990,000
Total	*569,450,000*	*998,250,000*	*1,293,290,000*
-Trains			
U-Bahn (HHA)	?	1,069,500,000	978,600,000
S-Bahn (DB)			
Electric	?	1,109,900,000	1,051,600,000
Diesel	?	307,400,000	297,000,000
AKN	?	39,200,000	38,700,000
ANB	?	6,900,000	9,000,000
EBO	?	6,700,000	6,500,000
Total	*2,127,500,000*	*2,539,600,000*	*2,381,400,000*

-Trams			
Municipal tramways (HHA)	911,900,000	269,700,000	0
-Ferries			
Alsterschiffe	?	5,300,000	4,500,000
Hadag schiffe (HADAG)	?	29,400,000	18,600,000
Total	*69,400,000*	*34,700,000*	*23,100,000*
Grand total	*3,678,250,000*	*3,842,250,000*	*3,697,790,000*

AVERAGE SPEED (km/h)

-Buses			
HHA stadt-buses	?	21.5	20.9
HHA schnell-bus	?	23.5	20.9
DB-bus (1970) PVG (1980)	?	28.6	24.5
VHH-bus	?	24.9	26.1
DBP-bus	?	28.6	29.5
Sub-average	**23.5**	**22.9**	**22.4**
Private	30.0	30.0	30.0
Overall bus speed	*23.5*	*22.9*	*22.4*
-Trains			
U-Bahn (HHA)	?	31.1	31.3
S-Bahn (DB)			
Electric	?	40.4	38.6
Diesel	?	51.2	47.4
AKN	?	34.6	44.4
ANB	?	32.2	35.8
EBO	?	34.1	37.1
Overall train speed	*36.0*	*36.2*	*35.7*
-Trams			
Municipal tramways (HHA)	20.0	18.0	0.0
-Ferries			
Alsterschiffe (HHA)	?	10.0	10.4
Hadag schiffe (HADAG)	?	10.9	12.2
Overall ferry speed	*10.0*	*10.7*	*11.9*
All modes average	*29.6*	*31.2*	*30.9*

ENERGY CONSUMPTION

-Buses

HHA stadt-bus & schnell-bus			
Diesel (litres)	?	13,700,000	21,300,000
DB-bus (1970) PVG (1980)			
Diesel (litres)	?	555,000	430,000
VHH-bus			
Diesel (litres)	?	3,630,000	5,500,000
DBP-bus			
Diesel (litres)	?	150,000	220,000
Private			
Diesel (litres)	?	4,000,000	7,720,000
Total (Joules)	$4.7166*10^{14}$	$8.4353*10^{14}$	$1.3467*10^{15}$

-Trains

U-Bahn (HHA)			
Elec.(kWh)	?	90,300,000	86,900,000
S-Bahn (DB)			
Electric (kWh)	?	111,700,000	125,000,000
Diesel (litres)	?	5,660,000	5,030,000
AKN			
Diesel (litres)	?	740,000	1,040,000
ANB			
Diesel (litres)	?	160,000	230,000
EBO			
Diesel (litres)	?	110,000	120,000
Total (Joules)	$4.4135*10^{14}$	$9.8260*10^{14}$	$1.0087*10^{15}$

-Trams

Municipal tramways (HHA)			
Elec.(kWh)	74,357,000	27,600,000	0
Total (Joules)	$2.6769*10^{14}$	$9.9360*10^{13}$	*0*

-Ferries

Alsterschiffe(HHA)			
Diesel (litres)	?	200,000	140,000
Hadag schiffe (HADAG)			
Diesel (litres)	?	4,550,000	2,919,000
Total (Joules)	$2.7576*10^{14}$	$1.8188*10^{14}$	$1.1713*10^{14}$
Grand total(Joules)	$1.4565*10^{15}$	$2.1074*10^{15}$	$2.4725*10^{15}$

Note:
(1) All public transport in Hamburg is controlled by the Hamburg Transport Community, a union of nine organisations known as the Hamburger Verkehrsverbund.
(2) HHA is the abbreviation for Hamburger Hochbahn Aktiengesellschaft.
(3) DB is the abbreviation for Deutsche Bundesbahn, the national railways who also run some bus services in Hamburg.
(4) PVG is the abbreviation for Pinneberger Verkehrsgesellschaft A. u . H. Reimers Autobus KG.
(5) VHH is the abbreviation for Verkehrsbetriebe Hamburg-Holstein Aktiengesellschaft.
(6) DBP is the abbreviation for Deutsche Bundespost.
(7) AKN is the abbreviation for Eisenbahngesellschaft Altona-Kaltenkirchen-Neümunster.
(8) ANB is the abbreviation for Alsternordbahn GmbH.
(9) EBO is the abbreviation for Elmshorn-Barmstedt-Oldesloer Eisenbahn Aktiengesellschaft.
(10) HADAG stands for HADAG Seetouristik und Fährdienst AG.

Hong Kong

POPULATION AND AREA	1960	1970	1980
Total population	3,129,648	3,936,630	4,986,560
Urbanised area(ha)	12,200	14,400	17,000
Population of the CBD	47,799	22,892	17,287
Area of the CBD(ha)	102	102	108
Population of the inner city	?	1,466,173	1,495,070
Area of the inner city(ha)	?	1,398	1,442

EMPLOYMENT LOCATION			
Number of jobs in the CBD	?	?	135,674
Number of jobs in the inner city	?	?	845,366
Number of jobs in the outer area	?	?	1,020,022
Number of jobs in the metro.area	?	1,716,300	1,865,388

PARKING SUPPLY IN THE CBD			
Off street parking spaces	?	?	?
On street parking spaces	?	?	?
Total parking spaces	?	2,708	5,076

ROAD NETWORK(km)			
Total roads in the metro.area	?	976	1,141

MOTOR VEHICLES ON REGISTER			
Private cars	35,778	105,874	211,556
Taxis and public hire cars	1,431	4,290	11,061
Motor cycles	4,095	16,692	27,443
Goods vehicles	10,270	25,790	64,214
Crown vehicles	1,549	3,277	5,041
Buses and Trams	1,153	3,259	5,383
Public light buses	0	3,813	4,350
Private light buses	0	1,567	924
Total vehicles on register	54,276	164,562	330,472

PRIVATE TRANSPORT INDICATORS			
Total annual V.K.T.	?	$1.8400*10^9$	$4.4845*10^9$
Total annual V.K.T.in cars	?	$7.1072*10^8$	$1.7322*10^9$
Average vehicle occupancy	?	1.95	1.77
Car occupant kilometres	?	$1.7002*10^9$	$3.0660*10^9$
Average road network speed(km/h)	?	25.9	20.6

TRANSPORTATION ENERGY USE			
Motor spirit consumption (Joules)	?	$5.1760*10^{15}$	$9.9099*10^{15}$
Diesel fuel consumption (Joules)	?	$5.5670*10^{15}$	$1.2787*10^{16}$
Total fuel consumption (Joules)	?	$1.0743*10^{16}$	$2.2697*10^{16}$

MODAL SPLIT FOR THE JOURNEY TO WORK (% of workers)			
Public transport	?	?	62.2
Private transport	?	?	3.3
Walking and cycling	?	?	34.5

AVERAGE TRIP LENGTHS (km)

Journey to work	?	?	?
Other trip purposes	?	?	?

PUBLIC TRANSPORT INDICATORS

VEHICLE KILOMETRES

-Buses

Kowloon Motor Bus Co.	?	?	121,046,000
China Motor Bus Co.	?	?	42,781,200
New Lantao Bus Co.	0	?	1,870,000
Public light buses[1]	?	?	378,760,000
Total	*?*	*?*	*544,457,200*

-Trains

Kowloon-Canton Railway	?	?	3,600,000
Mass Transit Railway	0	0	19,100,000
Total	*?*	*?*	*22,700,000*

-Trams

Hong Kong Tramways	?	?	8,100,000
Peak Tramways	?	?	ca 100,000
Total	*?*	*?*	*8,200,000*

-Ferries

Hong Kong and Yaumati, Star & minor ferries	?	?	3,943,919
Total	*?*	*?*	*3,943,919*
Grand total	*?*	*?*	*579,301,119*

PASSENGERS CARRIED

-Buses

Kowloon Motor Bus Co.	435,515,000	568,014,000	911,657,000
China Motor Bus Co.	121,120,000	185,795,000	275,533,000
New Lantao Bus Co.	0	974,000	2,802,000
Public light buses	77,200,000	415,500,000	545,675,000
Total	*632,835,000*	*1,170,283,000*	*1,735,667,000*

-Trains

Kowloon-Canton Railway	5,867,000	10,274,000	19,341,000
Mass Transit Railway	0	0	223,000,000
Total	*5,867,000*	*10,274,000*	*242,341,000*

-Trams

Hong Kong Tramways	180,585,000	158,533,000	159,183,000
Peak Tramways	1,886,000	2,239,000	2,041,000
Total	*182,471,000*	*160,772,000*	*161,224,000*

-Ferries

Hong Kong and Yaumati	106,765,000	182,201,000	131,994,000
Star Ferry Co.	41,864,000	56,646,000	46,551,000
Minor ferries	0	0	7,557,000
Total	*148,629,000*	*238,847,000*	*186,102,000*
Grand total	*969,802,000*	*1,580,176,000*	*2,325,334,000*

AVERAGE TRIP LENGTH (km)

-Buses

Kowloon Motor Bus Co.	?	?	3.1
China Motor Bus Co.	?	?	3.1
New Lantao Bus Co.	0.0	?	3.1
Public light buses	?	?	6.1

-Trains

Kowloon-Canton Railway	21.6	17.9	22.3
Mass Transit Railway	0.0	0.0	5.9

-Trams

Hong Kong Tramways	?	2.9	2.9
Peak Tramways	?	2.9	2.9

-Ferries

Ferries overall	*?*	*3.6*	*5.0*

PASSENGER KILOMETRES

-Buses

Kowloon Motor Bus Co.	?	?	?
China Motor Bus Co.	?	?	?
New Lantao Bus Co.	?	?	8,742,240
Sub-total	?	5,322,795,000	3,712,775,040
Public light buses	?	275,940,000	3,328,617,500
Total	*?*	*5,598,735,000*	*7,041,392,540*

-Trains

Kowloon-Canton Railway	126,727,200	183,904,600	431,304,300
Mass Transit Railway	0	0	1,311,240,000
Total	*126,727,200*	*183,904,600*	*1,742,544,300*

-Trams

Hong Kong and Peak Tramways	?	466,238,800	464,325,120

-Ferries

All ferries	?	859,849,200	936,093,060
Grand total	*?*	*7,108,727,600*	*10,184,350,000*

AVERAGE SPEED (km/h)

-Buses

Overall bus speed	?	?	14.8

-Trains

Kowloon-Canton Railway	?	?	27.3
Mass Transit Railway	0.0	0.0	33.0
Overall train speed	*?*	*?*	*31.3*

-Trams

Overall tram speed	?	?	9.9

-Ferries

Overall ferry speed	?	?	13.5
All modes average	*?*	*?*	*16.8*

ENERGY CONSUMPTION

-Buses
Kowloon & China Motor Bus Co's.

Diesel (litres)	?	33,749,699	69,306,138
New Lantao Bus Co.			
Diesel (litres)	0	negligible	792,000
Public light buses			
Diesel (litres)	?	32,436,668	?
Total(Joules)[2]	?	*2.5343*10^{15}*	*2.6840*10^{15}*

-Trains
Kowloon-Canton Railway

Diesel(litres)	?	2,684,500	4,031,300
Mass Transit Railway			
Elec.(kWh)	0	0	76,900,000
Total(Joules)	?	*1.0279*10^{14}*	*4.3120*10^{14}*

-Trams
Hong Kong &Peak Tramways

Elec.(kWh)	21,522,162	16,037,160	12,888,290
Total(Joules)	*7.7480*10^{13}*	*5.7734*10^{13}*	*4.6398*10^{13}*

-Ferries
Hong Kong , Yaumati and Star
Ferries only

Diesel(litres)	?	18,673,283	29,065,678
Total(Joules)	?	*0.7150*10^{15}*	*1.1129*10^{15}*
Grand total(Joules)	?	*3.4098*10^{15}*	*4.2745*10^{15}*

Note:

(1) In 1961 the equivalents of public light buses were known as miscellaneous small buses.

(2) The total bus energy figure for 1980 excudes PLBs because their energy use is included in private transport energy use and is inseparable.

Houston

POPULATION AND AREA	1960	1970	1980
Total population			
SMSA	1,430,394	1,999,316	2,905,353
Urbanised area	1,139,678	1,677,863	2,412,664
Urbanised area(ha)	111,500	139,601	271,696
Population of the CBD	2,786	3,719	2,145
Area of the CBD(ha)	392	392	392
Population of the inner city	503,836	526,089	480,819
Area of the inner city(ha)	23,310	23,310	23,310
EMPLOYMENT LOCATION			
Number of jobs in the CBD	56,900	96,200	173,543
Number of jobs in the inner city	?	?	615,190
Number of jobs in the outer area	?	?	880,110
Number of jobs in the metro.area	556,600	860,000	1,495,300
PARKING SUPPLY IN THE CBD			
Off street parking spaces	24,696	30,528	58,994
Parking garages	10,125	14,093	35,210
Parking lots	14,571	16,435	23,784
On street parking spaces	3,597	4,400	5,200
Total parking spaces	**28,293**	**34,928**	**64,194**
ROAD NETWORK (km)			
Total roads in the metro.area	?	23,329	30,674
MOTOR VEHICLES ON REGISTER			
Passenger cars	555,195	953,349	1,750,633
Other vehicles(eg commecial trucks,motor cycles,etc.)	161,353	341,962	565,019
Total vehicles on register	**716,548**	**1,295,311**	**2,315,652**
PRIVATE TRANSPORT INDICATORS			
Total annual V.K.T.	$1.0282*10^{10}$	$1.7752*10^{10}$	$3.3507*10^{10}$
Total annual V.K.T.in cars	$9.7680*10^{9}$	$1.6509*10^{10}$	$2.8816*10^{10}$
Average vehicle occupancy	?	?	1.61
Car occupant kilometres	?	?	$4.6394*10^{10}$
Average road network speed(km/h)	?	56.2	51.1
TRANSPORTATION ENERGY USE			
Motor spirit consumption (Joules)	$6.5512*10^{16}$	$1.2522*10^{17}$	$1.9190*10^{17}$
Diesel fuel consumption (Joules)	$3.2310*10^{15}$	$9.7150*10^{15}$	$3.0206*10^{16}$
Total fuel consumption (Joules)	$6.8743*10^{16}$	$1.3493*10^{17}$	$2.2211*10^{17}$
MODAL SPLIT FOR THE JOURNEY TO WORK (%of workers)			
SMSA			
Public transport	11.8	5.8	3.3
Private transport	83.0	90.6	93.9
Walking and cycling	5.2	3.6	2.8

City of Houston only

Public transport	14.3	7.9	3.3
Private transport	80.3	88.2	93.9
Walking and cycling	5.4	3.9	3.4

AVERAGE TRIP LENGTHS

Journey to work	?	?	14.7
Other trip purposes			
Family and personal business	?	?	8.9
Civic,educational and religious	?	?	10.3
Social/recreational	?	?	11.3
Work related trips(excluding J to W)	?	?	18.5
Other	?	?	9.5
All non-work trips	?	?	10.5

PUBLIC TRANSPORT INDICATORS

VEHICLE KILOMETRES
-Buses

Houston Rapid Transit Co.	25,339,643	25,143,671	0
Pioneer Bus Co.	4,066,538	0	0
MTA[1] of Harris County	0	0	26,414,106
Total	*29,406,181*	*25,143,671*	*26,414,106*

-Trains	0	0	0

-Trams	0	0	0

-Ferries	0	0	0
Grand Total	*29,406,181*	*25,143,671*	*26,414,106*

PASSENGERS CARRIED
-Buses

Houston Rapid Transit Co.	36,048,465	32,800,000	0
Pioneer Bus Co.	4,800,000	0	0
MTA of Harris County	0	0	42,774,866
Total	*40,848,465*	*32,800,000*	*42,774,866*

-Trains	0	0	0

-Trams	0	0	0

-Ferries	0	0	0
Grand Total	*40,848,465*	*32,800,000*	*42,774,866*

AVERAGE TRIP LENGTH (km)
-Buses

Houston Rapid Transit Co.	8.2	8.5	0.0
Pioneer Bus Co.	8.2	0.0	0.0
MTA of Harris County	0.0	0.0	8.7

-Trains	0.0	0.0	0.0

-Trams	0.0	0.0	0.0

-Ferries	0.0	0.0	0.0

PASSENGER KILOMETRES
-Buses

Houston Rapid Transit Co.	295,597,413	278,800,000	0
Pioneer Bus Co.	39,360,000	0	0
MTA of Harris County	0	0	372,662,215
Total	*334,957,413*	*278,800,000*	*372,662,215*

-Trains	0	0	0
-Trams	0	0	0
-Ferries	0	0	0
Grand Total	*334,957,413*	*278,800,000*	*372,662,215*

AVERAGE SPEED (km/h)
-Buses

Houston Rapid Transit Co.	18.4	20.8	0.0
Pioneer Bus Co.	?	0.0	0.0
MTA of Harris County	0.0	0.0	21.8
Overall bus speed	*18.4*	*20.8*	*21.8*

-Trains	0.0	0.0	0.0
-Trams	0.0	0.0	0.0
-Ferries	0.0	0.0	0.0
All modes average	*18.4*	*20.8*	*21.8*

ENERGY CONSUMPTION
-Buses

Houston Rapid Transit Co.			
Diesel (litres)	15,697,786	15,514,711	0
Pioneer Bus Co.			
Diesel (litres)	2,597,868	0	0
MTA of Harris County			
Diesel (litres)	0	0	21,658,413
Petrol(litres)	0	0	321,869
Total(Joules)	$7.0054*10^{14}$	$5.9406*10^{14}$	$8.4047*10^{14}$

-Trains	0	0	0
-Trams	0	0	0
-Ferries	0	0	0
Grand Total(Joules)	$7.0054*10^{14}$	$5.9406*10^{14}$	$8.4047*10^{14}$

Note:
(1) MTA is the Metropolitan Transit Authority.

London

POPULATION AND AREA	1960	1970	1980
Total population	7,992,400	7,452,300	6,713,200
Urbanised area(ha)	122,226	120,937	119,321
Population of the CBD	269,600	230,000	179,000
Area of the CBD(ha)	2,697	2,697	2,697
Population of the inner city	3,492,900	3,031,900	2,498,000
Area of the inner city(ha)			

EMPLOYMENT LOCATION			
Number of jobs in the CBD	1,402,260	1,250,030	1,070,170
Number of jobs in the inner city	2,683,760	2,331,530	1,983,990
Number of jobs in the outer area	1,700,010	1,747,750	1,616,060
Number of jobs in the metro.area	4,383,770	4,079,280	3,600,050

PARKING SUPPLY IN THE CBD			
Off street parking spaces	?	?	?
On street parking spaces	?	?	?
Total parking spaces	?	158,156	138,843

ROAD NETWORK (km)			
Motorways	?	25	44
All purpose	?	216	208
Principal roads	?	1,411	1,404
Classified roads	?	1,442	1,463
Sub-total	3,112	3,094	3,119
Unclassified roads	9,016	9,491	9,731
Total roads in the metro.area	12,128	12,585	12,850

MOTOR VEHICLES ON REGISTER			
Private vans and cars	1,249,450	1,660,141	1,932,000
Goods vehicles	?	277,427	257,100
Motor cycles,scooters and mopeds	?	121,004	127,300
Other vehicles	?	41,317	374,400
Crown exempt vehicles	?	41,256	32,900
Total vehicles on register	1,493,000	2,141,145	2,386,700

PRIVATE TRANSPORT INDICATORS			
Total annual V,KT.	$1.4319*10^{10}$	$1.8435*10^{10}$	$2.2451*10^{10}$
Total annual V.K.T.in cars	$1.0717*10^{10}$	$1.3826*10^{10}$	$1.6980*10^{10}$
Average vehicle occupancy[1]	1.79	1.79	1.76
Car occupant kilometres	$1.9183*10^{10}$	$2.4749*10^{10}$	$2.9885*10^{10}$
Average road network speed(km/h)	31.3	32.5	31.3

TRANSPORTATION ENERGY USE			
Motor spirit consumption (Joules)	$5.2372*10^{16}$	$6.7565*10^{16}$	$8.3420*10^{16}$
Diesel fuel consumption (Joules)[2]	$2.2853*10^{16}$	$2.7597*10^{16}$	$3.4711*10^{16}$
Total fuel consumption (Joules)	$7.5225*10^{16}$	$9.5162*10^{16}$	$1.1813*10^{17}$

MODAL SPLIT FOR THE JOURNEY TO WORK (% of workers)			
Public transport	51.0	44.0	39.0
Private transport	28.0	38.0	38.0
Walking and cycling	21.0	18.0	23.0

AVERAGE TRIP LENGTHS (km)

Journey to work	6.0	6.9	7.5
Other trip purposes	?	?	?

PUBLIC TRANSPORT INDICATORS

VEHICLE KILOMETRES

-Buses			
London Transport buses[3]	411,900,000	320,200,000	279,000,000
-Trains			
Underground(LT)	355,038,810	341,320,000	336,000,000
Suburban rail(National:BR)	203,500,000	193,800,000	189,100,000
Total	*558,538,810*	*535,120,000*	*525,100,000*
-Trams	0	0	0
-Ferries	0	0	0
Grand total	*970,438,810*	*855,320,000*	*804,100,000*

PASSENGERS CARRIED

-Buses			
London Transport buses			
Motor buses	2,281,000,000	1,502,000,000	1,183,000,000
Trolley buses	312,000,000	0	0
Total	*2,593,000,000*	*1,502,000,000*	*1,183,000,000*
-Trains			
Underground(LT)	674,000,000	672,000,000	541,000,000
Suburban rail(National:BR)	220,400,000	246,500,000	185,600,000
Total	*894,400,000*	*918,500,000*	*726,600,000*
-Trams	0	0	0
-Ferries	0	0	0
Grand total	*3,487,400,000*	*2,420,500,000*	*1,909,600,000*

AVERAGE TRIP LENGTH (km)

-Buses			
London Transport buses	3.7	3.7	3.5
-Trains			
Underground(LT)	7.7	7.9	7.6
Suburban rail(National:BR)	14.0	16.6	17.5
-Trams	0.0	0.0	0.0
-Ferries	0.0	0.0	0.0

PASSENGER KILOMETRES

-Buses

London Transport buses	9,568,000,000	5,482,000,000	4,188,000,000

-Trains

Underground(LT)	5,163,000,000	5,295,000,000	4,090,000,000
Suburban rail(National:BR)	3,086,000,000	4,092,000,000	3,248,000,000
Total	*8,249,000,000*	*9,387,000,000*	*7,338,000,000*

-Trams	0	0	0
-Ferries	0	0	0
Grand total	*17,817,000,000*	*14,869,000,000*	*11,526,000,000*

AVERAGE SPEED (km/h)

-Buses

Overall bus speed (LT buses)	20.9	18.5	17.7

-Trains

Underground (LT)	32.8	32.8	32.8
Suburban rail (National:BR)	43.8	44.6	45.4
Overall train speed	*36.9*	*37.9*	*38.4*

-Trams	0.0	0.0	0.0
-Ferries	0.0	0.00	0.0
All modes average	*28.3*	*30.7*	*30.9*

ENERGY CONSUMPTION

-Buses

LT motor bus

Diesel (litres)	?	129,618,700	112,940,716
LT trolley bus			
Elec.(kWh)	?	0	0
Total(Joules)	*$5.7666*10^{15}$*	*$4.9631*10^{15}$*	*$4.3245*10^{15}$*

-Trains

Underground(LT)

Elec.(kWh)	763,888,889	659,722,222	590,000,000
Suburban rail(National:BR)			
(Joules)[4]	$8.5800*10^{14}$	$8.1700*10^{14}$	$1.0992*10^{15}$
Total(Joules)	*$3.6080*10^{12}$*	*$3.1920*10^{15}$*	*$3.2232*10^{15}$*

-Trams	0	0	0

-Ferries	0	0	0
Grand total(Joules)	*$9.3746*10^{15}$*	*$8.1551*10^{15}$*	*$7.5477*10^{15}$*

Note:
(1)The average occupancy for all vehicles in London is 1.69,1.68,1.66 in 1960,1970 and 1980 respectively.
(2) London energy use is not specified by fuel type but according to vehicle type (private vehicles and goods vehicles). For conformity with other cities, the goods vehicles figures are shown as being all diesel and the private vehicles as all motor spirit, whereas each would have a mixture of the two fuel types.
(3) In 1960 the bus figures include a small component of trolley buses but these were gone by 1962/63.
(4) The British Rail energy data are only available in Joules (no split according to fuel type).

Los Angeles

POPULATION AND AREA	1960	1970	1980
Total population			
SMSA	6,038,771	7,041,980	7,477,503
Urbanised area	6,488,791	8,351,266	9,479,436
Urbanised area(ha)	354,830	407,148	473,278
Urbanised area of SMSA(ha)	270,537	281,679	305,830
Population of the CBD	16,651	8,340	9,516
Area of the CBD(ha)	324	324	324
Population of the inner city	2,479,015	2,811,801	2,966,850
Area of the inner city(ha)	91,971	93,071	100,322

EMPLOYMENT LOCATION			
Number of jobs in the CBD	174,096	128,698	152,919
Number of jobs in the inner city	1,013,000	1,174,000	1,394,419
Number of jobs in the outer area	1,602,000	1,566,000	1,828,153
Number of jobs in the metro.area	2,615,000	2,740,000	3,222,572

PARKING SUPPLY IN THE CBD			
Off street parking spaces	?	66,821	77,877
On street parking spaces	?	2,005	2,197
Total parking spaces	64,900	68,826	80,074

ROAD NETWORK (km)			
State highways	1,441	1,426	1,462
County maintained	6,630	6,598	5,965
Not county maintained	1,321	11	40
City streets	18,935	24,248	24,623
Nationals not overlapping the State or Local systems	1,244	1,562	1,739
Total roads in the metro.area	29,571	33,845	33,829

MOTOR VEHICLES ON REGISTER			
Autos	2,772,523	3,670,496	4,048,996
Trucks	297,762	477,075	743,629
Motor cycles	27,649	183,444	192,902
Trailers	226,404	290,231	345,584
Total	3,324,338	4,621,246	5,331,111
Total without trailers	3,097,934	4,331,015	4,985,527

PRIVATE TRANSPORT INDICATORS			
Total annual V.K.T.	$4.6927*10^{10}$	$5.9441*10^{10}$	$7.4799*10^{10}$
Total annual V.K.T.in cars	$4.4581*10^{10}$	$5.5280*10^{10}$	$6.7319*10^{10}$
Average vehicle occupancy	1.51	1.51	1.54
Car occupant kilometres	$6.7317*10^{10}$	$8.3473*10^{10}$	$1.0367*10^{11}$
Average road network speed(km/h)[1]	49.9	45.1	45.1

TRANSPORTATION ENERGY USE			
Motor spirit consumption (Joules)	$2.5460*10^{17}$	$4.0966*10^{17}$	$4.3724*10^{17}$
Diesel fuel consumption (Joules)	$2.6531*10^{16}$	$3.1884*10^{16}$	$4.7828*10^{16}$
Total fuel consumption (Joules)	$2.8113*10^{17}$	$4.4155*10^{17}$	$4.8506*10^{17}$

MODAL SPLIT FOR THE JOURNEY TO WORK (% of workers)

SMSA			
Public transport	8.7	5.8	7.7
Private transport	85.2	89.2	88.0
Walking and cycling	6.1	5.0	4.2
City of Los Angeles only			
Public transport	14.7	9.7	10.5
Private transport	79.2	85.1	85.5
Walking and cycling	6.1	5.2	4.0

AVERAGE TRIP LENGTHS (km)

Journey to work	12.1	15.3	15.3
Other trip purposes (all trips)	11.1	11.6	11.6

PUBLIC TRANSPORT INDICATORS

VEHICLE KILOMETRES

-Buses			
SCRTD motor bus	?	92,540,474	172,916,785
Long Beach Public Trans.Co.	?	8,116,026	10,685,095
Santa Monica Mun. Bus Lines	?	5,338,217	6,191,567
Others[2]	?	7,725,000	10,318,712
Total	116,056,956	113,719,717	200,112,159
-Trains			
LA-Long Beach interurban[3]	1,127,000	0	0
-Trams	0	0	0
-Ferries	0	0	0
Grand Total	117,183,956	113,719,717	200,112,159

PASSENGERS CARRIED

-Buses			
SCRTD motor bus	?	141,912,000	389,123,000
Long Beach Public Trans.Co.	?	9,852,905	18,187,700
Santa Monica Mun. Bus Lines	?	10,940,600	21,852,400
Others	?	10,850,073	13,598,900
Total	222,692,525	173,555,578	442,762,000
-Trains			
LA-Long Beach interurban	1,600,000	0	0
-Trams	0	0	0
-Ferries	0	0	0
Grand Total	224,292,525	173,555,578	442,762,000

AVERAGE TRIP LENGTH (km)
-Buses

SCRTD motor bus	?	?	6.7
Long Beach Public Trans.Co.	?	?	4.8
Santa Monica Mun. Bus Lines	?	?	4.8
Others	?	?	5.4
Overall	*6.5*	*6.5*	*6.5*

-Trains

LA-Long Beach interurban	20.0	0.0	0.0

-Trams

	0.0	0.0	0.0

-Ferries

	0.0	0.0	0.0

PASSENGER KILOMETRES
-Buses

SCRTD motor bus	?	?	2,602,245,737
Long Beach Public Trans.Co.	?	?	87,846,591
Santa Monica Mun. Bus Lines	?	?	105,033,502
Others	?	?	73,322,137
Total	*1,443,047,562*	*1,124,640,145*	*2,868,447,967*

-Trains

LA-Long Beach interurban	32,000,000	0	0

-Trams

	0	0	0

-Ferries

	0	0	0
Grand total	*1,475,047,562*	*1,124,640,145*	*2,868,447,967*

AVERAGE SPEED (km/h)
-Buses

SCRTD motor bus	?	20.9	22.9
Long Beach Public Trans.Co.	?	19.4	23.2
Santa Monica Mun. Bus Lines	?	19.6	23.2
Others	?	?	19.0
Overall bus speed	*20.0*	*20.3*	*21.6*

-Trains

LA-Long Beach interurban	?(4)	0.0	0.0

-Trams

	0.0	0.0	0.0

-Ferries

	0.0	0.0	0.0
All modes average	*20.0*	*20.3*	*21.6*

ENERGY CONSUMPTION

-Buses

SCRTD motor bus

Diesel (litres)	?	47,954,201	105,728,298
Long Beach Public Trans.Co.			
Diesel (litres)	?	3,822,373	6,681,661
Santa Monica Mun. Bus Lines			
Diesel (litres)	?	2,789,356	4,755,096
Others			
Diesel (litres)	?	3,576,389	4,780,077
Petrol(litres)(Total for all operators)	0	0	4,383,030
Total(Joules)	$2.2219*10^{15}$	$2.2263*10^{15}$	$4.8213*10^{15}$

-Trains			
LA-Long Beach interurban	?	0	0

-Trams	0	0	0

-Ferries	0	0	0
Grand total(Joules)	$2.2219*10^{15}$	$2.2263*10^{15}$	$4.8213*10^{15}$

Note:

(1) The LA Multi-County Area (which includes Orange and Ventura Counties) had average speeds for the journey to work in cars of 47.1 and 43.1km/h in 1967 and 1976 respectively.

(2) In 1960 there were approximately twenty-four bus operators and details of these have been provided by SCRTD. Also in 1970 and 1980 there were quite a large numbers of operators and details of these are also available.

(3) This was part of the Pacific-Electric system and was closed in March 1961.

(4) This has an undetectable affect on the overall speed of public transportation in LA.

Melbourne

POPULATION AND AREA	1960	1970	1980
Total population	1,984,815	2,503,450	2,722,817
Urbanised area(ha)	97,851	138,236	165,961
Population of the CBD	5,534	4,082	4,216
Area of the CBD(ha)	172	172	172
Area of the CAD(ha)[1]	238	238	238
Population of the inner city	315,142	307,570	245,019
Area of the inner city(ha)	8,365	8,365	8,365

EMPLOYMENT LOCATION			
Number of jobs in the CBD(CAD)	148,000	158,000	153,857
Number of jobs in the inner city	395,899	340,062	336,995
Number of jobs in the outer area	382,209	576,785	677,707
Number of jobs in the metro.area	778,108	916,847	1,014,702

PARKING SUPPLY IN THE CBD (CAD)			
Off street parking spaces	13,031	21,063	35,400
On street parking spaces	9,996	9,282	6,200
Total parking spaces	**23,027**	**30,345**	**41,600**

ROAD NETWORK (km)			
Sealed	?	12,475	15,893
Formed and surfaced	?	?	3,673
Formed only	?	?	852
Unformed	?	?	963
Total roads in the metro.area	**16,158**	**17,089**	**21,381**

MOTOR VEHICLES ON REGISTER			
Cars and station wagons	444,608	739,296	1,213,787
Utilities and panel vans	56,797	64,941	85,859
Rigid trucks	?	?	81,757
Articulated trucks	?	?	5,040
Other truck types	1,855	2,259	7,784
Total trucks(***)	36,851	42,819	94,581
Total commercial vehicles(***)	93,648	107,760	180,440
Motor cycles	9,741	16,358	36,647
Buses	1,698	2,555	6,995
Total vehicles on register	**549,695**	**865,969**	**1,437,869**

(Items marked***are sub totals)

PRIVATE TRANSPORT INDICATORS			
Total annual V.K.T.	$7.6670*10^9$	$1.2591*10^{10}$	$1.9029*10^{10}$
Total annual V.K.T.in cars	$6.1560*10^9$	$1.0584*10^{10}$	$1.5834*10^{10}$
Average vehicle occupancy	1.73	1.74	1.74
Car occupant kilometres	$1.0650*10^{10}$	$1.8416*10^{10}$	$2.7551*10^{10}$
Average road network speed(km/h)	48.6	48.2	47.5

TRANSPORTATION ENERGY USE			
Motor spirit consumption (Joules)	$3.7136*10^{16}$	$5.9041*10^{16}$	$8.2562*10^{16}$
Diesel fuel consumption (Joules)	$3.4810*10^{15}$	$4.3077*10^{15}$	$1.2885*10^{16}$
Total fuel consumption (Joules)	$4.0617*10^{16}$	$6.3349*10^{16}$	$9.5447*10^{16}$

MODAL SPLIT FOR THE JOURNEY TO WORK (% of workers)

Public transport	36.8	30.9	20.6
Private transport	53.4	58.7	73.7
Walking and cycling	9.8	10.4	5.7

AVERAGE TRIP LENGTHS (km)

Journey to work (all modes)	10.2	11.2	13.7
Journey to work (cars only)	11.1	12.3	14.4

PUBLIC TRANSPORT INDICATORS

VEHICLE KILOMETRES

-Buses			
Municipal motor bus	9,400,000	11,100,000	13,162,612
Private motor bus	33,100,000	37,200,000	36,077,000
Total	*42,500,000*	*48,300,000*	*49,239,612*
-Trains			
Suburban rail(Vic Rail)	75,224,000	70,577,000	69,569,000
-Trams			
Municipal tramways	31,800,000	24,600,000	24,062,000
-Ferries	0	0	0
Grand total	*149,524,000*	*143,477,000*	*142,870,612*

PASSENGERS CARRIED

-Buses			
Municipal motor bus	31,200,000	22,400,000	21,018,000
Private motor bus	78,538,000	81,000,000	50,787,000
Total	*109,738,000*	*103,400,000*	*71,805,000*
-Trains			
Suburban rail(Vic Rail)	153,700,000	140,400,000	85,754,000
-Trams			
Municipal tramways	177,900,000	110,700,000	100,474,000
-Ferries	0	0	0
Grand total	*441,338,000*	*354,500,000*	*258,033,000*

AVERAGE TRIP LENGTH (km)

-Buses			
Municipal motor bus	6.5	6.5	6.5
Private motor bus	4.0	4.0	4.0
-Trains			
Suburban rail(Vic Rail)	14.0	15.0	15.6
-Trams			
Municipal tramways	4.4	4.4	4.4
-Ferries	0.0	0.0	0.0

PASSENGER KILOMETRES
-Buses
Municipal motor bus	202,800,000	145,600,000	136,617,000
Private motor bus	314,152,000	324,000,000	203,148,000
Total	*516,952,000*	*469,600,000*	*339,765,000*

-Trains
Suburban rail(Vic Rail)	2,151,800,000	2,101,788,000	1,337,762,400

-Trams
Municipal tramways	782,760,000	487,080,000	442,085,600

-Ferries
-Ferries	0	0	0
Grand total	*3,451,512,000*	*3,058,468,000*	*2,119,613,000*

AVERAGE SPEED (km/h)
-Buses
Municipal motor buses	?	21.0	21.0
Private motor bus	?	21.0	21.0
Overall bus speed	*17.7*	*21.0*	*21.0*

-Trains
Suburban rail(Vic Rail)	33.0	33.0	33.0

-Trams
Municipal tramways	17.7	17.6	17.5

-Ferries
-Ferries	0.0	0.0	0.0
All modes average	*27.2*	*28.7*	*27.8*

ENERGY CONSUMPTION
-Buses
Municipal motor bus			
Diesel (litres)	3,133,333	4,254,000	5,795,954
Private motor bus			
Diesel (litres)	10,781,759	12,117,264	11,751,466
Total(Joules)	*5.3281*10^{14}*	*6.2686*10^{14}*	*6.7189*10^{14}*

-Trains
Suburban rail (Vic Rail)			
Elec.(kWh)	145,125,000	151,842,000	210,491,000
Total(Joules)	*5.2245*10^{14}*	*5.4663*10^{14}*	*7.5777*10^{14}*

-Trams
Municipal tramways			
Elec.(kWh)	64,648,000	56,088,000	54,264,610
Total(Joules)	*2.3273*10^{14}*	*2.0192*10^{14}*	*1.9535*10^{14}*

-Ferries
-Ferries	0	0	0
Grand total(Joules)	*1.2880*10^{15}*	*1.3754*10^{15}*	*1.6250*10^{15}*

Note:
(1) The Melbourne City Council defines a broader central area known as the
Central Activities District. Parking data were available only for this area
and not the traditional CBD.

Moscow

POPULATION AND AREA	1960	1970	1980
Total population			
City of Moscow	6,242,000	7,061,000	8,015,000
Moscow agglomeration	8,799,000	11,034,000	12,862,000
Urbanised area(ha) (City of Moscow)	29,830	50,550	57,840
Population of the CBD	900,000	540,000	294,000
Area of the CBD(ha)	1,900	1,900	1,900
Population of the inner city	?	?	?
Area of the inner city(ha)	?	?	?
EMPLOYMENT LOCATION			
Number of jobs in the CBD	?	?	?
Number of jobs in the inner city	?	?	?
Number of jobs in the outer area	?	?	?
Number of jobs in the metro.area	?	?	?
PARKING SUPPLY IN THE CBD			
Off street parking spaces	?	?	?
On street parking spaces	?	?	?
Total parking spaces	**?**	**?**	**?**
ROAD NETWORK (km)			
Total roads in the metro.area	2,400	3,300	3,441
MOTOR VEHICLES ON REGISTER			
Motor cars	?	?	160,300
Trucks/lorries	?	?	?
Motor cycles	?	?	?
Other vehicles	?	?	?
Total vehicles on register	**?**	**?**	**320,600**
PRIVATE TRANSPORT INDICATORS			
Total annual V.K.T.	?	?	?
Total annual V.K.T.in cars	?	?	$9.7000*10^8$
Average vehicle occupancy	?	?	1.9
Car occupant kilometres	?	?	$1.8430*10^9$
Average road network speed(km/h)	?	?	45.0
TRANSPORTATION ENERGY USE			
Motor spirit consumption (Joules)	?	?	$3.0621*10^{15}$
Diesel fuel consumption (Joules)	?	?	?
Total fuel consumption (Joules)	?	?	?
MODAL SPLIT FOR THE JOURNEY TO WORK (% of workers)			
Public transport	?	74.0	?
Private transport	?	2.0	?
Walking and cycling	?	24.0	?
AVERAGE TRIP LENGTHS (km)			
Journey to work	?	?	?
Other trip purposes	?	?	?

PUBLIC TRANSPORT INDICATORS

VEHICLE KILOMETRES

-Buses

Municipal motor bus	?	?	457,000,000
Municipal trolley bus	?	?	113,000,000
Total	*?*	*?*	*570,000,000*

-Trains

Metro	?	?	406,800,000
Suburban rail	?	?	?
Total	*?*	*?*	*?*

-Trams

Municipal tramways	?	?	70,000,000

-Ferries	0	0	0
Grand total	*?*	*?*	*?*

PASSENGERS CARRIED

-Buses

Municipal motor bus	990,000,000	1,519,000,000	1,787,000,000
Municipal trolley bus	793,000,000	785,000,000	806,000,000
Total	*1,783,000,000*	*2,304,000,000*	*2,593,000,000*

-Trains

Metro	1,038,000,000	1,628,000,000	2,318,000,000
Suburban rail	?	?	?
Total	*?*	*?*	*?*

-Trams

Municipal tramways	838,000,000	630,000,000	525,000,000

-Ferries	0	0	0
Grand total	*?*	*?*	*?*

AVERAGE TRIP LENGTH (km)

-Buses

Municipal motor bus	3.9	4.0	3.6
Municipal trolley bus	2.9	3.0	2.7

-Trains

Metro	7.0	9.8	10.5
Suburban rail	?	?	12.3

-Trams

Municipal tramways	3.1	3.0	2.3

-Ferries	0.0	0.0	0.0

PASSENGER KILOMETRES

-Buses

Municipal motor bus	3,861,000,000	6,076,000,000	6,433,000,000
Municipal trolley bus	2,300,000,000	2,355,000,000	2,176,000,000
Total	*6,161,000,000*	*8,431,000,000*	*8,609,000,000*

-Trains

Metro	7,266,000,000	15,954,000,000	24,339,000,000
Suburban rail	?	?	?
Total	*?*	*?*	*?*

-Trams

Municipal tramways	2,598,000,000	1,890,000,000	1,208,000,000

-Ferries	0	0	0
Grand total	*?*	*?*	*?*

AVERAGE SPEED (km/h)

-Buses

Municipal motor buses	?	21.6	22.2
Municipal trolley bus	?	18.2	18.7
Overall bus speed	*?*	*20.7*	*21.3*

-Trains

Metro	?	40.7	41.1
Suburban rail	44.3	42.0	40.5
Overall train speed	*?*	*41.4*	*40.8*

-Trams

Municipal tramways	?	17.4	17.5

-Ferries	0.0	0.0	0.0
All modes average	*?*	*?*	*?*

ENERGY CONSUMPTION

-Buses

Municipal motor bus			
Diesel (litres)	?	?	?
Municipal trolley bus			
Elec.(kWh)	?	?	?
Total(Joules)	*?*	*?*	*?*

-Trains

Metro			
Elec.(kWh)	?	?	1,006,000,000
Suburban rail			
Elec.(kWh)	?	?	?
Total(Joules)	*?*	*?*	*?*

-Trams

Municipal tramways			
Elec.(kWh)	?	?	?
Total(Joules)	*?*	*?*	*?*

-Ferries	0	0	0
Grand total(Joules)	*?*	*?*	*?*

Munich

POPULATION AND AREA	1960	1970	1980
Total population	1,046,000	1,311,798	1,298,941
Urbanised area(ha)	18,749	19,228	22,842
Population of the CBD	96,488	85,712	77,172
Area of the CBD(ha)	694	694	694
Population of the inner city	342,901	312,169	277,610
Area of the inner city(ha)	1,744	1,744	1,744

EMPLOYMENT LOCATION			
Number of jobs in the CBD	191,369	186,395	160,292
Number of jobs in the inner city	329,623	332,256	335,495
Number of jobs in the outer area	326,860	397,723	446,533
Number of jobs in the metro.area	656,483	729,979	782,028

PARKING SUPPLY IN THE CBD			
Not open to public	?	?	26,060
Open to public	?	?	8,870
Off street parking spaces (total)	?	?	34,930
Long term	?	?	7,960
Metered	?	?	2,310
Parking disk required	?	?	550
On street parking spaces (total)	?	?	10,820
Total parking spaces	?	?	45,750

ROAD NETWORK (km)			
Total roads in the metro.area	1,522	1,918	2,167

MOTOR VEHICLES ON REGISTER			
Motor cars	136,965	343,380	467,442
Trucks/lorries	15,312	22,793	24,374
Motor bikes and scooters	26,274	3,755	13,857
Omnibuses	544	959	1,302
Tractors (traction machines)	1,426	2,345	3,061
Other	1,037	3,357	6,613
Total vehicles on register	181,558	376,589	516,649

PRIVATE TRANSPORT INDICATORS			
Total annual V.K.T.	$2.0573*10^9$	$4.0635*10^9$	$4.8348*10^9$
Total annual V.K.T.in cars	$1.5858*10^9$	$3.5128*10^9$	$4.2500*10^9$
Average vehicle occupancy	1.6	1.6	1.6
Car occupant kilometres	$2.5373*10^9$	$5.6205*10^9$	$6.8000*10^9$
Average road network speed(km/h)	?	?	35.0

TRANSPORTATION ENERGY USE			
Motor spirit consumption (Joules)	$4.8410*10^{15}$	$1.2552*10^{16}$	$1.6070*10^{16}$
Diesel fuel consumption (Joules)	?	?	?
Total fuel consumption (Joules)	?	?	?

MODAL SPLIT FOR THE JOURNEY TO WORK (% of workers)			
Public transport	35.0	38.0	42.0
Private transport	25.0	32.0	38.0
Walking and cycling	40.0	30.0	20.0

AVERAGE TRIP LENGTHS (km)

Journey to work	?	?	4.0
Other trip purposes	?	?	?

PUBLIC TRANSPORT INDICATORS[1]

VEHICLE KILOMETRES

-Buses

Stadtwerke motor bus	10,361,000	25,291,000	27,796,000
Regional bus	0	0	8,054,000
Private motor bus	11,824,400	12,631,200	12,151,500
Oberbayern GmbH	0	0	1,216,000
Railway and postal buses	4,619,600	4,947,500	0
Total	*26,805,000*	*42,869,700*	*49,217,500*

-Trains

S-Bahn	0	0	61,160,000
U-Bahn	0	0	14,600,000
Pre S-Bahn suburban rail	?	23,360,000	0
Total	*?*	*23,360,000*	*75,760,000*

-Trams

Stadtwerke tramways	43,100,000	41,938,000	27,300,000

-Ferries

-Ferries	0	0	0
Grand total	*?*	*108,167,700*	*152,277,500*

PASSENGERS CARRIED

-Buses

Stadtwerke motor bus	56,193,000	83,049,000	142,800,000
Regional bus	0	0	(2)
Private motor bus	24,163,500	11,002,300	6,475,600
Oberbayern GmbH	0	0	900,000
Railway and postal buses	4,956,800	7,243,400	0
Total	*85,313,300*	*101,294,700*	*150,175,600*

-Trains

S-Bahn	0	0	158,000,000
U-Bahn	0	0	115,100,000
Pre S-Bahn suburban rail	?	58,400,000	0
Total	*?*	*58,400,000*	*273,100,000*

-Trams

Stadtwerke tramways	261,500,000	188,143,000	160,100,000

-Ferries

-Ferries	0	0	0
Grand total	*?*	*347,837,700*	*583,375,600*

AVERAGE TRIP LENGTH (km)
-Buses

Stadtwerke motor bus	3.2	3.2	3.2
All other buses	6.0	7.0	8.0

-Trains

S-Bahn	0.0	0.0	11.6
U-Bahn	0.0	0.0	3.6
Pre S-Bahn suburban rail	?	11.6	0.0

-Trams

Stadtwerke tramways	3.2	3.2	3.2

-Ferries

	0.0	0.0	0.0

PASSENGER KILOMETRES
-Buses

Stadtwerke motor bus	179,255,670	264,926,310	455,532,000
All other buses	174,721,800	127,719,900	59,004,800
Total	*353,977,470*	*392,646,210*	*514,536,800*

-Trains

S-Bahn	0	0	1,828,000,000
U-Bahn	0	0	416,662,000
Pre S-Bahn suburban rail	?	675,688,000	0
Total	*?*	*675,688,000*	*2,244,662,000*

-Trams

Stadtwerke tramways	839,415,000	603,939,030	513,921,000

-Ferries

	0	0	0
Grand total	*?*	*1,672,273,240*	*3,273,119,800*

AVERAGE SPEED (km/h)
-Buses

Stadtwerke motor bus	21.0	20.4	19.8
All other buses	?	?	25.0
Overall bus speed	*?*	*?*	*20.4*

-Trains

S-Bahn	0.0	0.0	60.0
U-Bahn	0.0	0.0	35.0
Pre S-Bahn suburban rail	?	?	0.0
Overall train speed	*?*	*?*	*55.4*

-Trams

Stadtwerke tramways	15.7	17.1	17.3

-Ferries

	0.0	0.0	0.0
All modes average	*?*	*?*	*43.9*

ENERGY CONSUMPTION

-Buses

Stadtwerke motor bus
Diesel (litres)

2,474,000	6,318,000	8,453,000

All other motor buses
Diesel (litres)

4,409,000	4,395,000	6,511,094

Total(Joules)

$2.6355*10^{14}$	$4.1020*10^{14}$	$5.7298*10^{14}$

-Trains

S-Bahn
Elec.(kWh)

0	0	191,125,000

U-Bahn
Elec.(kWh)

0	0	59,191,000

Pre S-Bahn suburban rail

?	?	0

Total(Joules)

?	?	$9.0114*10^{14}$

-Trams

Stadtwerke tramways
Elec.(kWh)

63,407,000	87,935,000	60,360,000

Total(Joules)

$2.2827*10^{14}$	$3.1657*10^{14}$	$2.1730*10^{14}$

-Ferries

0	0	0

Grand total(Joules)

?	?	$1.6914*10^{15}$

Note:

(1) The populations applicable to the various public tranport modes are as follows:

	1960	1970	1980
All buses-Planungsregion 14	1,714,337	2,074,244	2,305,444
S-Bahn-Planungsregion 14	1,714,337	2,074,244	2,305,444
U-Bahn-Planungsregion 14	1,714,337	2,074,244	2,305,444
Tramways-City of Munich	1,046,000	1,311,798	1,298,941

(2) Included in Stadtwerke motor bus.

234

New York

POPULATION AND AREA	1960	1970	1980
Total population			
New York/North Eastern New Jersey			
urbanised area	14,114,927	16,206,841	15,590,274
Tri-State Regional Planning Area	16,834,500	18,731,600	17,925,200
New York/North Eastern New Jersey			
urbanised area (ha)	489,899	628,075	726,324
Tri-State Regional Planning Area (ha)	747,922	829,300	906,000
Population of the CBD	543,300	517,400	506,100
Area of the CBD(ha)	2,331	2,331	2,331
Population of the inner city	7,781,984	7,895,563	7,071,639
Area of the inner city(ha)	66,952	66,952	66,220

EMPLOYMENT LOCATION			
Number of jobs in the CBD	2,183,400	2,201,000	1,930,000
Number of jobs in the inner city	3,954,000	4,078,400	3,537,300
Number of jobs in the outer area	3,358,200	4,330,200	4,905,000
Number of jobs in the metro.area	7,312,200	8,408,600	8,442,300

PARKING SUPPLY IN THE CBD			
Off street parking spaces	?	?	128,201
On street parking spaces	?	?	16,725
Total parking spaces	**?**	**?**	**144,926**

ROAD NETWORK (km)			
Freeway	1,760	2,159	2,506
Arterial	12,302	12,824	?
Local	58,358	61,906	?
Total roads in the metro.area	**72,420**	**76,889**	**83,559**

MOTOR VEHICLES ON REGISTER			
Motor cars (passenger and rental)	4,556,098	6,522,777	7,383,106
Commercial vehicles	451,303	623,047	719,582
Buses	11,828	22,857	13,885
Taxis	24,219	77,722	26,154
Motor cycles	10,235	53,591	88,262
Total vehicles on register	**5,053,683**	**7,299,994**	**8,230,989**

PRIVATE TRANSPORT INDICATORS			
Total annual V.K.T.	$7.6060*10^{10}$	$1.0237*10^{11}$	$1.1766*10^{11}$
Total annual V.K.T.in cars	$6.8450*10^{10}$	$9.1110*10^{10}$	$1.0589*10^{11}$
Average vehicle occupancy	1.42	1.34	1.33
Car occupant kilometres	$9.7199*10^{10}$	$1.2209*10^{11}$	$1.4083*10^{11}$
Average road network speed(km/h)			
Manhattan Hub (CBD)	?	?	16.1
New York City	?	?	25.8
New York suburbs	?	?	37.0
New York part of Tri-State Region	32.2	32.2	32.2
Whole Tri-State Region	?	35.1	34.9

TRANSPORTATION ENERGY USE

Motor spirit consumption (Joules)	$6.1686*10^{17}$	$7.5506*10^{17}$	$7.8930*10^{17}$
Diesel fuel consumption (Joules)	$7.9655*10^{16}$	$1.2081*10^{17}$	$1.1060*10^{17}$
Total fuel consumption (Joules)	$6.9651*10^{17}$	$8.7587*10^{17}$	$8.9990*10^{17}$

MODAL SPLIT FOR THE JOURNEY TO WORK (% of workers)

Whole Tri-State Region			
Public transport	44.6	35.9	28.3
Private transport	44.7	55.4	63.6
Walking and cycling	10.7	8.7	8.1
New York City only			
Public transport	67.4	62.4	57.6
Private transport	21.8	27.1	30.5
Walking and cycling	10.8	10.4	11.9

AVERAGE TRIP LENGTHS (km)

Journey to work (New York SMSA only)	?	?	16.7
Other trip purposes	?	?	?

PUBLIC TRANSPORT INDICATORS

VEHICLE KILOMETRES

-Buses			
NYCTA[1] motor buses	97,908,389	109,413,076	96,761,000
NYCTA trolley buses	3,408,517	0	0
MABSTOA[2]	46,672,362	69,874,000	60,858,000
New York City private buses	?	23,345,000	43,470,000
NY State buses outside NY City	?	50,393,000	52,647,000
New Jersey Transit/TNJ	150,718,553	82,432,000	69,230,000
New Jersey independents	?	88,067,000	91,448,000
Connecticut bus transit	?	28,980,000	21,413,000
Total	*469,819,000*	*452,504,076*	*435,827,000*
-Trains			
NYCTA underground	49,689,430	63,595,000	48,461,000
SIRTOA[3]	1,085,140	966,000	966,000
Suburban rail transit(NY State)	10,628,000	18,354,000	19,320,000
PATH[4]	1,709,820	2,415,000	2,254,000
Newark subway	1,022,350	973,000	914,480
New Jersey suburban rail	2,714,460	8,855,000	8,050,000
Total (train kms)	*66,849,200*	*94,836,000*	*80,034,710*
Equivalent car kms[5]	*554,848,360*	*780,682,927*	*606,065,180*
-Trams			
Roosevelt Island Tramway[6]	0	0	69,230
-Ferries			
Staten Island Ferry	429,870	322,000	322,000
Grand total	*1,025,097,230*	*1,233,509,003*	*1,042,214,180*

PASSENGERS CARRIED

-Buses			
NYCTA motor buses	417,216,552	409,000,904	?
NYCTA trolley buses	15,657,807	0	0
MABSTOA	257,611,933	?	?
New York City private buses	?	?	?
NY State buses outside NY City	?	?	?

236

New Jersey Transit/TNJ	268,955,408	?	?
New Jersey independents	?	?	?
Connecticut bus transit	?	?	?
Total	*1,796,892,720*	*1,234,000,000*	*937,000,000*
-Trains			
NYCTA underground	1,348,920,795	1,257,569,124	?
SIRTOA	5,607,000	5,205,263	?
Suburban rail transit(NY State)			
and New Jersey suburban rail	183,463,625	149,000,000	166,000,000
PATH	38,690,000	38,953,885	?
Newark subway	3,705,000	4,271,728	?
Total	*1,580,386,420*	*1,455,000,000*	*1,219,000,000*
-Trams			
Roosevelt Island Tramway	0	0	?
-Ferries			
Staten Island Ferry	26,280,000	22,000,000	22,000,000[7]
Grand total	*3,403,559,140*	*2,711,000,000*	*2,178,000,000*

AVERAGE TRIP LENGTH (km)

-Buses			
NYCTA motor buses	?	3.9	?
Other buses	?	5.4	?
Buses overall	*5.2*	*4.9*	*5.2*
-Trains			
NYCTA underground	?	11.2	?
SIRTOA	?	10.2	?
PATH	?	6.3	?
Newark subway	?	2.8	?
Rapid transit overall	*10.6*	*11.0*	*11.1*
Suburban rail transit(NY State)			
and New Jersey suburban rail	36.0	37.2	37.7
-Trams			
Roosevelt Island Tramway	0.0	0.0	?
-Ferries			
Staten Island Ferry [7]	8.5	9.8	8.2

PASSENGER KILOMETRES

-Buses			
NYCTA motor buses	?	1,574,650,000	1,262,400,000
NYCTA trolley buses	?	0	0
MABSTOA	?	1,189,150,000	840,740,000
New York City private buses	?	649,150,000	476,080,000
NY State buses outside NY City	?	211,880,000	374,650,000
New Jersey Transit/TNJ	?	1,280,430,000	943,620,000
New Jersey independents	?	957,470,000	794,540,000
Connecticut bus transit	?	177,260,000	198,190,000
Total	*9,379,780,000*	*6,039,990,000*	*4,890,220,000*

-Trains			
NYCTA underground	?[8]14,028,900,000		11,371,910,000
SIRTOA	?[8] 52,970,000		68,100,000
Suburban rail transit(NY State)			
and New Jersey suburban rail	6,088,320,000	5,542,910,000[9]	6,258,550,000[9]
PATH	?[10] 243,270,000		258,410,000
Newark subway	?[10] 12,080,000		12,080,000
Total	*20,938,580,000*	*19,880,130,000*	*17,970,820,000*
-Trams			
Roosevelt Island Tramway	0	0	1,770,000[11]
-Ferries			
Staten Island Ferry	222,920,000	215,580,000	177,740,000
Grand total	*30,541,280,000*	*26,135,700,000*	*23,038,780,000*

AVERAGE SPEED (km/h)

-Buses			
NYCTA motor buses[12]	12.2	12.4	10.4
NYCTA trolley buses	10.8	0.0	0.0
MABSTOA	10.9	?	?
New York City private buses	?	?	?
NY State buses outside NY City	?	?	17.0
New Jersey Transit/TNJ	19.6	20.9	25.0
New Jersey independents	?	?	?
Connecticut bus transit	?	?	?
Overall bus speed	*13.9*	*16.2*	*15.2*
-Trains			
NYCTA underground	29.5	29.7	31.6
SIRTOA	?	?	34.5
Suburban rail transit(NY State)	?	?	?
New Jersey suburban rail	?	?	?
PATH	?	35.2	?
Newark subway	?	19.7	23.4
Overall train speed	*35.4*	*35.4*	*35.4*
-Trams			
Roosevelt Island Tramway	0.0	0.0	?
-Ferries			
Staten Island Ferry	20.1	20.1	20.1
All modes average	*28.7*	*30.8*	*31.0*

ENERGY CONSUMPTION

-Buses			
NYCTA motor buses			
Diesel (litres)	58,051,170	65,708,429	?
NYCTA trolley buses			
Elec.(kWh)	7,952,302	0	0
MABSTOA			
Diesel (litres)	32,738,183	41,482,071	?
Petrol (litres)	914,581	0	0
New York City private buses			
Diesel (litres)	?	13,965,013	26,003,817
NY State buses outside NY City			
Diesel (litres)	?	29,916,793	36,726,855
New Jersey Transit/TNJ			
Diesel (litres)	66,742,264	38,073,084	37,850,000

New Jersey independents			
Diesel (litres)	?	39,662,739	41,185,441
Connecticut bus transit			
Diesel (litres)	?	14,434,322	10,665,360
Total(Joules)	$9.6286*10^{15}$	$9.3138*10^{15}$	$9.7998*10^{15}$

-Trains

NYCTA underground			
Elec.(kWh)	1,677,170,000	1,991,090,000	1,765,140,000
SIRTOA	18,339,000	16,325,000	16,325,000
PATH			
Elec.(kWh)	28,896,000	40,814,000	38,093,000
Newark subway			
Elec.(kWh)	2,852,000	2,715,000	2,548,000
Suburban rail transit(NY State)			
(Joules)	$1.6930*10^{16}$	$1.1570*10^{16}$	$1.3620*10^{16}$
New Jersey suburban rail[13]			
(Joules)	?	$3.8940*10^{15}$	$3.8410*10^{15}$
Total	$2.3148*10^{16}$	$2.2847*10^{16}$	$2.4021*10^{16}$

-Trams

Roosevelt Island Tramway [14]	0	0	?

-Ferries

Staten Island Ferry[14]	?	?	?
Grand total	$3.2777*10^{16}$	$3.2161*10^{16}$	$3.3821*10^{16}$

Notes:

(1) NYCTA is the abbreviation for *New York City Transit Authority*.

(2) MABSTOA is the abbreviation for *Manhattan and Bronx Surface Transit Operating Authority*.

(3) SIRTOA is the abbreviation for *Staten Island Rapid Transit Operating Authority*.

(4) PATH is the abbreviation for *Port Authority Trans-Hudson* .

(5) Only train kms were available for the individual operators but a total car kms figure could be calculated for each year through an overall train consist size.

(6) The Roosevelt Island Tramway data is included in the train data.

(7) The data for the Staten Island Ferry includes the Roosevelt Island Tramway.

(8) 1960 passenger km data for NYCTA and SIRTOA combined was 14,638,380,000.

(9) 1970 and1980 passenger km data for suburban rail transit (NY State) were 4,147,680,000 and 4,882,160,000 respectively. The data for New Jersey suburban rail were 1,395,230,000 and 1,376,390,000 respectively.

(10) 1960 passenger km data for PATH and the Newark subway combined was 211,880,000.

(11) The data for Roosevelt Island Tramway is included in the total figure for trains.

(12) The average speed shown for NYCTA buses includes MABSTOA buses.

(13) New Jersey suburban rail energy is included in suburban rail transit (NY State) in 1960.

(14) The Roosevelt Island Tramway and Staten Island Ferry energy use is negligible in the overall context of public transportation energy consumption in the Tri-State Region.

Paris

POPULATION AND AREA	1960	1970	1980
Total population	8,400,000	9,246,000	10,094,000
Urbanised area(ha)	122,450	149,805	209,392
Population of the CBD	776,595	693,000	548,620
Area of the CBD(ha)	2,333	2,333	2,333
Population of the inner city	6,000,000	6,258,000	6,148,000
Area of the inner city(ha)	45,150	49,600	57,800
EMPLOYMENT LOCATION			
Number of jobs in the CBD	994,088	1,029,828	932,148
Number of jobs in the inner city	3,326,780	3,434,000	3,465,600
Number of jobs in the outer area	660,908	872,000	1,148,000
Number of jobs in the metro.area	3,987,688	4,306,000	4,613,600
PARKING SUPPLY IN THE CBD			
Off street parking spaces	?	?	?
On street parking spaces	?	?	?
Total parking spaces	**127,000**	**170,275**	**187,000**
ROAD NETWORK (km)			
All roads in the Ville de Paris	900	1,000	1,245
Freeways and "rapid" roads	70	260	447
National highways	1,450	1,600	1,784
Ordinary departmental roads	3,000	3,700	5,951
Total roads in the metro.area	**5,420**	**6,560**	**9,427**
MOTOR VEHICLES ON REGISTER			
Motor cars	1,280,600	2,363,500	3,412,500
Other vehicles	271,155	410,740	451,730
Total vehicles on register	**1,551,755**	**2,774,240**	**3,864,230**
PRIVATE TRANSPORT INDICATORS			
Total annual V.K.T.[1]	$1.4732*10^{10}$	$2.0828*10^{10}$	$3.2000*10^{10}$
Total annual V.K.T.in cars	$1.2158*10^{10}$	$1.7744*10^{10}$	$2.8259*10^{10}$
Average vehicle occupancy	1.7	1.6	1.5
Car occupant kilometres	$2.0669*10^{10}$	$2.8390*10^{10}$	$4.2389*10^{10}$
Average road network speed(km/h)	?	?	28.0
TRANSPORTATION ENERGY USE			
Motor spirit consumption (Joules)	$6.4333*10^{16}$	$8.5147*10^{16}$	$1.4223*10^{17}$
Diesel fuel consumption (Joules)	$1.5435*10^{16}$	$2.3208*10^{16}$	$4.9011*10^{16}$
Total fuel consumption (Joules)	$7.9768*10^{16}$	$1.0836*10^{17}$	$1.9124*10^{17}$
MODAL SPLIT FOR THE JOURNEY TO WORK[2] (% of workers)			
Region d'Ile- de- France			
Public transport	?	?	39.8
Private transport	?	?	36.4
Walking and cycling	?	?	23.8
Ville de Paris only			
Public transport	?	?	60.1
Private transport	?	?	17.8
Walking and cycling	?	?	22.1

AVERAGE TRIP LENGTHS (km)

Journey to work	6.9	7.6	8.3
Other trip purposes	?	?	?

PUBLIC TRANSPORT INDICATORS

VEHICLE KILOMETRES

-Buses

Paris (RATP[3] motor bus)	?	39,400,000	42,100,000
Suburbs (RATP motor bus)	?	79,900,000	89,500,000
RATP motor bus (total)	120,500,000	119,300,000	131,600,000
APTR[4] motor bus (private)	39,000,000	47,000,000	56,000,000
Total	*159,500,000*	*166,300,000*	*187,600,000*

-Trains

Metro (RATP)	167,400,000	170,600,000	192,100,000
RER (RATP)	10,000,000	20,200,000	51,800,000
Suburban rail (National:SNCF[5])	23,200,000	28,700,000	43,800,000
Total	*200,600,000*	*219,500,000*	*287,700,000*

-Trams	0	0	0

-Ferries	0	0	0
Grand total	*360,100,000*	*385,800,000*	*475,300,000*

PASSENGERS CARRIED

-Buses

Paris (RATP motor bus)	?	179,200,000	313,200,000
Suburbs (RATP motor bus)	?	349,200,000	393,600,000
RATP motor bus (total)	852,100,000	528,400,000	706,800,000
APTR motor bus (private)	100,000,000	120,000,000	144,000,000
Total	*952,100,000*	*648,400,000*	*850,800,000*

-Trains

Metro (RATP)	1,166,000,000	1,128,300,000	1,109,500,000
RER (RATP)	43,000,000	98,300,000	222,900,000
Suburban rail (National:SNCF)	318,300,000	374,400,000	432,400,000
Total	*1,527,300,000*	*1,601,000,000*	*1,764,800,000*

-Trams	0	0	0

-Ferries	0	0	0
Grand total	*2,479,400,000*	*2,249,400,000*	*2,615,600,000*

AVERAGE TRIP LENGTH (km)

-Buses

Paris (RATP motor bus)	?	3.4	2.4
Suburbs (RATP motor bus)	?	4.3	3.1
RATP motor bus (overall)	4.0	4.0	2.8
APTR motor bus (private)	10.0	10.0	7.0

-Trains

Metro (RATP)	5.3	5.3	4.9
RER (RATP)	9.1	9.1	11.1
Suburban rail (National:SNCF)	14.2	16.3	17.6

-Trams	0.0	0.0	0.0

-Ferries	0.0	0.0	0.0

PASSENGER KILOMETRES

-Buses

Paris (RATP motor bus)	?	609,300,000	756,000,000
Suburbs (RATP motor bus)	?	1,501,600,000	1,221,200,000
RATP motor bus (total)	3,408,400,000	2,110,900,000	1,977,200,000
APTR motor bus (private)	1,000,000,000	1,200,000,000	1,008,000,000
Total	*4,408,400,000*	*3,310,900,000*	*2,985,200,000*

-Trains

Metro (RATP)	6,179,800,000	5,980,000,000	5,381,100,000
RER (RATP)	391,300,000	894,530,000	2,465,300,000
Suburban rail (National:SNCF)	4,530,000,000	6,090,000,000	7,610,000,000
Total	*11,101,100,000*	*12,964,530,000*	*15,456,400,000*

-Trams	0	0	0
-Ferries	0	0	0
Grand total	*15,509,500,000*	*16,275,430,000*	*18,441,600,000*

AVERAGE SPEED (km/h)

-Buses

Paris (RATP motor bus)	11.8	9.8	9.9
Suburbs (RATP motor bus)	16.5	13.9	13.9
RATP motor bus (overall)	15.0	12.5	12.6
APTR motor bus (private)	?	?	?
Overall bus speed	*15.0*	*12.5*	*12.6*

-Trains

Metro (RATP)	22.4	22.4	24.9
RER (RATP)	37.3	37.3	42.9
Suburban rail (National:SNCF)	50.0	55.0	60.0
Overall train speed	*34.2*	*38.7*	*45.1*

-Trams	0.0	0.0	0.0
-Ferries	0.0	0.0	0.0
All modes average	*28.7*	*33.4*	*39.8*

ENERGY CONSUMPTION

-Buses

RATP motor bus

Diesel(litres)	50,208,932	46,900,300	52,534,000
Petrol(litres)	?	?[6]	587,900

APTR motor bus (private)

Diesel(litres)	16,250,000	19,583,333	22,580,645
Total(Joules)	$2.5447*10^{15}$	$2.6372*10^{15}$	$2.8965*10^{15}$

-Trains

Metro (RATP)

Elec.(kWh)	410,100,000	420,800,000	499,200,000

RER (RATP)

Elec.(kWh)	42,500,000	86,400,000	222,200,000

Suburban rail (National:SNCF)

Diesel (litres)	?	?	3,900,000
Elec.(kWh)	?	?	639,000,000

Suburban rail (National:SNCF)

Total (Joules)	$1.2976*10^{15}$	$1.6052*10^{15}$	$2.4497*10^{15}$
Total(Joules)	$2.9270*10^{15}$	$3.4311*10^{15}$	$5.0467*10^{15}$

-Trams	0	0	0
-Ferries	0	0	0
Grand total(Joules)	$5.4717*10^{15}$	$6.0683*10^{15}$	$7.9432*10^{15}$

Note:

(1) For the Ville de Paris only the VKT figures are $3.3*10^9$, $6.0*10^9$, and $8.0*10^9$ in 1960,1970 and 1980 respectively. In 1980 the figures for the Petite Couronne and Grand Couronne only are $9.1662*10^9$ and $1.4834*10^{10}$ respectively.

(2) For 1980, the modal split for all other types of trips is available in both the Ile-de-France (greater Paris region) and for the Ville de Paris only. Figures are also available in many years for all trips collectively.

(3) RATP is the abbreviation for *Regie Autonome des Transports Parisiens.*

(4) APTR is a private bus organisation known as *Association Professionelle des Transports Publics Routiers.*

(5) SNCF is the National railway system known as *Societe Nationale des Chemins de fer Francais.*

(6) In 1970 the petrol component for RATP motor buses was comprised of 2,649,300 litres of ethanol/petrol mixture and 803,000 litres of petrol. Appropriate conversion factors were applied to these data to get the equivalent energy in Joules.

Perth

POPULATION AND AREA	1960	1970	1980
Total population	475,398	703,199	898,918
Urbanised area(ha)	30,503	57,734	83,545
Population of the CBD	14,331	10,759	6,392
Area of the CBD(ha)	759	761	759
Population of the inner city	231,547	238,245	205,840
Area of the inner city(ha)	10,814	13,154	13,317
EMPLOYMENT LOCATION			
Number of jobs in the CBD	66,312	88,835	91,593
Number of jobs in the inner city	125,253	175,987	194,011
Number of jobs in the outer area	40,640	108,634	186,117
Number of jobs in the metro.area	165,893	284,621	380,128
PARKING SUPPLY IN THE CBD			
Off street parking spaces	25,978	37,610	?
On street parking spaces	11,227	9,217	?
Total parking spaces	37,205	46,827	51,500
ROAD NETWORK (km)			
Formed and surfaced	5,632	6,855	9,036
Formed but not otherwise prepared	423	150	147
Unformed public roads	631	2,639	2,740
Total roads in the metro.area	6,686	9,644	11,923
MOTOR VEHICLES ON REGISTER			
Cars and station wagons	113,543	251,000	426,935
Utilities and panel vans	21,011	?	67,667
Rigid trucks	?	?	25,687
Articulated trucks	?	?	2,269
Other truck types	325	?	3,782
Total trucks(***)	9,168	?	31,738
Total commercial vehicles(***)	30,179	52,500	99,405
Motor cycles	9,028	8,800	22,759
Buses	732	?(1)	3,226
Total vehicles on register	153,478	312,300	552,325

(Items marked***are sub totals)

PRIVATE TRANSPORT INDICATORS			
Total annual V.K.T.	$2.1147*10^9$	$4.5796*10^9$	$7.5234*10^9$
Total annual V.K.T.in cars	$1.6727*10^9$	$3.6735*10^9$	$5.9304*10^9$
Average vehicle occupancy	1.89	1.79	1.74
Car occupant kilometres	$3.1614*10^9$	$6.5756*10^9$	$1.0319*10^{10}$
Average road network speed(km/h)	?	?	43.1

TRANSPORTATION ENERGY USE			
Motor spirit consumption (Joules)	$8.9632*10^{15}$	$2.1051*10^{16}$	$3.0941*10^{16}$
Diesel fuel consumption (Joules)	$1.0056*10^{15}$	$2.3650*10^{15}$	$6.4724*10^{15}$
Total fuel consumption (Joules)	$9.9688*10^{15}$	$2.3416*10^{16}$	$3.7413*10^{16}$

MODAL SPLIT FOR THE JOURNEY TO WORK (% of workers)

Public transport	?	21.0	12.0
Private transport	?	71.1	84.0
Walking and cycling	?	7.9	4.0

AVERAGE TRIP LENGTHS (km)

Journey to work	?	7.7	9.5
Other trip purposes	?	?	?

PUBLIC TRANSPORT INDICATORS

VEHICLE KILOMETRES

-Buses			
MTT motor bus	26,488,229	35,453,810	42,413,000
-Trains			
Suburban rail (Westrail)	5,400,000	4,700,000	4,800,000
-Trams	0	0	0
-Ferries			
MTT ferries	34,615	36,051	39,656
Grand total	*31,922,844*	*40,189,861*	*47,252,656*

PASSENGERS CARRIED

-Buses			
MTT motor bus	52,248,887	57,181,000	56,819,792
-Trains			
Suburban rail (Westrail)	12,026,000	10,557,000	6,505,100
-Trams	0	0	0
-Ferries			
MTT ferries	179,851	357,372	334,542
Grand total	*64,454,738*	*68,095,372*	*63,659,434*

AVERAGE TRIP LENGTH (km)

-Buses			
MTT motor bus	6.0	7.0	8.0
-Trains			
Suburban rail (Westrail)	9.8	10.8	11.8
-Trams	0.0	0.0	0.0
-Ferries			
MTT Ferries	1.4	1.4	1.4

PASSENGER KILOMETRES
-Buses
MTTmotor bus

313,493,322	400,267,000	454,558,336

-Trains
Suburban rail (Westrail)

117,854,800	114,015,600	76,760,180

-Trams

0	0	0

-Ferries
MTT ferries

251,791	500,321	468,359
Grand total		
431,599,913	*514,782,921*	*531,786,875*

AVERAGE SPEED (km/h)
-Buses
MTT motor buses

19.0	20.5	22.0

-Trains
Suburban rail (Westrail)

34.4	34.4	35.2

-Trams

0.0	0.0	0.0

-Ferries
MTT ferries

14.4	14.4	14.4
All modes average		
23.2	*23.6*	*23.9*

ENERGY CONSUMPTION
-Buses
MTT motor bus
Diesel (litres)

7,677,748	11,622,445	16,164,405
Total(Joules)		
$2.9398*10^{14}$	$4.4502*10^{14}$	$6.1894*10^{14}$

-Trains
Suburban rail (Westrail)
Diesel(litres)

5,000,000	3,000,000	2,909,000
Total(Joules)		
$1.9145*10^{14}$	$1.1487*10^{14}$	$1.1139*10^{14}$

-Trams

0	0	0

-Ferries
MTT ferries
Diesel(litres)

71,860	74,841	82,320
Total(Joules)		
$2.7515*10^{12}$	$2.8657*10^{12}$	$3.1520*10^{12}$
Grand total(Joules)		
$4.8818*10^{14}$	$5.6276*10^{14}$	$7.3348*10^{14}$

Note:
(1) Buses are included in the trucks figure for 1970.

Phoenix

POPULATION AND AREA	1960	1970	1980
Total population			
SMSA	663,510	967,522	1,509,052
Urbanised area	552,043	863,357	1,409,279
Urbanised area(ha)	64,336	100,492	165,991
Population of the CBD	8,400	8,019	6,724
Area of the CBD(ha)	389	389	389
Population of the inner city	73,000	68,192	55,917
Area of the inner city(ha)	2,934	2,934	2,934
EMPLOYMENT LOCATION			
Number of jobs in the CBD	22,892	26,306	25,918
Number of jobs in the inner city	50,842	60,984	70,418
Number of jobs in the outer area	167,826	272,374	595,582
Number of jobs in the metro.area	218,668	333,358	666,000
PARKING SUPPLY IN THE CBD			
Off street parking spaces	?	?	?
On street parking spaces	?	?	?
Total parking spaces	14,174	22,000	26,772
ROAD NETWORK (km)			
Total roads in the metro.area	10,195	12,323	15,763
MOTOR VEHICLES ON REGISTER			
Passenger vehicles	244,041	482,930	752,800
Commercial vehicles	57,066	68,985	120,857
Non-commercial vehicles	?	58,370	116,034
Buses and taxis	1,018	490	840
Motor bikes	3,436	19,768	48,545
Other (non-motorised)	34,747	96,166	102,496
Total vehicles on register	340,308	726,709	1,141,572
Total without non-motorised portion	305,561	630,543	1,039,076
PRIVATE TRANSPORT INDICATORS			
Total annual V.K.T.	$5.1842*10^9$	$9.3219*10^9$	$1.4860*10^{10}$
Total annual V.K.T.in cars	$4.7695*10^9$	$8.5761*10^9$	$1.3672*10^{10}$
Average vehicle occupancy	1.58	1.46	1.43
Car occupant kilometres	$7.5358*10^9$	$1.2521*10^{10}$	$1.8449*10^{10}$
Average road network speed(km/h)	45.0	45.6	41.6
TRANSPORTATION ENERGY USE			
Motor spirit consumption (Joules)	$3.4082*10^{16}$	$6.3012*10^{16}$	$8.8323*10^{16}$
Diesel fuel consumption (Joules)	$4.6897*10^{15}$	$8.0018*10^{15}$	$1.2386*10^{16}$
Total fuel consumption (Joules)	$3.8772*10^{16}$	$7.1014*10^{16}$	$1.1031*10^{17}$

MODAL SPLIT FOR THE JOURNEY
TO WORK (% of workers)
SMSA

Public transport	4.3	1.6	2.2
Private transport	88.7	93.8	94.6
Walking and cycling	7.0	4.6	3.2

City of Phoenix only

Public transport	5.1	2.0	3.2
Private tranport	89.6	93.9	93.4
Walking and cycling	5.3	4.1	3.4

AVERAGE TRIP LENGTHS (km)

Journey to work	?	?	13.0
Other trip purposes			
Shopping (hb)	?	?	6.4
School (hb)	?	?	7.6
Other (hb)	?	?	9.3
Non-home based	?	?	9.5
Overall average trip length (all trips)	**8.1**	**8.7**	**9.7**

PUBLIC TRANSPORT INDICATORS

VEHICLE KILOMETRES
-Buses

Phoenix Transit motor bus	?	4,796,126	10,915,903
Valley Transit Lines	?	0	0
Total	*6,355,940*	*4,796,126*	*10,915,903*
-Trains	0	0	0
-Trams	0	0	0
-Ferries	0	0	0
Grand total	*6,355,940*	*4,796,126*	*10,915,903*

PASSENGERS CARRIED
-Buses

Phoenix Transit motor bus	?	4,786,130	13,745,233
Valley Transit Lines	?	0	0
Total	*9,309,573*	*4,786,130*	*13,745,233*
-Trains	0	0	0
-Trams	0	0	0
-Ferries	0	0	0
Grand total	*9,309,573*	*4,786,130*	*13,745,233*

AVERAGE TRIP LENGTH (km)
-Buses

Buses overall	7.3	7.3	7.3
-Trains	0.0	0.0	0.0
-Trams	0.0	0.0	0.0
-Ferries	0.0	0.0	0.0

PASSENGER KILOMETRES
-Buses

Phoenix Transit motor bus	?	34,699,443	99,584,214
Valley Transit Lines	?	0	0
Total	*67,494,404*	*34,699,443*	*99,584,214*

-Trains	0	0	0
-Trams	0	0	0
-Ferries	0	0	0
Grand total	*67,494,404*	*34,699,443*	*99,584,214*

AVERAGE SPEED(km/h)
-Buses

Phoenix Transit motor bus	21.0	22.8	23.3
Valley Transit Lines	22.4	0.0	0.0
Overall bus speed	*21.7*	*22.8*	*23.3*

-Trains	0.0	0.0	0.0
-Trams	0.0	0.0	0.0
-Ferries	0.0	0.0	0.0
All modes average	*21.7*	*22.8*	*23.3*

ENERGY CONSUMPTION
-Buses

Phoenix Transit motor bus			
Diesel (litres)	?	2,592,844	7,127,072
Valley Transit Lines			
Diesel (litres)	?	0	0
Total(Joules)	$9.9153*10^{13}$	$9.9280*10^{13}$	$2.7290*10^{14}$

-Trains	0	0	0
-Trams	0	0	0
-Ferries	0	0	0
Grand total(Joules)	$9.9153*10^{13}$	$9.9280*10^{13}$	$2.7290*10^{14}$

San Francisco

POPULATION AND AREA	1960	1970	1980
Total population			
SMSA	2,648,762	3,109,249	3,250,630
Urbanised area	2,430,663	2,987,850	3,190,690
Urbanised area(ha)	147,242	176,379	206,045
Population of the CBD	36,620	35,039	34,338
Area of the CBD(ha)	383	383	383
Population of the inner city	740,316	715,674	678,974
Area of the inner city(ha)	10,700	10,700	11,549
EMPLOYMENT LOCATION			
Number of jobs in the CBD	216,800	235,570	273,164
Number of jobs in the inner city	475,900	536,300	552,200
Number of jobs in the outer area	620,400	879,600	1,052,800
Number of jobs in the metro.area	1,096,300	1,415,900	1,605,000
PARKING SUPPLY IN THE CBD			
Off street parking spaces	27,500	35,000	38,752
On street parking spaces	1,800	1,400	913
Total parking spaces	**29,300**	**36,400**	**39,665**
ROAD NETWORK (km)			
State highway	1,025	1,038	1,054
County maintained	3,834	3,850	3,771
Not county maintained	485	122	211
City streets	7,207	9,441	10,649
National roads (not overlapping)	8	34	140
Total roads in the metro.area	**12,559**	**14,485**	**15,825**
MOTOR VEHICLES ON REGISTER			
Passenger cars	1,079,080	1,516,920	1,766,270
Light duty trucks and vans	193,963	273,403	354,750
Motor cycles (and other)	48,198	69,426	92,390
Total vehicles on register	**1,321,241**	**1,859,749**	**2,213,410**
PRIVATE TRANSPORT INDICATORS			
Total annual V.K.T.	$1.6645*10^{10}$	$2.7635*10^{10}$	$3.3814*10^{10}$
Total annual V.K.T.in cars	$1.4981*10^{10}$	$2.4872*10^{10}$	$3.0433*10^{10}$
Average vehicle occupancy	1.44	1.41	1.41
Car occupant kilometres	$2.1573*10^{10}$	$3.5816*10^{10}$	$4.2911*10^{10}$
Average road network speed(km/h)	?	?	45.6
TRANSPORTATION ENERGY USE			
Motor spirit consumption (Joules)	$9.5051*10^{16}$	$1.6596*10^{17}$	$1.7997*10^{17}$
Diesel fuel consumption (Joules)	$1.8800*10^{16}$	$2.9636*10^{16}$	$3.1781*10^{16}$
Total fuel consumption (Joules)	$1.1385*10^{17}$	$1.9560*10^{17}$	$2.1175*10^{17}$
MODAL SPLIT FOR THE JOURNEY TO WORK (% of workers)			
SMSA			
Public transport	19.6	16.0	17.0
Private transport	71.4	77.3	77.5
Walking and cycling	9.0	6.7	5.5

City (County) of San Francisco only			
Public transport	42.0	37.0	39.6
Private transport	45.6	51.4	49.0
Walking and cycling	12.4	11.6	11.4

AVERAGE TRIP LENGTHS (km)

Journey to work (SMSA)	?	?	12.2
Journey to work (9 County Bay Region)	14.2	15.1	17.2
Other trip purposes	?	?	?

PUBLIC TRANSPORT INDICATORS

VEHICLE KILOMETRES

-Buses

"MUNI" motor bus[1]	22,921,380	22,379,000	28,951,210
"MUNI" trolley bus	13,588,394	12,125,111	11,604,711
AC Transit motor bus	31,738,170	38,620,501	51,356,585
Golden Gate Transit motor bus	9,500,000	11,659,620	14,317,373
SAM Trans motor bus[2]	0	1,851,500	14,427,435
Total	_77,747,944_	_86,635,732_	_120,657,314_

-Trains

BART[3]	0	0	32,274,060
Southern Pacific commuter rail[4]	5,182,300	3,802,820	3,802,820
Total	_5,182,300_	_3,802,820_	_36,076,880_

-Trams

"MUNI" tramways	6,298,030	6,108,139	6,326,070

-Ferries

Golden Gate Transit	0	22,540	187,298
Grand total	_89,228,274_	_96,569,231_	_163,247,562_

PASSENGERS CARRIED

-Buses

"MUNI" motor bus	89,620,660	86,255,000	98,775,000
"MUNI" trolley bus	73,439,824	74,921,000	71,705,000
AC Transit motor bus	57,743,986	56,061,167	79,000,000
Golden Gate Transit motor bus	5,940,000	7,290,000	10,615,000
SAM Trans motor bus	0	1,120,000	18,324,876
Total	_226,744,470_	_225,647,167_	_278,419,876_

-Trains

BART	0	0	45,300,000
Southern Pacific commuter rail	7,000,000	5,826,000	6,113,000
Total	_7,000,000_	_5,826,000_	_51,413,000_

-Trams

"MUNI" tramways	38,443,725	56,672,000	43,018,000

-Ferries

Golden Gate Transit	0	274,000	1,126,734
Grand total	_272,188,195_	_288,419,617_	_373,977,610_

AVERAGE TRIP LENGTH (km)

-Buses

"MUNI" motor bus	4.0	4.0	4.0
"MUNI" trolley bus	4.0	4.0	4.0
AC Transit motor bus	8.1	8.1	8.1
Golden Gate Transit motor bus	20.0	20.0	25.2
SAM Trans motor bus	0.0	10.2	10.2

-Trains

BART	0.0	0.0	19.4
Southern Pacific commuter rail	24.8	24.8	23.3

-Trams

"MUNI" tramways	4.4	4.4	4.6

-Ferries

Golden Gate Transit	0.0	10.2	16.0

PASSENGER KILOMETRES

-Buses

"MUNI" motor bus	361,171,260	347,607,650	398,063,250
"MUNI" trolley bus	293,759,296	299,684,000	286,820,000
AC Transit motor bus	464,839,087	603,114,050	635,950,000
Golden Gate Transit motor bus	118,800,000	145,800,000	267,073,400
SAM Trans motor bus	0	11,412,800	186,730,486
Total	*1,238,569,643*	*1,407,618,500*	*1,774,637,136*

-Trains

BART	0	0	876,555,000
Southern Pacific commuter rail	173,530,000	144,426,540	142,188,380
Total	*173,530,000*	*144,426,540*	*1,018,743,380*

-Trams

"MUNI" tramways	168,352,761	248,223,360	198,115,330

-Ferries

Golden Gate Transit	0	2,792,060	18,016,477
Grand total	*1,580,452,404*	*1,803,060,460*	*3,009,512,323*

AVERAGE SPEED(km/h)

-Buses

"MUNI" motor bus	16.4	16.3	16.2
"MUNI" trolley bus	13.5	13.5	12.9
AC Transit motor bus	21.4	22.9	23.3
Golden Gate Transit motor bus	35.9	35.9	35.9
SAM Trans motor bus	0.0	22.0	22.0
Overall bus speed	*19.5*	*20.6*	*21.8*

-Trains

BART	0.0	0.0	43.5
Southern Pacific commuter rail	55.2	55.2	55.2
Overall train speed	*55.2*	*55.2*	*45.1*

-Trams

"MUNI" tramways	14.4	16.2	15.0

-Ferries

Golden Gate Transit	0.0	20.4	25.1
All modes average	*22.9*	*22.8*	*29.3*

ENERGY CONSUMPTION

-Buses

"MUNI" motor bus			
Diesel (litres)	13,684,225	14,919,333	20,566,339
Petrol(litres)	695,244	0	0
"MUNI" trolley bus			
Elec.(kWh)	40,890,143	30,434,029	23,353,579
AC Transit motor bus			
Diesel (litres)	14,426,441	18,036,195	28,976,597
Golden Gate Transit motor bus			
Diesel (litres)	4,460,000	5,474,000	6,733,140
SAM Trans motor bus			
Diesel (litres)	0	881,667	7,440,087
Total(Joules)	$1.4185*10^{15}$	$1.6148*10^{15}$	$2.5238*10^{15}$

-Trains

BART			
Elec.(kWh)	0	0	139,412,000
Southern Pacific commuter rail			
Diesel(litres)	10,186,937	7,470,420	7,470,420
Total(Joules)	$3.9006*10^{14}$	$2.8604*10^{14}$	$7.8792*10^{14}$

-Trams

"MUNI" tramways			
Elec.(kWh)	21,911,489	34,564,765	49,586,958
Total(Joules)	$7.8881*10^{13}$	$1.2443*10^{14}$	$1.7851*10^{14}$

-Ferries

Golden Gate Transit			
Diesel(litres)	0	253,595	5,129,432
Total(Joules)	*0*	$9.7102*10^{12}$	$1.9641*10^{14}$
Grand total(Joules)	$1.8874*10^{15}$	$2.0350*10^{15}$	$3.6866*10^{15}$

Note:

(1) MUNI is the common name for *Municipal Railway of San Francisco.*

(2) SAM Trans is the abbreviation for *San Mateo County Transit.*

(3) BART is the abbreviation for *Bay Area Rapid Transit.*

(4)*Southern Pacific* commuter rail service runs between San Francisco and San Jose.

Singapore

POPULATION AND AREA	1960	1970	1980
Total population	1,646,000	2,074,507	2,413,945
Urbanised area(ha)	15,757	22,377	28,997
Population of the CBD	234,000	231,000	157,300
Area of the CBD (ha)	772	772	772
Population of the inner city	615,784	1,003,797	850,358
Area of the inner city(ha)	2,460	4,000	4,220

EMPLOYMENT LOCATION			
Number of jobs in the CBD	391,000	217,000	262,000
Number of jobs in the inner city	?	?	?
Number of jobs in the outer area	?	?	?
Number of jobs in the metro.area	?	650,892	1,077,090

PARKING SUPPLY IN THE CBD			
Off street parking spaces	?	?	?
On street parking spaces	?	?	?
Total parking spaces	?	12,119	25,327

ROAD NETWORK (km)			
Expressway	?	4	39
Major arterial	?	236	313
Collector road	?	113	157
Local improved road	?	1,011	1,539
Local unimproved road	?	574	308
Total roads in the metro.area	?	1,938	2,356

MOTOR VEHICLES ON REGISTER			
Motor cars	63,344	142,568	155,020
Goods vehicles	13,645	34,336	78,038
Public buses and school buses[1]	1,003	2,942	5,486
Motor cycles	18,931	105,214	118,345
Taxis	5	5,048	9,462
Total vehicles on register	96,928	290,108	371,341

PRIVATE TRANSPORT INDICATORS			
Total annual V.K.T.	?	?	?
Total annual V.K.T.in cars	$7.0070*10^8$	$1.5772*10^9$	$1.7149*10^9$
Average vehicle occupancy	?	1.66	2.50
Car occupant kilometres	?	$2.6182*10^9$	$4.2873*10^9$
Average road network speed(km/h)	?	33.2	30.0

TRANSPORTATION ENERGY USE			
Motor spirit consumption (Joules)	?	$1.1320*10^{16}$	$1.4382*10^{16}$
Diesel fuel consumption (Joules)[2]	?	$5.8300*10^{15}$	$8.4450*10^{15}$
Total fuel consumption (Joules)	?	$1.7150*10^{16}$	$2.2827*10^{16}$

MODAL SPLIT FOR THE JOURNEY TO WORK (% of workers)			
Public transport	?	?	59.6
Private transport	?	?	24.6
Walking and cycling	?	?	15.8

AVERAGE TRIP LENGTHS (km)

Journey to work	?	?	?
Other trip purposes	?	?	?

PUBLIC TRANSPORT INDICATORS

VEHICLE KILOMETRES
-Buses

Singapore Bus Service	?	?	217,731,511
City Shuttle Service	?	?	9,559,000
Scheme buses	?	?	7,709,489
Total	*?*	*?*	*235,000,000*
-Trains	0	0	0
-Trams	0	0	0
-Ferries	0	0	0
Grand total	*?*	*?*	*235,000,000*

PASSENGERS CARRIED
-Buses

Singapore Bus Service	?	?	816,000,000
City Shuttle Service	?	?	22,000,000
Scheme buses	?	?	8,000,000
Total	*?*	*?*	*846,000,000*
-Trains	0	0	0
-Trams	0	0	0
-Ferries	0	0	0
Grand total	*?*	*?*	*846,000,000*

AVERAGE TRIP LENGTH (km)
-Buses

Buses overall	?	?	5.5
-Trains	0.0	0.0	0.0
-Trams	0.0	0.0	0.0
-Ferries	0.0	0.0	0.0

PASSENGER KILOMETRES
-Buses

Overall buses	?	?	4,653,000,000
-Trains	0	0	0
-Trams	0	0	0
-Ferries	0	0	0
Grand total	*?*	*?*	*4,653,000,000*

AVERAGE SPEED (km/h)
-Buses

Overall bus speed	?	?	18.7
-Trains	0.0	0.0	0.0
-Trams	0.0	0.0	0.0
-Ferries	0.0	0.0	0.0
All modes average	*?*	*?*	*18.7*

ENERGY CONSUMPTION
-Buses
Overall buses

Diesel (litres)	?	?	99,576,271
Total(Joules)	*?*	*?*	$3.8128*10^{15}$
-Trains	0	0	0
-Trams	0	0	0
-Ferries	0	0	0
Grand total(Joules)	*?*	*?*	$3.8128*10^{15}$

Note:
(1) In 1980 there were 3,041 public buses and 2,445 school buses (no split for earlier years).
(2) The energy data shown for 1970 are actually 1976, the earliest year for which data were available.

Stockholm

POPULATION AND AREA	1960	1970	1980
Total population			
Municipality of Stockholm	808,294	740,486	647,214
County of Stockholm	1,271,014	1,477,234	1,528,200
Urbanised area(ha) (Municipality)	12,340	12,496	12,613
Population of the CBD	72,062	50,459	41,146
Area of the CBD(ha)	424	424	424
Population of the inner city	476,049	388,725	319,036
Area of the inner city(ha)	5,396	5,430	5,476

EMPLOYMENT LOCATION			
Number of jobs in the CBD	151,843	121,785	118,536
Number of jobs in the inner city	354,979	332,818	336,535
Number of jobs in the outer area	75,950	109,061	113,979
Number of jobs in the metro.area[1]	430,929	441,879	450,514

PARKING SUPPLY IN THE CBD			
Off street parking spaces	?	?	11,000
On street parking spaces	?	?	1,000
Total parking spaces[2]	10,000	10,500	12,000

ROAD NETWORK (km)			
2 lanes	?	1,150	1,250
4 lanes	?	130	140
6 and 8 lanes	?	85	90
Total roads in the metro.area	1,243	1,365	1,480

MOTOR VEHICLES ON REGISTER			
Passenger cars			
Municipality of Stockholm	115,781	203,405	224,231
County of Stockholm	?	368,497	540,513
Motor lorries (trucks)			
Municipality of Stockholm	14,708	16,126	22,309
County of Stockholm	?	25,220	43,169
Motor cycles			
Municipality of Stockholm	9,515	2,792	6,149
County of Stockholm	?	5,924	16,210
Buses			
Municipality of Stockholm	769	1,501	2,334
County of Stockholm	?	2,374	2,778
Total vehicles on register			
Municipality of Stockholm	140,004	222,323	252,689
County of Stockholm	?	402,015	602,670

PRIVATE TRANSPORT INDICATORS

Total annual V.K.T.			
Municipality of Stockholm	$1.7640*10^9$	$2.9400*10^9$	$3.4300*10^9$
County of Stockholm	$2.8420*10^9$	$5.4880*10^9$	$8.0360*10^9$
Total annual V.K.T.in cars			
Municipality of Stockholm	$1.4580*10^9$	$2.6100*10^9$	$3.1500*10^9$
County of Stockholm	$2.2910*10^9$	$4.8160*10^9$	$6.9700*10^9$
Average vehicle occupancy	1.40	1.35	1.35
Car occupant kilometres			
Municipality of Stockholm	$2.0412*10^9$	$3.5235*10^9$	$4.2525*10^9$
County of Stockholm	$3.2074*10^9$	$6.5016*10^9$	$9.4095*10^9$
Average road network speed(km/h)			
Municipality of Stockholm	?	?	30.0
County of Stockholm	?	?	43.0

TRANSPORTATION ENERGY USE

Motor spirit consumption (Joules)			
Municipality of Stockholm	?	?	$1.0080*10^{16}$
County of Stockholm	?	$1.6079*10^{16}$	$2.1074*10^{16}$
Diesel fuel consumption (Joules)			
Municipality of Stockholm	?	?	$3.6000*10^{15}$
County of Stockholm[3]	?	?	$4.5360*10^{14}$
Total fuel consumption (Joules)	?		
Municipality of Stockholm	?	?	$1.3680*10^{16}$
County of Stockholm[3]	?	?	$2.1528*10^{16}$

MODAL SPLIT FOR THE JOURNEY TO WORK (% of workers)

Public transport	?	57.0	46.0
Private transport	?	26.0	34.0
Walking and cycling	?	17.0	20.0

AVERAGE TRIP LENGTHS (km)

Journey to work	9.5	10.3	11.0
Other trip purposes	?	?	?

PUBLIC TRANSPORT INDICATORS

VEHICLE KILOMETRES

-Buses			
Municipal motor bus (SL)[4]	15,761,500	22,678,000	21,800,000
Municipal trolley bus (SS)[7]	5,803,800	0	0
County buses[5]	31,422,000		?
Other buses (SJ etc)[5]	?	15,416,000	?
Total	*54,565,300*	*69,516,000*	*88,800,000*
-Trains			
Tunnelbana (underground)	29,178,100	43,652,000	59,400,000
Local trains (SJ)[6]	12,896,000	23,223,000	32,800,000
Total	*42,074,100*	*66,875,000*	*92,200,000*
-Trams			
Municipal tramways (SL)[7]	14,551,300	922,000	600,000
-Ferries	0	0	0
Grand total	*111,190,700*	*137,313,000*	*181,600,000*

PASSENGERS CARRIED

-Buses

Municipal motor bus (SL)	22,012,400	39,623,900	?
Municipal trolley bus (SS)	13,229,500	0	0
County and other buses	39,503,200	36,756,300	?
Total	*74,745,100*	*76,380,200*	*214,000,000*

-Trains

Tunnelbana (underground)	42,840,900	172,000,000	195,000,000
Local trains (SJ etc)	19,840,100	42,000,000	53,000,000
Total	*62,681,000*	*214,000,000*	*248,000,000*

-Trams

Municipal tramways (SL)	40,158,500	752,400	incl in trains

-Ferries

	0	0	0
Grand total	*177,584,600*	*291,132,600*	*462,000,000*

AVERAGE TRIP LENGTH (km)

-Buses

All SL buses	3.2	3.6	4.0
County and other buses	6.5	7.2	8.0

-Trains

Tunnelbana (underground)	5.5	6.1	6.8
Local Trains (SJ etc)	9.8	10.8	12.0

-Trams

Municipal tramways (SL)	3.5	3.0	?

-Ferries

	0.0	0.0	0.0

PASSENGER KILOMETRES

-Buses

All SL buses	112,774,080	142,646,040	?
County and other buses	256,770,800	264,645,360	?
Total	*369,544,880*	*407,291,400*	*1,284,000,000*

-Trains

Tunnelbana (underground)	235,624,950	1,049,200,000	1,326,000,000
Local Trains (SJ)	194,432,980	453,600,000	636,000,000
Total	*430,057,930*	*1,502,800,000*	*1,962,000,000*

-Trams

Municipal tramways (SL)	140,554,750	2,257,200	incl in trains

-Ferries

	0	0	0
Grand total	*940,157,560*	*1,912,348,600*	*3,246,000,000*

AVERAGE SPEED (km/h)

-Buses

SL buses

Urban	15.1	14.6	14.7
Suburban	?	?	22.7
Overall bus speed	*20.0*	*23.0*	*25.4*

-Trains			
Tunnelbana (underground)	30.0	33.0	36.0
Local Trains (SJ)	?	?	?
Overall train speed	*?*	*?*	*?*

-Trams			
Municipal tramways (SL)	?	25.9	25.9

-Ferries	0.0	0.0	0.0
All modes average	*?*	*30.9*	*31.8*

ENERGY CONSUMPTION

-Buses			
Municipal motor bus (SL)			
Diesel (litres)	8,140,228	10,699,481	?[8]
Municipal trolley bus (SS)			
Elec.(kWh)	11,027,220	0	0
County and other buses[9]			
Diesel (litres)	12,540,000	17,798,440	?
Total(Joules)	*8.3154*10^{14}*	*1.0912*10^{15}*	*1.4281*10^{15}*

-Trains			
Tunnelbana (underground)			
Elec.(kWh)	96,288,000	137,940,000	184,140,000
Local Trains (SJ)			
Elec.(kWh)	51,584,000	85,751,400	104,960,000
Total(Joules)	*5.3234*10^{14}*	*8.0529*10^{14}*	*1.0408*10^{15}*

-Trams			
Municipal tramways (SL)			
Elec.(kWh)	24,737,210	1,567,400	960,000
Total(Joules)	*8.9054*10^{13}*	*5.6426*10^{12}*	*3.4560*10^{12}*

-Ferries	0	0	0
Grand total(Joules)	*1.4529*10^{15}*	*1.9021*10^{15}*	*2.4723*10^{15}*

Note:
(1) The number of jobs in the *County of Stockholm* was as follows: 1960 = 600,911 ; 1970 = 711,609 ;1980 = 749,338.
(2) Parking data were not available for the CBD as generally defined. The parking data shown above cannot therefore be related to the number of jobs shown in the employment data. Relevant employment data to match the parking data are as follows: 1960 = 100,300 ; 1970 = 80,500 ; 1980 = 78,300.
(3) The diesel fuel use figure for the County of Stockholm is obviously too low and probably only includes motor cars, not all vehicles. Diesel fuel use in the case of the Municipality of Stockholm includes all vehicles. Total fuel use for the County is also clearly too low.
(4) SL is the abbreviation for *ab storsStockholms Lokaltrafik* or the Greater Stockholm Transit Co.
(5) County buses and other buses in 1960 amounted to 33,000,000 vehicle kilometres. In 1980 the figure was 67,000,000.
(6) SJ is the *Swedish National Railway Co.* and SL contracts it to provide commuter rail services in the Stockholm region (*SJ Entreprenadtrafik* comprising the Lidingo, Roslags - and Saltsjobbanorna).
(7) SL was not formed until 1967. Prior to this the trams (and buses) were operated by *Stockholms Sparvagars* (SS) or the Stockholm Tramway Co.
(8) The overall fuel use in buses was 37,296,000 litres.
(9) In 1970 County buses used 11,940,360 litres and SJ and other buses used 5,858,080 litres.

Sydney

POPULATION AND AREA	1960	1970	1980
Total population	2,289,747	2,807,828	3,204,696
Urbanised area(ha)	107,389	146,394	182,559
Population of the CBD	7,565	6,063	4,440
Area of the CBD(ha)	416	416	416
Population of the inner city	613,219	610,462	536,031
Area of the inner city(ha)	13,701	13,701	13,701

EMPLOYMENT LOCATION			
Number of jobs in the CBD	195,000	210,000	180,500
Number of jobs in the inner city	573,294	584,643	535,968
Number of jobs in the outer area	386,546	621,779	827,610
Number of jobs in the metro.area	959,840	1,206,422	1,363,578

PARKING SUPPLY IN THE CBD			
Off street parking spaces	?	14,555	23,554
On street parking spaces	?	3,625	4,597
Total parking spaces	**?**	**18,180**	**28,151**

ROAD NETWORK (km)			
Sealed and surfaced	8,654	12,479	17,916
Formed only	1,156	834	1,044
Unformed	917	918	852
Total roads in the metro.area	**10,727**	**14,232**	**19,812**

MOTOR VEHICLES ON REGISTER			
Cars and station wagons	502,322	860,478	1,319,220
Utilities and panel vans	77,716	84,633	160,035
Rigid trucks	?	?	64,460
Articulated trucks	?	?	6,152
Other truck types	1,639	?	7,006
Total trucks(***)	34,352	46,238	77,618
Total commercial vehicles(***)	112,068	130,871	237,653
Motor cycles	10,746	32,474	53,771
Buses	3,192	4,995	9,269
Total vehicles on register	**628,328**	**1,028,818**	**1,619,913**

*(Items marked***are sub totals)*

PRIVATE TRANSPORT INDICATORS			
Total annual V.K.T.	$9.0063*10^9$	$1.5262*10^{10}$	$2.1326*10^{10}$
Total annual V.K.T. in cars	$7.3353*10^9$	$1.2604*10^{10}$	$1.7253*10^{10}$
Average vehicle occupancy	?	1.81	1.76
Car occupant kilometres	?	$2.2813*10^{10}$	$3.0365*10^{10}$
Average road network speed(km/h)	?	?	39.0

TRANSPORTATION ENERGY USE			
Motor spirit consumption (Joules)	$4.3727*10^{16}$	$6.9676*10^{16}$	$9.2648*10^{16}$
Diesel fuel consumption (Joules)	$3.6601*10^{15}$	$6.3066*10^{15}$	$1.8842*10^{16}$
Total fuel consumption (Joules)	$4.7387*10^{16}$	$7.5983*10^{16}$	$1.1149*10^{17}$

MODAL SPLIT FOR THE JOURNEY TO WORK (% of workers)

Public transport	?	32.4	29.5
Private transport	?	60.1	65.1
Walking and cycling	?	7.5	5.4

AVERAGE TRIP LENGTHS (km)

Journey to work	?	12.5	12.9
All trip purposes (morning peak)	?	8.7	8.8

PUBLIC TRANSPORT INDICATORS

VEHICLE KILOMETRES

-Buses			
Municipal motor bus	59,590,930	62,426,140	57,561,000
Private motor bus	33,069,400	42,353,032	48,287,000
Total	*92,660,330*	*104,779,172*	*105,848,000*
-Trains			
Suburban rail	143,944,000	92,231,000	139,726,000
-Trams			
Municipal tramways	2,093,000	0	0
-Ferries	1,000,000	965,000	972,348
Grand total	*239,697,330*	*197,975,172*	*246,546,348*

PASSENGERS CARRIED

-Buses			
Municipal motor bus	237,965,000	208,008,000	170,575,000
Private motor bus	77,700,000	111,179,474	65,039,000
Total	*315,665,000*	*319,187,474*	*235,614,000*
-Trains			
Suburban rail	237,636,706	238,800,205	207,862,000
-Trams			
Municipal tramways	11,051,000	0	0
-Ferries	15,093,000	15,305,000	12,593,000
Grand total	*579,445,706*	*573,292,679*	*456,069,000*

AVERAGE TRIP LENGTH (km)

-Buses			
Buses overall	4.5	4.7	5.6
-Trains			
Suburban rail	14.0	15.0	16.3
-Trams			
Municipal tramways	3.5	0.0	0.0
-Ferries	10.3	10.3	10.3

PASSENGER KILOMETRES

-Buses
All buses	1,420,492,500	1,490,605,504	1,328,862,960

-Trains
Suburban rail	3,326,913,884	3,574,839,069	3,381,914,740

-Trams
	38,678,500	0	0

-Ferries
	155,457,900	157,641,500	129,707,900
Grand total	*4,941,542,784*	*5,223,086,073*	*4,840,485,600*

AVERAGE SPEED (km/h)

-Buses
Overall bus speed	18.6	18.3	20.3

-Trains
Suburban rail	35.4	35.4	44.6

-Trams
Municipal tramways	19.3	0.0	0.0

-Ferries
	?	?	23.1
All modes average	*?*	*?*	*37.4*

ENERGY CONSUMPTION

-Buses
Municipal motor bus
Diesel (litres)	25,221,035	26,074,000	28,256,897
Petrol(litres)	0	0	217,859

Private motor bus
Diesel (litres)	14,012,458	20,966,848	20,203,766
Total(Joules)	$1.5023*10^{15}$	$1.8012*10^{15}$	$1.8631*10^{15}$

-Trains
Suburban rail
Elec.(kWh)	236,787,472	220,700,000	285,000,000
Total(Joules)	$8.5243*^{14}$	$7.9452*10^{14}$	$1.0260*10^{15}$

-Trams
Municipal tramways
Elec.(kWh)	4,667,390	0	0
Total(Joules)	$1.6803*10^{13}$	*0*	*0*

-Ferries
Diesel(litres)	6,743,088	6,507,080	6,556,551
Total(Joules)	$2.5819*10^{14}$	$2.4916*10^{14}$	$2.5105*10^{14}$
Grand total(Joules)	$2.6297*10^{15}$	$2.8449*10^{15}$	$3.1402*10^{15}$

Tokyo

POPULATION AND AREA	1960	1970	1980
Total population			
Tokyo metropolis	9,683,802	11,408,071	11,597,211
Tokyo metropolitan transportation area	15,520,000	21,471,000	25,839,000
Urbanised area(ha)			
Tokyo metropolis	73,900	97,800	110,900
Tokyo metropolitan transportation area	181,200	287,155	360,155
Population of the CBD	545,267	402,013	337,644
Area of the CBD(ha)	4,018	4,105	4,105
Population of the inner city	8,310,027	8,840,942	8,336,303
Area of the inner city(ha)	41,233	48,995	54,518

EMPLOYMENT LOCATION			
Number of jobs in the CBD	1,266,000	1,720,000	1,958,000
Number of jobs in the inner city	4,526,000	5,891,000	6,234,000
Number of jobs in the outer area	374,000	709,000	1,116,000
Number of jobs in the metro.area	4,900,000	6,600,000	7,350,000

PARKING SUPPLY IN THE CBD			
Off street parking spaces	?	64,578	?
On street parking spaces	?	48,420	?
Total parking spaces	?	**112,998**	?

ROAD NETWORK (km)			
Total roads in the metro.area	18,881	20,573	22,098

MOTOR VEHICLES ON REGISTER			
Passenger cars	154,240	1,199,176	1,811,227
Lorries	276,860	840,389	1,041,031
Special vehicles	11,854	36,244	55,803
Motor cycles	159,060	102,466	166,882
Buses	6,369	18,646	15,791
Total vehicles on register	**608,392**	**2,196,921**	**3,090,734**

PRIVATE TRANSPORT INDICATORS			
Total annual V.K.T.	$1.5458*10^{10}$	$2.8425*10^{10}$	$3.2065*10^{10}$
Total annual V.K.T.in cars	$1.0542*10^{10}$	$2.0512*10^{10}$	$2.4796*10^{10}$
Average vehicle occupancy	1.6	1.5	1.4
Car occupant kilometres	$1.6867*10^{10}$	$3.0768*10^{10}$	$3.4714*10^{10}$
Average road network speed (km/h)			
Tokyo metropolis	?	?	21.4
Tokyo metropolitan area[1]	?	?	20.1

TRANSPORTATION ENERGY USE			
Motor spirit consumption (Joules)	$6.5515*10^{16}$	$1.2461*10^{17}$	$1.1351*10^{17}$
Diesel fuel consumption (Joules)	$2.6072*10^{16}$	$4.4025*10^{16}$	$5.3147*10^{16}$
LPG fuel consumption (Joules)	0.0	0.0	$1.7297*10^{16}$
Total fuel consumption (Joules)	$9.1587*10^{16}$	$1.6864*10^{17}$	$1.8396*10^{17}$

MODAL SPLIT FOR THE JOURNEY
TO WORK (% of workers)

Tokyo metropolitan transportation area

Public transport	?	61.3	51.9
Private transport	?	12.9	25.0
Walking and cycling	?	25.8	23.1
Tokyo metropolis (prefecture) only			
Public transport	?	62.9	59.0
Private transport	?	11.6	16.1
Walking and cycling	?	25.5	24.9
CBD work trips only			
Public transport	?	89.1	91.6
Private transport	?	7.7	6.1
Walking and cycling	?	3.2	2.3

AVERAGE TRIP LENGTHS (km)

Journey to work	?	?	?
Other trip purposes	?	?	?

PUBLIC TRANSPORT INDICATORS

VEHICLE KILOMETRES
-Buses

All motor buses	285,000,000	511,000,000	509,928,000
All trolley buses	6,100,000	1,000,000	0
Total	*291,100,000*	*512,000,000*	*509,928,000*

-Trains

Subways (TRTA and TBTMG)[2]	29,000,000	143,000,000	217,948,000
Suburban rail (National:JNR)	439,000,000	731,000,000	994,235,000
Private railways	327,000,000	535,000,000	697,438,000
Total	*795,000,000*	*1,409,000,000*	*1,909,621,000*

-Trams

Municipal tramways	55,800,000	12,000,000	2,938,000

-Ferries	0	0	0
Grand total	*1,141,900,000*	*1,933,000,000*	*2,422,487,000*

PASSENGERS CARRIED
-Buses

All motor buses	1,437,454,000	2,554,980,000	2,257,234,000
All trolley buses	55,000,000	9,000,000	0
Total	*1,492,454,000*	*2,563,980,000*	*2,257,234,000*

-Trains

Subways (TRTA and TBTMG)	315,774,000	1,329,850,000	2,021,439,000
Suburban rail (National:JNR)	2,592,401,000	3,600,225,000	3,938,290,000
Private railways	1,749,444,000	3,199,771,000	3,928,935,000
Total	*4,657,619,000*	*8,129,846,000*	*9,888,664,000*

-Trams

Municipal tramways	781,210,000	170,418,000	43,771,000

-Ferries	0	0	0
Grand total	*6,931,283,000*	*10,864,200,000*	*12,189,700,000*

AVERAGE TRIP LENGTH (km)

-Buses			
All motor buses	2.7	2.8	3.0
Alltrolley buses	2.5	2.5	0.0
-Trains			
Subways (TRTA and TBTMG)	7.0	7.1	6.1
Suburban rail (National:JNR)	14.0	15.9	17.0
Private railways	9.4	11.4	12.3
-Trams			
Municipal tramways	2.5	2.5	2.5
-Ferries	0.0	0.0	0.0

PASSENGER KILOMETRES

-Buses			
All motor buses	3,881,125,800	7,153,944,000	6,771,702,000
All trolley buses	137,500,000	22,500,000	0
Total	*4,018,625,800*	*7,176,444,000*	*6,771,702,000*
-Trains			
Subways (TRTA and TBTMG)	2,186,000,000	9,485,000,000	12,351,000,000
Suburban rail (National:JNR)	36,351,000,000	57,284,000,000	66,786,000,000
Private railways	16,462,000,000	36,442,000,000	48,115,000,000
Total	*54,999,000,000*	*103,211,000,000*	*127,252,000,000*
-Trams	1,953,025,000	426,045,000	109,427,500
-Ferries	0	0	0
Grand total	*60,970,700,000*	*110,813,000,000*	*134,133,000,000*

AVERAGE SPEED (km/h)

-Buses			
Overall bus speed	15.3	13.2	12.0
-Trains			
Subways (TRTA and TBTMG)	30.4	34.8	34.3
Suburban rail (National:JNR)	38.8	38.8	38.9
Private railways	42.5	42.5	42.5
Overall train speed	*39.6*	*39.7*	*39.8*
-Trams			
Municipal tramways	13.3	11.4	13.0
-Ferries	0.0	0.0	0.0
All modes average	*37.2*	*37.9*	*38.4*

ENERGY CONSUMPTION

-Buses

All motor buses

Diesel (litres)	87,993,941	154,753,791	170,223,405
All trolley buses			
Elec.(kWh)	15,860,000	2,400,000	0
Total(Joules)	$3.4264*10^{15}$	$5.9342*10^{15}$	$6.5179*10^{15}$

-Trains

Subways (TRTA andTBTMG)			
Elec.(kWh)	120,000,000	427,000,000	706,000,000
Suburban rail (National:JNR)			
Elec.(kWh)[3]	1,167,611,111	1,944,250,000	2,644,444,444
Private railways			
Elec.(kWh)[3]	993,416,667	1,591,861,111	1,830,166,667
Total(Joules)	$8.2117*10^{15}$	$1.4267*10^{16}$	$1.8650*10^{16}$

-Trams

Municipal tramways			
Elec.(kWh)	115,106,021	39,728,152	7,996,748
Total(Joules)	$4.1438*10^{14}$	$1.4302*10^{14}$	$2.8788*10^{13}$

-Ferries	0	0	0
Grand total(Joules)	$1.2053*10^{16}$	$2.0344*10^{16}$	$2.5199*10^{16}$

Note:

(1) The Tokyo metropolitan area consists of the prefectures: Tokyo,Kanagawa, Saitama and Chiba.

(2) TRTA is the abbreviation for *Teito Rapid Transit Authority* and TBTMG is the abbreviation for *Transportation Bureau of Tokyo Metropolitan Government.*

(3) Energy used in the national and private railways in Tokyo is not all electrical. The totals shown here are based on actual total energy use (all fuels) converted to electric energy equivalent.

Toronto

POPULATION AND AREA	1960	1970	1980
Total population			
Municipality of Metropolitan Toronto	1,620,861	2,089,729	2,137,395
Metropolitan region	2,105,792	2,920,250	3,417,701
Urbanised area(ha)			
Municipality of Metropolitan Toronto	43,989	50,447	53,970
Metropolitan region	?	?	?
Population of the CBD (MPD 1e)	5,413	3,650	4,742
Area of the CBD(ha) (MPD 1e)	188	188	188
Population of the "central area"	124,983	121,165	121,093
Area of the "central area" (ha)	2,697	2,716	2,775
Population of the inner city	890,174	904,325	762,921
Area of the inner city(ha)	12,000	12,594	13,500

EMPLOYMENT LOCATION			
Number of jobs in the CBD	122,179	135,815	142,645
Number of jobs in the "central area"	297,179	318,430	335,739
Number of jobs in the inner city	488,205	514,468	508,418
Number of jobs in the outer area	186,495	407,016	553,773
Number of jobs in the metro.area	674,700	921,484	1,062,191

PARKING SUPPLY IN THE CBD			
Off street parking spaces	22,436	25,913	27,187
On street parking spaces	1,000	1,000	1,006
Total parking spaces	**23,436**	**26,913**	**28,193**

ROAD NETWORK (km)			
Highways and arterials	615	?	824
Municipal streets and roads	2,157	?	4,991
Total roads in the metro.area	**2,772**	**4,875**	**5,815**

MOTOR VEHICLES ON REGISTER			
Cars and station wagons	482,705	748,521	988,538
Trucks	75,913	95,089	172,132
Motor cycles and mopeds	?	?	24,275
Buses[1]	?	?	4,943
Total vehicles on register	**558,618**	**843,610**	**1,189,888**

PRIVATE TRANSPORT INDICATORS			
Total annual V.K.T.	?	?	$1.5864 * 10^{10}$
Total annual V.K.T.in cars	?	?	$1.3157 * 10^{10}$
Average vehicle occupancy	1.5	1.6	1.6
Car occupant kilometres	?	?	$2.1051 * 10^{10}$
Average road network speed(km/h)	?	?	?

TRANSPORTATION ENERGY USE			
Motor spirit consumption (Joules)	?	?	$7.4410 * 10^{16}$
Diesel fuel consumption (Joules)	?	?	$2.6018 * 10^{16}$
Total fuel consumption (Joules)	?	?	$1.0043 * 10^{17}$

MODAL SPLIT FOR THE JOURNEY
TO WORK (% of workers)

Public transport	22.9	?	31.2
Private transport	70.3	?	63.0
Walking and cycling	6.3	?	5.8

AVERAGE TRIP LENGTHS (km)

Journey to work	8.5	10.7	13.1
All trip purposes	?	?	10.7

PUBLIC TRANSPORT INDICATORS

VEHICLE KILOMETRES
-Buses

Municipal motor bus (TTC)[2]	24,472,000	52,969,000	79,373,000
Municipal trolley bus (TTC)	6,601,000	6,601,000	6,601,000
Private motor bus (Go Transit)	0	4,000,000	6,206,000
Total	*31,073,000*	*63,570,000*	*92,180,000*

-Trains

Subway (TTC)	11,431,000	36,547,000	62,146,000
Commuter rail (Go Transit)	0	5,000,000	8,156,835
Total	*11,431,000*	*41,547,000*	*70,302,835*

-Trams

Municipal tramways (TTC)	35,581,000	18,354,000	15,134,000

-Ferries	0	0	0
Grand total	*78,085,000*	*123,471,000*	*177,616,835*

PASSENGERS CARRIED
-Buses

Municipal motor bus (TTC)	66,500,000	119,000,000	153,900,000
Municipal trolley bus (TTC)	22,600,000	17,700,000	19,400,000
Private motor bus (Go Transit)	0	5,000,000	8,305,273
Total	*89,100,000*	*141,700,000*	*181,605,273*

-Trains

Subway (TTC)	31,300,000	84,200,000	136,000,000
Commuter rail (Go Transit)	0	7,000,000	12,530,980
Total	*31,300,000*	*91,200,000*	*148,530,980*

-Trams

Municipal tramways (TTC)	134,300,000	55,600,000	57,200,000

-Ferries	0	0	0
Grand total	*254,700,000*	*288,500,000*	*387,336,253*

AVERAGE TRIP LENGTH (km)[3]
-Buses
All TTC buses	8.5	9.8	10.8
Private motor bus (Go Transit)	0.0	6.0	7.0

-Trains
Subway (TTC)	8.5	9.8	10.8
Commuter rail (Go Transit)	0.0	26.0	29.6

-Trams
Municipal tramways (TTC)	8.5	9.8	10.8

-Ferries
	0.0	0.0	0.0

PASSENGER KILOMETRES
-Buses
Municipal motor bus (TTC)	565,250,000	1,166,200,000	1,660,581,000
Municipal trolley bus (TTC)	192,100,000	173,460,000	209,326,000
Private motor bus (Go Transit)	0	30,000,000	58,137,000
Total	*757,350,000*	*1,369,660,000*	*1,928,044,000*

-Trains
Subway (TTC)	266,050,000	825,160,000	1,467,440,000
Commuter rail (Go Transit)	0	182,000,000	370,917,008
Total	*266,050,000*	*1,007,160,000*	*1,838,357,008*

-Trams
Municipal tramways (TTC)	1,141,550,000	544,880,000	617,188,000

-Ferries
	0	0	0
Grand total	*2,164,950,000*	*2,921,700,000*	*4,383,589,008*

AVERAGE SPEED (km/h)
-B uses
Municipal motor bus (TTC)	18.2	19.0	20.3
Municipal trolley bus (TTC)	15.8	15.5	14.8
Private motor bus (Go Transit)	0.0	?	?
Overall bus speed[4]	*17.6*	*18.5*	*19.7*

-Trains
Subway (TTC)	24.2	30.8	32.4
Commuter rail (Go Transit)	0.0	50.0	55.1
Overall train speed	*24.2*	*32.3*	*34.3*

-Trams
Municipal tramways (TTC)	16.1	16.3	15.8

-Ferries
	0.0	0.0	0.0
All modes average	*17.6*	*22.5*	*24.8*

ENERGY CONSUMPTION

-Buses

Municipal motor bus (TTC)			
Diesel (litres)	12,880,000	27,900,000	40,800,000
Municipal trolley bus (TTC)			
Elec.(kWh)	16,502,500	16,800,000	18,300,000
Private motor bus (Go Transit)			
Diesel (litres)	0	1,869,000	2,900,000
Total(Joules)	$5.5258*10^{14}$	$1.2003*10^{15}$	$1.7392*10^{15}$

-Trains

Subway (TTC)			
Elec.(kWh)	35,436,100	157,000,000	232,100,000
Commuter rail			
Diesel(litres)	0	11,770,000	19,200,000
Total(Joules)	$1.2757*10^{14}$	$1.0159*10^{15}$	$1.5767*10^{15}$

-Trams

Municipal tramways (TTC)			
Elec.(kWh)	113,859,200	58,100,000	51,800,000
Total(Joules)	$4.0989*10^{14}$	$2.0916*10^{14}$	$1.8648*10^{14}$

-Ferries	0	0	0
Grand total(Joules)	$1.0900*10^{15}$	$2.4254*10^{15}$	$3.4964*10^{15}$

Note:

(1) Buses are included in the totals in 1960 and1970.

(2) TTC is the abbreviation for *Toronto Transit Commission.*

(3) Average trip lengths for the various modes operated by the TTC are not available. However, for 1980, TTC provide a system average of 10.79 km which can be used in conjunction with total system passengers. They suggest for earlier years that the figure would be lower, hence values of 8.5 km and 9.8 km for 1960 and 1970 respectively have been adopted. In the absence of better data these systems averages have been applied uniformly for each mode. This may therefore not give a very accurate picture of the relative importance of each mode within the total system.

(4) Go Transit buses have an almost negligible effect on the overall bus speed in Toronto.

Vienna

POPULATION AND AREA	1960	1970	1980
Total population	1,627,566	1,614,841	1,531,346
Urbanised area(ha)	17,805	18,906	21,242
Population of the CBD	32,243	25,134	19,537
Area of the CBD(ha)	301	301	301
Population of the inner city	634,558	565,429	487,759
Area of the inner city(ha)	3,652	3,652	3,680

EMPLOYMENT LOCATION			
Number of jobs in the CBD	148,461	126,879	121,368
Number of jobs in the inner city	480,930	426,891	414,685
Number of jobs in the outer area	384,053	359,318	401,368
Number of jobs in the metro.area	864,983	786,209	816,053

PARKING SUPPLY IN THE CBD			
Off street parking spaces	?	?	?
On street parking spaces	?	?	?
Total parking spaces	?	?	23,000

ROAD NETWORK (km)			
Total roads in the metro.area	1,935	2,410	2,650

MOTOR VEHICLES ON REGISTER			
Cars and station wagons	152,334	345,434	476,553
Trucks	21,829	30,299	40,309
Motor cycles and mopeds	85,612	57,074	47,223
Buses	2,852	3,147	3,608
Other types of vehicles	3,336	3,730	4,635
Total vehicles on register	265,963	439,684	572,328

PRIVATE TRANSPORT INDICATORS			
Total annual V.K.T.	?	?	$4.9000*10^9$
Total annual V.K.T.in cars	?	?	$4.0800*10^9$
Average vehicle occupancy	?	?	1.6
Car occupant kilometres	?	?	$6.5280*10^9$
Average road network speed(km/h)	?	?	30.0

TRANSPORTATION ENERGY USE			
Motor spirit consumption (Joules)	?	?	$1.5247*10^{16}$
Diesel fuel consumption (Joules)	?	?	$1.8232*10^{15}$
Total fuel consumption (Joules)	?	?	$1.7250*10^{16}$

MODAL SPLIT FOR THE JOURNEY TO WORK (% of workers)			
Public transport	?	40.9	44.9
Private transport	?	41.8	40.4
Walking and cycling	?	17.3	14.7

AVERAGE TRIP LENGTHS (km)			
Journey to work	?	?	5.7
Other trip purposes	?	?	?

PUBLIC TRANSPORT INDICATORS

VEHICLE KILOMETRES
-Buses

Stadtbusses (WVB)[1]	7,888,762	12,323,049	18,044,435
Private motor bus[2]	0	2,153,740	3,746,705
Total	*7,888,762*	*14,476,789*	*21,791,140*

-Trains

S-Bahn (National:OBB)	0	7,204,892	9,938,468
U-Bahn (WVB)	0	0	5,231,791
Total	*0*	*7,204,892*	*15,170,259*

-Trams

Strassenbahn (WVB)	89,003,081	61,057,064	52,303,652
Stadtbahn (WVB)	19,753,356	18,396,401	16,411,318
Total	*108,756,437*	*79,453,465*	*68,714,970*

-Ferries	0	0	0
Grand total	*116,645,199*	*101,135,146*	*105,676,369*

PASSENGERS CARRIED
-Buses

Stadtbusses (WVB)	41,252,530	57,479,444	83,986,268
Private motor bus	0	incl in WVB	incl in WVB
Total	*41,252,530*	*57,479,444*	*83,986,268*

-Trains

S-Bahn (National:OBB)	0	34,701,206	36,571,156
U-Bahn (WVB)	0	0	68,864,917
Total	*0*	*34,701,206*	*105,436,073*

-Trams

Strassenbahn (WVB)	377,256,714	289,973,476	230,357,508
Stadtbahn (WVB)	85,900,439	72,489,459	59,319,692
Total	*463,157,153*	*362,462,935*	*289,677,425*

-Ferries	0	0	0
Grand total	*504,409,683*	*454,643,585*	*479,099,766*

AVERAGE TRIP LENGTH (km)
-Buses

Buses overall	5.5	5.5	5.5

-Trains

S-Bahn (National:OBB)	0.0	10.0	10.0
U-Bahn (WVB)	0.0	0.0	5.5

-Trams

Strassenbahn (WVB)	5.5	5.5	5.5
Stadtbahn (WVB)	5.5	5.5	5.5

-Ferries	0.0	0.0	0.0

PASSENGER KILOMETRES
-Buses

All buses	226,888,915	316,136,942	461,924,474

-Trains			
S-Bahn (National:OBB)	0	347,012,000	365,712,000
U-Bahn (WVB)	0	0	378,757,044
Total	*0*	*347,012,000*	*744,469,044*
-Trams			
Strassenbahn (WVB)	2,074,911,927	1,594,854,118	1,266,966,294
Stadtbahn (WVB)	472,452,415	398,692,025	326,258,306
Total	*2,547,364,342*	*1,993,546,143*	*1,593,224,600*
-Ferries	0	0	0
Grand total	*2,774,253,257*	*2,656,695,085*	*2,799,618,118*

AVERAGE SPEED (km/h)

-Buses			
Overall bus speed	19.1	18.5	19.2
-Trains			
S-Bahn (National:OBB)	0.0	40.6	40.6
U-Bahn (WVB)	0.0	0.0	34.7
Overall train speed	*0.0*	*40.6*	*37.6*
-Trams			
Strassenbahn (WVB)	14.2	14.7	14.9
Stadtbahn (WVB)	24.5	24.3	24.7
Overall tram speed	*16.1*	*16.6*	*16.9*
-Ferries	0.0	0.0	0.0
All modes average	*16.3*	*20.0*	*22.8*

ENERGY CONSUMPTION

-Buses			
Stadtbusses (WVB)			
Diesel (litres)	2,857,864	6,156,067	11,503,419
Private motor bus			
Diesel (litres)	0	1,076,870	2,386,436
Total(Joules)	*$1.0943*10^{14}$*	*$2.7695*10^{14}$*	*$5.3184*10^{14}$*
-Trains			
S-Bahn (National:OBB)			
Elec.(kWh)	0	31,845,623	43,928,029
U-Bahn			
Elec.(kWh)	0	0	38,922,739
Total(Joules)	*0*	*$1.1464*10^{14}$*	*$2.9826*10^{14}$*
-Trams			
Strassenbahn (WVB)			
Elec.(kWh)	85,584,158	99,544,763	128,249,049
Stadtbahn (WVB)			
Elec.(kWh)	14,866,732	17,321,385	12,441,653
Total(Joules)	*$3.6162*10^{14}$*	*$4.2072*10^{14}$*	*$5.0649*10^{14}$*
-Ferries	0	0	0
Grand total(Joules)	*$4.7105*10^{14}$*	*$8.1231*10^{14}$*	*$1.3366*10^{14}$*

Note:
(1) WVB is the abbreviation for *Wiener Stadtwerke Verkehrsbetriebe.*
(2) Private buses are run under contract from WVB.

Washington

POPULATION AND AREA	1960	1970	1980
Total population			
SMSA	2,076,610	2,861,748	2,988,100
Urbanised area	1,808,423	2,481,489	2,763,105
Urbanised area(ha)	88,241	128,205	208,933
Population of the CBD	10,500	6,046	3,458
Area of the CBD(ha)	460	460	460
Population of the inner city	763,956	756,610	638,300
Area of the inner city(ha)	14,789	14,789	14,452

EMPLOYMENT LOCATION			
Number of jobs in the CBD	225,000	220,510	268,700
Number of jobs in the inner city	502,000	515,100	541,679
Number of jobs in the outer area	346,671	588,900	1,123,524
Number of jobs in the metro.area	848,671	1,104,000	1,665,203

PARKING SUPPLY IN THE CBD			
Off street parking spaces	42,627	60,074	62,243
On street parking spaces	6,402	4,987	8,700
Total parking spaces	**49,029**	**65,061**	**70,943**

ROAD NETWORK (km)			
Freeway/expressway/parkway	?	397	464
Arterials	?	5,508	2,520
Collectors and local streets	?	8,759	12,202
Total roads in the metro.area	**?**	**14,664**	**15,186**

MOTOR VEHICLES ON REGISTER			
Private automobiles	601,788	1,147,360	1,677,425
Other vehicle types	76,603	146,051	250,465
Total vehicles on register	**678,391**	**1,293,411**	**1,927,890**

PRIVATE TRANSPORT INDICATORS			
Total annual V.K.T.	?	$1.8518*10^{10}$	$2.7069*10^{10}$
Total annual V.K.T.in cars	?	$1.6230*10^{10}$	$2.3724*10^{10}$
Average vehicle occupancy	?	1.5	1.47
Car occupant kilometres	?	$2.4345*10^{10}$	$3.4874*10^{10}$
Average road network speed(km/h)	?	?	38.6

TRANSPORTATION ENERGY USE			
Motor spirit consumption (Joules)	?	$1.0379*10^{17}$	$1.5311*10^{17}$
Diesel fuel consumption (Joules)	?	$1.4895*10^{16}$	$0.6340*10^{16}$
Total fuel consumption (Joules)	?	$1.1869*10^{17}$	$1.5945*10^{17}$

MODAL SPLIT FOR THE JOURNEY TO WORK (% of workers)			
SMSA			
Public transport	25.1	16.4	14.1
Private trans.	66.8	76.7	80.7
Walking and cycling	8.1	6.9	5.2

Washington D.C. only (inner area)

Public transport	43.2	37.0	38.9
Private transport	46.2	52.4	49.0
Walking and cycling	10.5	10.6	12.1

AVERAGE TRIP LENGTHS (km)

Journey to work	?	11.3	13.5
Other trip purposes	?	?	?

PUBLIC TRANSPORT INDICATORS

VEHICLE KILOMETRES

-Buses

DC Transit Co. motor bus (total)	43,652,305	?	0
Diesel	31,237,503	?	0
Petrol	12,414,802	?	0
Private motor buses			
Wash.,Virg. and MD.Coach Co. [1](tot.)	6,938,886	?	0
Diesel	4,218,200	?	0
Petrol	2,720,686	?	0
Alex., Barcroft,Wash. Transit Co.[2]	6,745,325	?	0
WMA Transit Co.[3]	2,698,130	7,751,073	0
Sub total - private buses	**16,382,341**	**?**	**0**
Total	*60,034,646*	*75,566,477*	*89,313,580*[4]

-Trains

Rapid transit (metro)	0	0	28,640,290
Commuter rail	920,800	789,300	1,192,500
Total	*920,800*	*789,300*	*29,832,790*

-Trams

DC Transit Co. tramways	7,023,118	0	0

-Ferries

	0	0	0
Grand total	*67,978,564*	*76,355,777*	*119,146,370*

PASSENGERS CARRIED

-Buses

DC Transit Co. motor bus	134,701,479	116,910,372	0
Private motor buses			
Wash.,Virg.and MD.Coach Co.	12,649,197	6,000,000	0
Alex.,Barcroft,Wash. Transit Co.	12,000,000	8,000,000	0
WMA Transit Co.	4,000,000	5,894,328	0
Sub total - private buses	**28,649,197**	**19,894,328**	**0**
Total	*163,350,676*	*137,909,700*	*193,952,960*

-Trains

Rapid transit (metro)	0	0	76,776,000
Commuter rail	1,105,000	1,105,000	1,908,000
Total	*1,105,000*	*1,105,000*	*78,684,000*

-Trams

DC Transit Co. tramways	40,875,902	0	0

-Ferries

	0	0	0
Grand total	*205,331,578*	*137,909,700*	*272,636,960*

AVERAGE TRIP LENGTH (km)

-Buses			
All buses	6.0	6.0	6.0
-Trains			
Rapid transit (metro)	0.0	0.0	8.0
Commuter rail	36.5	36.5	36.5
-Trams			
DC Transit Co. tramways	4.0	0.0	0.0
-Ferries	0.0	0.0	0.0

PASSENGER KILOMETRES

-Buses			
All buses	980,104,056	820,828,200	1,155,377,783
-Trains			
Rapid transit (metro)	0	0	615,765,430
Commuter rail	40,385,240	40,385,240	69,732,320
Total	*40,385,240*	*40,385,240*	*685,497,750*
-Trams			
DC Transit Co. tramways	163,503,608	0	0
-Ferries	0	0	0
Grand total	*1,183,992,904*	*861,213,440*	*1,840,875,533*

AVERAGE SPEED (km/h)

-Buses			
DC Transit Co. motor bus	16.0	?	0.0
Private motor buses			
Wash.,Virg.and MD.Coach Co.	17.0	?	0.0
Alex.,Barcroft,Wash. Transit Co.	?	?	0.0
WMA Transit Co.	?	21.1	0.0
Overall bus speed	*17.8*	*17.8*	*17.8*
-Trains			
Rapid transit (metro)	0.0	0.0	38.6
Commuter rail	55.0	55.0	55.0
Overall train speed	*55.0*	*55.0*	*40.3*
-Trams			
DC Transit Co. tramways	12.3	0.0	0.0
-Ferries	0.0	0.0	0.0
All modes average	*18.3*	*19.5*	*26.2*

ENERGY CONSUMPTION

-Buses

DC Transit Co. motor bus (total)

Diesel (litres)	18,353,620	?	0
Petrol (litres)	9,229,370	?	0
Private motor buses			
Wash.,Virg.and MD.Coach Co. (total)			
Diesel (litres)	1,983,249	?	0
Petrol (litres)	2,643,747	?	0
Alex.,Barcroft,Wash. Transit Co.			
Diesel (litres)	4,253,163	?	0
WMA Transit Co.			
Diesel (litres)	1,390,789	?	0
Total(Joules)	$1.4067*10^{15}$	$1.8324*10^{15}$	$2.2721*10^{15}$

-Trains

Rapid transit (metro)

Elec.(kWh)	0	0	161,012,000
Commuter rail			
(Joules)	$4.8987*10^{13}$	$4.5464*10^{13}$	$7.5724*10^{13}$
Total(Joules)	$4.8987*10^{13}$	$4.5464*10^{13}$	$6.5537*10^{14}$

-Trams

DC Transit Co. tramways

Elec.(kWh)	32,343,266	0	0
Total(Joules)	$1.1644*10^{14}$	*0*	*0*

-Ferries	0	0	0
Grand total(Joules)	$1.5721*10^{15}$	$1.8779*10^{15}$	$2.9275*10^{15}$

Note:

(1) The full name of this company was *Washington,Virginia and Maryland Coach Co.*

(2) The full name of this company was *Alexandria, Barcroft,Washington Transit Co.*

(3) WMA Transit Co. is the abbreviation for *Washington Metropolitan Area Transit Co.*

(4) By 1980 all transit services in the Washington area were under one authority: *Washington Metropolitan Area Transit Authority (WMATA).*

West Berlin

POPULATION AND AREA	1960	1970	1980
Total population	2,204,000	2,122,000	2,001,000
Urbanised area(ha)	25,750	27,997	31,486
Population of the CBD	?	15,000	16,000
Area of the CBD(ha)	120	120	120
Population of the inner city	945,252	809,377	635,463
Area of the inner city(ha)	7,130	7,082	7,608

EMPLOYMENT LOCATION			
Number of jobs in the CBD	48,016	39,000	40,000
Number of jobs in the inner city	502,717	437,020	349,500
Number of jobs in the outer area	534,917	515,838	487,500
Number of jobs in the metro.area	1,037,634	952,858	837,000

PARKING SUPPLY IN THE CBD			
Off street parking spaces	?	?	?
On street parking spaces	?	?	?
Total parking spaces	**?**	**16,000**	**17,500**

ROAD NETWORK (km)			
City streets/roads	2,605	2,809	2,907
Autobahn	18	23	36
Total roads in the metro.area	**2,623**	**2,832**	**2,943**

MOTOR VEHICLES ON REGISTER			
Cars and station wagons	145,793	373,233	538,094
Trucks, buses and other special vehicles	29,860	40,134	57,446
Motor cycles	19,150	2,676	16,564
Total vehicles on register	**194,803**	**416,043**	**612,104**

PRIVATE TRANSPORT INDICATORS			
Total annual V.K.T.	?	$4.6370*10^9$	$6.1870*10^9$
Total annual V.K.T.in cars	?	$4.0810*10^9$	$5.4450*10^9$
Average vehicle occupancy	1.7	1.68	1.68
Car occupant kilometres	?	$6.8561*10^9$	$9.1476*10^9$
Average road network speed(km/h)	?	?	27.8

TRANSPORTATION ENERGY USE			
Motor spirit consumption (Joules)	?	$1.7632*10^{16}$	$2.2674*10^{16}$
Diesel fuel consumption (Joules)	?	$7.6010*10^{15}$	$8.1050*10^{15}$
Total fuel consumption (Joules)	?	$2.5233*10^{16}$	$3.0779*10^{16}$

MODAL SPLIT FOR THE JOURNEY TO WORK (% of workers)			
Public transport	57.0	50.0	37.0
Private transport	16.0	34.0	48.0
Walking and cycling	27.0	16.0	15.0

AVERAGE TRIP LENGTHS (km)			
Journey to work	?	?	8.0
Other trip purposes			
Shopping	?	?	4.7
School/education	?	?	6.4

Social/recreational	?	?	6.3
Trips to home	?	?	7.1
Overall (all trips)	?	?	6.7

PUBLIC TRANSPORT INDICATORS

VEHICLE KILOMETRES

-Buses			
Municipal motor bus (BVG)[1]	57,402,000	81,851,000	77,800,000
Municipal trolley bus (BVG)	1,947,000	0	0
Total	*59,349,000*	*81,851,000*	*77,800,000*
-Trains			
S-Bahn (DR)[2]	44,512,000	24,013,000	19,200,000
U-Bahn (BVG)	34,451,000	47,162,000	69,600,000
Total	*78,963,000*	*71,175,000*	*88,800,000*
-Trams			
Municipal tramways (BVG)	44,179,000	0	0
-Ferries	42,000	negligible	negligible
Grand total	*182,533,000*	*153,026,000*	*166,600,000*

PASSENGERS CARRIED

-Buses			
Municipal motor bus (BVG)	287,556,000	450,600,000	406,200,000
Municipal trolley bus (BVG)	14,230,000	0	0
Total	*301,786,000*	*450,600,000*	*406,200,000*
-Trains			
S-Bahn (DR)	182,500,000	45,625,000	36,500,000
U-Bahn (BVG)	141,286,000	232,900,000	346,500,000
Total	*323,786,000*	*278,525,000*	*383,000,000*
-Trams			
Municipal tramways (BVG)	219,762,000	0	0
-Ferries	277,000	100,000	200,000
Grand total	*845,611,000*	*729,225,000*	*789,400,000*

AVERAGE TRIP LENGTH (km)

-Buses			
Municipal motor bus (BVG)	4.6	5.0	4.4
Municipal trolley bus (BVG)	3.5	0.0	0.0
-Trains			
S-Bahn (DR)	10.0	10.0	10.0
U-Bahn (BVG)	6.0	6.0	6.2
-Trams			
Municipal tramways (BVG)	3.6	0.0	0.0
-Ferries	3.8	3.8	3.8

PASSENGER KILOMETRES

-Buses			
Municipal motor bus (BVG)	1,308,380,000	2,243,990,000	1,799,470,000
Municipal trolley bus (BVG)	49,950,000	0	0
Total	*1,358,330,000*	*2,243,990,000*	*1,799,470,000*

-Trains

S-Bahn (DR)	1,825,000,000	456,250,000	365,000,000
U-Bahn (BVG)	853,370,000	1,406,720,000	2,155,230,000
Total	*2,678,370,000*	*1,862,970,000*	*2,520,230,000*

-Trams

Municipal tramways (BVG)	797,740,000	0	0

-Ferries

	1,050,000	380,000	760,000
Grand total	*4,835,490,000*	*4,107,340,000*	*4,320,460,000*

AVERAGE SPEED (km/h)
-Buses

Municipal motor bus (BVG)	20.6	20.3	20.0
Municipal trolley bus (BVG)	19.8	0.0	0.0
Overall bus speed	*20.6*	*20.3*	*20.0*

-Trains

S-Bahn (DR)	37.0	37.0	37.0
U-Bahn (BVG)	26.2	30.5	31.3
Overall train speed	*33.6*	*32.1*	*32.1*

-Trams

Municipal tramways (BVG)	16.6	0.0	0.0

Ferries

	11.4	11.4	11.4
All modes average	*27.1*	*25.7*	*27.1*

ENERGY CONSUMPTION
-Buses

Municipal motor bus (BVG)

Diesel (litres)	20,994,000	35,484,000	35,937,000

Municipal trolley bus (BVG)

Elec.(kWh)	3,535,000	0	0
Total(Joules)	*$8.1663*10^{14}$*	*$1.3590*10^{15}$*	*$1.3760*10^{15}$*

-Trains

S-Bahn (DR)

Elec.(kWh)	139,100,000	75,041,000	60,000,000

U-Bahn (BVG)

Elec.(kWh)	46,683,000	99,613,000	159,893,000
Total(Joules)	*$6.6882*10^{14}$*	*$6.2876*10^{14}$*	*$7.9162*10^{14}$*

-Trams

Municipal tramways (BVG)

Elec.(kWh)	40,512,00	0	0
Total(Joules)	*$1.4584*10^{14}$*	*0*	*0*

-Ferries

Diesel(litres)	negligible	negligible	negligible
Total(Joules)	negligible	negligible	negligible
Grand total(Joules)	*$1.6313*10^{15}$*	*$1.9878*10^{15}$*	*$2.1676*10^{15}$*

Note:

(1) BVG is the abbreviation for *Berliner Verkehrs -Betriebe.*

(2) DR is the abbreviation for *Deutsche Reichsbahn.* In the period 1960 to 1980 the S-Bahn was under East German administration. However, on January 9, 1984 the S-Bahn was handed over to West German administration.

Zürich

POPULATION AND AREA	1960	1970	1980
Total population (agglomeration)	697,434	791,761	780,502
Urbanised area(ha)	11,955	13,715	14,544
Population of the CBD	14,514	10,436	6,750
Area of the CBD(ha)	152	152	152
Population of the inner city	437,273	417,972	369,688
Area of the inner city(ha)	4,686	4,686	4,686

EMPLOYMENT LOCATION			
Number of jobs in the CBD	61,184	66,516	64,155
Number of jobs in the inner city	270,561	302,595	308,341
Number of jobs in the outer area	95,969	141,309	164,901
Number of jobs in the metro.area	366,530	443,904	473,242

PARKING SUPPLY IN THE CBD			
Off street parking spaces	?	?	?
On street parking spaces	?	?	?
Total parking spaces	?	?	**9,000**

ROAD NETWORK (km)			
City of Zürich	?	?	728
Rest of agglomeration	?	?	1,317
Total roads in the metro.area	?	?	**2,045**

MOTOR VEHICLES ON REGISTER			
Agglomeration of Zürich			
Cars and station wagons	87,900	201,020	292,406
Other vehicles[1]	42,900	35,480	44,854
Total vehicles on register	**130,800**	**236,500**	**337,260**
City of Zürich only			
Cars and station wagons	55,171	109,555	127,492
Trucks and vans	6,123	11,082	11,656
Motor bikes	20,836	8,327	7,913
Total vehicles on register	**82,130**	**128,964**	**147,061**

PRIVATE TRANSPORT INDICATORS			
Total annual V.K.T.	?	?	?
Total annual V.K.T.in cars	?	?	$3.3700*10^9$
Average vehicle occupancy	?	?	1.68
Car occupant kilometres	?	?	$5.6616*10^9$
Average road network speed(km/h)			
City of Zürich	30.0	30.0	26.0
Kanton of Zürich[2]	50.0	50.0	45.0
Agglomeration of Zürich	40.0	40.0	36.0

TRANSPORTATION ENERGY USE			
Motor spirit consumption (Joules)	?	?	$1.2261*10^{16}$
Diesel fuel consumption (Joules)	?	?	$1.6330*10^{15}$
Total fuel consumption (Joules)	?	?	$1.3894*10^{16}$

MODAL SPLIT FOR THE JOURNEY TO WORK (% of workers)

Public transport	?	?	34.0
Private transport	?	?	45.0
Walking and cycling	?	?	21.0

AVERAGE TRIP LENGTHS (km)

Journey to work	?	?	?
Other trip purposes	?	?	?

PUBLIC TRANSPORT INDICATORS

VEHICLE KILOMETRES

-Buses

Municipal motor bus (VBZ)[3]	5,470,000	6,885,000	8,087,000
Municipal trolley bus (VBZ)	3,123,000	2,145,000	3,483,000
Total	*8,593,000*	*9,030,000*	*11,570,000*

-Trains

Suburban rail (National:SBB)[4]	14,276,000	11,507,000	17,506,000
SZU[5]	505,000	540,000	700,000
FB[6]	169,700	242,500	493,400
Funicular railways[7]			
Polybahn	?	?	?
Seilbahnen Dolder	?	?	?
Luftseilbahn Adliswil - Felsenegg	?	?	?
Total	*14,950,700*	*12,289,500*	*18,699,400*

-Trams

Municipal tramways (VBZ)	21,786,000	19,566,000	18,407,000

-Ferries[8]

Zurichsee - Schiffahrts - Gesellschaft	?	?	?
Grand total	*45,329,700*	*40,885,500*	*48,676,400*

PASSENGERS CARRIED

-Buses

Municipal motor bus (VBZ)[9]	26,906,800	38,639,300	47,132,400
Municipal trolley bus (VBZ)	20,425,600	15,981,700	27,150,000
Total	*47,332,400*	*54,621,000*	*74,282,400*

-Trains

Suburban rail (National:SBB)	59,475,280	44,559,000	56,600,000
SZU	3,954,049	4,181,300	4,196,234
FB	1,328,469	1,877,434	2,957,696
Funicular railways			
Polybahn	731,398	788,217	746,190
Seilbahnen Dolder	319,612	482,735	615,265
Luftseilbahn Adliswil - Felsenegg	140,126	178,487	169,878
Total	*65,948,934*	*52,067,173*	*65,285,263*

-Trams

Municipal tramways (VBZ)	149,067,600	147,679,000	142,917,600

-Ferries[10]

Zurichsee - Schiffahrts - Gesellschaft	1,088,753	1,152,255	1,093,798
Grand total	*263,437,687*	*255,519,428*	*283,579,061*

AVERAGE TRIP LENGTH (km)

-Buses
Municipal motor bus (VBZ)

VBZ main services	3.6	3.6	3.4
Regional buses	4.0	4.0	4.0
Municipal trolley bus (VBZ)	3.6	3.6	3.4

-Trains

Suburban rail (National:SBB)	14.5	15.0	15.6
SZU	5.5	5.5	7.9
FB	6.0	6.0	6.1
Funicular railways			
Polybahn	0.2	0.2	0.2
Seilbahnen Dolder	0.5	0.5	0.5
Luftseilbahn Adliswil - Felsenegg	1.0	1.0	1.0

-Trams

Municipal tramways (VBZ)	3.6	3.6	3.4

-Ferries

Zurichsee - Schiffahrts - Gesellschaft	?	?	?

PASSENGER KILOMETRES

-Buses

Municipal motor bus (VBZ)	96,864,480	139,101,480	169,270,560
Municipal trolley bus (VBZ)	73,532,160	57,534,120	92,310,000
Total	*170,396,640*	*196,635,600*	*261,580,560*

-Trains

Suburban rail (National:SBB)	862,391,560	668,385,000	883,400,000
SZU	21,747,270	22,997,150	33,276,136
FB	7,970,814	11,264,604	19,000,000
Funicular railways			
Polybahn	117,024	126,115	119,390
Seilbahnen Dolder	159,806	241,368	307,633
Luftseilbahn Adliswil - Felsenegg	140,126	178,487	169,878
Total	*892,526,600*	*703,192,724*	*936,273,037*

-Trams

Municipal tramways (VBZ)	536,643,360	531,644,400	485,919,840

-Ferries

Zurichsee - Schiffahrts - Gesellschaft	negligible	negligible	negligible
Grand total	*1,599,566,600*	*1,431,472,724*	*1,683,773,437*

AVERAGE SPEED (km/h)

-Buses

Municipal motor buses (VBZ)	?	23.0	21.9
Municipal trolley bus(VBZ)	?	19.0	17.3
Overall bus speed	*22.5*	*21.8*	*20.3*

-Trains

Suburban rail (National:SBB)	41.0	45.7	46.2
SZU	25.0	30.0	33.0
FB	?	?	?
Funicular railways [11]			
Polybahn	?	?	?
Seilbahnen Dolder	?	?	?
Luftseilbahn Adliswil - Felsenegg	?	?	?
Overall train speed	*40.6*	*45.2*	*45.7*

-Trams

Municipal tramways (VBZ)	16.0	14.5	15.3

-Ferries

Zurichsee - Schiffahrts - Gesellschaft[11]	?	?	?
All modes average	*30.4*	*30.5*	*32.8*

ENERGY CONSUMPTION

-Buses

Municipal motor bus (VBZ)			
Diesel (litres)	2,557,143	3,211,000	3,270,000
Municipal trolley bus (VBZ)			
Elec.(kWh)	12,231,667	8,388,000	12,842,000
Total(Joules)	*$1.4195*10^{14}$*	*$1.5315*10^{14}$*	*$1.6374*10^{14}$*

-Trains

Suburban rail (National:SBB)			
Elec.(kWh)	134,194,000	105,864,000	154,053,000
SZU			
Elec.(kWh)	3,968,000	4,243,000	5,500,000
FB			
Elec.(kWh)	1,333,000	1,905,000	3,877,000
Funicular railways			
Elec.(kWh)	negligible	negligible	negligible
Total(Joules)	*$5.0218*10^{14}$*	*$4.0324*10^{14}$*	*$5.8835*10^{14}$*

-Trams

Municipal tramways (VBZ)			
Elec.(kWh)	49,113,000	60,062,000	57,820,000
Total(Joules)	*$1.7681*10^{14}$*	*$2.1622*10^{14}$*	*$2.0815*10^{14}$*

-Ferries

Diesel(litres)	?	?	?
Total(Joules)	?	?	?
Grand total(Joules)	*$8.2094*10^{14}$*	*$7.7261*10^{14}$*	*$9.6024*10^{14}$*

285

Note:

(1) The decline in "other" vehicles from 1960 to 1970 is due to a reduction in motor bikes as in many other cities over this period. The decline is evident in the more detailed data for the City of Zürich only.

(2) The Kanton of Zürich is a much larger area than the Agglomeration or City of Zürich and embraces large sections of undeveloped and sparsely developed land.

(3) VBZ is the abbreviation for *Verkehrsbetriebe Zürich*. The vehicle kms data for motor buses include the main VBZ services plus the regional bus services in the areas further out.

(4) SBB is the abbreviation for the National railway system, *Schweizerischen Bundesbahnen.*

(5) SZU is the abbreviation for *Sihltal - Zürich - Uetliberg - bahn.*

(6) FB is the abbreviation for *Adhasionsbahnen Forch.*

(7) The funicular railways' vehicle kms data are not available, but as the routes are only between about 0.16 km and 1.25 km, these data are negligible in the overall context of Zürich's public transport system.

(8) Ferry services do operate on Lake Zürich at the foot of the central area and there are also car ferries that operate across the lake and also carry passengers ,but no data are available on actual kilometres operated. A significant amount of travel on the passenger ferries, however, is tourist oriented and therefore not directly relevant, and as far as local needs are concerned,the ferries are minor in the overall context of public transport.

(9) In 1980 the bus passengers were comprised of 15,034,000 on regional buses and 32,098,400 on the VBZ's main services. Comparable data are not available for 1960 and1970.

(10) Passenger data only are available on the ferry system.

(11) The funicular railways and ferries would have a negligible affect on public transport speeds because of their small contribution to public transport operations overall.

SOURCEBOOK OF URBAN LAND USE, TRANSPORT AND ENERGY DATA FOR PRINCIPAL CITIES OF NORTH AMERICA, EUROPE, ASIA AND AUSTRALIA, 1960, 1970 AND 1980

PART II   STANDARDISED DATA

Adelaide

POPULATION PARAMETERS	1960	1970	1980
Urban density (persons / ha)	16.8	14.6	12.9
Inner area density (persons / ha)	24.5	22.3	18.8
Outer area density (persons / ha)	15.3	13.7	12.4
CBD density (persons / ha)	18.6	12.0	8.2
Proportion of population in CBD (%)	0.7	0.3	0.2
Proportion of population in inner area (%)	24.0	15.2	11.6
EMPLOYMENT PARAMETERS			
Employment density (jobs / ha)	?	5.8	5.4
Inner area employment density (jobs / ha)	?	24.3	25.1
Outer area employment density (jobs / ha)	?	3.7	3.7
CBD employment density (jobs / ha)	254.5	253.0	250.7
Proportion of jobs in CBD (%)	?	16.8	14.4
Proportion of jobs in inner area (%)	?	41.9	37.3
ACTIVITY INTENSITY PARAMETERS (Pop. & Jobs / ha)			
CBD activity intensity	273.1	264.9	258.9
Inner area activity intensity	?	46.6	43.9
Outer area activity intensity	?	17.5	16.0
City - wide activity intensity	?	20.4	18.3
VEHICLE OWNERSHIP PARAMETERS			
Total vehicles / 1000 people	293.0	347.8	568.4
Passenger cars / 1000 people	228.4	288.5	475.3
PRIVATE MOBILITY PARAMETERS			
Total per capita vehicle kms.	3,339	5,402	6,795
Per capita car kms.	2,633	4,602	5,833
Total per capita occupant kms.	7,503	10,264	12,403
Per capita car occupant kms.	5,916	8,743	10,722
Total vehicle kms. per vehicle	12,351	15,530	11,954
Car kms. per car	12,494	15,951	12,272
TRAFFIC RESTRAINT PARAMETERS			
Parking spaces / 1000 CBD workers	247.1	302.7	379.9
Length of road per person (m)	5.8	9.0	9.1
Total vehicles per km of road	55.0	38.6	64.2
Total vehicle kms. per km. of road	678,889	599,118	767,705
Car kms. per km. of road	535,322	510,371	658,970
TRANSPORT ENERGY PARAMETERS			
Motor spirit use / person (MJ)	15,352	24,474	28,791
Total private energy use / person (MJ)	16,959	26,865	34,193
Public trans. energy use / person (MJ)	752	585	1,014
Total energy use / person (MJ)	17,711	27,450	35,207

PUBLIC TRANSPORT PARAMETERS

Vehicle kilometres per person

Buses	39.7	32.6	39.9
Rail	29.6	14.1	10.3
Trams	1.5	0.8	0.9
Ferries	0.0	0.0	0.0
Total	*70.8*	*47.5*	*51.1*

Passenger trips per person

Buses	113.3	63.4	65.5
Rail	24.8	15.9	14.8
Trams	4.7	3.2	2.9
Ferries	0.0	0.0	0.0
Total	*142.8*	*82.5*	*83.2*

Passenger trips per vehicle kilometre

Buses	2.9	1.9	1.6
Rail	0.8	1.1	1.4
Trams	3.2	4.0	3.3
Ferries	0.0	0.0	0.0
Overall	*2.0*	*1.7*	*1.6*

Passenger kilometres per person

Buses	536.7	347.4	416.4
Rail	321.5	202.6	219.4
Trams	30.6	20.8	18.7
Ferries	0.0	0.0	0.0
Total	*888.8*	*570.8*	*654.5*

Average speed of public transport

Buses (km/h)	18.9	19.8	21.0
Rail (km/h)	28.0	30.0	45.0
Trams (km/h)	29.0	28.0	28.0
Ferries (km/h)	0.0	0.0	0.0
Overall	*22.5*	*23.7*	*29.2*

Vehicular energy efficiency

Buses (MJ / km)	11.8	11.9	15.7
Rail (MJ / km)	9.1	13.5	36.7
Trams (MJ / km)	8.6	8.8	8.0
Ferries (MJ / km)	0.0	0.0	0.0
Overall	*10.6*	*12.3*	*19.8*

Modal energy efficiency

Buses (MJ / passenger km.)	0.87	1.12	1.51
Rail (MJ / passenger km.)	0.84	0.94	1.73
Trams (MJ / passenger km.)	0.42	0.34	0.37
Ferries (MJ / passenger km.)	0.00	0.00	0.00
Overall	*0.85*	*1.02*	*1.55*

Amsterdam

POPULATION PARAMETERS	1960	1970	1980
Urban density (persons / ha)	97.5	64.2	50.8
Inner area density (persons / ha)	117.0	97.8	83.3
Outer area density (persons / ha)	71.5	42.4	32.4
CBD density (persons / ha)	205.8	146.1	108.4
Proportion of population in CBD (%)	15.1	11.2	9.7
Proportion of population in inner area (%)	68.6	60.0	59.2
EMPLOYMENT PARAMETERS			
Employment density (jobs / ha)	39.9	29.3	23.2
Inner area employment density (jobs / ha)	57.8	60.8	46.1
Outer area employment density (jobs / ha)	15.8	8.9	10.3
CBD employment density (jobs / ha)	281.3	262.5	153.1
Proportion of jobs in CBD (%)	50.6	44.2	29.9
Proportion of jobs in inner area (%)	83.0	81.6	71.7
ACTIVITY INTENSITY PARAMETERS **(Pop. & Jobs / ha)**			
CBD activity intensity	487.0	408.6	261.6
Inner area activity intensity	174.9	158.5	129.3
Outer area activity intensity	87.3	51.3	42.7
City - wide activity intensity	137.4	93.5	74.0
VEHICLE OWNERSHIP PARAMETERS			
Total vehicles / 1000 people	97.8	233.3	342.1
Passenger cars / 1000 people	64.7	210.0	307.8
PRIVATE MOBILITY PARAMETERS			
Total per capita vehicle kms.	?	?	?
Per capita car kms.	692	2073	2582
Total per capita occupant kms.	?	?	?
Per capita car occupant kms.[1]	1,190	3,565	4,441
Total vehicle kms. per vehicle	?	?	?
Car kms. per car	10,939	10,257	9,508
TRAFFIC RESTRAINT PARAMETERS			
Parking spaces / 1000 CBD workers	61.0	93.5	208.2
Length of road per person (m)	0.5	1.7	2.1
Total vehicles per km of road	208.9	141.1	161.2
Total vehicle kms. per km. of road	?	?	?
Car kms. per km. of road	1,511,278	1,384,916	1,378,489
TRANSPORT ENERGY PARAMETERS			
Motor spirit use / person (MJ)	2,064	7,321	9,171
Total private energy use / person (MJ)	?	?	?
Public trans. energy use / person (MJ)	468	670	1,158
Total energy use / person (MJ)	?	?	?

PUBLIC TRANSPORT PARAMETERS

Vehicle kilometres per person

Buses	12.2	19.9	30.0
Rail	19.6	22.6	30.0
Trams	18.3	9.8	14.2
Ferries	0.0	0.0	0.0
Total	*50.1*	*52.3*	*74.2*

Passenger trips per person

Buses	55.7	82.9	112.8
Rail	22.5	19.7	63.5
Trams	111.3	133.9	169.1
Ferries	0.0	0.0	0.0
Total	*189.5*	*236.5*	*345.4*

Passenger trips per vehicle kilometre

Buses	4.6	4.2	3.8
Rail	1.1	0.9	2.0
Trams	6.1	13.6	11.9
Ferries	0.0	0.0	0.0
Overall	*3.8*	*4.4*	*4.5*

Passenger kilometres per person

Buses	223.0	348.2	507.5
Rail	449.7	473.8	819.6
Trams	278.3	348.2	473.6
Ferries	0.0	0.0	0.0
Total	*951.0*	*1,170.2*	*1,800.7*

Average speed of public transport

Buses (km/h)	15.4	17.4	18.0
Rail (km/h)	65.0	65.0	57.2
Trams (km/h)	17.3	15.8	15.0
Ferries (km/h)	0.0	0.0	0.0
Overall	*39.7*	*37.4*	*36.0*

Vehicular energy efficiency

Buses (MJ / km)	16.0	16.5	19.6
Rail (MJ / km)	8.0	8.0	10.0
Trams (MJ / km)	6.3	16.4	18.3
Ferries (MJ / km)	0.0	0.0	0.0
Overall	*9.3*	*12.6*	*15.2*

Modal energy efficiency

Buses (MJ / passenger km.)	0.88	0.94	1.16
Rail (MJ / passenger km.)	0.35	0.38	0.38
Trams (MJ / passenger km.)	0.41	0.46	0.55
Ferries (MJ / passenger km.)	0.0	0.0	0.0
Overall	*0.49*	*0.56*	*0.63*

(1) Amsterdam has a significant component of bicycle travel and the per capita passenger kms were as follows:

1960: 1,283
1970: 796
1980: 918

292

Boston

POPULATION PARAMETERS	1960	1970	1980
Urban density (persons / ha)	18.1	15.4	12.1
Inner area density (persons / ha)	54.6	50.7	44.8
Outer area density (persons / ha)	13.6	12.2	9.8
CBD density (persons / ha)	139.7	114.2	125.5
Proportion of population in CBD (%)	3.3	2.5	2.7
Proportion of population in inner area (%)	32.8	27.7	24.3

EMPLOYMENT PARAMETERS			
Employment density (jobs / ha)	6.9	6.2	6.2
Inner area employment density (jobs / ha)	29.3	29.6	32.7
Outer area employment density (jobs / ha)	4.1	4.0	4.3
CBD employment density (jobs / ha)	478.9	430.9	382.8
Proportion of jobs in CBD (%)	29.7	23.1	15.9
Proportion of jobs in inner area (%)	46.2	40.5	34.6

ACTIVITY INTENSITY PARAMETERS (Pop. & Jobs / ha)			
CBD activity intensity	618.6	545.1	508.3
Inner area activity intensity	83.9	80.3	77.5
Outer area activity intensity	17.7	16.2	14.1
City - wide activity intensity	25.0	21.6	18.3

VEHICLE OWNERSHIP PARAMETERS			
Total vehicles / 1000 people	328.5	404.5	556.8
Passenger cars / 1000 people	272.6	336.5	465.3

PRIVATE MOBILITY PARAMETERS			
Total per capita vehicle kms.	4,569	7,083	9,836
Per capita car kms.	4,112	6,375	8,852
Total per capita occupant kms.	6,900	10,058	13,967
Per capita car occupant kms.	6,209	9,052	12,570
Total vehicle kms. per vehicle	13,910	17,512	17,521
Car kms. per car	15,083	18,946	17,529

TRAFFIC RESTRAINT PARAMETERS			
Parking spaces / 1000 CBD workers	107.3	219.1	321.7
Length of road per person (m)	?	?	5.2
Total vehicles per km of road	?	?	111.5
Total vehicle kms. per km. of road	?	?	1,762,971
Car kms. per km. of road	?	?	1,586,674

TRANSPORT ENERGY PARAMETERS			
Motor spirit use / person (MJ)	23,486	38,284	54,185
Total private energy use / person (MJ)	28,652	45,887	64,223
Public trans. energy use / person (MJ)	?	?	?
Total energy use / person (MJ)	?	?	?

PUBLIC TRANSPORT PARAMETERS

Vehicle kilometres per person

Buses	13.0	14.6	14.9
Rail	7.0	8.0	8.3
Trams	6.1	4.8	2.9
Ferries	0.0	0.0	0.0
Total	*26.1*	*27.4*	*26.1*

Passenger trips per person

Buses	40.9	33.8	24.1
Rail	41.9	35.0	36.3
Trams	22.6	18.8	19.5
Ferries	0.0	0.0	0.0
Total	*105.4*	*87.6*	*79.9*

Passenger trips per vehicle kilometre

Buses	3.1	2.3	1.6
Rail	5.9	4.3	4.2
Trams	3.7	3.9	6.7
Ferries	0.0	0.0	0.0
Overall	*4.0*	*3.2*	*3.0*

Passenger kilometres per person

Buses	245.3	219.8	168.9
Rail	282.2	247.5	270.5
Trams	90.8	75.6	78.3
Ferries	0.0	0.0	0.0
Total	*618.3*	*542.9*	*517.7*

Average speed of public transport

Buses (km/h)	18.0	18.0	18.2
Rail (km/h)	?	?	38.5
Trams (km/h)	21.3	20.7	20.2
Ferries (km/h)	0.0	0.0	0.0
Overall	*?*	*?*	*29.6*

Vehicular energy efficiency

Buses (MJ / km)	?	?	?
Rail (MJ / km)	?	?	?
Trams (MJ / km)	?	?	?
Ferries (MJ / km)	0.0	0.0	0.0
Overall	*?*	*?*	*?*

Modal energy efficiency

Buses (MJ / passenger km.)	?	?	?
Rail (MJ / passenger km.)	?	?	?
Trams (MJ / passenger km.)	?	?	?
Ferries (MJ / passenger km.)	0.0	0.0	0.0
Overall	*?*	*?*	*?*

Brisbane

POPULATION PARAMETERS	1960	1970	1980
Urban density (persons / ha)	21.0	11.3	10.2
Inner area density (persons / ha)	25.2	24.2	18.5
Outer area density (persons / ha)	18.4	9.1	9.1
CBD density (persons / ha)	?	11.0	15.3
Proportion of population in CBD (%)	?	0.2	0.3
Proportion of population in inner area (%)	45.1	31.1	21.7

EMPLOYMENT PARAMETERS			
Employment density (jobs / ha)	7.2	?	4.1
Inner area employment density (jobs / ha)	14.4	?	15.6
Outer area employment density (jobs / ha)	2.8	?	2.5
CBD employment density (jobs / ha)	335.3	344.5	345.8
Proportion of jobs in CBD (%)	26.1	?	13.9
Proportion of jobs in inner area (%)	75.9	?	45.7

ACTIVITY INTENSITY PARAMETERS (Pop. & Jobs / ha)			
CBD activity intensity	?	355.5	361.2
Inner area activity intensity	39.6	?	34.1
Outer area activity intensity	21.4	?	11.6
City - wide activity intensity	28.1	?	14.3

VEHICLE OWNERSHIP PARAMETERS			
Total vehicles / 1000 people	260.7	372.3	595.2
Passenger cars / 1000 people	192.3	294.3	458.1

PRIVATE MOBILITY PARAMETERS			
Total per capita vehicle kms.	3,341	4,685	7,293
Per capita car kms.	2,608	3,788	5,861
Total per capita occupant kms.	7,911	9,042	14,588
Per capita car occupant kms.	6,174	7,311	11,724
Total vehicle kms. per vehicle	13,770	12,584	12,254
Car kms. per car	14,570	12,871	12,794

TRAFFIC RESTRAINT PARAMETERS			
Parking spaces / 1000 CBD workers	162.2	227.6	268.4
Length of road per person (m)	7.8	7.5	6.9
Total vehicles per km of road	36.3	49.9	94.4
Total vehicle kms. per km. of road	499,627	627,586	1,157,355
Car kms. per km. of road	389,967	507,425	930,096

TRANSPORT ENERGY PARAMETERS			
Motor spirit use / person (MJ)	15,496	21,167	30,653
Total private energy use / person (MJ)	16,682	23,008	36,448
Public trans. energy use / person (MJ)	2,981	1,010	855
Total energy use / person (MJ)	19,663	24,018	37,303

PUBLIC TRANSPORT PARAMETERS

Vehicle kilometres per person

Buses	27.1	37.0	26.6
Rail	30.2	20.2	21.7
Trams	20.6	0.0	0.0
Ferries	0.0	0.0	0.0
Total	*77.9*	*57.2*	*48.3*

Passenger trips per person

Buses	73.8	94.6	49.8
Rail	39.5	31.8	29.5
Trams	118.5	0.0	0.0
Ferries	0.0	0.0	0.0
Total	*231.8*	*126.4*	*79.3*

Passenger trips per vehicle kilometre

Buses	2.7	2.6	1.9
Rail	1.3	1.6	1.4
Trams	5.8	0.0	0.0
Ferries	0.0	0.0	0.0
Overall	*3.0*	*2.2*	*1.6*

Passenger kilometres per person

Buses	324.7	520.2	328.9
Rail	506.2	432.9	415.8
Trams	521.4	0.0	0.0
Ferries	0.0	0.0	0.0
Total	*1,352.3*	*953.1*	*744.7*

Average speed of public transport

Buses (km/h)	21.3	20.0	23.0
Rail (km/h)	28.4	33.8	37.0
Trams (km/h)	17.6	0.0	0.0
Ferries (km/h)	0.0	0.0	0.0
Overall	*22.5*	*26.3*	*30.8*

Vehicular energy efficiency

Buses (MJ / km)	13.4	15.3	16.9
Rail (MJ / km)	81.8	22.0	18.7
Trams (MJ / km)	7.3	0.0	0.0
Ferries (MJ / km)	0.0	0.0	0.0
Overall	*38.3*	*17.7*	*17.7*

Modal energy efficiency

Buses (MJ / passenger km.)	1.12	1.09	1.37
Rail (MJ / passenger km.)	4.88	1.03	0.98
Trams (MJ / passenger km.)	0.29	0.0	0.0
Ferries (MJ / passenger km.)	0.0	0.0	0.0
Overall	*2.20*	*1.06*	*1.15*

Brussels

POPULATION PARAMETERS	1960	1970	1980
Urban density (persons / ha)	100.3	79.6	67.4
Inner area density (persons / ha)	115.8	113.2	100.5
Outer area density (persons / ha)	84.5	59.0	49.8
CBD density (persons / ha)	197.1	74.9	74.1
Proportion of population in CBD (%)	5.0	1.8	1.9
Proportion of population in inner area (%)	58.2	54.2	51.8
EMPLOYMENT PARAMETERS			
Employment density (jobs / ha)	66.7	49.5	42.1
Inner area employment density (jobs / ha)	105.0	101.8	91.8
Outer area employment density (jobs / ha)	27.8	17.3	15.6
CBD employment density (jobs / ha)	?	?	591.5
Proportion of jobs in CBD (%)	?	?	24.6
Proportion of jobs in inner area (%)	79.4	78.4	75.9
ACTIVITY INTENSITY PARAMETERS (Pop. & Jobs / ha)			
CBD activity intensity	?	?	665.6
Inner area activity intensity	220.8	215.0	192.3
Outer area activity intensity	112.3	76.3	65.4
City - wide activity intensity	167.0	129.1	109.4
VEHICLE OWNERSHIP PARAMETERS			
Total vehicles / 1000 people	191.0	298.3	407.8
Passenger cars / 1000 people	157.3	262.3	361.1
PRIVATE MOBILITY PARAMETERS			
Total per capita vehicle kms.	2,491	3,603	4,636
Per capita car kms.	1,793	2,918	3,935
Total per capita occupant kms.	3,986	5,404	6,723
Per capita car occupant kms	2,869	4,377	5,706
Total vehicle kms. per vehicle	13,042	12,076	11,370
Car kms. per car	11,400	11,125	10,900
TRAFFIC RESTRAINT PARAMETERS			
Parking spaces / 1000 CBD workers	?	?	185.5
Length of road per person (m)	1.4	1.4	1.7
Total vehicles per km of road	134.7	206.9	246.3
Total vehicle kms. per km. of road	1,757,241	2,499,032	2,800,157
Car kms. per km. of road	1,264,759	2,024,194	2,376,794
TRANSPORT ENERGY PARAMETERS			
Motor spirit use / person (MJ)	5,474	10,427	14,744
Total private energy use / person (MJ)	12,157	16,980	21,454
Public trans. energy use / person (MJ)	722	814	1,339
Total energy use / person (MJ)	12,879	17,794	22,793

PUBLIC TRANSPORT PARAMETERS

Vehicle kilometres per person

Buses	10.5	18.1	26.6
Rail	6.6	6.3	11.5
Trams	46.9	22.5	15.5
Ferries	0.0	0.0	0.0
Total	*64.0*	*46.9*	*53.6*

Passenger trips per person

Buses	62.4	65.9	95.3
Rail	59.6	53.7	67.6
Trams	209.8	114.1	102.9
Ferries	0.0	0.0	0.0
Total	*331.8*	*233.7*	*265.8*

Passenger trips per vehicle kilometre

Buses	5.9	3.6	3.6
Rail	9.0	8.4	5.9
Trams	4.5	5.1	6.6
Ferries	0.0	0.0	0.0
Overall	*5.2*	*5.0*	*5.0*

Passenger kilometres per person

Buses	218.3	250.5	381.3
Rail	835.0	751.3	603.3
Trams	734.4	433.6	411.5
Ferries	0.0	0.0	0.0
Total	*1,787.7*	*1,435.4*	*1,396.1*

Average speed of public transport

Buses (km/h)	18.8	18.7	19.8
Rail (km/h)	40.7	40.7	38.4
Trams (km/h)	17.1	16.1	17.3
Ferries (km/h)	0.0	0.0	0.0
Overall	*28.3*	*29.4*	*27.1*

Vehicular energy efficiency

Buses (MJ / km)	16.5	19.5	21.6
Rail (MJ / km)	28.6	30.8	37.4
Trams (MJ / km)	7.7	11.8	21.6
Ferries (MJ / km)	0.0	0.0	0.0
Overall	*11.3*	*17.4*	*25.0*

Modal energy efficiency

Buses (MJ / passenger km.)	0.80	1.41	1.51
Rail (MJ / passenger km.)	0.23	0.26	0.71
Trams (MJ / passenger km.)	0.49	0.61	0.81
Ferries (MJ / passenger km.)	0.00	0.00	0.00
Overall	*0.40*	*0.57*	*0.96*

Chicago

POPULATION PARAMETERS	1960	1970	1980
Urban density (persons / ha)	24.0	20.3	17.5
Inner area density (persons / ha)	71.1	63.9	54.1
Outer area density (persons / ha)	12.1	12.0	11.4
CBD density (persons / ha)	10.6	11.9	15.6
Proportion of population in CBD (%)	0.07	0.07	0.09
Proportion of population in inner area (%)	57.1	48.2	42.3
EMPLOYMENT PARAMETERS			
Employment density (jobs / ha)	9.8	8.5	8.1
Inner area employment density (jobs / ha)	32.5	28.0	25.5
Outer area employment density (jobs / ha)	4.1	4.8	5.2
CBD employment density (jobs / ha)	779.5	880.6	937.9
Proportion of jobs in CBD (%)	13.2	12.9	12.3
Proportion of jobs in inner area (%)	66.5	52.4	44.9
ACTIVITY INTENSITY PARAMETERS			
(Pop. & Jobs / ha)			
CBD activity intensity	790.1	892.5	953.5
Inner area activity intensity	103.6	91.9	79.6
Outer area activity intensity	16.2	16.8	16.6
City - wide activity intensity	33.8	28.8	25.6
VEHICLE OWNERSHIP PARAMETERS			
Total vehicles / 1000 people	324.1	435.4	518.4
Passenger cars / 1000 people	307.7	391.0	445.0
PRIVATE MOBILITY PARAMETERS			
Total per capita vehicle kms.	4,306	6,073	7,965
Per capita car kms.	4,095	5,769	7,566
Total per capita occupant kms.	6,717	8,927	11,708
Per capita car occupant kms.	6,381	8,481	11,122
Total vehicle kms. per vehicle	12,718	13,949	15,364
Car kms. per car	13,308	14,757	17,003
TRAFFIC RESTRAINT PARAMETERS			
Parking spaces / 1000 CBD workers	83.0	96.3	91.1
Length of road per person (m)	4.8	5.0	5.0
Total vehicles per km of road	70.0	87.5	103.2
Total vehicle kms. per km. of road	889,664	1,219,830	1,584,879
Car kms. per km. of road	845,191	1,158,843	1,505,631
TRANSPORT ENERGY PARAMETERS			
Motor spirit use / person (MJ)	26,731	41,737	48,246
Total private energy use / person (MJ)	29,165	44,994	51,988
Public trans. energy use / person (MJ)	1,334	1,203	1,392
Total energy use / person (MJ)	30,499	46,197	53,380

PUBLIC TRANSPORT PARAMETERS

Vehicle kilometres per person

Buses	31.8	25.8	23.2
Rail	20.3	19.0	18.4
Trams	0.0	0.0	0.0
Ferries	0.0	0.0	0.0
Total	*52.1*	*44.8*	*41.6*

Passenger trips per person

Buses	107.7	76.7	81.1
Rail	37.7	32.5	33.5
Trams	0.0	0.0	0.0
Ferries	0.0	0.0	0.0
Total	*145.4*	*109.2*	*114.6*

Passenger trips per vehicle kilometre

Buses	3.4	3.0	3.5
Rail	1.9	1.7	1.8
Trams	0.0	0.0	0.0
Ferries	0.0	0.0	0.0
Overall	*2.8*	*2.4*	*2.8*

Passenger kilometres per person

Buses	413.1	295.4	323.7
Rail	602.2	560.2	647.4
Trams	0.0	0.0	0.0
Ferries	0.0	0.0	0.0
Total	*1,015.3*	*855.6*	*971.1*

Average speed of public transport

Buses (km/h)	16.4	15.0	18.2
Rail (km/h)	44.1	45.1	46.9
Trams (km/h)	0.0	0.0	0.0
Ferries (km/h)	0.0	0.0	0.0
Overall	*32.9*	*34.7*	*37.4*

Vehicular energy efficiency

Buses (MJ / km)	23.7	25.8	34.2
Rail (MJ / km)	28.7	28.2	32.5
Trams (MJ / km)	0.0	0.0	0.0
Ferries (MJ / km)	0.0	0.0	0.0
Overall	*25.6*	*26.8*	*33.5*

Modal energy efficiency

Buses (MJ / passenger km.)	1.82	2.26	2.45
Rail (MJ / passenger km.)	0.96	0.96	0.92
Trams (MJ / passenger km.)	0.0	0.0	0.0
Ferries (MJ / passenger km.)	0.0	0.0	0.0
Overall	*1.31*	*1.41*	*1.43*

Copenhagen

POPULATION PARAMETERS	1960	1970	1980
Urban density (persons / ha)	40.1	33.4	30.4
Inner area density (persons / ha)	93.6	79.6	59.3
Outer area density (persons / ha)	22.6	22.4	23.6
CBD density (persons / ha)	142.9	115.6	84.8
Proportion of population in CBD (%)	4.0	3.0	2.2
Proportion of population in inner area (%)	57.5	45.8	37.3
EMPLOYMENT PARAMETERS			
Employment density (jobs / ha)	17.9	15.5	16.2
Inner area employment density (jobs / ha)	52.0	44.3	37.9
Outer area employment density (jobs / ha)	6.7	8.6	11.1
CBD employment density (jobs / ha)	408.3	341.1	325.1
Proportion of jobs in CBD (%)	25.9	19.1	16.0
Proportion of jobs in inner area (%)	71.6	55.0	44.8
ACTIVITY INTENSITY PARAMETERS			
(Pop. & Jobs / ha)			
CBD activity intensity	551.2	456.7	409.9
Inner area activity intensity	145.6	123.9	97.2
Outer area activity intensity	29.3	31.0	34.7
City - wide activity intensity	58.0	48.9	46.6
VEHICLE OWNERSHIP PARAMETERS			
Total vehicles / 1000 people	138.0	255.2	296.2
Passenger cars / 1000 people	88.5	199.5	246.4
PRIVATE MOBILITY PARAMETERS			
Total per capita vehicle kms.	1,575	3,581	4,166
Per capita car kms.	1,263	3,069	3,462
Total per capita occupant kms.	4,253	6,088	7,499
Per capita car occupant kms.	3,411	5,217	6,231
Total vehicle kms. per vehicle	11,411	14,034	14,065
Car kms. per car	14,283	15,385	14,049
TRAFFIC RESTRAINT PARAMETERS			
Parking spaces / 1000 CBD workers	150.7	198.5	212.3
Length of road per person (m)	2.8	3.4	4.3
Total vehicles per km of road	49.3	74.1	69.3
Total vehicle kms. per km. of road	563,000	1,040,106	974,849
Car kms. per km. of road	451,000	891,448	810,087
TRANSPORT ENERGY PARAMETERS			
Motor spirit use / person (MJ)	6,711	10,649	11,106
Total private energy use / person (MJ)	8,474	15,047	16,152
Public trans. energy use / person (MJ)	662	717	1,131
Total energy use / person (MJ)	9,136	15,764	17,283

PUBLIC TRANSPORT PARAMETERS

Vehicle kilometres per person

Buses	17.5	34.2	50.2
Rail	35.0	48.7	59.3
Trams	19.8	3.1	0.0
Ferries	0.0	0.0	0.0
Total	*72.3*	*86.0*	*109.5*

Passenger trips per person

Buses	60.3	108.4	143.7
Rail	52.4	44.0	57.2
Trams	80.6	12.5	0.0
Ferries	0.0	0.0	0.0
Total	*193.3*	*164.9*	*200.9*

Passenger trips per vehicle kilometre

Buses	3.4	3.2	2.9
Rail	1.5	0.9	1.0
Trams	4.1	4.0	0.0
Ferries	0.0	0.0	0.0
Overall	*2.7*	*1.9*	*1.8*

Passenger kilometres per person

Buses	331.6	617.9	862.1
Rail	861.6	708.7	795.9
Trams	354.5	54.8	0.0
Ferries	0.0	0.0	0.0
Total	*1,547.7*	*1,381.4*	*1,657.2*

Average speed of public transport

Buses (km/h)	?	21.8	23.8
Rail (km/h)	59.1	59.0	54.3
Trams (km/h)	?	?	0.0
Ferries (km/h)	0.0	0.0	0.0
Overall	*?*	*?*	*38.4*

Vehicular energy efficiency

Buses (MJ / km)	12.4	14.6	16.8
Rail (MJ / km)	9.6	6.8	8.0
Trams (MJ / km)	9.5	9.5	0.0
Ferries (MJ / km)	0.0	0.0	0.0
Overall	*10.5*	*11.1*	*13.1*

Modal energy efficiency

Buses (MJ / passenger km.)	0.65	0.81	0.98
Rail (MJ / passenger km.)	0.25	0.40	0.54
Trams (MJ / passenger km.)	0.53	0.54	0.00
Ferries (MJ / passenger km.)	0.00	0.00	0.00
Overall	*0.46*	*0.63*	*0.81*

Denver

POPULATION PARAMETERS	1960	1970	1980
Urban density (persons / ha)	18.6	13.8	11.9
Inner area density (persons / ha)	28.5	22.7	19.3
Outer area density (persons / ha)	12.0	10.0	9.8
CBD density (persons / ha)	40.6	23.7	18.5
Proportion of population in CBD (%)	1.7	0.7	0.4
Proportion of population in inner area (%)	53.1	41.9	30.9
EMPLOYMENT PARAMETERS			
Employment density (jobs / ha)	8.9	6.8	7.6
Inner area employment density (jobs / ha)	13.5	13.1	16.8
Outer area employment density (jobs / ha)	5.8	4.1	4.9
CBD employment density (jobs / ha)	139.9	176.0	262.6
Proportion of jobs in CBD (%)	13.9	13.0	11.6
Proportion of jobs in inner area (%)	61.0	42.2	49.7
ACTIVITY INTENSITY PARAMETERS (Pop. & Jobs / ha)			
CBD activity intensity	180.5	199.7	281.1
Inner area activity intensity	42.0	35.8	36.1
Outer area activity intensity	17.8	14.1	14.7
City - wide activity intensity	27.5	20.6	19.5
VEHICLE OWNERSHIP PARAMETERS			
Total vehicles / 1000 people	573.2	648.7	852.5
Passenger cars / 1000 people	479.1	522.7	666.2
PRIVATE MOBILITY PARAMETERS			
Total per capita vehicle kms.	6,374	8,080	9,927
Per capita car kms.	5,888	7,148	9,455
Total per capita occupant kms.	9,561	11,312	12,210
Per capita car occupant kms.	8,832	10,007	11,630
Total vehicle kms. per vehicle	11,119	12,455	11,645
Car kms. per car	12,290	13,674	14,192
TRAFFIC RESTRAINT PARAMETERS			
Parking spaces / 1000 CBD workers	595.2	578.3	497.6
Length of road per person (m)	8.8	11.0	9.4
Total vehicles per km of road	65.1	69.3	106.5
Total vehicle kms. per km. of road	626,315	736,787	1,052,541
Car kms. per km. of road	578,626	651,807	1,002,509
TRANSPORT ENERGY PARAMETERS			
Motor spirit use / person (MJ)	46,620	62,313	63,466
Total private energy use / person (MJ)	53,880	69,445	76,660
Public trans. energy use / person (MJ)	351	183	542
Total energy use / person (MJ)	54,231	69,628	77,202

PUBLIC TRANSPORT PARAMETERS

Vehicle kilometres per person

Buses	15.6	9.1	24.9
Rail	0.0	0.0	0.0
Trams	0.0	0.0	0.0
Ferries	0.0	0.0	0.0
Total	*15.6*	*9.1*	*24.9*

Passenger trips per person

Buses	43.0	13.4	26.9
Rail	0.0	0.0	0.0
Trams	0.0	0.0	0.0
Ferries	0.0	0.0	0.0
Total	*43.0*	*13.4*	*26.9*

Passenger trips per vehicle kilometre

Buses	2.8	1.5	1.1
Rail	0.0	0.0	0.0
Trams	0.0	0.0	0.0
Ferries	0.0	0.0	0.0
Overall	*2.8*	*1.5*	*1.1*

Passenger kilometres per person

Buses	245.3	92.7	217.6
Rail	0.0	0.0	0.0
Trams	0.0	0.0	0.0
Ferries	0.0	0.0	0.0
Total	*245.3*	*92.7*	*217.6*

Average speed of public transport

Buses (km/h)	?	17.7	21.1
Rail (km/h)	0.0	0.0	0.0
Trams (km/h)	0.0	0.0	0.0
Ferries (km/h)	0.0	0.0	0.0
Overall	*?*	*17.7*	*21.1*

Vehicular energy efficiency

Buses (MJ / km)	22.5	20.1	21.7
Rail (MJ / km)	0.0	0.0	0.0
Trams (MJ / km)	0.0	0.0	0.0
Ferries (MJ / km)	0.0	0.0	0.0
Overall	*22.5*	*20.1*	*21.7*

Modal energy efficiency

Buses (MJ / passenger km.)	1.43	1.97	2.49
Rail (MJ / passenger km.)	0.00	0.00	0.00
Trams (MJ / passenger km.)	0.00	0.00	0.00
Ferries (MJ / passenger km.)	0.00	0.00	0.00
Overall	*1.43*	*1.97*	*2.49*

Detroit

POPULATION PARAMETERS	1960	1970	1980
Urban density (persons / ha)	18.7	17.6	14.1
Inner area density (persons / ha)	67.7	61.4	48.1
Outer area density (persons / ha)	11.3	12.2	10.6
CBD density (persons / ha)	25.6	21.4	11.2
Proportion of population in CBD (%)	0.2	0.2	0.1
Proportion of population in inner area (%)	47.2	38.1	31.6
EMPLOYMENT PARAMETERS			
Employment density (jobs / ha)	6.9	6.8	6.2
Inner area employment density (jobs / ha)	30.2	24.8	19.9
Outer area employment density (jobs / ha)	3.5	4.6	4.8
CBD employment density (jobs / ha)	?	345.7	305.8
Proportion of jobs in CBD (%)	?	6.8	6.6
Proportion of jobs in inner area (%)	56.6	39.8	29.6
ACTIVITY INTENSITY PARAMETERS			
(Pop. & Jobs / ha)			
CBD activity intensity	?	367.1	317.0
Inner area activity intensity	97.9	86.2	68.0
Outer area activity intensity	14.8	16.8	15.4
City - wide activity intensity	25.6	24.4	20.3
VEHICLE OWNERSHIP PARAMETERS			
Total vehicles / 1000 people	401.6	511.0	691.0
Passenger cars / 1000 people	365.5	451.1	593.8
PRIVATE MOBILITY PARAMETERS			
Total per capita vehicle kms.	?	9,086	11,573
Per capita car kms.	?	8,022	9,941
Total per capita occupant kms.	?	13,266	16,318
Per capita car occupant kms.	?	11,712	14,017
Total vehicle kms. per vehicle	?	17,783	16,748
Car kms. per car	?	17,783	16,748
TRAFFIC RESTRAINT PARAMETERS			
Parking spaces / 1000 CBD workers	?	429.0	473.4
Length of road per person (m)	5.2	5.2	5.8
Total vehicles per km of road	77.7	98.5	119.1
Total vehicle kms. per km. of road	?	1,749,381	1,995,395
Car kms. per km. of road	?	1,544,513	1,714,024
TRANSPORT ENERGY PARAMETERS			
Motor spirit use / person (MJ)	?	57,000	65,978
Total private energy use / person (MJ)	?	59,674	68,591
Public trans. energy use / person (MJ)	421	315	377
Total energy use / person (MJ)	?	59,989	68,968

PUBLIC TRANSPORT PARAMETERS

Vehicle kilometres per person

Buses	17.3	14.2	16.4
Rail	0.0	0.1	0.1
Trams	0.9	0.0	0.0
Ferries	0.0	0.0	0.0
Total	*18.2*	*14.3*	*16.5*

Passenger trips per person

Buses	45.4	37.8	25.6
Rail	0.0	0.1	0.1
Trams	3.2	0.0	0.0
Ferries	0.0	0.0	0.0
Total	*48.6*	*37.9*	*25.7*

Passenger trips per vehicle kilometre

Buses	2.6	2.7	1.6
Rail	0.0	1.2	1.2
Trams	3.6	0.0	0.0
Ferries	0.0	0.0	0.0
Overall	*2.7*	*2.7*	*1.6*

Passenger kilometres per person

Buses	115.1	97.8	108.8
Rail	0.0	1.6	3.0
Trams	8.0	0.0	0.0
Ferries	0.0	0.0	0.0
Total	*123.1*	*99.4*	*111.8*

Average speed of public transport

Buses (km/h)	20.2	20.5	21.4
Rail (km/h)	0.0	41.9	41.9
Trams (km/h)	15.2	0.0	0.0
Ferries (km/h)	0.0	0.0	0.0
Overall	*19.9*	*20.5*	*21.5*

Vehicular energy efficiency

Buses (MJ / km)	23.9	21.8	22.4
Rail (MJ / km)	0.0	99.9	99.9
Trams (MJ / km)	10.1	0.0	0.0
Ferries (MJ / km)	0.0	0.0	0.0
Overall	*23.2*	*22.1*	*22.8*

Modal energy efficiency

Buses (MJ / passenger km.)	3.58	3.16	3.70
Rail (MJ / passenger km.)	0.00	3.44	2.94
Trams (MJ / passenger km.)	1.10	0.00	0.00
Ferries (MJ / passenger km.)	0.00	0.00	0.00
Overall	*3.42*	*3.17*	*3.68*

Frankfurt

POPULATION PARAMETERS	1960	1970	1980
Urban density (persons / ha)	87.2	74.6	54.0
Inner area density (persons / ha)	120.1	88.6	62.5
Outer area density (persons / ha)	60.8	65.2	48.9
CBD density (persons / ha)	105.5	81.3	65.2
Proportion of population in CBD (%)	3.6	2.9	2.5
Proportion of population in inner area (%)	61.4	47.7	43.3
EMPLOYMENT PARAMETERS			
Employment density (jobs / ha)	63.3	60.0	43.2
Inner area employment density (jobs / ha)	112.4	110.7	74.3
Outer area employment density (jobs / ha)	23.9	26.0	24.7
CBD employment density (jobs / ha)	511.7	480.8	389.1
Proportion of jobs in CBD (%)	23.9	21.3	18.4
Proportion of jobs in inner area (%)	79.1	74.0	64.2
ACTIVITY INTENSITY PARAMETERS			
(Pop. & Jobs / ha)			
CBD activity intensity	617.2	562.1	454.3
Inner area activity intensity	232.5	199.3	136.8
Outer area activity intensity	84.7	91.2	73.6
City - wide activity intensity	150.5	134.6	97.2
VEHICLE OWNERSHIP PARAMETERS			
Total vehicles / 1000 people	176.6	310.1	426.9
Passenger cars / 1000 people	133.3	280.0	386.9
PRIVATE MOBILITY PARAMETERS			
Total per capita vehicle kms.	?	?	?
Per capita car kms.	2,000	3,485	4,256
Total per capita occupant kms.	?	?	?
Per capita car occupant kms.	3,199	5,576	6,810
Total vehicle kms. per vehicle	?	?	?
Car kms. per car	15,000	12,500	11,000
TRAFFIC RESTRAINT PARAMETERS			
Parking spaces / 1000 CBD workers	110.4	189.2	241.8
Length of road per person (m)	1.3	1.5	2.0
Total vehicles per km of road	132.4	204.9	214.2
Total vehicle kms. per km. of road	?	?	?
Car kms. per km. of road	1,498,825	2,303,009	2,136,111
TRANSPORT ENERGY PARAMETERS			
Motor spirit use / person (MJ)	6,104	12,452	16,093
Total private energy use / person (MJ)	?	?	?
Public trans. energy use / person (MJ)	?	?	733
Total energy use / person (MJ)	?	?	?

PUBLIC TRANSPORT PARAMETERS

Vehicle kilometres per person

Buses	?	?	14.7
Rail	?	?	19.6
Trams	45.0	40.2	20.2
Ferries	0.0	0.0	0.0
Total	*?*	*?*	*54.5*

Passenger trips per person

Buses	?	?	48.1
Rail	?	?	99.4
Trams	248.6	211.8	158.8
Ferries	0.0	0.0	0.0
Total	*?*	*?*	*306.3*

Passenger trips per vehicle kilometre

Buses	?	?	2.9
Rail	?	?	4.4
Trams	5.5	5.3	7.8
Ferries	0.0	0.0	0.0
Overall	*?*	*?*	*4.6*

Passenger kilometres per person

Buses	?	?	214.0
Rail	?	?	879.5
Trams	969.4	826.0	619.5
Ferries	0.0	0.0	0.0
Total	*?*	*?*	*1,713.0*

Average speed of public transport

Buses (km/h)	?	?	21.5
Rail (km/h)	?	?	43.8
Trams (km/h)	?	?	16.7
Ferries (km/h)	0.0	0.0	0.0
Overall	*?*	*?*	*36.7*

Vehicular energy efficiency

Buses (MJ / km)	?	?	12.8
Rail (MJ / km)	?	?	19.4
Trams (MJ / km)	?	?	13.7
Ferries (MJ / km)	0.0	0.0	0.0
Overall	*?*	*?*	*16.4*

Modal energy efficiency

Buses (MJ / passenger km.)	?	?	0.88
Rail (MJ / passenger km.)	?	?	0.39
Trams (MJ / passenger km.)	?	?	0.45
Ferries (MJ / passenger km.)	0.00	0.00	0.00
Overall	*?*	*?*	*0.46*

Hamburg

POPULATION PARAMETERS	1960	1970	1980
Urban density (persons / ha)	68.3	57.5	41.7
Inner area density (persons / ha)	139.6	109.1	88.4
Outer area density (persons / ha)	52.1	47.7	35.0
CBD density (persons / ha)	59.0	36.3	26.4
Proportion of population in CBD (%)	1.5	0.9	0.7
Proportion of population in inner area (%)	37.8	30.2	26.8

EMPLOYMENT PARAMETERS			
Employment density (jobs / ha)	37.5	31.1	23.8
Inner area employment density (jobs / ha)	114.1	108.6	105.5
Outer area employment density (jobs / ha)	20.1	16.4	12.0
CBD employment density (jobs / ha)	443.3	432.9	407.4
Proportion of jobs in CBD (%)	20.1	20.5	20.0
Proportion of jobs in inner area (%)	56.4	55.6	56.0

ACTIVITY INTENSITY PARAMETERS (Pop. & Jobs / ha)			
CBD activity intensity	502.3	469.2	433.8
Inner area activity intensity	253.7	217.7	193.9
Outer area activity intensity	72.2	64.1	47.0
City - wide activity intensity	105.8	88.6	65.5

VEHICLE OWNERSHIP PARAMETERS			
Total vehicles / 1000 people	129.9	267.1	382.4
Passenger cars / 1000 people	95.7	241.4	344.4

PRIVATE MOBILITY PARAMETERS			
Total per capita vehicle kms.	2,031	3,987	4,998
Per capita car kms.	1,560	3,477	4,409
Total per capita occupant kms.	3,411	6,698	8,397
Per capita car occupant kms.	2,620	5,841	7,407
Total vehicle kms. per vehicle	15,666	14,924	13,071
Car kms. per car	16,300	14,400	12,800

TRAFFIC RESTRAINT PARAMETERS			
Parking spaces / 1000 CBD workers	123.7	139.1	148.9
Length of road per person (m)	1.8	2.0	2.2
Total vehicles per km of road	74.1	135.8	171.2
Total vehicle kms. per km. of road	1,158,014	2,027,069	2,238,160
Car kms. per km. of road	889,418	1,767,659	1,974,143

TRANSPORT ENERGY PARAMETERS			
Motor spirit use / person (MJ)	4,761	12,422	16,671
Total private energy use / person (MJ)	?	?	?
Public trans. energy use / person (MJ)	795	937	1,013
Total energy use / person (MJ)	?	?	?

PUBLIC TRANSPORT PARAMETERS

Vehicle kilometres per person

Buses	22.0	30.0	38.8
Rail	24.4	44.2	41.4
Trams	19.3	5.6	0.0
Ferries	0.8	0.4	0.2
Total	*66.5*	*80.2*	*80.4*

Passenger trips per person

Buses	57.3	84.0	111.6
Rail	154.8	148.0	133.6
Trams	115.7	28.1	0.0
Ferries	12.2	5.0	3.1
Total	*340.0*	*265.1*	*248.3*

Passenger trips per vehicle kilometre

Buses	2.6	2.8	2.9
Rail	6.4	3.4	3.2
Trams	6.0	5.0	0.0
Ferries	16.0	12.2	12.8
Overall	*5.1*	*3.3*	*3.1*

Passenger kilometres per person

Buses	310.8	443.7	530.0
Rail	1,161.1	1,128.7	976.0
Trams	497.7	119.9	0.0
Ferries	37.9	15.4	9.5
Total	*2,007.5*	*1,707.7*	*1,515.5*

Average speed of public transport

Buses (km/h)	23.5	22.9	22.4
Rail (km/h)	36.0	36.2	35.7
Trams (km/h)	20.0	18.0	0.0
Ferries (km/h)	10.0	10.7	11.9
Overall	*29.6*	*31.2*	*30.9*

Vehicular energy efficiency

Buses (MJ / km)	11.7	12.5	14.2
Rail (MJ / km)	9.9	9.9	10.0
Trams (MJ / km)	7.6	7.9	0.0
Ferries (MJ / km)	197.6	197.7	199.9
Overall	*12.0*	*11.7*	*12.6*

Modal energy efficiency

Buses (MJ / passenger km.)	0.83	0.85	1.04
Rail (MJ / passenger km.)	0.21	0.39	0.42
Trams (MJ / passenger km.)	0.29	0.37	0.00
Ferries (MJ / passenger km.)	3.97	5.24	5.07
Overall	*0.40*	*0.55*	*0.67*

Hong Kong

POPULATION PARAMETERS	1960	1970	1980
Urban density (persons / ha)	256.5	273.4	293.3
Inner area density (persons / ha)	?	1,048.8	1,036.8
Outer area density (persons / ha)	?	190.0	224.4
CBD density (persons / ha)	470.9	225.5	160.4
Proportion of population in CBD (%)	1.5	0.6	0.4
Proportion of population in inner area (%)	?	37.2	30.0
EMPLOYMENT PARAMETERS			
Employment density (jobs / ha)	?	119.2	109.7
Inner area employment density (jobs / ha)	?	?	478.3
Outer area employment density (jobs / ha)	?	?	65.6
CBD employment density (jobs / ha)	?	?	1,258.6
Proportion of jobs in CBD (%)	?	?	7.3
Proportion of jobs in inner area (%)	?	?	45.3
ACTIVITY INTENSITY PARAMETERS			
(Pop. & Jobs / ha)			
CBD activity intensity	?	?	1,419.0
Inner area activity intensity	?	?	1,515.1
Outer area activity intensity	?	?	290.0
City - wide activity intensity	?	392.6	403.0
VEHICLE OWNERSHIP PARAMETERS			
Total vehicles / 1000 people	17.3	41.8	66.3
Passenger cars / 1000 people	11.4	26.9	42.4
PRIVATE MOBILITY PARAMETERS			
Total per capita vehicle kms.	?	467	899
Per capita car kms.	?	181	347
Total per capita occupant kms.	?	828	1,592
Per capita car occupant kms.	?	432	615
Total vehicle kms. per vehicle	?	11,683	13,982
Car kms. per car	?	6,713	8,188
TRAFFIC RESTRAINT PARAMETERS			
Parking spaces / 1000 CBD workers	?	?	37.4
Length of road per person (m)	?	0.25	0.23
Total vehicles per km of road	?	168.6	289.6
Total vehicle kms. per km. of road	?	1,885,246	3,930,351
Car kms. per km. of road	?	728,197	1,518,142
TRANSPORT ENERGY PARAMETERS			
Motor spirit use / person (MJ)	?	1,315	1,987
Total private energy use / person (MJ)	?	2,729	4,552
Public trans. energy use / person (MJ)	?	866	852
Total energy use / person (MJ)	?	3,595	5,404

PUBLIC TRANSPORT PARAMETERS

Vehicle kilometres per person

Buses	?	?	109.2
Rail	?	?	4.6
Trams	?	?	1.6
Ferries	?	?	0.8
Total	*?*	*?*	*116.2*

Passenger trips per person

Buses	202.2	297.3	348.1
Rail	1.9	2.6	48.6
Trams	58.3	40.8	32.3
Ferries	47.5	60.7	37.3
Total	*309.9*	*401.4*	*466.3*

Passenger trips per vehicle kilometre

Buses	?	?	3.2
Rail	?	?	10.7
Trams	?	?	19.7
Ferries	?	?	47.2
Overall	*?*	*?*	*4.0*

Passenger kilometres per person

Buses	?	1,422.2	1,412.1
Rail	40.5	46.7	349.9
Trams	?	118.4	93.1
Ferries	?	218.4	187.7
Total	*?*	*1,805.7*	*2,042.8*

Average speed of public transport

Buses (km/h)	?	?	14.8
Rail (km/h)	?	?	31.3
Trams (km/h)	?	?	9.9
Ferries (km/h)	?	?	13.5
Overall	*?*	*?*	*16.8*

Vehicular energy efficiency

Buses (MJ / km)	?	?	16.2
Rail (MJ / km)	?	?	19.0
Trams (MJ / km)	?	?	5.7
Ferries (MJ / km)	?	?	282.2
Overall	*?*	*?*	*21.3*

Modal energy efficiency

Buses (MJ / passenger km.)	?	0.45	0.72
Rail (MJ / passenger km.)	?	0.56	0.25
Trams (MJ / passenger km.)	?	0.12	0.10
Ferries (MJ / passenger km.)	?	0.83	1.19
Overall	*?*	*0.48*	*0.62*

Houston

POPULATION PARAMETERS	1960	1970	1980
Urban density (persons / ha)	10.2	12.0	8.9
Inner area density (persons / ha)	21.6	22.6	20.6
Outer area density (persons / ha)	7.2	9.9	7.8
CBD density (persons / ha)	7.1	9.5	5.5
Proportion of population in CBD (%)	0.2	0.2	0.1
Proportion of population in inner area (%)	35.2	26.3	16.6
EMPLOYMENT PARAMETERS			
Employment density (jobs / ha)	5.0	6.2	5.5
Inner area employment density (jobs / ha)	?	?	26.4
Outer area employment density (jobs / ha)	?	?	3.5
CBD employment density (jobs / ha)	145.2	245.4	442.7
Proportion of jobs in CBD (%)	10.2	11.2	11.6
Proportion of jobs in inner area (%)	?	?	41.1
ACTIVITY INTENSITY PARAMETERS			
(Pop. & Jobs / ha)			
CBD activity intensity	152.3	254.9	448.2
Inner area activity intensity	?	?	47.0
Outer area activity intensity	?	?	11.3
City - wide activity intensity	15.2	18.2	14.4
VEHICLE OWNERSHIP PARAMETERS			
Total vehicles / 1000 people	500.9	647.9	797.0
Passenger cars / 1000 people	388.1	476.8	602.6
PRIVATE MOBILITY PARAMETERS			
Total per capita vehicle kms.	7,188	8,879	11,533
Per capita car kms.	6,829	8,257	9,918
Total per capita occupant kms.	?	?	18,568
Per capita car occupant kms.	?	?	15,968
Total vehicle kms. per vehicle	14,349	13,705	14,470
Car kms. per car	17,594	17,317	16,460
TRAFFIC RESTRAINT PARAMETERS			
Parking spaces / 1000 CBD workers	497.2	363.1	369.9
Length of road per person (m)	?	11.7	10.6
Total vehicles per km of road	?	55.5	75.5
Total vehicle kms. per km. of road	?	760,941	1,092,358
Car kms. per km. of road	?	707,660	939,428
TRANSPORT ENERGY PARAMETERS			
Motor spirit use / person (MJ)	45,800	62,629	74,510
Total private energy use / person (MJ)	47,569	67,192	83,618
Public trans. energy use / person (MJ)	490	297	289
Total energy use / person (MJ)	48,059	67,489	83,907

PUBLIC TRANSPORT PARAMETERS

Vehicle kilometres per person

Buses	20.6	12.6	9.1
Rail	0.0	0.0	0.0
Trams	0.0	0.0	0.0
Ferries	0.0	0.0	0.0
Total	*20.6*	*12.6*	*9.1*

Passenger trips per person

Buses	28.6	16.4	14.7
Rail	0.0	0.0	0.0
Trams	0.0	0.0	0.0
Ferries	0.0	0.0	0.0
Total	*28.6*	*16.4*	*14.7*

Passenger trips per vehicle kilometre

Buses	1.4	1.3	1.6
Rail	0.0	0.0	0.0
Trams	0.0	0.0	0.0
Ferries	0.0	0.0	0.0
Overall	*1.4*	*1.3*	*1.6*

Passenger kilometres per person

Buses	234.2	139.4	128.3
Rail	0.0	0.0	0.0
Trams	0.0	0.0	0.0
Ferries	0.0	0.0	0.0
Total	*234.2*	*139.4*	*128.3*

Average speed of public transport

Buses (km/h)	18.4	20.8	21.8
Rail (km/h)	0.0	0.0	0.0
Trams (km/h)	0.0	0.0	0.0
Ferries (km/h)	0.0	0.0	0.0
Overall	*18.4*	*20.8*	*21.8*

Vehicular energy efficiency

Buses (MJ / km)	23.8	23.6	31.8
Rail (MJ / km)	0.0	0.0	0.0
Trams (MJ / km)	0.0	0.0	0.0
Ferries (MJ / km)	0.0	0.0	0.0
Overall	*23.8*	*23.6*	*31.8*

Modal energy efficiency

Buses (MJ / passenger km.)	2.09	2.13	2.26
Rail (MJ / passenger km.)	0.00	0.00	0.00
Trams (MJ / passenger km.)	0.00	0.00	0.00
Ferries (MJ / passenger km.)	0.00	0.00	0.00
Overall	*2.09*	*2.13*	*2.26*

London

POPULATION PARAMETERS	1960	1970	1980
Urban density (persons / ha)	65.4	61.6	56.3
Inner area density (persons / ha)	108.9	94.6	77.9
Outer area density (persons / ha)	49.9	49.7	48.3
CBD density (persons / ha)	100.0	85.3	66.4
Proportion of population in CBD (%)	3.4	3.1	2.7
Proportion of population in inner area (%)	43.7	40.7	37.2
EMPLOYMENT PARAMETERS			
Employment density (jobs / ha)	35.9	33.7	30.2
Inner area employment density (jobs / ha)	83.7	72.7	61.9
Outer area employment density (jobs / ha)	18.9	19.7	18.5
CBD employment density (jobs / ha)	519.9	463.5	396.8
Proportion of jobs in CBD (%)	32.0	30.6	29.7
Proportion of jobs in inner area (%)	61.2	57.2	55.1
ACTIVITY INTENSITY PARAMETERS			
(Pop. & Jobs / ha)			
CBD activity intensity	619.9	548.8	463.2
Inner area activity intensity	192.6	167.3	139.8
Outer area activity intensity	68.8	69.4	66.8
City - wide activity intensity	101.3	95.3	86.5
VEHICLE OWNERSHIP PARAMETERS			
Total vehicles / 1000 people	186.8	287.3	355.5
Passenger cars / 1000 people	156.3	222.8	287.8
PRIVATE MOBILITY PARAMETERS			
Total per capita vehicle kms.	1,792	2,474	3,344
Per capita car kms.	1,341	1,855	2,529
Total per capita occupant kms.	3,028	4,156	5,552
Per capita car occupant kms.	2,400	3,321	4,452
Total vehicle kms. per vehicle	9,591	8,610	9,407
Car kms. per car	8,577	8,328	8,789
TRAFFIC RESTRAINT PARAMETERS			
Parking spaces / 1000 CBD workers	?	126.5	129.7
Length of road per person (m)	1.5	1.7	1.9
Total vehicles per km of road	123.1	170.1	185.7
Total vehicle kms. per km. of road	1,180,656	1,464,816	1,747,160
Car kms. per km. of road	883,658	1,098,592	1,321,401
TRANSPORT ENERGY PARAMETERS			
Motor spirit use / person (MJ)	6,553	9,066	12,426
Total private energy use / person (MJ)	9,412	12,769	17,597
Public trans. energy use / person (MJ)	1,173	1,094	1,124
Total energy use / person (MJ)	10,585	13,863	18,721

PUBLIC TRANSPORT PARAMETERS

Vehicle kilometres per person

Buses	51.5	43.0	41.6
Rail	69.9	71.8	78.2
Trams	0.0	0.0	0.0
Ferries	0.0	0.0	0.0
Total	*121.4*	*114.8*	*119.8*

Passenger trips per person

Buses	324.4	201.5	176.2
Rail	111.9	123.3	108.2
Trams	0.0	0.0	0.0
Ferries	0.0	0.0	0.0
Total	*436.3*	*324.8*	*284.4*

Passenger trips per vehicle kilometre

Buses	6.3	4.7	4.2
Rail	1.6	1.7	1.4
Trams	0.0	0.0	0.0
Ferries	0.0	0.0	0.0
Overall	*3.6*	*2.8*	*2.4*

Passenger kilometres per person

Buses	1,197.1	735.6	623.8
Rail	1,032.1	1,259.6	1,093.1
Trams	0.0	0.0	0.0
Ferries	0.0	0.0	0.0
Total	*2,229.2*	*1,995.2*	*1,716.9*

Average speed of public transport

Buses (km/h)	20.9	18.5	17.7
Rail (km/h)	36.9	37.9	38.4
Trams (km/h)	0.0	0.0	0.0
Ferries (km/h)	0.0	0.0	0.0
Overall	*28.3*	*30.7*	*30.9*

Vehicular energy efficiency

Buses (MJ / km)	14.0	15.5	15.5
Rail (MJ / km)	6.5	6.0	6.1
Trams (MJ / km)	0.0	0.0	0.0
Ferries (MJ / km)	0.0	0.0	0.0
Overall	*9.7*	*9.5*	*9.4*

Modal energy efficiency

Buses (MJ / passenger km.)	0.60	0.91	1.03
Rail (MJ / passenger km.)	0.44	0.42	0.44
Trams (MJ / passenger km.)	0.00	0.00	0.00
Ferries (MJ / passenger km.)	0.00	0.00	0.00
Overall	*0.53*	*0.62*	*0.66*

Los Angeles

POPULATION PARAMETERS	1960	1970	1980
Urban density (persons / ha)	18.3	20.5	20.0
Inner area density (persons / ha)	27.0	30.2	29.6
Outer area density (persons / ha)	15.3	17.6	17.5
CBD density (persons / ha)	51.4	25.7	29.4
Proportion of population in CBD (%)	0.3	0.1	0.1
Proportion of population in inner area (%)	38.2	33.7	31.3
EMPLOYMENT PARAMETERS			
Employment density (jobs / ha)	9.7	9.7	10.5
Inner area employment density (jobs / ha)	11.0	12.6	13.9
Outer area employment density (jobs / ha)	9.0	8.3	8.9
CBD employment density (jobs / ha)	537.3	397.2	472.0
Proportion of jobs in CBD (%)	6.7	4.7	4.8
Proportion of jobs in inner area (%)	38.7	42.9	43.3
ACTIVITY INTENSITY PARAMETERS (Pop. & Jobs / ha)			
CBD activity intensity	588.7	422.9	501.4
Inner area activity intensity	38.0	42.8	43.5
Outer area activity intensity	24.3	25.9	26.4
City - wide activity intensity	28.0	30.2	30.5
VEHICLE OWNERSHIP PARAMETERS			
Total vehicles / 1000 people	513.0	615.0	666.7
Passenger cars / 1000 people	459.1	521.2	541.5
PRIVATE MOBILITY PARAMETERS			
Total per capita vehicle kms.	7,771	8,441	10,003
Per capita car kms.	7,382	7,850	9,003
Total per capita occupant kms.	11,734	12,746	15,405
Per capita car occupant kms.	11,147	11,854	13,865
Total vehicle kms. per vehicle	15,148	13,724	15,003
Car kms. per car	16,080	15,061	16,626
TRAFFIC RESTRAINT PARAMETERS			
Parking spaces / 1000 CBD workers	372.8	534.8	523.6
Length of road per person (m)	4.9	4.8	4.5
Total vehicles per km of road	112.4	136.5	157.6
Total vehicle kms. per km. of road	1,586,926	1,756,271	2,211,091
Car kms. per km. of road	1,507,592	1,633,328	1,989,979
TRANSPORT ENERGY PARAMETERS			
Motor spirit use / person (MJ)	42,161	58,174	58,474
Total private energy use / person (MJ)	46,554	62,702	64,870
Public trans. energy use / person (MJ)	368	316	645
Total energy use / person (MJ)	46,922	63,018	65,515

PUBLIC TRANSPORT PARAMETERS

Vehicle kilometres per person

Buses	19.2	16.1	26.8
Rail	0.2	0.0	0.0
Trams	0.0	0.0	0.0
Ferries	0.0	0.0	0.0
Total	*19.4*	*16.1*	*26.8*

Passenger trips per person

Buses	36.9	24.6	59.2
Rail	0.3	0.0	0.0
Trams	0.0	0.0	0.0
Ferries	0.0	0.0	0.0
Total	*37.2*	*24.6*	*59.2*

Passenger trips per vehicle kilometre

Buses	1.9	1.5	2.2
Rail	1.4	0.0	0.0
Trams	0.0	0.0	0.0
Ferries	0.0	0.0	0.0
Overall	*1.9*	*1.5*	*2.2*

Passenger kilometres per person

Buses	239.0	159.7	383.6
Rail	5.3	0.0	0.0
Trams	0.0	0.0	0.0
Ferries	0.0	0.0	0.0
Total	*244.3*	*159.7*	*383.6*

Average speed of public transport

Buses (km/h)	20.0	20.3	20.6
Rail (km/h)	?	0.0	0.0
Trams (km/h)	0.0	0.0	0.0
Ferries (km/h)	0.0	0.0	0.0
Overall	*20.0*	*20.3*	*20.6*

Vehicular energy efficiency

Buses (MJ / km)	19.1	19.6	24.1
Rail (MJ / km)	?	0.0	0.0
Trams (MJ / km)	0.0	0.0	0.0
Ferries (MJ / km)	0.0	0.0	0.0
Overall	*19.1*	*19.6*	*24.1*

Modal energy efficiency

Buses (MJ / passenger km.)	1.50	2.00	1.70
Rail (MJ / passenger km.)	?	0.00	0.00
Trams (MJ / passenger km.)	0.00	0.00	0.00
Ferries (MJ / passenger km.)	0.00	0.00	0.00
Overall	*1.50*	*2.00*	*1.70*

Melbourne

POPULATION PARAMETERS	1960	1970	1980
Urban density (persons / ha)	20.3	18.1	16.4
Inner area density (persons / ha)	37.7	36.8	29.3
Outer area density (persons / ha)	18.7	16.9	15.7
CBD density (persons / ha)	32.2	23.7	24.5
Proportion of population in CBD (%)	0.3	0.2	0.2
Proportion of population in inner area (%)	15.9	12.3	9.0
EMPLOYMENT PARAMETERS			
Employment density (jobs / ha)	8.0	6.6	6.1
Inner area employment density (jobs / ha)	47.3	40.7	40.3
Outer area employment density (jobs / ha)	4.3	4.4	4.3
CBD employment density (jobs / ha)	621.8	663.9	646.5
Proportion of jobs in CBD (%)	19.0	17.2	15.2
Proportion of jobs in inner area (%)	50.9	37.1	33.2
ACTIVITY INTENSITY PARAMETERS (Pop. & Jobs / ha)			
CBD activity intensity	654.0	687.6	671.0
Inner area activity intensity	85.0	77.5	69.6
Outer area activity intensity	23.0	21.3	20.0
City - wide activity intensity	28.3	24.7	22.5
VEHICLE OWNERSHIP PARAMETERS			
Total vehicles / 1000 people	277.0	345.9	528.1
Passenger cars / 1000 people	224.0	295.3	445.8
PRIVATE MOBILITY PARAMETERS			
Total per capita vehicle kms.	3,863	5,029	6,989
Per capita car kms.	3,102	4,228	5,815
Total per capita occupant kms.	6,683	8,751	12,160
Per capita car occupant kms.	5,366	7,356	10,119
Total vehicle kms. per vehicle	13,948	14,540	13,234
Car kms. per car	13,846	14,316	13,045
TRAFFIC RESTRAINT PARAMETERS			
Parking spaces / 1000 CBD workers	155.6	192.1	270.4
Length of road per person (m)	8.1	6.8	7.9
Total vehicles per km of road	34.0	50.7	67.2
Total vehicle kms. per km. of road	474,502	736,790	889,996
Car kms. per km. of road	380,988	619,346	740,564
TRANSPORT ENERGY PARAMETERS			
Motor spirit use / person (MJ)	18,710	23,584	29,104
Total private energy use / person (MJ)	20,464	25,305	33,646
Public trans. energy use / person (MJ)	649	549	597
Total energy use / person (MJ)	21,113	25,854	34,243

PUBLIC TRANSPORT PARAMETERS

Vehicle kilometres per person

Buses	21.4	19.3	18.1
Rail	37.9	28.2	25.6
Trams	16.0	9.8	8.8
Ferries	0.0	0.0	0.0
Total	*75.3*	*57.3*	*52.5*

Passenger trips per person

Buses	55.3	41.3	26.4
Rail	77.4	56.1	31.5
Trams	89.6	44.2	36.9
Ferries	0.0	0.0	0.0
Total	*222.4*	*141.6*	*94.8*

Passenger trips per vehicle kilometre

Buses	2.6	2.1	1.5
Rail	2.0	2.0	1.2
Trams	5.6	4.5	4.2
Ferries	0.0	0.0	0.0
Overall	*3.0*	*2.5*	*1.8*

Passenger kilometres per person

Buses	260.5	187.6	124.8
Rail	1,084.1	839.6	491.3
Trams	394.4	194.6	162.4
Ferries	0.0	0.0	0.0
Total	*1,739.0*	*1,221.7*	*778.5*

Average speed of public transport

Buses (km/h)	17.7	21.0	21.0
Rail (km/h)	33.0	33.0	33.0
Trams (km/h)	17.7	17.6	17.5
Ferries (km/h)	0.0	0.0	0.0
Overall	*27.2*	*28.7*	*27.8*

Vehicular energy efficiency

Buses (MJ / km)	12.5	13.0	13.6
Rail (MJ / km)	6.9	7.7	10.9
Trams (MJ / km)	7.3	8.2	8.1
Ferries (MJ / km)	0.0	0.0	0.0
Overall	*8.6*	*9.6*	*11.4*

Modal energy efficiency

Buses (MJ / passenger km.)	1.03	1.33	1.98
Rail (MJ / passenger km.)	0.24	0.26	0.57
Trams (MJ / passenger km.)	0.30	0.41	0.44
Ferries (MJ / passenger km.)	0.00	0.00	0.00
Overall	*0.37*	*0.45*	*0.77*

Moscow

POPULATION PARAMETERS	1960	1970	1980
Urban density (persons / ha)	209.3	139.7	138.6
Inner area density (persons / ha)	?	?	?
Outer area density (persons / ha)	?	?	?
CBD density (persons / ha)	473.7	284.2	154.7
Proportion of population in CBD (%)	14.4	7.7	3.7
Proportion of population in inner area (%)	?	?	?
EMPLOYMENT PARAMETERS			
Employment density (jobs / ha)	?	?	?
Inner area employment density (jobs / ha)	?	?	?
Outer area employment density (jobs / ha)	?	?	?
CBD employment density (jobs / ha)	?	?	?
Proportion of jobs in CBD (%)	?	?	?
Proportion of jobs in inner area (%)	?	?	?
ACTIVITY INTENSITY PARAMETERS **(Pop. & Jobs / ha)**			
CBD activity intensity	?	?	?
Inner area activity intensity	?	?	?
Outer area activity intensity	?	?	?
City - wide activity intensity	?	?	?
VEHICLE OWNERSHIP PARAMETERS			
Total vehicles / 1000 people	?	?	40.0
Passenger cars / 1000 people	?	?	20.0
PRIVATE MOBILITY PARAMETERS			
Total per capita vehicle kms.	?	?	?
Per capita car kms.	?	?	121
Total per capita occupant kms.	?	?	?
Per capita car occupant kms.	?	?	230
Total vehicle kms. per vehicle	?	?	?
Car kms. per car	?	?	6,051
TRAFFIC RESTRAINT PARAMETERS			
Parking spaces / 1000 CBD workers	?	?	?
Length of road per person (m)	0.4	0.5	0.4
Total vehicles per km of road	?	?	93.2
Total vehicle kms. per km. of road	?	?	?
Car kms. per km. of road	?	?	281,895
TRANSPORT ENERGY PARAMETERS			
Motor spirit use / person (MJ)	?	?	380
Total private energy use / person (MJ)	?	?	?
Public trans. energy use / person (MJ)	?	?	?
Total energy use / person (MJ)	?	?	?

PUBLIC TRANSPORT PARAMETERS

Vehicle kilometres per person

Buses	?	?	71.1
Rail	?	?	?
Trams	?	?	8.7
Ferries	0.0	0.0	0.0
Total	?	?	?

Passenger trips per person

Buses	285.6	326.3	323.5
Rail	?	?	?
Trams	134.2	89.2	65.5
Ferries	0.0	0.0	0.0
Total	?	?	?

Passenger trips per vehicle kilometre

Buses	?	?	4.5
Rail	?	?	?
Trams	?	?	7.5
Ferries	0.0	0.0	0.0
Overall	?	?	?

Passenger kilometres per person

Buses	987.0	1,194.0	1,074.1
Rail	?	?	?
Trams	416.2	267.7	150.7
Ferries	0.0	0.0	0.0
Total	?	?	?

Average speed of public transport

Buses (km/h)	?	20.7	21.3
Rail (km/h)	?	41.4	40.8
Trams (km/h)	?	17.4	17.5
Ferries (km/h)	0.0	0.0	0.0
Overall	?	?	?

Vehicular energy efficiency

Buses (MJ / km)	?	?	?
Rail (MJ / km)	?	?	?
Trams (MJ / km)	?	?	?
Ferries (MJ / km)	0.0	0.0	0.0
Overall	?	?	?

Modal energy efficiency

Buses (MJ / passenger km.)	?	?	?
Rail (MJ / passenger km.)	?	?	?
Trams (MJ / passenger km.)	?	?	?
Ferries (MJ / passenger km.)	0.0	0.0	0.0
Overall	?	?	?

322

Munich

POPULATION PARAMETERS	1960	1970	1980
Urban density (persons / ha)	56.6	68.2	56.9
Inner area density (persons / ha)	196.6	179.0	159.2
Outer area density (persons / ha)	42.0	57.2	48.4
CBD density (persons / ha)	139.0	123.5	111.2
Proportion of population in CBD (%)	9.2	6.5	5.9
Proportion of population in inner area (%)	32.8	23.8	21.4
EMPLOYMENT PARAMETERS			
Employment density (jobs / ha)	35.5	38.0	34.2
Inner area employment density (jobs / ha)	189.0	190.5	192.4
Outer area employment density (jobs / ha)	19.5	22.7	21.2
CBD employment density (jobs / ha)	275.7	268.5	230.9
Proportion of jobs in CBD (%)	29.2	25.5	20.5
Proportion of jobs in inner area (%)	52.0	45.5	42.9
ACTIVITY INTENSITY PARAMETERS **(Pop. & Jobs / ha)**			
CBD activity intensity	414.7	392.0	342.1
Inner area activity intensity	385.6	369.5	351.6
Outer area activity intensity	61.5	79.9	69.6
City - wide activity intensity	92.1	106.2	91.1
VEHICLE OWNERSHIP PARAMETERS			
Total vehicles / 1000 people	173.6	287.1	397.7
Passenger cars / 1000 people	130.9	261.8	359.9
PRIVATE MOBILITY PARAMETERS			
Total per capita vehicle kms.	1,967	3,098	3,722
Per capita car kms.	1,516	2,678	3,272
Total per capita occupant kms.	3,147	4,956	5,955
Per capita car occupant kms.	2,426	4,285	5,235
Total vehicle kms. per vehicle	11,456	10,886	9,438
Car kms. per car	11,578	10,230	9,092
TRAFFIC RESTRAINT PARAMETERS			
Parking spaces / 1000 CBD workers	?	?	285.4
Length of road per person (m)	1.5	1.5	1.7
Total vehicles per km of road	119.3	196.3	238.4
Total vehicle kms. per km. of road	1,351,708	2,118,613	2,231,103
Car kms. per km. of road	1,041,919	1,831,491	1,961,237
TRANSPORT ENERGY PARAMETERS			
Motor spirit use / person (MJ)	4,628	9,568	12,372
Total private energy use / person (MJ)	?	?	?
Public trans. energy use / person (MJ)	?	?	807
Total energy use / person (MJ)	?	?	?

PUBLIC TRANSPORT PARAMETERS

Vehicle kilometres per person

Buses	15.6	20.7	21.3
Rail	?	11.3	32.9
Trams	41.2	32.0	21.0
Ferries	0.0	0.0	0.0
Total	*?*	*64.0*	*75.2*

Passenger trips per person

Buses	49.8	48.8	65.1
Rail	?	28.2	118.5
Trams	250.0	143.4	123.3
Ferries	0.0	0.0	0.0
Total	*?*	*220.4*	*306.9*

Passenger trips per vehicle kilometre

Buses	3.2	2.4	3.1
Rail	?	2.5	3.6
Trams	6.1	4.5	5.9
Ferries	0.0	0.0	0.0
Overall	*?*	*3.2*	*3.8*

Passenger kilometres per person

Buses	206.5	189.3	223.2
Rail	?	325.8	973.6
Trams	802.5	460.4	395.6
Ferries	0.0	0.0	0.0
Total	*?*	*975.5*	*1,592.4*

Average speed of public transport

Buses (km/h)	?	?	20.4
Rail (km/h)	?	?	55.4
Trams (km/h)	15.7	17.1	17.3
Ferries (km/h)	0.0	0.0	0.0
Overall	*?*	*?*	*43.9*

Vehicular energy efficiency

Buses (MJ / km)	9.8	9.6	11.6
Rail (MJ / km)	?	?	11.9
Trams (MJ / km)	5.3	7.5	8.0
Ferries (MJ / km)	0.0	0.0	0.0
Overall	*?*	*?*	*11.1*

Modal energy efficiency

Buses (MJ / passenger km.)	0.74	1.04	1.11
Rail (MJ / passenger km.)	?	?	0.40
Trams (MJ / passenger km.)	0.27	0.52	0.42
Ferries (MJ / passenger km.)	0.00	0.00	0.00
Overall	*?*	*?*	*0.52*

New York

POPULATION PARAMETERS	1960	1970	1980
Urban density (persons / ha)	22.5	22.6	19.8
Inner area density (persons / ha)	116.2	117.9	106.8
Outer area density (persons / ha)	13.3	14.2	12.9
CBD density (persons / ha)	233.1	222.0	217.1
Proportion of population in CBD (%)	3.2	2.8	2.8
Proportion of population in inner area (%)	46.2	42.2	39.5
EMPLOYMENT PARAMETERS			
Employment density (jobs / ha)	9.8	10.1	9.3
Inner area employment density (jobs / ha)	59.1	60.9	53.4
Outer area employment density (jobs / ha)	4.9	5.7	5.8
CBD employment density (jobs / ha)	936.7	944.2	828.0
Proportion of jobs in CBD (%)	29.9	26.2	22.9
Proportion of jobs in inner area (%)	54.1	48.5	41.9
ACTIVITY INTENSITY PARAMETERS (Pop. & Jobs / ha)			
CBD activity intensity	1,169.8	1,166.2	1,045.1
Inner area activity intensity	175.3	178.8	160.2
Outer area activity intensity	18.2	19.9	18.7
City - wide activity intensity	32.3	32.7	29.1
VEHICLE OWNERSHIP PARAMETERS			
Total vehicles / 1000 people	300.2	389.7	459.2
Passenger cars / 1000 people	270.6	348.2	411.9
PRIVATE MOBILITY PARAMETERS			
Total per capita vehicle kms.	4,518	5,465	6,564
Per capita car kms.	4,066	4,864	5,907
Total per capita occupant kms.	6,415	7,323	8,730
Per capita car occupant kms.	5,774	6,518	7,856
Total vehicle kms. per vehicle	15,050	14,023	14,295
Car kms. per car	15,024	13,968	14,342
TRAFFIC RESTRAINT PARAMETERS			
Parking spaces / 1000 CBD workers	?	?	75.1
Length of road per person (m)	4.3	4.1	4.7
Total vehicles per km of road	69.8	94.9	98.5
Total vehicle kms. per km. of road	1,050,262	1,331,400	1,408,107
Car kms. per km. of road	945,181	1,184,955	1,267,248
TRANSPORT ENERGY PARAMETERS			
Motor spirit use / person (MJ)	33,963	40,310	44,033
Total private energy use / person (MJ)	38,349	46,759	50,203
Public trans. energy use / person (MJ)	1,947	1,717	1,887
Total energy use / person (MJ)	40,296	48,476	52,090

325

PUBLIC TRANSPORT PARAMETERS

Vehicle kilometres per person

Buses	27.9	24.2	24.3
Rail	33.0	41.7	33.8
Trams	0.0	0.0	0.0
Ferries	0.03	0.02	0.02
Total	*60.9*	*65.9*	*58.1*

Passenger trips per person

Buses	106.7	65.9	52.3
Rail	93.9	77.7	68.0
Trams	0.0	0.0	0.0
Ferries	1.6	1.2	1.2
Total	*202.2*	*144.8*	*121.5*

Passenger trips per vehicle kilometre

Buses	3.8	2.7	2.1
Rail	2.8	1.9	2.0
Trams	0.0	0.0	0.0
Ferries	61.1	68.3	68.3
Overall	*3.3*	*2.2*	*2.1*

Passenger kilometres per person

Buses	557.2	322.4	272.8
Rail	1,243.8	1,061.3	1,002.5
Trams	0.0	0.0	0.0
Ferries	13.2	11.5	9.9
Total	*1,814.2*	*1,395.2*	*1,285.2*

Average speed of public transport

Buses (km/h)	13.9	16.2	15.2
Rail (km/h)	35.4	35.4	35.4
Trams (km/h)	0.0	0.0	0.0
Ferries (km/h)	20.1	20.1	20.1
Overall	*28.7*	*30.8*	*31.0*

Vehicular energy efficiency

Buses (MJ / km)	20.5	20.6	22.5
Rail (MJ / km)	41.7	29.3	39.6
Trams (MJ / km)	0.0	0.0	0.0
Ferries (MJ / km)	?	?	?
Overall	*32.0*	*26.1*	*32.5*

Modal energy efficiency

Buses (MJ / passenger km.)	1.03	1.54	2.00
Rail (MJ / passenger km.)	1.11	1.15	1.34
Trams (MJ / passenger km.)	0.00	0.00	0.00
Ferries (MJ / passenger km.)	?	?	?
Overall	*1.07*	*1.23*	*1.47*

Paris

POPULATION PARAMETERS	1960	1970	1980
Urban density (persons / ha)	68.6	61.7	48.3
Inner area density (persons / ha)	132.9	126.2	106.4
Outer area density (persons / ha)	31.0	29.8	26.0
CBD density (persons / ha)	332.9	297.0	235.2
Proportion of population in CBD (%)	9.2	7.5	5.4
Proportion of population in inner area (%)	71.4	67.7	60.9

EMPLOYMENT PARAMETERS			
Employment density (jobs / ha)	32.6	28.7	22.0
Inner area employment density (jobs / ha)	73.7	69.2	60.0
Outer area employment density (jobs / ha)	8.5	8.7	7.6
CBD employment density (jobs / ha)	426.1	441.4	399.5
Proportion of jobs in CBD (%)	24.9	23.9	20.2
Proportion of jobs in inner area (%)	83.4	79.7	75.1

ACTIVITY INTENSITY PARAMETERS (Pop. & Jobs / ha)			
CBD activity intensity	759.0	738.4	634.7
Inner area activity intensity	206.6	195.4	166.4
Outer area activity intensity	39.5	38.5	33.6
City - wide activity intensity	101.2	90.4	70.3

VEHICLE OWNERSHIP PARAMETERS			
Total vehicles / 1000 people	184.7	300.0	382.8
Passenger cars / 1000 people	152.5	255.6	338.1

PRIVATE MOBILITY PARAMETERS			
Total per capita vehicle kms.	1,754	2,253	3,170
Per capita car kms.	1,447	1,919	2,800
Total per capita occupant kms.	2,981	3,604	4,755
Per capita car occupant kms.	2,461	3,071	4,199
Total vehicle kms. per vehicle	8,184	8,240	8,281
Car kms. per car	8,184	8,240	8,281

TRAFFIC RESTRAINT PARAMETERS			
Parking spaces / 1000 CBD workers	127.8	165.3	200.6
Length of road per person (m)	0.6	0.7	0.9
Total vehicles per km of road	286.3	422.9	409.9
Total vehicle kms. per km. of road	2,718,081	3,175,000	3,394,505
Car kms. per km. of road	2,243,173	2,704,878	2,997,666

TRANSPORT ENERGY PARAMETERS			
Motor spirit use / person (MJ)	7,659	9,209	14,091
Total private energy use / person (MJ)	9,496	11,719	18,946
Public trans. energy use / person (MJ)	651	656	787
Total energy use / person (MJ)	10,147	12,375	19,733

PUBLIC TRANSPORT PARAMETERS

Vehicle kilometres per person

Buses	19.0	18.0	18.6
Rail	23.9	23.7	28.5
Trams	0.0	0.0	0.0
Ferries	0.0	0.0	0.0
Total	*42.9*	*41.7*	*47.1*

Passenger trips per person

Buses	113.3	70.1	84.3
Rail	181.8	173.2	174.8
Trams	0.0	0.0	0.0
Ferries	0.0	0.0	0.0
Total	*295.1*	*243.3*	*259.1*

Passenger trips per vehicle kilometre

Buses	6.0	3.9	4.5
Rail	7.6	7.3	6.1
Trams	0.0	0.0	0.0
Ferries	0.0	0.0	0.0
Overall	*6.9*	*5.8*	*5.5*

Passenger kilometres per person

Buses	524.8	358.1	295.7
Rail	1,321.6	1,402.2	1,531.2
Trams	0.0	0.0	0.0
Ferries	0.0	0.0	0.0
Total	*1,846.4*	*1,760.3*	*1,826.9*

Average speed of public transport

Buses (km/h)	15.0	12.5	12.6
Rail (km/h)	34.2	38.7	45.1
Trams (km/h)	0.0	0.0	0.0
Ferries (km/h)	0.0	0.0	0.0
Overall	*28.7*	*33.4*	*39.8*

Vehicular energy efficiency

Buses (MJ / km)	16.0	15.9	15.4
Rail (MJ / km)	14.6	15.6	17.5
Trams (MJ / km)	0.0	0.0	0.0
Ferries (MJ / km)	0.0	0.0	0.0
Overall	*15.2*	*15.7*	*16.7*

Modal energy efficiency

Buses (MJ / passenger km.)	0.58	0.80	0.97
Rail (MJ / passenger km.)	0.26	0.27	0.33
Trams (MJ / passenger km.)	0.00	0.00	0.00
Ferries (MJ / passenger km.)	0.00	0.00	0.00
Overall	*0.35*	*0.37*	*0.43*

Perth

POPULATION PARAMETERS	1960	1970	1980
Urban density (persons / ha)	15.6	12.2	10.8
Inner area density (persons / ha)	21.4	18.1	15.5
Outer area density (persons / ha)	12.4	10.4	9.9
CBD density (persons / ha)	18.9	14.1	8.4
Proportion of population in CBD (%)	3.0	1.5	0.7
Proportion of population in inner area (%)	48.7	33.9	22.9
EMPLOYMENT PARAMETERS			
Employment density (jobs / ha)	5.4	4.9	4.6
Inner area employment density (jobs / ha)	11.6	13.4	14.6
Outer area employment density (jobs / ha)	2.1	2.4	2.7
CBD employment density (jobs / ha)	87.4	116.7	120.7
Proportion of jobs in CBD (%)	40.0	31.2	24.1
Proportion of jobs in inner area (%)	45.5	61.8	51.0
ACTIVITY INTENSITY PARAMETERS			
(Pop. & Jobs / ha)			
CBD activity intensity	106.3	130.8	129.1
Inner area activity intensity	33.0	31.5	30.1
Outer area activity intensity	14.5	12.8	12.6
City - wide activity intensity	21.0	17.1	15.4
VEHICLE OWNERSHIP PARAMETERS			
Total vehicles / 1000 people	322.8	444.1	614.4
Passenger cars / 1000 people	238.8	356.9	474.9
PRIVATE MOBILITY PARAMETERS			
Total per capita vehicle kms.	4,155	6,513	7,929
Per capita car kms.	3,287	5,224	6,250
Total per capita occupant kms.	8,407	11,657	14,563
Per capita car occupant kms.	6,650	9,351	11,479
Total vehicle kms. per vehicle	13,779	14,664	13,621
Car kms. per car	14,732	14,635	13,891
TRAFFIC RESTRAINT PARAMETERS			
Parking spaces / 1000 CBD workers	561.1	527.1	562.3
Length of road per person (m)	14.1	13.7	13.3
Total vehicles per km of road	23.0	32.4	46.3
Total vehicle kms. per km. of road	316,288	474,865	631,000
Car kms. per km. of road	250,179	380,910	497,392
TRANSPORT ENERGY PARAMETERS			
Motor spirit use / person (MJ)	17,613	29,937	32,610
Total private energy use / person (MJ)	19,589	33,300	39,432
Public trans. energy use / person (MJ)	1,027	800	816
Total energy use / person (MJ)	20,616	34,100	40,248

PUBLIC TRANSPORT PARAMETERS

Vehicle kilometres per person			
Buses	55.7	50.4	47.2
Rail	11.4	6.7	5.3
Trams	0.0	0.0	0.0
Ferries	0.1	0.1	0.0
Total	*67.2*	*57.2*	*52.5*

Passenger trips per person			
Buses	109.9	81.3	63.2
Rail	25.3	15.0	7.2
Trams	0.0	0.0	0.0
Ferries	0.4	0.5	0.4
Total	*135.6*	*96.8*	*70.8*

Passenger trips per vehicle kilometre			
Buses	2.0	1.6	1.3
Rail	2.2	2.2	1.4
Trams	0.0	0.0	0.0
Ferries	5.2	9.9	8.4
Overall	*2.0*	*1.7*	*1.3*

Passenger kilometres per person			
Buses	659.4	569.2	505.7
Rail	247.9	162.1	85.4
Trams	0.0	0.0	0.0
Ferries	0.5	0.7	0.5
Total	*907.8*	*732.0*	*591.6*

Average speed of public transport			
Buses (km/h)	19.0	20.5	22.0
Rail (km/h)	34.4	34.4	35.2
Trams (km/h)	0.0	0.0	0.0
Ferries (km/h)	14.4	14.4	14.4
Overall	*23.2*	*23.6*	*23.9*

Vehicular energy efficiency			
Buses (MJ / km)	11.1	12.6	14.6
Rail (MJ / km)	35.5	24.4	23.2
Trams (MJ / km)	0.0	0.0	0.0
Ferries (MJ / km)	79.5	79.5	79.5
Overall	*15.3*	*14.0*	*15.5*

Modal energy efficiency			
Buses (MJ / passenger km.)	0.94	1.11	1.36
Rail (MJ / passenger km.)	1.62	1.01	1.45
Trams (MJ / passenger km.)	0.00	0.00	0.00
Ferries (MJ / passenger km.)	10.93	5.73	6.73
Overall	*1.13*	*1.09*	*1.38*

Phoenix

POPULATION PARAMETERS	1960	1970	1980
Urban density (persons / ha)	8.6	8.6	8.5
Inner area density (persons / ha)	24.9	23.2	19.1
Outer area density (persons / ha)	7.8	8.2	8.3
CBD density (persons / ha)	21.6	20.6	17.3
Proportion of population in CBD (%)	1.3	0.8	0.5
Proportion of population in inner area (%)	11.0	7.1	3.7
EMPLOYMENT PARAMETERS			
Employment density (jobs / ha)	3.4	3.3	4.0
Inner area employment density (jobs / ha)	17.3	20.8	24.0
Outer area employment density (jobs / ha)	2.7	2.8	3.7
CBD employment density (jobs / ha)	58.8	67.6	66.6
Proportion of jobs in CBD (%)	10.5	7.9	3.9
Proportion of jobs in inner area (%)	23.3	18.3	10.6
ACTIVITY INTENSITY PARAMETERS (Pop. & Jobs / ha)			
CBD activity intensity	80.4	88.2	83.9
Inner area activity intensity	42.2	44.0	43.1
Outer area activity intensity	10.5	11.0	12.0
City - wide activity intensity	12.0	11.9	12.5
VEHICLE OWNERSHIP PARAMETERS			
Total vehicles / 1000 people	460.5	651.7	688.6
Passenger cars / 1000 people	367.8	499.1	499.0
PRIVATE MOBILITY PARAMETERS			
Total per capita vehicle kms.	7,813	9,635	10,609
Per capita car kms.	7,188	8,864	9,210
Total per capita occupant kms.	12,345	14,067	15,171
Per capita car occupant kms.	11,357	12,941	13,170
Total vehicle kms. per vehicle	16,966	14,784	13,496
Car kms. per car	19,544	17,758	17,138
TRAFFIC RESTRAINT PARAMETERS			
Parking spaces / 1000 CBD workers	619.2	836.3	1,033.0
Length of road per person (m)	15.4	12.7	10.4
Total vehicles per km of road	30.0	51.2	65.9
Total vehicle kms. per km. of road	508,504	756,464	889,621
Car kms. per km. of road	467,827	695,943	818,455
TRANSPORT ENERGY PARAMETERS			
Motor spirit use / person (MJ)	51,367	65,127	69,908
Total private energy use / person (MJ)	58,435	73,398	78,751
Public trans. energy use / person (MJ)	149	103	181
Total energy use / person (MJ)	58,584	73,501	78,932

PUBLIC TRANSPORT PARAMETERS

Vehicle kilometres per person

Buses	9.6	5.0	7.2
Rail	0.0	0.0	0.0
Trams	0.0	0.0	0.0
Ferries	0.0	0.0	0.0
Total	*9.6*	*5.0*	*7.2*

Passenger trips per person

Buses	14.0	4.9	9.1
Rail	0.0	0.0	0.0
Trams	0.0	0.0	0.0
Ferries	0.0	0.0	0.0
Total	*14.0*	*4.9*	*9.1*

Passenger trips per vehicle kilometre

Buses	1.5	1.0	1.3
Rail	0.0	0.0	0.0
Trams	0.0	0.0	0.0
Ferries	0.0	0.0	0.0
Overall	*1.5*	*1.0*	*1.3*

Passenger kilometres per person

Buses	101.7	35.9	66.0
Rail	0.0	0.0	0.0
Trams	0.0	0.0	0.0
Ferries	0.0	0.0	0.0
Total	*101.7*	*35.9*	*66.0*

Average speed of public transport

Buses (km/h)	21.7	22.8	23.3
Rail (km/h)	0.0	0.0	0.0
Trams (km/h)	0.0	0.0	0.0
Ferries (km/h)	0.0	0.0	0.0
Overall	*21.7*	*22.8*	*23.3*

Vehicular energy efficiency

Buses (MJ / km)	15.6	20.7	25.0
Rail (MJ / km)	0.0	0.0	0.0
Trams (MJ / km)	0.0	0.0	0.0
Ferries (MJ / km)	0.0	0.0	0.0
Overall	*15.6*	*20.7*	*25.0*

Modal energy efficiency

Buses (MJ / passenger km.)	1.47	2.86	2.74
Rail (MJ / passenger km.)	0.00	0.00	0.00
Trams (MJ / passenger km.)	0.00	0.00	0.00
Ferries (MJ / passenger km.)	0.00	0.00	0.00
Overall	*1.47*	*2.86*	*2.74*

San Francisco

POPULATION PARAMETERS	1960	1970	1980
Urban density (persons / ha)	16.5	16.9	15.5
Inner area density (persons / ha)	69.2	66.9	58.8
Outer area density (persons / ha)	12.4	13.7	12.9
CBD density (persons / ha)	95.6	91.5	89.7
Proportion of population in CBD (%)	1.5	1.2	1.1
Proportion of population in inner area (%)	30.5	24.0	21.3
EMPLOYMENT PARAMETERS			
Employment density (jobs / ha)	7.4	8.0	7.8
Inner area employment density (jobs / ha)	44.5	50.1	47.8
Outer area employment density (jobs / ha)	4.5	5.3	5.4
CBD employment density (jobs / ha)	566.1	615.1	713.2
Proportion of jobs in CBD (%)	19.8	16.6	17.0
Proportion of jobs in inner area (%)	43.4	37.9	34.4
ACTIVITY INTENSITY PARAMETERS			
(Pop. & Jobs / ha)			
CBD activity intensity	661.7	706.6	802.9
Inner area activity intensity	113.7	117.0	106.6
Outer area activity intensity	16.9	19.0	18.3
City - wide activity intensity	23.9	24.9	23.3
VEHICLE OWNERSHIP PARAMETERS			
Total vehicles / 1000 people	498.8	598.1	680.9
Passenger cars / 1000 people	407.4	487.9	543.4
PRIVATE MOBILITY PARAMETERS			
Total per capita vehicle kms.	6,284	8,888	10,402
Per capita car kms.	5,656	8,000	9,362
Total per capita occupant kms.	9,049	12,800	14,667
Per capita car occupant kms.	8,145	11,520	13,200
Total vehicle kms. per vehicle	12,598	14,860	15,277
Car kms. per car	13,883	16,396	17,230
TRAFFIC RESTRAINT PARAMETERS			
Parking spaces / 1000 CBD workers	135.1	154.5	145.2
Length of road per person (m)	4.7	4.7	4.9
Total vehicles per km of road	105.2	128.4	139.9
Total vehicle kms. per km. of road	1,325,344	1,907,836	2,136,746
Car kms. per km. of road	1,192,850	1,717,087	1,923,096
TRANSPORT ENERGY PARAMETERS			
Motor spirit use / person (MJ)	35,885	53,375	55,365
Total private energy use / person (MJ)	42,983	62,909	65,141
Public trans. energy use / person (MJ)	713	654	1,134
Total energy use / person (MJ)	43,696	63,563	66,275

PUBLIC TRANSPORT PARAMETERS

Vehicle kilometres per person

Buses	29.4	27.9	37.1
Rail	2.0	1.2	11.1
Trams	2.4	2.0	1.9
Ferries	0.0	0.0	0.1
Total	*33.8*	*31.1*	*50.2*

Passenger trips per person

Buses	85.6	72.6	85.7
Rail	2.6	1.9	15.8
Trams	14.5	18.2	13.2
Ferries	0.0	0.1	0.3
Total	*102.7*	*92.8*	*115.0*

Passenger trips per vehicle kilometre

Buses	2.9	2.6	2.3
Rail	1.4	1.5	1.4
Trams	6.1	9.3	6.8
Ferries	0.0	12.2	6.0
Overall	*3.1*	*3.0*	*2.3*

Passenger kilometres per person

Buses	467.6	452.7	545.9
Rail	65.5	46.5	313.4
Trams	63.6	79.8	60.9
Ferries	0.0	0.9	5.5
Total	*596.7*	*579.9*	*925.7*

Average speed of public transport

Buses (km/h)	19.5	20.6	21.8
Rail (km/h)	55.2	55.2	45.1
Trams (km/h)	14.4	16.2	15.0
Ferries (km/h)	0.0	20.4	25.1
Overall	*22.9*	*22.8*	*29.3*

Vehicular energy efficiency

Buses (MJ / km)	18.2	18.6	20.9
Rail (MJ / km)	75.3	75.2	21.8
Trams (MJ / km)	12.5	20.4	28.2
Ferries (MJ / km)	0.0	430.8	1,048.6
Overall	*21.2*	*21.1*	*22.6*

Modal energy efficiency

Buses (MJ / passenger km.)	1.15	1.15	1.42
Rail (MJ / passenger km.)	2.25	1.98	0.77
Trams (MJ / passenger km.)	0.47	0.50	0.90
Ferries (MJ / passenger km.)	0.00	3.48	10.90
Overall	*1.19*	*1.13*	*1.22*

Singapore

POPULATION PARAMETERS	1960	1970	1980
Urban density (persons / ha)	104.5	92.7	83.2
Inner area density (persons / ha)	250.3	250.9	201.5
Outer area density (persons / ha)	77.5	58.3	63.1
CBD density (persons / ha)	303.0	299.1	203.7
Proportion of population in CBD (%)	14.2	11.1	6.6
Proportion of population in inner area (%)	37.4	48.4	35.2
EMPLOYMENT PARAMETERS			
Employment density (jobs / ha)	?	29.1	37.1
Inner area employment density (jobs / ha)	?	?	?
Outer area employment density (jobs / ha)	?	?	?
CBD employment density (jobs / ha)	506.3	281.0	339.3
Proportion of jobs in CBD (%)	?	33.3	24.3
Proportion of jobs in inner area (%)	?	?	?
ACTIVITY INTENSITY PARAMETERS **(Pop. & Jobs / ha)**			
CBD activity intensity	809.3	580.1	543.0
Inner area activity intensity	?	?	?
Outer area activity intensity	?	?	?
City - wide activity intensity	?	121.8	120.3
VEHICLE OWNERSHIP PARAMETERS			
Total vehicles / 1000 people	58.9	139.8	155.0
Passenger cars / 1000 people	38.5	68.7	64.7
PRIVATE MOBILITY PARAMETERS			
Total per capita vehicle kms.	?	?	?
Per capita car kms.	426	760	716
Total per capita occupant kms.	?	?	?
Per capita car occupant kms.	?	1,262	1,789
Total vehicle kms. per vehicle	?	?	?
Car kms. per car	11,062	11,062	11,062
TRAFFIC RESTRAINT PARAMETERS			
Parking spaces / 1000 CBD workers	?	62.1	96.7
Length of road per person (m)	?	0.9	1.0
Total vehicles per km of road	?	149.7	157.6
Total vehicle kms. per km. of road	?	?	?
Car kms. per km. of road	?	813,829	727,886
TRANSPORT ENERGY PARAMETERS			
Motor spirit use / person (MJ)	?	?	6,003
Total private energy use / person (MJ)	?	?	9,527
Public trans. energy use / person (MJ)	?	?	1,591
Total energy use / person (MJ)	?	?	11,118

PUBLIC TRANSPORT PARAMETERS

Vehicle kilometres per person

Buses	?	?	98.1
Rail	0.0	0.0	0.0
Trams	0.0	0.0	0.0
Ferries	0.0	0.0	0.0
Total	*?*	*?*	*98.1*

Passenger trips per person

Buses	?	?	353.1
Rail	0.0	0.0	0.0
Trams	0.0	0.0	0.0
Ferries	0.0	0.0	0.0
Total	*?*	*?*	*353.1*

Passenger trips per vehicle kilometre

Buses	?	?	3.6
Rail	0.0	0.0	0.0
Trams	0.0	0.0	0.0
Ferries	0.0	0.0	0.0
Overall	*?*	*?*	*3.6*

Passenger kilometres per person

Buses	?	?	1,942.0
Rail	0.0	0.0	0.0
Trams	0.0	0.0	0.0
Ferries	0.0	0.0	0.0
Total	*?*	*?*	*1,942.0*

Average speed of public transport

Buses (km/h)	?	?	18.7
Rail (km/h)	0.0	0.0	0.0
Trams (km/h)	0.0	0.0	0.0
Ferries (km/h)	0.0	0.0	0.0
Overall	*0.0*	*0.0*	*18.7*

Vehicular energy efficiency

Buses (MJ / km)	?	?	16.2
Rail (MJ / km)	0.0	0.0	0.0
Trams (MJ / km)	0.0	0.0	0.0
Ferries (MJ / km)	0.0	0.0	0.0
Overall	*?*	*?*	*16.2*

Modal energy efficiency

Buses (MJ / passenger km.)	?	?	0.82
Rail (MJ / passenger km.)	0.00	0.00	0.00
Trams (MJ / passenger km.)	0.00	0.00	0.00
Ferries (MJ / passenger km.)	0.00	0.00	0.00
Overall	*?*	*?*	*0.82*

Stockholm

POPULATION PARAMETERS	1960	1970	1980
Urban density (persons / ha)	65.5	59.3	51.3
Inner area density (persons / ha)	88.2	71.6	58.3
Outer area density (persons / ha)	47.8	49.8	46.0
CBD density (persons / ha)	170.0	119.0	97.0
Proportion of population in CBD (%)	8.9	6.8	6.4
Proportion of population in inner area (%)	58.9	52.5	49.3
EMPLOYMENT PARAMETERS			
Employment density (jobs / ha)	34.0	34.2	34.4
Inner area employment density (jobs / ha)	65.8	61.3	61.5
Outer area employment density (jobs / ha)	10.9	15.4	16.0
CBD employment density (jobs / ha)	358.1	287.2	279.6
Proportion of jobs in CBD (%)	35.2	27.6	26.3
Proportion of jobs in inner area (%)	82.4	75.3	74.7
ACTIVITY INTENSITY PARAMETERS (Pop. & Jobs / ha)			
CBD activity intensity	528.1	406.2	376.6
Inner area activity intensity	154.0	132.9	119.8
Outer area activity intensity	58.7	65.2	62.0
City - wide activity intensity	99.5	93.5	85.7
VEHICLE OWNERSHIP PARAMETERS			
Total vehicles / 1000 people	173.2	300.2	390.4
Passenger cars / 1000 people	143.2	274.7	346.5
PRIVATE MOBILITY PARAMETERS			
Total per capita vehicle kms.	2,182	3,970	5,300
Per capita car kms.	1,804	3,525	4,867
Total per capita occupant kms.	3,055	5,360	7,155
Per capita car occupant kms.	2,525	4,758	6,570
Total vehicle kms. per vehicle	12,600	13,224	13,574
Car kms. per car	12,593	12,832	14,048
TRAFFIC RESTRAINT PARAMETERS			
Parking spaces / 1000 CBD workers	100.0	130.4	153.3
Length of road per person (m)	1.5	1.8	2.3
Total vehicles per km of road	112.6	162.9	170.7
Total vehicle kms. per km. of road	1,419,147	2,153,846	2,317,568
Car kms. per km. of road	1,172,968	1,912,088	2,128,378
TRANSPORT ENERGY PARAMETERS			
Motor spirit use / person (MJ)	?	?	15,574
Total private energy use / person (MJ)	?	?	21,136
Public trans. energy use / person (MJ)	1,143	1,288	1,618
Total energy use / person (MJ)	?	?	22,754

PUBLIC TRANSPORT PARAMETERS

Vehicle kilometres per person

Buses	42.9	47.1	58.1
Rail	33.1	45.3	60.3
Trams	11.4	0.6	0.4
Ferries	0.0	0.0	0.0
Total	*87.4*	*93.0*	*118.8*

Passenger trips per person

Buses	58.8	51.7	140.0
Rail	49.3	144.9	162.3
Trams	31.6	0.5	?
Ferries	0.0	0.0	0.0
Total	*139.7*	*196.6*	*302.3*

Passenger trips per vehicle kilometre

Buses	1.4	1.1	2.4
Rail	1.5	3.2	2.7
Trams	2.8	0.8	?
Ferries	0.0	0.0	0.0
Overall	*1.6*	*2.1*	*2.5*

Passenger kilometres per person

Buses	290.7	275.7	840.4
Rail	338.4	1,017.3	1,283.9
Trams	110.6	1.5	?
Ferries	0.0	0.0	0.0
Total	*739.7*	*1,294.5*	*2,124.3*

Average speed of public transport

Buses (km/h)	20.0	23.0	25.4
Rail (km/h)	30.0	33.0	36.0
Trams (km/h)	?	25.9	25.9
Ferries (km/h)	0.0	0.0	0.0
Overall	*?*	*30.9*	*31.8*

Vehicular energy efficiency

Buses (MJ / km)	15.2	15.7	16.1
Rail (MJ / km)	12.7	12.0	11.3
Trams (MJ / km)	6.1	6.1	5.8
Ferries (MJ / km)	0.0	0.0	0.0
Overall	*13.1*	*13.9*	*13.6*

Modal energy efficiency

Buses (MJ / passenger km.)	2.25	2.68	1.11
Rail (MJ / passenger km.)	1.24	0.54	0.53
Trams (MJ / passenger km.)	0.63	2.50	?
Ferries (MJ / passenger km.)	0.00	0.00	0.00
Overall	*1.55*	*0.99*	*0.76*

Sydney

POPULATION PARAMETERS	1960	1970	1980
Urban density (persons / ha)	21.3	19.2	17.6
Inner area density (persons / ha)	44.8	44.6	39.1
Outer area density (persons / ha)	17.9	16.6	15.8
CBD density (persons / ha)	18.2	14.6	10.7
Proportion of population in CBD (%)	0.3	0.2	0.1
Proportion of population in inner area (%)	26.8	21.7	16.7
EMPLOYMENT PARAMETERS			
Employment density (jobs / ha)	8.9	8.2	7.5
Inner area employment density (jobs / ha)	41.8	42.3	39.1
Outer area employment density (jobs / ha)	4.1	4.7	4.9
CBD employment density (jobs / ha)	468.8	504.8	433.9
Proportion of jobs in CBD (%)	20.3	17.4	13.2
Proportion of jobs in inner area (%)	59.7	48.5	39.3
ACTIVITY INTENSITY PARAMETERS (Pop. & Jobs / ha)			
CBD activity intensity	487.0	519.4	444.6
Inner area activity intensity	86.6	86.9	78.2
Outer area activity intensity	22.0	21.3	20.7
City - wide activity intensity	30.2	27.4	25.1
VEHICLE OWNERSHIP PARAMETERS			
Total vehicles / 1000 people	268.1	366.4	489.3
Passenger cars / 1000 people	219.4	306.5	411.7
PRIVATE MOBILITY PARAMETERS			
Total per capita vehicle kms.	3,757	5,436	6,442
Per capita car kms.	3,060	4,489	5,212
Total per capita occupant kms.	7,119	9,838	11,712
Per capita car occupant kms.	5,798	8,125	9,475
Total vehicle kms. per vehicle	14,334	14,834	13,165
Car kms. per car	14,603	14,648	13,078
TRAFFIC RESTRAINT PARAMETERS			
Parking spaces / 1000 CBD workers	?	86.6	156.0
Length of road per person (m)	4.7	5.1	6.2
Total vehicles per km of road	58.6	72.3	81.8
Total vehicle kms. per km. of road	839,592	1,072,372	1,076,418
Car kms. per km. of road	683,817	885,610	870,836
TRANSPORT ENERGY PARAMETERS			
Motor spirit use / person (MJ)	18,346	24,815	27,986
Total private energy use / person (MJ)	19,768	27,061	33,678
Public trans. energy use / person (MJ)	1,148	1,013	980
Total energy use / person (MJ)	20,916	28,074	34,658

PUBLIC TRANSPORT PARAMETERS

Vehicle kilometres per person

Buses	40.5	37.3	33.0
Rail	62.9	32.8	43.6
Trams	0.9	0.0	0.0
Ferries	0.4	0.3	0.3
Total	*104.7*	*70.4*	*76.9*

Passenger trips per person

Buses	137.9	113.7	73.5
Rail	103.8	85.0	64.9
Trams	4.8	0.0	0.0
Ferries	6.6	5.5	3.9
Total	*253.1*	*204.2*	*142.3*

Passenger trips per vehicle kilometre

Buses	3.4	3.0	2.2
Rail	1.7	2.6	1.5
Trams	5.3	0.0	0.0
Ferries	15.1	15.9	13.0
Overall	*2.4*	*2.9*	*1.8*

Passenger kilometres per person

Buses	620.4	530.9	414.7
Rail	1,453.0	1,273.2	1,055.3
Trams	16.9	0.0	0.0
Ferries	67.9	56.1	40.5
Total	*2,158.2*	*1,860.2*	*1,510.5*

Average speed of public transport

Buses (km/h)	18.6	18.3	20.3
Rail (km/h)	35.4	35.4	44.6
Trams (km/h)	19.3	0.0	0.0
Ferries (km/h)	?	?	23.1
Overall	*?*	*?*	*37.4*

Vehicular energy efficiency

Buses (MJ / km)	16.2	17.2	17.6
Rail (MJ / km)	5.9	8.6	7.3
Trams (MJ / km)	8.0	0.0	0.0
Ferries (MJ / km)	258.2	258.2	258.2
Overall	*11.0*	*14.4*	*12.7*

Modal energy efficiency

Buses (MJ / passenger km.)	1.06	1.21	1.40
Rail (MJ / passenger km.)	0.26	0.22	0.30
Trams (MJ / passenger km.)	0.43	0.00	0.00
Ferries (MJ / passenger km.)	1.66	1.58	1.94
Overall	*0.53*	*0.54*	*0.65*

Tokyo

POPULATION PARAMETERS	1960	1970	1980
Urban density (persons / ha)	131.0	116.6	104.6
Inner area density (persons / ha)	201.5	180.4	152.9
Outer area density (persons / ha)	42.1	52.6	57.8
CBD density (persons / ha)	135.7	97.9	82.3
Proportion of population in CBD (%)	3.5	1.9	1.3
Proportion of population in inner area (%)	53.5	41.2	32.3
EMPLOYMENT PARAMETERS			
Employment density (jobs / ha)	66.3	67.5	66.3
Inner area employment density (jobs / ha)	109.8	120.2	114.3
Outer area employment density (jobs / ha)	11.4	14.5	19.8
CBD employment density (jobs / ha)	315.1	419.0	477.0
Proportion of jobs in CBD (%)	25.8	26.1	26.6
Proportion of jobs in inner area (%)	92.4	89.3	84.8
ACTIVITY INTENSITY PARAMETERS			
(Pop. & Jobs / ha)			
CBD activity intensity	450.8	516.9	559.3
Inner area activity intensity	311.3	300.6	267.2
Outer area activity intensity	53.5	67.1	77.6
City - wide activity intensity	197.3	184.1	170.9
VEHICLE OWNERSHIP PARAMETERS			
Total vehicles / 1000 people	62.8	192.6	266.5
Passenger cars / 1000 people	15.9	105.1	156.2
PRIVATE MOBILITY PARAMETERS			
Total per capita vehicle kms.	1,466	2,492	2,765
Per capita car kms.	1,000	1,798	2,138
Total per capita occupant kms.	2,345	3,737	3,871
Per capita car occupant kms.	1,600	2,697	2,993
Total vehicle kms. per vehicle	13,089	12,132	10,375
Car kms. per car	17,274	15,697	13,690
TRAFFIC RESTRAINT PARAMETERS			
Parking spaces / 1000 CBD workers	?	65.7	?
Length of road per person (m)	1.9	1.8	1.9
Total vehicles per km of road	32.2	106.8	139.9
Total vehicle kms. per km. of road	818,707	1,381,665	1,451,036
Car kms. per km. of road	558,339	997,035	1,122,092
TRANSPORT ENERGY PARAMETERS			
Motor spirit use / person (MJ) (passenger)	3,740	7,064	8,488
Motor spirit use / person (MJ) (total)	6,212	11,972	11,279
Total private energy use / person (MJ)	8,684	14,782	15,862
Public trans. energy use / person (MJ)	777	948	967
Total energy use / person (MJ)	9,461	15,730	16,829

341

PUBLIC TRANSPORT PARAMETERS

Vehicle kilometres per person

Buses	18.8	23.8	19.7
Rail	51.2	65.6	73.9
Trams	3.6	0.6	0.1
Ferries	0.0	0.0	0.0
Total	*73.6*	*90.0*	*93.7*

Passenger trips per person

Buses	96.2	119.4	87.4
Rail	300.1	378.6	382.7
Trams	50.3	7.9	1.7
Ferries	0.0	0.0	0.0
Total	*446.6*	*505.9*	*471.8*

Passenger trips per vehicle kilometre

Buses	5.1	5.0	4.4
Rail	5.9	5.8	5.2
Trams	14.0	14.2	14.9
Ferries	0.0	0.0	0.0
Overall	*6.1*	*5.6*	*5.0*

Passenger kilometres per person

Buses	258.9	334.2	262.1
Rail	3,543.8	4,807.0	4,924.8
Trams	125.8	19.8	4.2
Ferries	0.0	0.0	0.0
Total	*3,928.5*	*5,161.0*	*5,191.1*

Average speed of public transport

Buses (km/h)	15.3	13.2	12.0
Rail (km/h)	39.6	39.7	39.8
Trams (km/h)	13.3	11.4	13.0
Ferries (km/h)	0.0	0.0	0.0
Overall	*37.2*	*37.9*	*38.4*

Vehicular energy efficiency

Buses (MJ / km)	11.8	11.6	12.8
Rail (MJ / km)	10.4	10.1	9.8
Trams (MJ / km)	7.4	11.9	9.8
Ferries (MJ / km)	0.0	0.0	0.0
Overall	*10.6*	*10.5*	*10.4*

Modal energy efficiency

Buses (MJ / passenger km.)	0.85	0.83	0.96
Rail (MJ / passenger km.)	0.15	0.14	0.15
Trams (MJ / passenger km.)	0.21	0.34	0.26
Ferries (MJ / passenger km.)	0.00	0.00	0.00
Overall	*0.20*	*0.18*	*0.19*

Toronto

POPULATION PARAMETERS	1960	1970	1980
Urban density (persons / ha)	36.8	41.4	39.6
Inner area density (persons / ha)	74.2	71.8	56.5
Outer area density (persons / ha)	22.8	31.3	34.0
CBD density (persons / ha)	28.7	19.4	25.2
Proportion of population in CBD (%)	0.3	0.2	0.2
Proportion of population in inner area (%)	54.9	43.3	35.7
EMPLOYMENT PARAMETERS			
Employment density (jobs / ha)	15.3	18.3	19.7
Inner area employment density (jobs / ha)	40.7	40.9	37.7
Outer area employment density (jobs / ha)	5.8	10.8	13.7
CBD employment density (jobs / ha)	648.5	720.9	757.1
Proportion of jobs in CBD (%)	18.1	14.7	13.4
Proportion of jobs in inner area (%)	72.4	55.8	47.9
ACTIVITY INTENSITY PARAMETERS (Pop. & Jobs / ha)			
CBD activity intensity	677.2	740.3	782.3
Inner area activity intensity	114.9	112.7	94.2
Outer area activity intensity	28.6	42.1	47.7
City - wide activity intensity	52.1	59.7	59.3
VEHICLE OWNERSHIP PARAMETERS			
Total vehicles / 1000 people	344.6	403.7	554.4
Passenger cars / 1000 people	297.8	358.2	462.5
PRIVATE MOBILITY PARAMETERS			
Total per capita vehicle kms.	?	?	7,422
Per capita car kms.	?	?	6,156
Total per capita occupant kms.	?	?	11,875
Per capita car occupant kms.	?	?	9,850
Total vehicle kms. per vehicle	?	?	13,388
Car kms. per car	?	?	13,310
TRAFFIC RESTRAINT PARAMETERS			
Parking spaces / 1000 CBD workers	191.8	198.2	197.6
Length of road per person (m)	1.7	2.3	2.7
Total vehicles per km of road	201.5	173.0	203.8
Total vehicle kms. per km. of road	?	?	2,728,117
Car kms. per km. of road	?	?	2,262,597
TRANSPORT ENERGY PARAMETERS			
Motor spirit use / person (MJ)	?	?	34,813
Total private energy use / person (MJ)	?	?	46,986
Public trans. energy use / person (MJ)	672	1,161	1,636
Total energy use / person (MJ)	?	?	48,622

PUBLIC TRANSPORT PARAMETERS

Vehicle kilometres per person

Buses	19.2	29.9	42.0
Rail	7.1	19.2	31.5
Trams	22.0	8.8	7.1
Ferries	0.0	0.0	0.0
Total	*48.3*	*57.9*	*80.6*

Passenger trips per person

Buses	55.0	67.1	83.5
Rail	19.3	42.7	67.3
Trams	82.9	26.6	26.8
Ferries	0.0	0.0	0.0
Total	*157.2*	*136.4*	*177.6*

Passenger trips per vehicle kilometre

Buses	2.9	2.2	2.0
Rail	2.7	2.2	2.1
Trams	3.8	3.1	3.8
Ferries	0.0	0.0	0.0
Overall	*3.3*	*2.3*	*2.2*

Passenger kilometres per person

Buses	467.3	651.3	891.9
Rail	164.1	457.2	795.1
Trams	704.3	260.7	288.8
Ferries	0.0	0.0	0.0
Total	*1,335.7*	*1,369.2*	*1,975.8*

Average speed of public transport

Buses (km/h)	17.6	18.5	19.7
Rail (km/h)	24.2	32.3	34.3
Trams (km/h)	16.1	16.3	15.8
Ferries (km/h)	0.0	0.0	0.0
Overall	*17.6*	*22.5*	*24.8*

Vehicular energy efficiency

Buses (MJ / km)	17.8	18.9	18.9
Rail (MJ / km)	11.2	24.5	22.3
Trams (MJ / km)	11.5	11.4	12.3
Ferries (MJ / km)	0.0	0.0	0.0
Overall	*14.0*	*19.6*	*19.7*

Modal energy efficiency

Buses (MJ / passenger km.)	0.73	0.88	0.90
Rail (MJ / passenger km.)	0.48	1.01	0.85
Trams (MJ / passenger km.)	0.36	0.38	0.30
Ferries (MJ / passenger km.)	0.00	0.00	0.00
Overall	*0.50*	*0.83*	*0.80*

Vienna

POPULATION PARAMETERS	1960	1970	1980
Urban density (persons / ha)	91.4	85.4	72.1
Inner area density (persons / ha)	173.8	154.8	132.5
Outer area density (persons / ha)	70.2	68.8	59.4
CBD density (persons / ha)	107.1	83.5	64.9
Proportion of population in CBD (%)	2.0	1.6	1.3
Proportion of population in inner area (%)	39.0	35.0	31.9
EMPLOYMENT PARAMETERS			
Employment density (jobs / ha)	48.6	41.6	38.4
Inner area employment density (jobs / ha)	131.7	116.9	112.7
Outer area employment density (jobs / ha)	27.1	23.6	22.9
CBD employment density (jobs / ha)	493.2	421.5	403.2
Proportion of jobs in CBD (%)	17.2	16.1	14.9
Proportion of jobs in inner area (%)	55.6	54.3	50.8
ACTIVITY INTENSITY PARAMETERS			
(Pop. & Jobs / ha)			
CBD activity intensity	600.3	505.0	468.1
Inner area activity intensity	305.5	271.7	245.2
Outer area activity intensity	97.3	92.4	82.3
City - wide activity intensity	140.0	127.0	110.5
VEHICLE OWNERSHIP PARAMETERS			
Total vehicles / 1000 people	163.4	272.3	373.7
Passenger cars / 1000 people	93.6	213.9	311.2
PRIVATE MOBILITY PARAMETERS			
Total per capita vehicle kms.	?	?	3,200
Per capita car kms.	?	?	2,664
Total per capita occupant kms.	?	?	5,120
Per capita car occupant kms.	?	?	4,262
Total vehicle kms. per vehicle	?	?	8,562
Car kms. per car	?	?	8,562
TRAFFIC RESTRAINT PARAMETERS			
Parking spaces / 1000 CBD workers	?	?	189.5
Length of road per person (m)	1.2	1.5	1.7
Total vehicles per km of road	137.4	182.4	216.0
Total vehicle kms. per km. of road	?	?	1,849,057
Car kms. per km. of road	?	?	1,539,623
TRANSPORT ENERGY PARAMETERS			
Motor spirit use / person (MJ)	?	?	10,074
Total private energy use / person (MJ)	?	?	11,265
Public trans. energy use / person (MJ)	289	503	873
Total energy use / person (MJ)	?	?	12,138

PUBLIC TRANSPORT PARAMETERS

Vehicle kilometres per person

Buses	4.8	9.0	14.2
Rail	0.0	4.5	9.9
Trams	66.8	49.2	44.9
Ferries	0.0	0.0	0.0
Total	*71.6*	*62.7*	*69.0*

Passenger trips per person

Buses	25.3	35.6	54.8
Rail	0.0	21.5	68.9
Trams	284.6	224.5	189.2
Ferries	0.0	0.0	0.0
Total	*309.9*	*281.6*	*312.9*

Passenger trips per vehicle kilometre

Buses	5.2	4.0	3.9
Rail	0.0	4.8	7.0
Trams	4.3	4.6	4.2
Ferries	0.0	0.0	0.0
Overall	*4.3*	*4.5*	*4.5*

Passenger kilometres per person

Buses	139.4	195.8	301.6
Rail	0.0	214.9	486.2
Trams	1,565.1	1,234.5	1,040.4
Ferries	0.0	0.0	0.0
Total	*1,704.5*	*1,645.2*	*1,828.2*

Average speed of public transport

Buses (km/h)	19.1	18.5	19.2
Rail (km/h)	0.0	40.6	37.6
Trams (km/h)	16.1	16.6	16.9
Ferries (km/h)	0.0	0.0	0.0
Overall	*16.3*	*20.0*	*22.8*

Vehicular energy efficiency

Buses (MJ / km)	13.9	19.1	24.4
Rail (MJ / km)	0.0	15.9	19.7
Trams (MJ / km)	3.3	5.3	7.4
Ferries (MJ / km)	0.0	0.0	0.0
Overall	*4.0*	*8.0*	*12.6*

Modal energy efficiency

Buses (MJ / passenger km.)	0.48	0.88	1.15
Rail (MJ / passenger km.)	0.00	0.33	0.40
Trams (MJ / passenger km.)	0.14	0.21	0.32
Ferries (MJ / passenger km.)	0.00	0.00	0.00
Overall	*0.17*	*0.31*	*0.48*

Washington

POPULATION PARAMETERS	1960	1970	1980
Urban density (persons / ha	20.5	19.4	13.2
Inner area density (persons / ha)	51.7	51.2	44.2
Outer area density (persons / ha)	14.2	15.2	10.9
CBD density (persons / ha)	22.8	13.1	7.5
Proportion of population in CBD (%)	0.5	0.2	0.1
Proportion of population in inner area (%)	36.8	26.4	21.4
EMPLOYMENT PARAMETERS			
Employment density (jobs / ha)	9.6	8.6	8.0
Inner area employment density (jobs / ha)	33.9	34.8	37.5
Outer area employment density (jobs / ha)	4.7	5.2	5.8
CBD employment density (jobs / ha)	489.1	479.4	584.1
Proportion of jobs in CBD (%)	26.5	20.0	16.1
Proportion of jobs in inner area (%)	59.2	46.7	32.5
ACTIVITY INTENSITY PARAMETERS			
(Pop. & Jobs / ha)			
CBD activity intensity	511.9	492.5	591.6
Inner area activity intensity	85.6	86.0	81.7
Outer area activity intensity	18.9	20.4	16.7
City - wide activity intensity	30.1	28.0	21.2
VEHICLE OWNERSHIP PARAMETERS			
Total vehicles / 1000 people	326.7	452.0	645.2
Passenger cars / 1000 people	289.8	400.9	561.4
PRIVATE MOBILITY PARAMETERS			
Total per capita vehicle kms.	?	6,471	9,058
Per capita car kms.	?	5,671	7,939
Total per capita occupant kms.	?	?	13,315
Per capita car occupant kms.	?	?	11,670
Total vehicle kms. per vehicle	?	14,317	14,041
Car kms. per car	?	14,146	14,143
TRAFFIC RESTRAINT PARAMETERS			
Parking spaces / 1000 CBD workers	217.9	295.0	264.0
Length of road per person (m)	?	5.1	5.1
Total vehicles per km of road	?	88.2	127.0
Total vehicle kms. per km. of road	?	1,262,821	1,782,497
Car kms. per km. of road	?	1,106,792	1,562,228
TRANSPORT ENERGY PARAMETERS			
Motor spirit use / person (MJ)	?	36,268	51,241
Total private energy use / person (MJ)	?	41,473	53,362
Public trans. energy use / person (MJ)	757	656	980
Total energy use / person (MJ)	?	42,129	54,342

PUBLIC TRANSPORT PARAMETERS

Vehicle kilometres per person

Buses	28.9	26.4	29.9
Rail	0.4	0.3	10.0
Trams	3.4	0.0	0.0
Ferries	0.0	0.0	0.0
Total	*32.7*	*26.7*	*39.9*

Passenger trips per person

Buses	78.7	47.8	64.9
Rail	0.5	0.4	26.3
Trams	19.7	0.0	0.0
Ferries	0.0	0.0	0.0
Total	*98.9*	*48.2*	*91.2*

Passenger trips per vehicle kilometre

Buses	2.7	1.8	2.2
Rail	1.2	1.4	2.6
Trams	5.8	0.0	0.0
Ferries	0.0	0.0	0.0
Overall	*3.0*	*1.8*	*2.3*

Passenger kilometres per person

Buses	472.0	286.8	386.7
Rail	19.4	14.1	229.4
Trams	78.7	0.0	0.0
Ferries	0.0	0.0	0.0
Total	*570.1*	*300.9*	*616.1*

Average speed of public transport

Buses (km/h)	17.8	17.8	17.8
Rail (km/h)	55.0	55.0	40.3
Trams (km/h)	12.3	0.0	0.0
Ferries (km/h)	0.0	0.0	0.0
Overall	*18.3*	*19.5*	*26.2*

Vehicular energy efficiency

Buses (MJ / km)	20.7	24.2	25.4
Rail (MJ / km)	53.2	57.6	22.0
Trams (MJ / km)	16.6	0.0	0.0
Ferries (MJ / km)	0.0	0.0	0.0
Overall	*23.1*	*24.6*	*24.6*

Modal energy efficiency

Buses (MJ / passenger km.)	1.44	2.23	1.97
Rail (MJ / passenger km.)	1.21	1.13	0.96
Trams (MJ / passenger km.)	0.71	0.00	0.00
Ferries (MJ / passenger km.)	0.00	0.00	0.00
Overall	*1.33*	*2.18*	*1.59*

348

West Berlin

POPULATION PARAMETERS	1960	1970	1980
Urban density (persons / ha)	85.6	75.8	63.6
Inner area density (persons / ha)	132.6	114.3	83.5
Outer area density (persons / ha)	67.6	62.8	57.2
CBD density (persons / ha)	?	125.0	133.3
Proportion of population in CBD (%)	?	0.7	0.8
Proportion of population in inner area (%)	42.9	38.1	31.8
EMPLOYMENT PARAMETERS			
Employment density (jobs / ha)	40.3	34.0	26.6
Inner area employment density (jobs / ha)	70.5	61.7	45.9
Outer area employment density (jobs / ha)	28.7	24.7	20.4
CBD employment density (jobs / ha)	400.1	325.0	333.3
Proportion of jobs in CBD (%)	4.6	4.1	4.8
Proportion of jobs in inner area (%)	48.5	45.9	41.8
ACTIVITY INTENSITY PARAMETERS (Pop. & Jobs / ha)			
CBD activity intensity	?	450.0	466.6
Inner area activity intensity	203.1	176.0	129.4
Outer area activity intensity	96.3	87.5	77.6
City - wide activity intensity	125.9	109.8	90.2
VEHICLE OWNERSHIP PARAMETERS			
Total vehicles / 1000 people	88.4	196.1	305.9
Passenger cars / 1000 people	66.1	175.9	268.9
PRIVATE MOBILITY PARAMETERS			
Total per capita vehicle kms.	?	2,185	3,092
Per capita car kms.	?	1,923	2,721
Total per capita occupant kms.	?	3,671	5,195
Per capita car occupant kms.	?	3,231	4,572
Total vehicle kms. per vehicle	?	11,145	10,108
Car kms. per car	?	10,934	10,119
TRAFFIC RESTRAINT PARAMETERS			
Parking spaces / 1000 CBD workers	?	410.3	437.5
Length of road per person (m)	1.2	1.3	1.5
Total vehicles per km of road	74.3	146.9	208.0
Total vehicle kms. per km. of road	?	1,637,359	2,102,277
Car kms. per km. of road	?	1,441,031	1,850,153
TRANSPORT ENERGY PARAMETERS			
Motor spirit use / person (MJ)	?	8,309	11,331
Total private energy use / person (MJ)	?	11,891	15,382
Public trans. energy use / person (MJ)	740	937	1,083
Total energy use / person (MJ)	?	12,828	16,465

PUBLIC TRANSPORT PARAMETERS

Vehicle kilometres per person

Buses	26.9	38.6	38.9
Rail	35.8	33.5	44.4
Trams	20.0	0.0	0.0
Ferries	0.0	0.0	0.0
Total	*82.7*	*72.1*	*83.3*

Passenger trips per person

Buses	136.9	212.3	203.0
Rail	146.9	131.3	191.4
Trams	99.7	0.0	0.0
Ferries	0.1	0.0	0.1
Total	*383.6*	*343.6*	*394.5*

Passenger trips per vehicle kilometre

Buses	5.1	5.5	5.2
Rail	4.1	3.9	4.3
Trams	5.0	0.0	0.0
Ferries	6.6	6.6	6.6
Overall	*4.6*	*4.8*	*4.7*

Passenger kilometres per person

Buses	616.3	1,057.5	899.3
Rail	1,215.2	877.9	1,259.5
Trams	362.0	0.0	0.0
Ferries	0.5	0.2	0.4
Total	*2,194.0*	*1,935.6*	*2,159.2*

Average speed of public transport

Buses (km/h)	20.6	20.3	20.0
Rail (km/h)	33.6	32.1	32.1
Trams (km/h)	16.6	0.0	0.0
Ferries (km/h)	11.4	11.4	11.4
Overall	*27.1*	*25.7*	*27.1*

Vehicular energy efficiency

Buses (MJ / km)	13.8	16.6	17.7
Rail (MJ / km)	8.5	8.8	8.9
Trams (MJ / km)	3.3	0.0	0.0
Ferries (MJ / km)	?	?	?
Overall	*8.9*	*13.0*	*13.0*

Modal energy efficiency

Buses (MJ / passenger km.)	0.60	0.61	0.76
Rail (MJ / passenger km.)	0.25	0.34	0.31
Trams (MJ / passenger km.)	0.18	0.0	0.0
Ferries (MJ / passenger km.)	?	?	?
Overall	*0.34*	*0.48*	*0.50*

Zürich

POPULATION PARAMETERS	1960	1970	1980
Urban density (persons / ha)	58.3	57.7	53.7
Inner area density (persons / ha)	93.3	89.2	78.9
Outer area density (persons / ha)	35.8	41.4	41.7
CBD density (persons / ha)	95.5	68.7	44.4
Proportion of population in CBD (%)	2.1	1.3	0.9
Proportion of population in inner area (%)	62.7	52.8	47.4
EMPLOYMENT PARAMETERS			
Employment density (jobs / ha)	30.7	32.4	32.5
Inner area employment density (jobs / ha)	57.7	64.6	65.8
Outer area employment density (jobs / ha)	13.2	15.7	16.7
CBD employment density (jobs / ha)	402.5	437.6	422.1
Proportion of jobs in CBD (%)	16.7	15.0	13.6
Proportion of jobs in inner area (%)	73.8	68.2	65.2
ACTIVITY INTENSITY PARAMETERS			
(Pop. & Jobs / ha)			
CBD activity intensity	498.0	506.3	466.5
Inner area activity intensity	151.0	153.8	144.7
Outer area activity intensity	49.0	57.1	58.4
City - wide activity intensity	89.0	90.1	86.2
VEHICLE OWNERSHIP PARAMETERS			
Total vehicles / 1000 people	187.5	298.7	432.1
Passenger cars / 1000 people	126.0	253.9	374.6
PRIVATE MOBILITY PARAMETERS			
Total per capita vehicle kms.	?	?	?
Per capita car kms.	?	?	4,318
Total per capita occupant kms.	?	?	?
Per capita car occupant kms.	?	?	7,254
Total vehicle kms. per vehicle	?	?	?
Car kms. per car	?	?	11,525
TRAFFIC RESTRAINT PARAMETERS			
Parking spaces / 1000 CBD workers	?	?	140.3
Length of road per person (m)	?	?	2.6
Total vehicles per km of road	?	?	164.9
Total vehicle kms. per km. of road	?	?	?
Car kms. per km. of road	?	?	1,647,922
TRANSPORT ENERGY PARAMETERS			
Motor spirit use / person (MJ)	?	?	15,709
Total private energy use / person (MJ)	?	?	17,800
Public trans. energy use / person (MJ)	1,177	976	1,230
Total energy use / person (MJ)	?	?	19,030

PUBLIC TRANSPORT PARAMETERS

Vehicle kilometres per person

Buses	12.3	11.4	14.8
Rail	21.4	15.5	24.0
Trams	31.2	24.7	23.6
Ferries	?	?	?
Total	*64.9*	*51.6*	*62.4*

Passenger trips per person

Buses	67.9	69.0	95.2
Rail	94.6	65.8	83.6
Trams	213.7	186.5	183.1
Ferries	1.6	1.5	1.4
Total	*377.7*	*322.7*	*363.3*

Passenger trips per vehicle kilometre

Buses	5.5	6.0	6.4
Rail	4.4	4.2	3.5
Trams	6.8	7.5	7.8
Ferries	?	?	?
Overall	*5.8*	*6.2*	*5.8*

Passenger kilometres per person

Buses	244.3	248.4	335.1
Rail	1,279.7	888.1	1,199.6
Trams	769.5	671.5	622.6
Ferries	?	?	?
Total	*2,293.5*	*1,808.0*	*2,157.3*

Average speed of public transport

Buses (km/h)	22.5	21.8	20.3
Rail (km/h)	40.6	45.2	45.7
Trams (km/h)	16.0	14.5	15.3
Ferries (km/h)	?	?	?
Overall	*30.4*	*30.5*	*32.8*

Vehicular energy efficiency

Buses (MJ / km)	16.5	17.0	14.2
Rail (MJ / km)	33.6	32.8	31.5
Trams (MJ / km)	8.1	11.1	11.3
Ferries (MJ / km)	?	?	?
Overall	*18.1*	*18.9*	*19.7*

Modal energy efficiency

Buses (MJ / passenger km.)	0.83	0.78	0.63
Rail (MJ / passenger km.)	0.56	0.57	0.63
Trams (MJ / passenger km.)	0.33	0.41	0.43
Ferries (MJ / passenger km.)	?	?	?
Overall	*0.51*	*0.54*	*0.57*

APPENDICES

APPENDIX 1: LIST OF CONTRIBUTORS TO SOURCEBOOK

ADELAIDE

Mark Nowosilskyj
Australian Bureau of Statistics
South Australia
10 Pulteney St
Adelaide, SA. 5000

Lindsay Oxlad, Nicole Ricketts
Director-General of Transport (SA)
State Administration Centre
Victoria Square
Adelaide, SA. 5000

Highways Department of
South Australia
PO Box 1
Walkerville, SA. 5081

Peter Bourke, John Hanna,
Mike Llewellyn-Smith
Adelaide City Council
Town Hall
King William St
Adelaide, SA. 5000

Martin Bell
Department of
Environment and Planning
and South Australian
Planning Commission
55 Grenfell St
Adelaide, SA. 5000

Adrian Gargett
State Transport Authority
Norwich Centre
55 King William Rd
North Adelaide, SA. 5006

AMSTERDAM

F le Clercq, Jos v.d. Kleij, Roel TerBrugge
Structural Planning Division
Dienst Ruimtelijke Ordening Amsterdam
Wibautstraat 3
109 EH Amsterdam
Netherlands

CJ Ruijgrok and
J P J M van Est
Organisatie Voor Toegepast
Natuurwetenschappelijk
Delft, Netherlands

Hans du Bois
Press, Publicity and
Information Department
gvb Municipal Transport
Stadhouderskade 1
1054 ES Amsterdam
Netherlands

BOSTON

Massachusetts Bay Transportation
Authority
Communications Directorate
10 Park Plaza
Boston, Mass. 02116

Massachusetts Department
of Public Works,
State Planning Bureau of
Transportation, Planning
and Development

Ian Harrington
Metropolitan Area Planning Council
110 Tremont St
Boston, Mass. 02108

Centre for Massachusetts Data
Office of Communities and
Development
100 Cambridge St
Boston, Mass. 02202

BRISBANE

Dr Peter Shilton, Derek Kemp, Jim
Eastwell, Neil Viney, John Dudgeon
Brisbane City Council
69 Ann St
Brisbane, Qld. 4001

Rowan Haigh
Australian Bureau of Statistics;
Queensland
Ann St
Brisbane, Qld. 4000

Transport Department
Urban Public Transport Division
Transport House - The Valley Centre
230 Brunswick St
Fortitude Valley, Qld. 4006

BRUSSELS

Vincent Carton
Agglomération de Bruxelles
Service Urbanisme
rue de la Loi 15
1040 Brussels, Belgium

Antoine Lombart
Traffic Department Manager
Société des Transports Intercomunaux
de Bruxelles

100 Nashua St
Boston, Mass. 02114

Office of the Secretary
Executive Office of
Transportation
and Construction
1 Ashburton Place
Boston, Mass. 02108

The Commonwealth of Exec.
Massachusetts
Registry of Motor Vehicles
100 Nashua St
Boston, Mass. 02114

Adrian McKeen
Queensland Railways
Railway Centre
305 Edward St
Brisbane, Qld. 4000

Len Johnston, Daniel Ng,
Geoff Middleton
Main Roads Department, 345
Queensland
GPO Box 1412
Brisbane, Qld. 4001

André J Jacobs
International Union of
Public Transport
Avenue de L'Uruguay 19
B-1050 Brussels, Belgium

Professor Jan Tanghe
Groep Planning
Sint-Jacobsstraat 68
8000 Brugge, Belgium

15 Avenue de la Toison d'Or
1050 Brussels, Belgium

Violette Vansteelandt
Van De Vlaamse Gemeenschap
Administratie voor Ruimtelijke
Ordening en Leefmilien

Belgian Ministry of Ministerie
Transport through the
Australian   Ambassador
Australian   Embassy
51-52 Avenue des Arts
1040 Brussels, Belgium

CHICAGO

Mehmet Civgin and Roy Bell
Chicago Area Transportation Study
300 W Adams St
Chicago, Ill. 60606

Margaret McGatby
City of Chicago
City Hall
121 N La Salle St
Chicago, Ill. 60602

Gary Foyle
Regional Transportation Authority
300 N State St
Chicago, Ill. 60610

Sarah La Belle
Argonne National Analysis
Laboratory
Center for Transportation
Research, Building 362, 9700
Cass Ave, Argonne, Ill. 60439
James Mulqueeny Jr
Operations Planning
Department
Chicago Transit Authority
Merchandise Mart Plaza
PO Box 3555
Chicago, Ill. 60654

Allen D Grossboll
Office of the Secretary of State
Vehicle Services Department
Springfield, Ill. 62756

John Paige
North Eastern Illinois Planning
Commission
400 W Madison
Chicago, Ill. 60606

Tom Kaiser
Department   of   Public
Works
Bureau of Traffic
Engineering
320 N Clark St
Chicago, Ill. 60610

COPENHAGEN

Wulf D Wätjen
Hovedstadsrådet
Sankt Annae Plads 26
DK-1250
København K, Denmark

Kai Lemberg
General Planning
Department
Town Hall 1599
København V, Denmark

Associate Professor Jørgen S Nørgård

Professor Tom Rallis

357

Energy Group
Physic Laboratory III
Building 309
The Technical University of Denmark
DK 2800 Lyngby, Denmark

Department for Road
Construction,
Transportation Engineering
and Town Planning
Building 115
Technical University of
Denmark
Lyngby, 2800 København,
Denmark

Danish State Railways
Sølvgade 40
1349 København K, Denmark

Niels A Thomsen
Vejkontoret
Islands Brygge 37
2300 København S,
Denmark

Erik Kjoergaard
Hovedstadsområdets Trafikselskab (HT)
Gothersgade 53
1123 København K, Denmark

Karl Lundberg
Københavns Statistik
Kontor
Vester Voldgade 87
1552 København V,
Denmark

Holger Pyndt
National Association of Local
Authorities in Denmark
11 Gyldenløvergade
DK 1600 Copenhagen V, Denmark

DENVER

Philip A. Plienis, William La Mont Jr.,
David H. Williams and Doug Groedert
City and County of Denver
Planning Office
1445 Cleveland Place
Denver, Colorado 80202

Stephen Millard,
Regional Transportation
District
1600 Blake St
Denver, Colorado 80202

Richard Gebhart, Steven D. Rudy,
George Shermstall and Geoff May
Denver Regional Council of Governments
2480 W 26th Ave
Denver, Colorado 80211

John A. Bruce
City and County of Denver
Department of Public
Works
Office of City Engineer
5440 Roslyn St
Denver, Colorado 80216

John Leary
Denver Air Pollution Control District
1101 Bellaire Rd

James W. Margolis
Colorado Office of Energy
Conservation

Denver, Colorado

112 E 14th Ave
Denver, Colorado 80203

Motor Vehicle Department
140 6th St West
Denver, Colorado

DETROIT

James Fryer,
Transportation Operations
City of Detroit
Department of Transportation
1301 East Warren
Detroit, Michigan 48207

South Eastern Michigan
Transportation Authority
First National Building
660 Woodward Ave
Detroit, Michigan 48226

Michael Tako, Jim Thomas and
Carmine Polombo
Southeast Michigan Council of
Governments
800 Book Building
1249 Washington Boulevard
Detroit, Michigan 48226

Mark P. Haas
Department of Commerce
Energy Administration
PO Box 30228
Lansing, Michigan 48909

George O. Stevens
State Secondary Complex
7064 Crowner Drive
Lansing, Michigan 48918

Lawrence S. Rosen PhD
Department of
Management and Budget
PO Box 30026
Lewis Cass Building
Lansing, Michigan 48909

R. F. Gregory and Ann Lang
Facilities Department
GM-D1 Leasing and New Center
Revitalization
485 West Milwaukee Ave
Detroit, Michigan 48202

Charles Ohno, Bob
Hoffman and Pat Becker
City of Detroit
Data Coordination Division
3400 Cadillac Tower
Detroit, Michigan 48226

Nancy Glenn
Michigan Department of Transportation
425 West Ottowa
Lansing, Michigan 48909

FRANKFURT

Herr Müller-Raemisch, Herr Haas,
Dr Schriever, Herr Eckhard and
Herr Klaus Janz
Stadt Frankfurt

Herr Henss and Herr
Dirmeier,
Bundesbahndirektion
Friedrich Ebert-Anlage 35

Technische Radhuis
Amt für Kommunale Gesamtent-
wicklung und Stadtplanung
Hausanschrift: Braubachstr 15
600 Frankfurt am Main
West Germany

Room 445 A
Frankfurt am Main
West Germany

Stadtwerke Frankfurt am Main
Börneplatz
Frankfurt am Main
West Germany

Günter J. Höhn (MCIT)
Frankfurter Verkehrs und
Tarifverbund
Mannheimer Strasse 15-19
6000 Fankfurt am Main
West Germany

HAMBURG

Herr Buch and Herr Heidebruch
Statistisches landesamt der Freien
und Hausestadt Hamburg
Steckelhörn 12
2000 Hamburg 11
West Germany

Herr Klaus Pehmöller
Hamburger
Verkehrsverbund
Hamburgerstr 11
D2000 Hamburg 76
West Germany

Frau Waldtraut Lohse
ADAC
Verkerhrsabteilung
Amsinckstr 39
2000 Hamburg 1
Postfach 100202
West Germany

Herr Ingelmann
Freie und Hansestadt
Hamburg
Baubehörde
Tiefbauamt TGO
Stadthausbrücke 8
2000 Hamburg 36
West Germany

HONG KONG

Dorothy Chan and Chiu
Tak-Kwong
Transport Department
Guardian House
32 Oi Kwan Rd
Hong Kong

Duncan Murray
Mass Transit Railway
Corporation
33 Wai Yip St
Kowloon Bay
PO Box 9916 GPO
Hong Kong

Gregory Chiu Fook-ching
Census and Statistics Department
317 Des Voeux Rd Central
Kai Tak Commercial Buildings
Hong Kong

Christopher Ki,
Census Planning Section
Census and Statistics
Department
74-77 Connaught Rd Central
Permanent Comfort
Buildings 5th floor

Alvan Li
Traffic and Transport Survey Division
Canton Rd Government Offices
393 Canton Rd
Kowloon, Hong Kong

Peter S. Leeds, F. K. Lai and K. C. Keung
Transport Department
Guardian House
32 Oi Kwan Rd
Hong Kong

HOUSTON

Hans C. Olavson
Houston-Galveston Regional
Transportation Study
PO Box 1386
Houston, Texas 77251

Laurie Huckaba
Houston Chamber of Commerce
Research Division
25th Floor, 1110 Milam Building
Houston, Texas 77002

Sharon Mathew and Joseph Chow
Department of Planning and
Development
City of Houston, Mayor's Office
PO Box 1562
Houston, Texas 77251

LONDON

David Bayliss
Chief Transport Planner
Greater London Council (abolished)
Transportation and Development Dept.
Room 412
The County Hall
London SE1 7PB

Dr Peter R. White
The Polytechnic of Central London

Hong Kong

Dr Peter K. S. Pun and Amy
Pow
Town Planning Division
Murray Building
Garden Rd
Hong Kong

Robert Bush and Rilla Ryan
Metropolitan Transit
Authority
500 Jefferson St
Houston, Texas 77002

Katy Liske
Rice Center for Community
Design and Research
9 Greenway Plaza
Office Suite 1900
Houston, Texas 77046

State Department of
Highways and Public
Transportation
Motor Vehicle Division
Austin, Texas 78779

Peter Collins
Group Planning
London Transport
55 Broadway
London SW1 HOBD

Transport 2000 Ltd
258 Pentonville Rd

35 Marylebone Rd
London NW1 5LS

London N19JY

LOS ANGELES

Glenn O. Johnson,
Lothar Van Schoenborn and
George E. Marr
Citywide Planning Division
Department of City Planning
City of Los Angeles
561 City Hall
200 N Spring St
Los Angeles, CA. 90012

Paul Shimazu
Department of
Transportation
Division of Transportation
Planning
1120 N St
PO Box 1499
Sacramento, CA. 95807

Ron Johnson
Southern California Rapid Transit
District
425 South Main St
Los Angeles, CA. 90013

Donald A. Dove
Transportation Analysis
and LARTS   Branch
Department of
Transportation
District 7, PO Box 2304
Los Angeles, CA. 90051

Jeffrey G. Davis
County of Los Angeles
Department of Regional Planning
320W Temple St
Los Angeles, CA. 90012

Department of Motor
Vehicles
Division of Registration
PO Box 11319
Sacramento, CA. 95853

Milly Yamada
Air Quality Division
Southern California Association of
Governments
600 S. Commonwealth
Suite 1000
Los Angeles, CA. 90005

Al Rifkin
Department of
Transportation
City of Los Angeles
200 N Spring St
Los Angeles, CA. 90012

MELBOURNE

Andrew McLean
Metropolitan Transit Authority
Corporate Planning
9th Floor, 50 Queen St
Melbourne, Vic. 3000

Douglas A. Bell and
Dr. Timothy A. Patton
Ministry of Transport
PO Box 4910
Melbourne, Vic. 3001

Australian Bureau of Statistics, Victoria
8th Floor, Cnr Flinders and Elizabeth Sts
Melbourne, Vic. 3000

David Ferguson
Road Construction
Authority
60 Denmark St

Kew, Vic. 3101

Ministry for Planning and Environment
Urban Strategy Task Force
Olderfleet Building
477 Collins St
Melbourne, Vic. 3000

MOSCOW

The Secretary
Embassy of the Union of Soviet
Socialists Republic
Canberra Ave
Griffith, ACT. 2603

Dr Gary J. Hausladen
Assistant Professor
Department of Geography 78
and Planning
Southwest Texas State
University
San Marcos, Texas   78666-4616

M. J. Levin
National Security Agency
Fort George G. Meade
Maryland 20755-6000

MUNICH

Herr Karl Auwärter and
Herr Breu
Landeshauptstadt München
Direktorium
Postfach, 8000 München 1
West Germany

Herr Werner Brög
Geschäftsführer
Socialdata GmbH
Hans-Grässel-Weg 1
D-8000 München 1
West Germany

Herr Manfred v Malapert-Neufville
Vertrieb und Marketing (App 6402)
ADAC (Allgemeiner Deutscher
Automobil-Club)
Am Westpark 8
8000 München 70
West Germany

Jürgen Bechmann
Münchner Verkehrs-und
Tarifverbund
Letter der Stabsstelle
Grundlagenforschung
Thierschstrasse 2
8000 München 22
West Germany

H. Schwerdtfeger and K. Tehnik
Planungsreferat
Brucknerstrasse 21
8000 München 80
West Germany

Verkehrs-Rauml
Entwicklungs und
Flachennutzungsplanung
Rindermarkt 5
D-8000 München 2
West Germany

Herr Glatzmeier
Regional Headquarters
Bundesbahndirektion
Richelstrasse 3
8000 München 19
West Germany

NEW YORK

Lawrence V. Hammel and
David Jordan
New York Metropolitan Transportation
Council
One World Trade Center
Suite 82E
New York, NY. 10048

Leonard M. Gaines
New York State Department
of Commerce
99 Washington Ave
Albany, NY. 12245

Research and Development
State of New York
Department of Motor Vehicles
The Governor Nelson A. Rockefeller
Empire State Plaza
Albany, NY. 12228

Robert Selsam
Metropolitan
Transportation Authority
347 Madison Ave
Manhattan, NY. 10007

New York City Transit Authority
370 Jay St
Brooklyn, NY. 11201

Boris Pushkarev and Robert
Cumella
New York Regional Plan
Association
1040 Ave of the Americas
New York, NY. 10018

Robert McCarthy
Office of Transportation Research
Bureau of Transportation Planning and
Research
NYC Department of Transportation
51 Chambers St Room 1427
New York, NY. 10007

PARIS

Claude Lescure
Chambre Syndicale des Constructeurs
D'Automobiles
2 Rue de Presbourg
75008 Paris
France

Le Directeur
Direction de
l'Aménagement Urbain
17 Boulevard Morland
75181 Paris
Cedex 04
France

O. Groret and J. P. Fradin,
Direction Régionale de l'Equipement
d'Ile de France
Départment Politique des Transports
19-23 rue Miollis
75732 Paris
Cedex 15
France

Monsieur De Creusefond
Entre de Documentation Statistique
RATP
53 Ter Quai des Grandes Augustins
Paris, France

Secrétariat de la Mairie de Paris
Hôtel de Ville
75196 Paris R P, France

Christine Fleurant, MR Soudieu and
MR Hattenberger
Atelier Parisien D'Urbanisme
Ville de Paris
17 Boulevard Morland
75181 Paris Cedex 04
France

Yves Farhi and MR Ballut
Direction Regionale de
l'Equipement
d'Ile de France
21 rue Miollis
75015 Paris
France

Luc Aliadiere and Marie de
Vaquet
SNCF (French National
Railways)
88 Rue St Lazare
Paris Cedex 09
France

RATP
41 rue Caumartin (2ndFl)
Paris, France

PERTH

Ray Karvinen, Mark Rogers and
Anna Di Rosso
State Planning Commission
22 St Georges Tce
Perth, WA. 6000

Helen Close
Transperth
10 Adelaide Tce
Perth, WA. 6000

Bob Lloyd
Main Roads Department of
Western Australia
Waterloo Crescent
East Perth, WA. 6000

David Leith
Westrail
Westrail Centre
West Parade
East Perth, WA. 6000

PHOENIX

Richard F. Counts
City of Phoenix
Planning Department
125 East Washington St
Phoenix, Arizona 85004

William E. Jacobson
City of Phoenix
Planning Department
Long Range Division
125 East Washington St
Phoenix, Arizona 85004

Russell J. Heisinger
Maricopa County Department of
Plannning and Development
111 South Third Ave
Phoenix, Arizona 85003

Dale Hardy
City of Phoenix, Public
Transit
Administration
251 W Washington St, 6th
Floor
Phoenix, Arizona 85003

Phoenix Transit
Cnr W Adams and 1st St
Phoenix, Arizona

Dr Terry Max Johnson
Maricopa Association of
Governments
Transportation Planning
Office
Arizona Department of
Transportation
1739 West Jackson St
Phoenix, Arizona 85007

Robert F. Ohnleiter
Transportation Planning Division
Arizona Department of Transportation
1651 W Jackson St
Phoenix, Arizona 85007

Arizona Department of
Transportation
Motor Vehicle Division
1801 West Jefferson St
Phoenix, Arizona
PO Box 2100
Phoenix, Arizona 85001

SAN FRANCISCO

Charles L. Purvis and
Hanna Kollo
Metropolitan Transportation Commission
Metrocenter
101 8th St
Oakland, CA. 94607

Ms Patricia Perry
Association of Bay Area
Governments
Metrocenter
101 8th St,
Oakland CA. 94607

San Francisco Municipal Railway (MUNI)
949 Presidio Ave
San Francisco, CA. 94115

Chi-Hsin Shao and M. F. Groat
SanFrancisco City Planning Department
450 McAllister St
San Francisco, CA. 94102

Michael Y. Kim
Bay Area Air Quality Management District
939 Ellis St
San Francisco, CA. 94109

Ms Sue Stropes
AC Transit
Research and Planning Department
508 16th St
Oakland, CA. 94612

Joy Dahlgren
Golden Gate Bridge and Highway District
PO Box 3474
San Rafael, CA. 94912

Ben Chuck
CAL TRAINS
PO Box 7310
San Francisco, CA. 94120

SINGAPORE

M. Mathews
National University of Singapore
Lower Kent Ridge Rd
Singapore 0511

Kenneth Goh
Department of Statistics
Maxwell Rd PO Box 3010
Singapore 9050

Lee Hock Guan
Public Works Department
Ministry of National Development
10th Floor, National Development Building
Maxwell Rd, Singapore 0106

Tan Tsu Haung
Statutory Planning
Ministry of National Devp.
6th Floor, National Development Building,
Maxwell Rd, Singapore 0106

Provisional MRT Authority
1 Maritime Square
02-70 World Trade Centre
Singapore 0409

D. Murugan
Singapore High Commission
17 Forster Crescent
Yarralumla, Canberra, ACT. 2600

Koh Lian Choon
Senior Assistant Registrar
Registry of Vehicles
Sin Ming Rd
Singapore 2057

Economics Officer
Ministry of Trade and Industry
40th Floor CPF Building
70 Robinson Rd
Singapore 0106

STOCKHOLM

Gunnel Horm and Lars Petersson
Stockholms läns landsting
Trafikkontoret
Sergels Torg 12
S-111 57 Stockholm
Sweden

Per Gullström and Christer
Pränting
Stockholms Kommun
Utrednings-och
Statistikkontoret
Box 8320
104 20 Stockholm
Sweden

FORSKNINGSRÅDSÄMNDEN
Secretariat for Future Studies
Wenner-Gren Center
Sveavägen 166
PO Box 6710
S-11385 Stockholm
Sweden

Bjorn Lindfelt, Stig
Nordquist
Stockholms läns landsting
Regionplane-och
Näringslivsnämnden
Regionplanekontoret
Sergels Torg 12
Box 7841
10398 Stockholm
Sweden

Stockholms Stadskansli
Finansavdelningen
Planeringsberedningens Kamsli
Stadsheset
105 35 Stockholm
Sweden

AB Storstockholms
Localtrafik (SL)
Tegnérgatan 2
Box 6301
S-113 81 Stockholm
Sweden

AP Gan Parmebry
Transportrådet (Transport Council)
Box 1339
17126 Solna,
Sweden

Statens väg-och trafikinstitut
Swedish Road and Traffic
Research
Institute
S-581 01 Linköping
Sweden

Herje Norrby, Rolf Gäfvert and
Anders Petterson
Trafik av dolningen - Tekniska byran
Fleminggatan 4, Box 8312,
10420 Stockholm, Sweden

SYDNEY

Robert Leavens
Ministry of Transport
State Transport Study Group
Aetna Life Tower
227 Elizabeth St
Sydney, NSW. 2000

P. Margison
Strategic Planning Section
Department of Main Roads, NSW
309 Castlereagh St
Sydney, NSW. 2000

Australian Bureau of Statistics, NSW
5th Floor, St Andrews House
Sydney Square
Sydney, NSW. 2000

N. Bidewell, K. Jamieson, K. Jones and
Neville Shoosmith
Urban Transity Authority of NSW
11 York St
Sydney, NSW. 2000

Martin Halliday
Strategic Planning Section
Sydney City Council
Town Hall House
Level 7, George St
Sydney, NSW. 2000

David Wilmoth
Central Policy Division
Environment and Planning
Commission of NSW
175 Liverpool St
Sydney, NSW. 2000

Alan Woodhouse
Passenger Development
Section
State Rail Authority
1st Floor, 509 Pitt St
Sydney, NSW, 2000

TOKYO

H. Hiyoki and A. G. Virili,
Government of Western Australia
7th Floor, Sankaido Building
9-13 Akasaka 1 - Chome
Minato-ku, Tokyo. 102
Japan

Tokyo Metropolitan Government
Statistics Division
Bureau of General Affairs
5-1 Marunouchi 3 - Chome
Chiyoda-ku, Tokyo 100, Japan

Professor Ryohei Kakumoto
Japan Transport Economics
Research Center
6-6 Toranomon 1- Chome
Minato-ku, Tokyo 100
Japan

TORONTO

T. P. Henry
GO Transit
555 Wilson Ave

Assistant Professor John B.
Robinson
University of Waterloo

Downsview, Ontario M3H 5Y6

Faculty of Environmental
Studies
Dept of Man-Environment
Studies
Waterloo, Ontario N2L 3G1

Public Works Department
City of Toronto
City Hall
Toronto, Ontario M5H 2N2

Juri Pill and Norm Funk
Toronto Transit Commission
1900 Yonge St
Toronto, Ontario M4S 1Z2

Ontario Ministry of Transportation and
Communications
1201 Wilson Ave
Downsview
Ontario M3M 1J 8

Dick Gordon, Robert
Stopnicki, Rhonda Petrella
and Angus Murray
The Municipality of
Metropolitan Toronto
Metropolitan Planning
Department
City Hall, East Tower, 11th
Floor
Toronto, Ontario M5H 2N1

VIENNA

Osterreichische Bundesbahnen
Bundesbahndirektion Wien
Präsident
Hofrat Dr Erwin Semmelrath
Nordbahnstrasse 50
A-1020 Wien
Austria

Der Direktor
der
Bundeswirtschaftskammer
der Gewerblichen Wirtschaft
Section Verkehr
1040 Wien
Wiedner Hauptstrasse 63
Austria

Dipl. In. Dr Jawecki, Herr Hansly,
Frau Weiss and Herr Koeberl
Senatsrat
Magistrat der Stadt Wien
Magistratsabteilung 18
Stadtstrukturplanung
Rathausstrasse 14-16
3 Stock, Tür 311
1082 Wien, Austria

Magistrat Der Stadt Wien
Büro der Geschäftsgruppe
Strasse
Verkehr und Energie
Ing. Kurt Windisch
Techn. Oberamtstrat
Wien, Austria

Magistrat Der Stadt Wien
Magistratsabteilung 66
Statistisches Amt der Stadt Wien
Volksgartenstrasse 3
1016 Wien
Austria

Wiener Stadtwerke
Verkehrsbetriebe
Favoritenstrasse 9-11
Postfach 40
1041 Wien
Austria

Dr Gerlinde Muhlgassner
Prof. Elisabeth Lichtenberger
Institut für Geographie der
Universität Wien
Universitätsstrasse 7
1010 Wien
Austria

WASHINGTON DC

Abdul R. Sleemi
Data Analysis Branch
Government of the District of Columbia
Department of Public Works
Transportation Systems Administration
Bureau of Traffic Services
613G St NW, Room 721
Washington DC 20001

John Fuarz, William Herman and
Dave Semendinger
Washington Metropolitan Area Transit
Authority
600 Fifth St NW
Washington DC 20001

John Neff
Director-Statistics
American Public Transit Association
1225 Connecticut Ave NW
Washington DC 20036

Dr Gabriel Roth
World Bank
Infrastructure Division
Economic Development Institute IBRD
1818 H St NW
Washington DC 20433

The Urban Institute
2100 M NW, Washington DC

Ronald G. Sarros, Chris
Neumann and Bill Mann
Department of Transportation
Planning
Metropolitan Washington
Council of
Governments
1875 Eye St NW Suite 200
Washington DC 20006-5454

Harry Gray
Motor Vehicles Department
Public Works
2000 14th St NW
Washington DC 20001

Irving Hoch
Senior Fellow
Resources for the Future
1755 Massachusetts Ave NW
Washington DC 20036

Department of
Transportation,
Washington DC
Information Systems Office
301C St NW
Washington DC

WEST BERLIN

Herrn Stein
Senator für Verkehr und Betriebe
III A II
Lindenstrasse 20-25

Statistisches Landesamt Der
Berlin
31 Fehrbelliner Platz 1
D-1000 Berlin 31

D-1000 Berlin 61, West Germany

Deutsches Institut für Urbanistik
Strasse des 17
Juni 112
Postfach 126224
1 Berlin 12
West Germany

ZURICH

Dr Giovanni Gottardi
Jenni + Gottardi AG
Beratende Ingenieure
Mutschellenstrasse 21
8002 Zürich
Switzerland

Bruno Waldispühl
Kundendienst Personeverkehr
Schweizerische Bundesbahnen
Kreisdirektion 111, Verkaufsleitung
Bahnhofplatz 15
8023 Zürich
Switzerland

Dr Ott
Statistisches Amt der Stadt Zürich
Naptgasse 6, Zürich
Switzerland

Dr Peter Keller, Prof H. Brändli
Institut für Orts, Regional und
Landesplanung
ETH, Hönggerberg
Zürich
Switzerland

R. Eggli
Gesundheitsinspektoriat der Stadt Zürich
Postfach, CH 8035, Zürich
Stampfenbachstrasse 144, Switzerland

West Germany

Generalkonsulat
der Bundesrepublik
Deutschland
Consulate General of the
Federal
Republic of Germany
480 Punt Rd
South Yarra, Vic. 3141
Australia

H. Kissling and Dr Meyer
Amt für Raumplanung des
Kantons Zürich
Fachstelle Wirtschaft und
Bevolkerung
Stampfenbachstrasse 30
8090 Zürich
Switzerland

Dr H. J. Sommer
Amt für Technische
Anlangen und
Lufthygiene
des Kantons Zürich
Weinbergerstrasse 15/17
8090 Zürich
Switzerland

Stadtplanungsamt Zürich
Amtshaus V
Werdmühheplatz 3
Postfach CH-8023 Zürich 1
Switzerland

Beat Cagienard
Verkehrsbetriebe Zürich
Postfach 8023
Zürich
Bahnhofquai 5
Switzerland

APPENDIX 2: DATA RETURN SHEET FOR INTERNATIONAL CITIES

Table A2.1

Data return sheet for international cities

City : ....

	1960	1970	1980
1. LAND USE DATA			
(i) Population and area data			
(a) Population (total)..........			
(b) Actual urbanised area (ha) - (excluding all large non-urban uses such as undeveloped land)..........			
(c) Area of the CBD (ha)..........			
(d) Population contained in the CBD			
(e) Inner urban area (ha)..........			
(f) Population contained in the inner urban area..........			
(ii) Parking availability in the CBD (number of spaces)			
(a) Off-street..........			
(b) On-street..........			
(iii) Employment location			
(a) Number of jobs located in the CBD..........			
(b) Number of jobs located in the inner urban area. (incl. CBD)..........			
(c) Total number of jobs in the whole metropolitan area..........			
2. TRANSPORTATION DATA			
(i) Road network..........			
(a) Total length of road in the metropolitan area (this figure includes all road types from inter-state highways and freeways down to local or municipal resedential streets.)..........			
(ii) Total vehicles on register			
(a) Passenger cars..........			
(b) Commercial vehicles..........			
(c) Trucks..........			
(d) Motor cycles..........			
(e) Others (or whatever other categories are available)..........			
(iii) Private transport indicators			
(a) Total annual vehicle kilometres (or vehicle miles) of travel..........			
(b) Average vehicle occupancy (persons per vehicle). (This figure covers the 24 hour period)..........			
(c) Average speed of travel in passenger vehicles for whole metro area..........			
(d) Total annual gasoline consumption for the metro area (incl. LPG)..........			
(e) Total annual diesel fuel consumption for the metro. area. Please note that any breakdown in (a) and (b) by vehicle type would be most valuable..........			
(iv) Modal split data			
(a) % of people taking public transportation for journey-to-work..........			
(b) % of people taking private transportation for journey-to-work..........			
(c) % of people walking and cycling for journey-to-work..........			
(d) Any other modal split data available; eg the above split for CBD orientated work trips compared to other types of work trips OR figures on modal split for other types of trips..........			
(v) Average trip lengths			
(a) Journey to work..........			
(b) Other trip types (whatever available) Note that these data include all modes (cars, public transportation, and walking/cycling)..........			

Public transport data continued overleaf

Table A2.1 (cont.)

City...................

	Annual vehicle kilometres (1)			Annual passengers carried			Average distance each passenger carried(2)			Average speed of travel (km/h)			Annual energy consumption(3)		
	1960	1970	1980	1960	1970	1980	1960	1970	1980	1960	1970	1980	1960	1970	1980
(vi) Public transport indicators															
(a)Buses															
Government...........															
Private..................															
(b)Trains															
Subway..................															
Surface..................															
Commuter rail........															
(c) Trams...............															
(d) Ferries.............															

Notes:
(1) The annual vehicle kilometres for trains is actual wagon or car kilometres not train kilometres. Similarly where articulated trams are used, actual wagon kilometres are used.
(2) Average distance travelled by each passenger is used to estimate passenger kilometres.
(3) In whatever energy units are applicable (eg kWh for electric transit, gallons or litres of diesel/petrol etc).

374

References

Abelson, P.W. (1986) **The economic evaluation of roads in Australia.** Australian Professional Publications, Sydney, 144pp

Allen, I. (1980) The ideology of dense neighbourhood redevelopment : Cultural diversity and transcendent community experience. **Urban Affairs Quarterly** 15(4), 409-428

Altshuler, A., Anderson, M., Jones, D., Roos, D. and Womack, J. (1985) **The future of the automobile: The report of MIT's international automobile program.** Unwin Paperbacks(Counterpoint), London , 321 pp

Amandon, S. (1973) We're doing what the Romans did. **Shelter** 1(8-9), 12

Antoniou, J. (1971) **Environmental management : Planning for traffic.** McGraw Hill

Archibald, R. and Gillingham, R. (1981) Decomposition of the price and income elasticities of the consumer demand for gasoline. **Southern Economic Journal** 47(4), 1021-1031

Ashworth, G. (1973) **Encyclopaedia of planning.** Barrie and Jenkins, London 120pp

Athens Centre of Ekistics (1980) HUCO: The human community in Athens. **Ekistics** 283, 232-263

Australian Bureau of Statistics (1981) **Housing survey 1978, Sydney, Newcastle and Wollongong : Part 3 Anticipated residential movement and satisfaction with current housing conditions.** ABS, NSW Office

Australian Institute of Urban Studies (1983) **Housing policy in the Perth** region: Density and form. AIUS Publication 110, Canberra

Badcock, B. (1984) **Unfairly structured cities.** Basil Blackwell, Oxford

Baldassare, M. (1979) **Residential crowding in urban America.** University of California Press, Berkeley, California

Barrett, B. (1967) **The inner suburbs.** Melbourne University Press, Melbourne

Baum, A., Harpin, R.E. and Valins, S. (1975) The role of group phenomena in the experience of crowding. **Environment and Behaviour** 7, 185-189

Bay Area Transportation Commission (1969) **Bay Area Transportation Report.** Berkeley, California

Beaumont, J.R. and Keys, P. (1982) **Future cities: Spatial analysis of energy issues.** Research Studies Press, Wiley, Chichester, England

Beed, C.S. (1981) **Melbourne's development and planning.** Clewara Press, Melbourne, 306pp

Behnman, J. and Belinger, R.E. (1976) Effect of energy shortage and land use on auto occupancy. **Transportation Engineering Journal of ASCE , Proceedings of the American Society of Civil Engineers** 102 (TE2), 255-270

Ben Bouanah, J. and Stein, M.M. (1978) Urban transportation models: A generalized process for international application. **Traffic Quarterly,** 32, 449-470

Berger, P.L. (1977) In praise of New York: A semi-secular homily. **Commentary** 63, 59-62

Berry , B.J.L., and 14 others, (1974) **Land use, urban form and environmental quality.** Research Paper No. 155 for the Office of Research and Development, Environment Protection Authority, University of Chicago Press, Chicago

Berry, B.J.L and Kasarda J.D. (1977) **Contemporary urban ecology.** Macmillan Publishing, New York, 497pp

Berry, B.J.L. (1985) Islands of renewal in seas of decay. in Peterson, P.E. (ed) **The new urban reality,** Brookings Institute, Washington DC.

Biderman, A., Louiro, M. and Bacchus, H. (1963) **Historical incidents of extreme overcrowding.** Bureau of Social Science Research, Washington D.C.

Black, J. (1981) **Urban transport planning.** Croom Helm, London, 221 pp

Blumenfeld, H. (1965) The modern metropolis. **Scientific American ,** November

Bowden, P., Campbell, R. and Newman, P. (1984) The potential for bike rail integration as a means of easing transport problems in Perth. **Transport Research Paper** 1/84 , Environmental Science , Murdoch University 25 pp

Bowyer, D.P., Akcelik, R. and Biggs,D.C. (1985) **Guide to fuel consumption analyses for urban traffic management.** ARRB Special Report No.32 , Australian Road Research Board, Melbourne

Briggs, A. (1963) **Victorian Cities.** Pelican, 59-71

Britten, J.R. (1977) **What is a satisfactory house? A report of some householders views.** Building Research Establishment, Current Paper No. 26/77, Department of the Environment, England

Brotchie, J.,Hall P. and Newton P.W. (eds.) (1987) **The spatial impact of technological change.** Croom Helm, 460pp

Brown, L.R. (1978) The worldwide loss of cropland. **Worldwatch Paper No.**

24 , WorldWatch Institute, Washington DC.

Bunker, R. (1983) **Urban consolidation: the experience of Sydney, Melbourne and Adelaide.** Australian Institute of Urban Studies , Publication No. 111, Canberra .

Burnley, I.H. (1980) **The Australian urban system: Growth, change, and differentiation.** Longman Cheshire, Melbourne, 339 pp

Button, K.J., Fowkes, A.S. and Pearman, A.D. (1980) Car ownership in West Yorkshire : The influence of public transport accessibility. **Urban Studies** 17, 211-215

Cargo, D.B. (1978) **Solid wastes: Factors influencing generation rates.** University of Chicago, Illinois

Carmichael, T.J. and Haley, C.E. (1950) A study of vehicle , roadway and traffic relationships by means of statistical instruments. **Highway Research Board Proceedings** 30 , 282-296

Carr, D. (1977) Health aspects of town planning. Australian Institute of Health Surveyors Conference, Perth,October

Castells, M. (1975) **The urban question: A Marxist approach.** (Sheridan, A., tr.), Edward Arnold, London

Cervero, R. (1986a) **Suburban gridlock** Centre for Urban Policy Research, Rutgers University, New Jersey, 188pp

Cervero, R. (1986b) Urban transit in Canada: Integration and innovation at its best. **Transport Quarterly,** Vol 40 (3), 293-316

Cham-Son, C. (1983) Hong Kong's planners dismiss Western bogeys. **Australian Planner** , April/May, 44-47

Chandler, T. and Fox, G. (1974) **3000 years of urban growth.** Academic Press , New York

Chandler, W. U . (1985) Energy productivity : Key to environmental protection and economic progress. **Worldwatch Paper 63 ,** Worldwatch Institute , Washington D.C.

Chang , M.F. and Horowitz, A.J. (1979) Estimates of fuel savings through improved traffic flow in seven US cities. **Traffic Engineering and Control** 20 (2) February

Chang, M.F. and Herman, R. (1978) An attempt to characterise traffic in metropolitan areas. **Transportation Science** 12(1) , 58-79

Cherry, G. (1969) The influence of 19th century thought on planning. **Journal of Contemporary History** 4, 45-54

Cheslow, M.D. (1978) **The effects of urban development patterns on transportation energy use.** The Urban Institute, Washington, D.C. Presented at: The Fifth National Conference on the Effects of Energy Constraints on Transportation Systems, July-Aug.

Chisholm, M. and Kivell, P. (1987) **Inner city wasteland: An assessment of government and market failure in land development.** Institute of Economic Affairs, 80pp

Clark, C. (1967) **Population growth and land use.** Macmillan , London

Clark, C. (1982) **Regional and urban location.** University of Queensland Press, St Lucia, Brisbane, Australia

Clark, R. (1987) **Transport and land use : Study packages I-IV** Course notes Geography 350-1, Department of Geography, University of New England, Armidale, NSW

Connell, R. (1986) Meet the obstacle to L.A. metro rail. **Los Angeles Times,** April 11, 1986

Conway, J. and Adams, B. (1977) The social effects of living off the ground. **Habitat International** 2 (5) and (6), 595-614

Cox, H. (1966) **The secular city.** Macmillan, New York

Cox, K. (ed.) (1978) **Urbanization and conflict in market societies.** Methuen and Co Ltd, London, 246pp

Cresswell, R. (ed) (1979) **Quality in urban planning and designes.** Newnes-Butterworths, London, 1979

Dahl, C.A. (1982) Do gasoline demand elasticities vary? **Land Economics** 58(3), 373-382

Davie, M. (1972) **In the future now: A report from California.** Hamish Hamilton, London

Davison, G. (1983) The city-bred child and urban reform in Melbourne 1900-1940. in Williams, P. (ed.), **Social process and the city,** Urban Studies Yearbook 1, George, Allen and Unwin, Sydney

Dean, I.A. (1976) Planning and the individual. in **Regional Planning in Victoria:** Symposium RAPI, RAIGS, I of E and National Trust , Melbourne

Department of City Planning, City and County of San Francisco and 10 others (1987) **The Mission Bay plan: Proposal for citizen review.** Department of City Planning , City and County of San Francisco, April

Department of Environment and Planning (1983) **Regional review of residential densities.** Department of Environmental Planning, Sydney

Duxbury, M.L., Neville, S.D., Campbell, R. and Newman, P.W.G. (1988) Mixed land-use and residential satisfaction : An evaluation. **Transport Research Paper** 2/88, Environmental Science, Murdoch University 19pp

Dynarski, M. (1986) Household formation and suburbanization, 1970-1980. **Journal of Urban Economics** 19, 71-87

Edmonston, B. (1975) **Population distribution in American cities.** Lexington Books,Lexington, Massachusetts

Edner, S.M. and Arrington, G.B., Jr. (1985) **Urban decision making for transportation investment : Portland's light rail transit line.** US Department of Transportation, Technology Sharing Program, Report N° DOT-I-85-03, US Government Printing office, Washington DC

Ellul, J. (1970) **The meaning of the city.** Eerdmans, Grand Rapids, New York

Energy and Environmental Analysis Inc. (1982) **Fuel efficiency of passenger cars.** Report to International Energy Agency, Washington DC

Eno Foundation (1988) Report of the 20th Annual Joint Conference Eno Foundation Board of Directors and Board of Consultants. **Transportation Quartlerly** Vol XLII (1), 141-154

Erskine, R. (1981) **The Byker Development.** City of Newcastle-upon-Tyne, England

Evans, L. and Herman, R. (1976) A simplified approach to calculations of fuel consumption in urban traffic sytems. **Traffic Engineering and Control** 17 (8) and (9), 352-354

Evans, L., Herman, R. and Lam, T. (1976) Multivariate analysis of traffic factors related to fuel consumption in urban driving, **Transportation Science,** 10(2), 205-215

Everitt, B. (1974) **Cluster analysis.** Heinemann Educational Books, London

Federal Highway Administration (1985) **Highway Statistics.** US Department of Transportation,Washington DC

Fels, M.F. and Munson,M.J. (1974) **Energy thrift in urban transportation: Options for the future,** in "The Energy Conservation Papers Ford Foundation Energy Policy Project Report".

Fisher, P.M.G. (1987) Globalisation-new technology and urban form: Australia's industrial and employment future. Paper to International Symposium on Transport, Communication and Urban Form. Monash University, August 24-25, 1987

Freedman, J.L. (1975) **Crowding and behavior.** Viking, New York

Freestone, R. (1986) Exporting the garden city: metropolitan images in Australia, 1900-1930. **Planning Perspectives** 1, 61-84

Fuguitt, G.V. and Zuickes, J.J. (1973) Residential preferences and population distribution : Results of a national survey. Paper presented to Annual Meeting of the Rural Sociological Society, College Park, Maryland, August 24

Gappert, G. (Ed.) (1987) **The future of winter cities.** Urban Affairs Annual Reviews Vol 31, Sage Publications Ltd, London, 320 pp

Goldberg, M.A. and Mercer, J. (1986) **The myth of the North American city: Continentalism challenged.** University of British Columbia Press, Vancouver

Grabow, S. (1977) Frank Lloyd Wright and the American city: The Broadacre debate. **American Institute of Planners Journal** (April), 115-124

Gratz, L. (1981) **The Vienna Underground construction.** Stadtbaudirektion, Wien, February

Gruen, V. (1973) **Centres for the urban environment: Survival of the cities .** Litton Educational Publishing Inc.,

Guest, A.M. (1972) Urban history, population densities, and higher status residential location. **Economic Geography** 48 , 375-387

Guest, A.M. and Cluett, C. (1976) Analysis of mass transit ridership using 1970 census data. **Traffic Quarterly,** 30, 143-161

Hall, P. (1977) **The world cities.** Weidenfeld and Nicolson, London, 271 pp

Hall, P. and Hass-Klau, C. (1985) **Can rail save the city? :The impacts of rail transit and pedestrianisation on British and German cities.** Gower, England, 241pp

Hall, P. and Hay, D. (1980) **Growth centres in the European urban system.** Heinemann Educational Books , London, 278 pp

Hall, P. et al. (1973) **The containment of urban England.** George Allen and Unwin, London

Hamer, M. (1987) **Wheels within wheels: A study of the Road Lobby.** Routledge, London, 162pp

Hardin, G. (1968) The tragedy of the commons. **Science** 162 : 1243-1248

Harrison, P. (1977) Major urban areas in **Atlas of Australian Resources,** Australian Government Publishing Service, Canberra

Harvey, D. (1973) **Social justice and the city.** Edward Arnold, Melbourne

Hatwell, G. (1976) Population, planning and agriculture in Victoria 1971-76: Interactions and implications. Master of Environmental Science Thesis, Monash University,Melbourne, Australia,170 pp

Heinritz, G. and Klingbeil, D. (1986) The take-off of suburbia in the Munich region.**The take-off of suburbia and the crisis of the central city** in International Symposium, Munich and Vienna, Heinritz, G. and Lichtenberger, E. (eds.) Franz Steiner Verlag, Wiesbaden, 33-53

Hempel, D.J. and Tucker, L.R. (1979) Citizen preferences for housing as community social indicators. **Environment and Behaviour** 11(3), 399-428

Hensher, D.A. (1977) **Formulation of an urban passenger tranport policy: A re-appraisal of some elements-accessiblity, energy and urban form.** Macquarie University, North Ryde, N.S.W, Australia

Hensher, D.A., Smith, N.C., Barnard P.O. and Milthorpe, F.W. (1987) **Dimensions of automobile project.** NERDDC End of Grant Report (Phase III, 1985-1987), School of Economic and Financial Studies, Macquarie University, N.S.W., 389pp

Herman, R. , Rule, R.G. and Jackson, M.W. (1978) Fuel economy and exhaust emissions under two conditions of traffic smoothness. Presented to Passenger Car Meeting, Troy Hilton, Troy, Michigan, June 5-9, SAE Technical Paper 780614

Hillman, M. and Whalley , A. (1979) **Walking is transport.** Policy Studies Institute , London, 120pp

Hillman, M. and Whalley, A. (1983) **Energy and personal travel: Obstacles to conservation.** Policy Studies Institute, London, 304pp

Ho, G.E. (1983) Predicting solid waste quantity and quality. **Transactions of the Institution of Engineers, Australia** CE25, 261-267

Illich, I. (1973) **Tools for conviviality.** Fantanna/Collins, Glasgow

International Statistical Institute (1972) **International Statistical Yearbook of Large Towns.** Volume 3(1964), 5 (1970) and 6 (1972) International Statistical Institute , The Hague, Netherlands

Jacobs, J. (1961) **The death and life of great American cities.** Random House, New York

Jefferson, M. (1909) The anthropography of some great cities. **Bulletin of the American Geographical Society** XC1(g), 537-566

Kendig, H. (1979) **New life for old suburbs.** George Allen and Unwin, Sydney

Kent, J.H. and Mudford, N.R. (1979) Motor vehicle emissions and fuel consumption modelling. **Transportation Research** 13A , 395-406

Kenworthy, J.R. (1978) **Roads and residential development in Perth.** Independent study contract, Environmental Science, Murdoch University

Kenworthy, J.R. (1986a) **Driving cycles , urban form and transport energy.** Ph.D. Thesis , Environmental Science ,Murdoch University, 546 pp

Kenworthy, J.R. (1986b) Transport energy conservation through urban planning and lifestyle changes : Some fundamental choices for Perth. in McDavitt, C. (Ed) **Towards a State Conservation Strategy:Invited Review Papers , Bulletin 251,** Department of Conservation and Environment, Western Australia , 69-99

Kenworthy, J.R. (1987a) An urban vision for an urban future : The Perth central area compared to thirty international cities. Presented to Australian Institute of Urban Studies Seminar-"How High The City? Density, Skyline, Space, and Function in Central Perth", Tawarri , Nedlands Foreshore, 18th June

Kenworthy, J.R. (1987b) Australian cities: Beyond the suburban dream.

Habitat Australia 15 (6) , 3-7

Kenworthy, J.R. and Newman, P.W.G. (1987) Learning from the best and worst: Transportation and land use lessons from thirty-two international cities with implications for gasoline use and emissions. Paper presented to Eighth Annual Pedestrian Conference , Boulder, Colorado, October 1-4

Kenworthy, J.R. and Newman, P.W.G. (1982) A driving cycle for Perth: Methodology and preliminary results. Presented to Joint SAE-A/ARRB "Second Conference on Traffic, Energy and emissions", Melbourne, May 19-21, Paper No. 82149

Kenworthy, J.R. and Newman, P.W.G. (1985) Congestion, public transport and energy : A preliminary examination of the public transport and energy implications of reducing congestion in Perth. **Transport Research Paper** 1/85 , Environmental Science , Murdoch University 60pp

Kenworthy, J.R. and Newman, P.W.G. (1986a) The potential of ethanol as a transport fuel: A review based on technological, economic and environmental criteria. **Issues in Energy Policy in Western Australia, Discussion Paper** Nº 6/86, Environmental Science , Murdoch University 40 pp

Kenworthy, J.R. and Newman, P.W.G. (1986b) From hype to mothballs: An assessment of synthetic crude oils from oil shale, coal and oil sands. **Issues in Energy Policy in Western Australia, Discussion Paper** Nº 7/86 , Environmental Science , Murdoch University 90pp

Kenworthy, J.R., Newman, P.W.G. and Lyons, T.J. (1983) **A driving cycle for Perth.** Final report to National Energy Research Development and Demonstration Council Project No. 79/9252 NERDDP/EG/83/129, April, Canberra 326pp

Kenworthy, J.R., Newman, P.W.G. and Lyons, T.J. (1987) **Transport energy conservation policies for Australian cities.** Progress report for NERDDC project number 86/6119, School of Biological and Environmental Sciences, Murdoch University, December, 11 pp

Kenworthy, J.R., Newman, P.W.G., Rainford H. and Lyons, T.J. (1986) Fuel consumption , time saving and freeway speed limits.**Traffic Engineering and Control** , 27(9), 455-459

King, A.D. (1976) **Colonial urban development, culture, social power and environment.** Routledge and Kegan Paul, London

King, A.D. (1978) Exporting planning:The colonial and neo-colonial experience. **Urbanism , Past and Present** 5, 12-22

King, A.D. (1980) Historical patterns of reaction to urbanism: The case of Britain 1880-1939. **International Journal of Urban and Regional Research** 4, 453-467

King, R. (1982) In Melbourne it will not pay to be poor. **RAPIJ** 20(3), 110

Klaassen, L.H., Bourdrez, J.A. and Volmuller , J. (1981) **Transport and reurbanisation.** Gower, England, 214 pp

Knox, J. (1982a) **Transport 2000: A Perth study.** Director General of Transport, Perth, 156pp

Knox, P. (1982b) **Urban social geography : An introduction .** Longman, New York

Korte, C. (1976) The impact of urbanization on social behavior : A comparison of the United States and the Netherlands. **Urban Affairs**

Quarterly 12(1), 21-36

Krause, O. and Hair, D. (1975) Trends in land use and competition for land to produce food and fiber. in US Department of Agriculture, **Perspectives on Prime Lands,** Washington DC.

Kristol, I. (1972) An urban civilization without cities? **Horizon** XIV(4), 41

La Belle, S.J. and Moses ,D.O. (1982) **Technology assessment of productive conservation in urban transportation (ANL/ES-130).** Energy and Environmental Systems Division, Argonne National Laboratory, Illinois

Landsberg, M. (1988) Profusion of handy shops makes Manhattan a pedestrian's delight. **The Globe and Mail** Saturday May 21, 1988, p A2

Lansing, J.B. and Hendricks, G. (1967) **Automobile ownership and residential density.** Survey Research Centre, Institute for Social Research , University of Michigan

Lee, T. (1971) The effect of the built environment on human behavior. **International Journal of Environmental Studies 1** 307-314

Lichtenberger, E. (1976) The changing nature of European urbanization in Berry, B.J.L. (ed), **Urbanization and Counter Urbanization.** Sage Publications , London

Logan, J.R. and Molotch, H.L. (1987) **Urban fortunes; The political economy of place.** California U.P., 383pp

Macauley, M.K. (1985) Estimation and recent behavior of urban population and employment density gradients. **Journal of Urban Economics 18,** 251-260

Maddox, D. (1978) **Exploring the housing attitude of future home buyers in four Australian cities.** A Project for the Committee of Inquiry into Housing Costs, PA Consulting Services, Pty Ltd, Australian Government Publishing Service, Canberra

Manning, I. (1978) **The journey to work.** George Allen and Unwin, Sydney

Marquand, R. (1988) U.S. discovers new black hole in intellectual life. **The Christian Science Monitor,** World Edition, January 4-10 (p1 and 28)

Maunder, D.A.C. (1983) Household and travel characteristics in two suburban residential areas of Delhi, India 1982. **Transport and Road Research Laboratory Supplementary Report** 767, Crowthorne, Berkshire, U.K.

Maunder, D.A.C., Fouracre, P.R. and Rao, C.H. (1981) Household and travel characteristics in two residential areas of Delhi, India 1979. **Transport and Road Research Laboratory Supplementary Report** 673, Crowthorne, Berkshire, U.K.

Maunsell and Partners (1975) **New structures for Australian cities.** Cities Commission, Canberra, Australian Capital Territory

McAsey, J. (1987) Inner-city households cost community less, says study. **The Age** Melbourne, 27/11/87

McNulty, R.H. , Penne ,R.L. , Jacobson ,D.R. and Partners for Livable Places (1986) **The return of the livable city :Learning from America's best.** Acropolis Books Ltd, Washington DC, 324 pp

Mercer, C. (1975) **Living in cities: Psychological and urban environment.** Penguin, Harmondsworth and Baltimore

Merlin, P. (1976) **Impact of the structure and extent of urban development on the choices of modes of transport.** European Conference of Ministers of Transport , Economic Research Centre, Paris

Metropolitan Washington Council of Governments (MWCOG) and National Capital Region Transportation Planning Board (NCRTPB) (1983) **Metrorail area planning : Metrorail before-and-after study.** Metropolitan Washington Council of Governments, August, 161 pp

Michelson, W. (1977) **Environmental choice, human behaviour, and residential satisfaction.** Oxford University Press,Oxford, England

Milkins, E.E. and Watson, H.C. (1983) Comparison of urban driving patterns. Presented to The 2nd International Pacific Conference, Tokyo, JSAE /SAE /SAE-A/IATO

Millas, A.J. (1980) Planning for the elderly within the context of a neighbourhood. **Ekistics** 283, 264-273

Mitchell, R.B. and Rapkin, C. (1954) **Urban traffic: A function of land use.** Columbia University Press, New York

Moore, E.F. (1959) The shortest path through a maze. **International Symposium on the Theory of Switching,** Harvard University

Moorhouse, F. (1980) **Days of wine and rage.** Penguin, Sydney

Mumford, L. (1961) **The city in history.** Penguin,Harmondsworth, England

National Association of Australian State Road Authorities (NAASRA) (1984) **Funding the future: Australian roads - The major findings of the NAASRA roads study 1984.** 25pp

Neels, K., Cheslow, M.D., Kirby, R.F. and Peterson, G.E. (1977) **An empirical investigation of the effects of land use on urban travel.** The Urban Institute, Washington D.C. Working Paper 5049-17-1, August 83p

Neilson Associates (1987) **Net community benefits of urban consolidation.** A Report Prepared by Neilson Associates Pty Ltd for the City of Melbourne, November, 73pp (plus appendices)

Neutze, M. (1977) **Urban development in Australia : A descriptive analysis.** George Allen and Unwin, Sydney, 259pp

Neville, S.D., Campell, R., Duxbury, M.L. and Newman P.W.G. (1988) Mixed land use and transport energy: Defining the connection. **Transport Research Paper** 1/88, Environmental Science, Murdoch University 22pp

Newman, P. and Hogan ,T. (1981) A review of urban density models: Towards a resolution of the conflict between populace and planner. **Human Ecology,** 9(3) , 269 - 303

Newman, P.W.G. (1978) Fremantle: A case study in inner city population decline. **Shire and Municipal Record** January, 438-485

Newman, P.W.G. (1986) Lessons from Liverpool. **Planning and Administration** 1, 32-42

Newman, P.W.G. (1987) The impact of the America's Cup on Fremantle - An insider's view. Paper for P.A.P.E.R. '87 Conference "The Effects of Hallmark Events on Cities" Perth, Western Australia, June

Newman, P.W.G. and Hogan ,T.L.F. (1987) Urban density and transport : A simple model based on 3 city types. **Transport Research Paper,** 1/87 , Environmental Science, Murdoch University, 36pp

Newman, P.W.G. and Kenworthy, J.R. (1980a) Land use planning for transport energy conservation in Australian cities. **Search** 11(11), 367-376

Newman, P.W.G. and Kenworthy, J.R. (1980b) Public and private transport in Australian cities: I. An analysis of existing patterns and their energy implications. **Transport Policy and Decision Making** 1, 133-148

Newman, P.W.G. and Kenworthy, J.R. (1980c) Public and private transport in Australian cities: II. The potential for energy conservation through land use change. **Transport Policy and Decision Making** 1, 149-167

Newman, P.W.G. and Kenworthy, J.R. (1984) The use and abuse of driving cycle research : Clarifying the relationship between traffic congestion, energy and emissions. **Transportation Quarterly** 38 (4), 615-635

Newman, P.W.G. and Kenworthy, J.R. (1986) The transport energy trade-off: Fuel-efficient traffic versus fuel-efficient cities. **Transport Research Paper** 1/86, Environmental Science ,Murdoch University, 24 pp

Newman, P.W.G. and Kenworthy, J.R. (1987a) Gasoline consumption and cities : A comparison of U.S. cities with a global survey and some implications. **Transport Research Paper** 8/87, Environmental Science, Murdoch University, 31 pp

Newman, P.W.G. and Kenworthy, J.R. (1987b) Transport and urban form in thirty-two of the world's principal cities. Presented to International Symposium on Transport, Communications and Urban Form, Monash University, Melbourne, 24-26 August

Newman, P.W.G. and Kenworthy, J.R. (1988) The transport energy trade-off: Fuel-efficient traffic versus fuel-efficient cities. **Transportation Research - A** 22A(3), 163 -174

Newman, P.W.G. and Muste, K. (1987) **Submission to Joint Government and Industry Committee investigating effect of State and Local Government regulations on the land and housing industry.** School of Environmental and Life Sciences, Murdoch University, June, 17pp

Newman, P.W.G., Annandale, D.D. and Duxbury, L. (1984) The rise or decline of the Australian inner city? An analysis of recent trends in population, housing, age structure and occupation. **Urban Policy and Research** 2(1), 7-16

Newman, P.W.G., Kenworthy, J.R. and Lyons, T.J. (1985) Transport energy use in the Perth metropolitan region: Some urban policy implications. **Urban Policy and Research** 3(2) , 4-15

Newman, P.W.G., Kenworthy, J.R. and Lyons, T.J. (1987) **Transport energy conservation policies for Australian cities - The perspective from an international comparison of thirty-two principal world cities.** End of Grant Report, Project No. 836, National Energy Research Development and Demonstration Council,Environmental Science, Murdoch University, August, 40pp

OECD Road Research Group (1978) **Integrated urban traffic management.** OECD, Paris

Organisation for Economic Co-operation and Development (OECD) (1973) **Techniques of improving urban conditions by restraint of road traffic.** OECD Symposium, Paris

Organisation for Economic Co-operation and Development (OECD) (1976) **Land use policies and agriculture.** OECD, Paris

Pawley, M. (1975) **The private future.** Pan Books, London

Pindyck, R.S. (1979) **The structure of world energy demand.** The MIT Press, Cambridge, Massachusetts

Pitt, D.R. (1983) Fuel consumption models - An evaluation based on Perth's transport patterns. Honours Thesis, Environmental Science, Murdoch

University, Perth, Western Australia, 82pp

Poelstra, H. (1987) Accessibility in historic cities:Amsterdam, in Papers and Proceedings of IFHP International Congress, Sevilla, Spain 26 -30 October Vol 1, 9-13

Powell, J.M. (1976) **Environmental management in Australia 1788-1914.** Oxford University Press, Oxford, England

Pun, P.K.S. (1979) Hong Kong tries participation. **Royal Australian Planning Institute Journal** 17(3), 211-215

Pushkarev, B.S. and Zupan, J.M. (1977) **Public transportation and land use policy.** Indiana University Press, Bloomington and London

Pushkarev, B.S., Zupan, J.M. and Cumella, R.S. (1982) **Urban rail in America : An exploration of criteria for fixed guideway transit.** Indiana University Press, Bloomington (A Regional Plan Association Book), 289pp

Ravetz, A. (1980) **Remaking cities: Contradictions of the recent urban environment.** Croom Helm, London, 348pp

Real Estate Institue of N.S.W. (1987) **Medium density housing.** Real Estate Institute of N.S.W Position Paper 7, Sydney, 18pp

Real Estate Research Corporation (1974) **The costs of sprawl - Environmental and economic cost of alternative residential development patterns at the fringe .** Prepared for the Council on Environmental Quality: The Office of Policy Department and Research Department of Housing and Urban Development and the Office of Planning and Management, USEPA

Reid, H.M. (ed.) (1981) **Urban consolidation for Sydney.** Papers and Workshop Reports Presented at the Conference held on 17 November 1979, Planning Research Centre, University of Sydney, Australia, 44pp

Rodriguez, C.G., McDonnell, J.J., Draper, R.W. and McGarry,E. (1985) **Transportation planning data for urbanized areas based on the 1980 Census.** Prepared for Urban Planning and Transportation Management Division, Office of Highway Planning, Federal Highway Administration, Washington, D.C. 20590, U.S. Department of Transportation, DOT-I-85-20, 89 pp.

Rourke, F.E. (1964) Urbanism and American democracy. **Ethnics** 74 , 255-268

Russell, J.C. (1958) Late ancient and medieval population. **Transactions of the American Philosophical Society** 48(3) 1-18

Safdie, M. (1970) **Beyond Habitat.** MIT Press, Cambridge, Masssachusetts

Safdie, M. (1974) **For everyone a garden.** MIT Press, Cambridge, Masssachusetts

Sandercock, L. (1975) **Cities for sale. Property, politics and urban planning in Australia.** Melbourne University Press, Melbourne, Australia

Sandercock, L. (1979) **The land racket. The real costs of property speculation.** Silverfish, O'Conner, Australian Capital Territory 113pp

SATS (1974) **Sydney area transport study 1974** Vol 2, Minister for Transport, NSW

Saunders, P. (1981) **Social theory and the urban question.** Hutchinson, London, 292pp

Schaeffer, K.H. and Sclar , E. (1975) **Access for all.** Penguin, Harmondsworth, England

Schedvin, C.B. and McCarthy, J.W. (eds) (1974) **Urbanization in Australia: The nineteenth century.** University of Sydney Press, Sydney

Schmitt, R. (1966) Density, health and social disorganization. **Journal of the American Institute of Planners** 29, 38-40

Schmitt, R.C., Zane, L.Y.S. and Nishi, S. (1978) Density, health and social disorganization revisited. **Journal of the American Institute of Planners** 44(2) , 209-211

Schneider, K.R. (1979) **On the nature of cities: Towards enduring and creative human environments.** Jossey Bass, San Francisco , 352 pp

Sharpe, R. (1982) Energy efficiency and equity of various urban land use patterns. **Urban Ecology** 7, 1-18

Shevky, E. and Bell, W. (1955) **Social area analysis.** Stanford University Press, California

Shevky, E. and Williams, M. (1949) **The social areas of Los Angeles.** University of California Press, Los Angeles

Small, K. (1986) Transportation and urban change. in Peterson, P.E. (ed.), **The new urban reality,** Brookings Institution, Washington D.C. 197-223

Small, K.A. (1980) Energy scarcity and urban development patterns. **International Regional Science Review** 5 (2) , 97-119

Smith, M.P. (1980) **The city and social theory.** Basil Blackwell, Oxford, 315 pp

Snell, B. (1974) **American ground transport: A proposal for restructuring the automobile, truck, bus and rail industries.** US Government Printing Office

Snell, B. (1975) **The Snell Report** Extract from "New Society" No. 86, Australian Broadcasting Commission, Tuesday 23/9/1975, 13pp

Squires (1974) **The pastoral novel.** University Press of Virginia, Charlottesville

Stockholms Stadsbyggnadskontor (1972) **Stockholm urban environment.** Stockholm, 169pp

Stokols, D., Ohlig, W. and Resnick, S.M. (1978) Perception of residential crowding, classroom experiences and student health. **Human Ecology** 6(3), 333-251

Stonex, K.A. (1957) Survey of Los Angeles traffic characteristics. 36th Annual Meeting ,U.S. Highway Research Board , 509-538

Stopher, P.R. and Meyburg, A.H. (1975) **Urban transportation modeling and planning.** Lexington Books, Lexington, Massachusetts

Summers, R. and Heston, A. (1984) Improved international comparisons of real product and its composition: 1950 - 1980. **Review of Income and Wealth** 30(2) , 207-262

Tanghe, J., Vlaeminck, S. and Berghoef, J. (1984) **Living cities: A case for urbanism and guidelines for re-urbanization.** Pergamon Press, Oxford, 373pp

Taylor, M.A.P. and Anderson ,B.E. (1982) Modelling pollution and energy use in urban road networks. in **Proceedings of 11th Annual Australian Road Research Board Conference** 11 (6), 1-17

Taylor, N. (1973) **The village in the city.** Temple Smith, London

The Municipality of Metropolitan Toronto,Toronto Transit Commission and Energy Ontario (1984) **Metropolitan Toronto area transportation energy study phase II 1984.** (i) Summary report , 44pp plus Appendix. (ii)Background report No.1 - Short term transportation energy conservation measures. 188pp. (iii) Background report No. 2 - Energy conservation through transportation land use. 82pp . (iv) Background report No. 3 - A contingency plan strategy.122 pp . Municipality of Metropolitan Toronto, Toronto Transit Commission and Energy Ontario

Thomson, J.M. (1977) **Great cities and their traffic.** Penguin , England, 344pp

Transport Canada (1984) **Fuel consumption trends.** Ottawa

United Nations (1976) **Global review of human settlements.** United Nations, Vols 1 and 2, Pergamon Press, New York

United Nations (1981) **Yearbook of world energy statistics.** United Nations, New York

US Bureau of the Census (1980) **Social indicators III . Selected data on social conditions and trends in the United States.** A publication of the Federal Statistical System, December, Washington DC

US Department of Transportation (1985) **Highway statistics.** Federal Highway Administration, Washington D.C.

van den Berg, L. , Burns, L.S. , and Klaassen , L.H. (1987) **Spatial cycles.** Gower, Aldershot, England, 277 pp

van den Berg, L. , Drewett, R. , Klaassen, L.H. , Rossi, A. and Vijverberg, C.H.T. (1982) **Urban Europe: A study of growth and decline Volume 1.** Pergamon Press, Oxford, 162 pp

van den Berg, L., Klaassen, L.H. and van der Meer, J. (1983/5) **Urban revival? Recent trends in the urban development of the Netherlands.** Series: Foundations of Empirical Economic Research, Netherlands Economic Institute, Rotterdam, 21pp

Van der Ryn, S. (1983) Fit for city living. **Solar Age** July, 39-42

Van der Ryn, S. and Calthorpe, P. (1986) **Sustainable communities: A new design synthesis for cities, suburbs and towns.** Sierra Club Books, San Francisco, 238pp

van Vliet, W. (1983) Children's travel behaviour. **Ekistics** 298, 61-65

Vogt, E., Raundalen, M. and Iversen, O. (1980) Selegrad: An experiment in environment design. **Ekistics** 281, 113-115

Vuchic, V.R. (1981) **Urban public transportation systems and technology.** Prentice Hall , Englewood Cliffs, New Jersey

Wagner, C. (1975) **Rural retreats: Urban investment in rural land for residential purposes.** Department of Urban and Regional Development , Canberra

Walker, R.A. (1978) The transformation of urban structure in the nineteenth century and the beginnings of suburbanization. in Cox, K. (ed.) **Urbanization and conflict in market societies** Methuen and Co Ltd, London, 165-205

Warner, S.B. , Jr. (1968) **The private city.** University of Pennsylvania Press , Philadelphia

Watson, H.C., Milkins, E. and Marshall, G.A. (1979) Controlling traffic flow for minimum energy consumption and emissions in Proceedings of The Institution of Engineers, Australia, Conference, Adelaide, 14-16 November, 116-124

Watt, K.E.F. and Ayers, C. (1974) Urban land use patterns and transportation energy cost. Presented to: "The Annual Meeting of the American Association for the Advancement of Science", San Francisco

Weaver, R. (1977) The suburbanization of America. **New York Affairs** 4(3), 24-33

Webber, M.M. (1963) Order in diversity: Community without propinquity in Wingo, L. (Ed), **Cities and space: The future use of urban land.** John Hopkins Press, Baltimore

Webber, M.M. (1964) The urban place and the non-place realm in **Explorations into urban structure** University of Pennsylvania Press, Philadelphia

Webber, M.M. (1968) The post city age. **Daedalus** 97(4), 1093-1099

Webber, M.M. (1973) Urbanization and communications. in Gobner, G.,Gross, L.P. and Melody, W.H. (Eds), **Communications, Technology and Social Policy.** Wiley, New York

Westerman, H.L. (1982) Report on the first phase of the project : planning and evaluation of energy efficient transport systems. ERDIC, N.S.W.

Weston, R.F. (1971) **New York waste management.** Planning Status Report 1970, USEPA, Washington DC.

Wheaton, W.C. (1982) The long-run structure of transportation and gasoline demand. **Bell Journal of Economics** 13(2), 439-454

White, D., Sutton, P., Pews, A., Mardon, C., Dick, J. and Crow, M. (1978) **Seeds for change: Creatively confronting the energy crisis.** Patchwork Press CCV, Melbourne, 540 pp

White, M. and White, L. (1962) **The intellectual versus the city: From Thomas Jefferson to Frank Lloyd Wright.** Harvard University Press, Cambridge, Massachusetts

Wickham, E.R. (1977) Social malaise in urban areas and the concept of the city in Millward, S. (ed.) **Urban Renewal in Retrospect and Prospect** Geographical Publications Ltd, Herts, UK, 266pp

Wilmoth , D. (1982) Urban consolidation policy and social equity in Conference on Urban Consolidation and Equity , Centre for Environmental Studies , Macquarie University , Sydney

Wilson, M.A. (1976) **Public housing for Australia.** University of Queensland Press, St Lucia, Brisbane, Queensland

Yeung, Y.M. (1977) High-rise, high-density housing: Myths and reality. **Habitat International** 2 (5) and(6), 587-594

HSN

AOFY/12

LUISN